Industrial Relations & Conflict Management

Series editors

Disseminating cutting edge theories and empirical research in the field of industrial relations and conflict management, from an interdisciplinary approach, and firmly based in theories on human behaviour in relation to work and organizations. Formally the series will publish monographs and contributed or edited volumes from leading psychology scholars. Specifically, the series integrates theories and research from industrial relations (sociology, business, law and psychology), with those on conflict management, mediation and more generally well-being and productive behaviour in the workplace. Volumes in this series respond to the demands of policymakers and the public, remaining relevant and applicable for science, industry and society. Delivering relevant research and conclusions from local, regional, national and international perspectives. The aim of the series is to contribute to cooperative and constructive relations in organizations at three levels: organizational level, team level and interpersonal level. The series will contribute to the existing academic research and literature by providing an advanced publication platform for improving the science of understanding industrial relations and conflict management. Publishing volumes which deliver valuable contributions from the range of developing perspectives on this subject.

More information about this series at http://www.springer.com/series/13458

Alicia Arenas · Donatella Di Marco
Lourdes Munduate · Martin C. Euwema
Editors

Shaping Inclusive Workplaces Through Social Dialogue

Springer

Editors
Alicia Arenas
University of Seville
Seville
Spain

Lourdes Munduate
University of Seville
Seville
Spain

Donatella Di Marco
University of Seville
Seville
Spain

Martin C. Euwema
KU Leuven
Leuven
Belgium

ISSN 2199-4544 ISSN 2199-4552 (electronic)
Industrial Relations & Conflict Management
ISBN 978-3-319-66392-0 ISBN 978-3-319-66393-7 (eBook)
DOI /10.1007/978-3-319-66393-7

Library of Congress Control Number: 2017952000

Printed on acid-free paper

This Springer imprint is published by Springer Nature
The registered company is Springer International Publishing AG
The registered company address is: Gewerbestrasse 11, 6330 Cham, Switzerland

Foreword

Diverse workforces are seen as a reflection of structural trends and as an asset for enterprises and societies. The rapid ageing of societies in industrialized and emerging economies requires that members of all social groups join the ranks of workers, if the shrinking of working age populations and economic output are to be countered. People's aspirations and desires are also changing. If given a choice, the majority of women, including those who are currently not working for pay or profit, would prefer to be in paid employment and look after their families, according to a recently-released ILO-Gallup world survey study, *Towards a Better Future for Women and Work: Voices of Women and Men:* http://www.ilo.org/global/publications/books/WCMS_546256/lang–en/index.htm. Many older workers, who are still fit for work, may be willing and ready to keep contributing to economies with their skills and experience, while people with disabilities await the chance to prove their talents and gain in autonomy and respect.

Diversity at the workplace is also a productive factor. A diverse and more representative pool of employees, for instance, is more likely to understand and address more effectively the equally diverse needs of their actual and potential clients. Diverse workplaces when inclusive, namely when representing equally the talents and aspirations of all groups of workers, can breed innovation, boost motivation and raise overall productivity. However, while the arguments in favour of diversity are compelling, the reality shows how elusive this goal is.

Everywhere in the world women, young and older workers and members of ethnic minorities are still under-represented in the labour force. This is even more so for people with disabilities or people living with HIV and AIDS. When in employment, they are over-represented at the lower end of the earnings distribution and are concentrated in a narrower range of occupations and sectors and in forms of employment, such as temporary employment or short-hours employment or agency employment, which are characterized by greater employment insecurity, fewer social security benefits, often lower hourly wages, and fewer prospects of skills upgrading and career advancement. (*Non-standard Employment around the World: Understanding Challenges, Shaping Prospects*, ILO, 2016: http://www.ilo.org/global/publications/books/WCMS_534326/lang–en/index.htm)

While managing diversity in the workplace brings many benefits, it is clearly not without efforts. Biases and prejudices regarding what members of particular groups are good or not good at or what is considered to be appropriate or inappropriate often unconsciously shape the rules, practices and institutions governing the organization of work and interpersonal relations in the workplace. These biases need to be identified, understood and properly managed if individual talents are to be valued and employed for the benefit of the organization.

This book makes an important contribution towards understanding what it takes to build diverse and inclusive workplaces. Drawing on a wide range of theoretical and empirical research in the field of industrial relations and conflict management (sociology, business, law and psychology), it makes two important points regarding how to achieve inclusiveness. First, it acknowledges that discrimination—direct or indirect—may arise at any time, during recruitment and selection, while assessing an employee's performance, while determining his or her remuneration or while preventing and addressing violence and harassment at work. Hence the need to embrace a cycle of inclusion approach which identifies and monitors each and every such stage, acknowledging their interconnection and mutually-reinforcing nature. Second, it rightly suggests that social dialogue, by fostering constructive and transparent relations between management, employees and trade unions, is key to advancing social innovation. Social dialogue—the authors contend—is not only a means to promote a change of attitudes and develop effective organizational responses, it is also the defining feature of a culture of diversity and inclusiveness at the workplace. Work patterns and work organization, which equally reflect and equally value the aspirations, talents and professional paths of a composite and varied workforce, need to empower workers of under-represented groups and provide the space for consultations and negotiations. Only through stronger representation and bargaining power will these groups be able to challenge and influence the reshaping of occupational structures and work culture and practices so as to make them socially inclusive.

This is consistent with the ILO's decent work agenda and the many international labour standards dealing with non-discrimination and equality, notably Convention No. 111 concerning Discrimination in Respect of Employment and Occupation, 1958 and its accompanying Recommendation; the Older Workers Recommendation, 1980 (No. 162) or the Vocational Rehabilitation and Employment (Disabled Persons) Recommendation, 1983 (No. 168). Empirical evidence shows that adaptability to change appears to be higher when equal employment opportunities act in combination with policies aimed at raising workers' participation in decision-making.

Embracing a diversity model means embracing a transformative agenda. The aim is to acknowledge diversity as an individual and societal asset and ensure inclusion without assimilation. This is clearly a goal that cannot be achieved overnight: the empowerment of disadvantaged individuals and groups and the promotion of an enabling policy environment that protect and reward social dialogue at all levels, at the organization level and beyond, is crucial to progress in that direction.

Manuela Tomei
Director Conditions of Work and Equality
Department (WORKQUALITY) ILO
Geneva, Switzerland

Contents

Part I
Reframing Inclusive Workplaces

Chapter 1
Dialogue for Inclusion: When Managing Diversity Is not Enough

Alicia Arenas, Donatella Di Marco, Lourdes Munduate and Martin C. Euwema

Diversity is inviting people to the party whereas inclusion is asking them to dance, as they are able. (Emily Hickey, Vanderbilt University)

"Employment is crucial for the effective inclusion of refugees as it allows for economic and social participation, as well as personal fulfillment. However, many skilled refugees experience high levels of unemployment and their skills are significantly underutilized as they are underemployed in low-skilled, temporary, or low-paying jobs" (Alice Beste, United Nations University, 2015).

"The Federal Employment Agency (BA) in Germany estimates that half of the refugees will remain unemployed within five years (Salikutluk et al. 2016). Everyday thousands of people leave everything to escape the war and persecution. More than a million refugees arrived in Europe last year, many of them fleeing the wars in Syria, Afghanistan and Iraq. When they arrive in the host countries things are not easy at all. They experience legal and social barriers to integration starting from an insecure legal status, prejudices, and employment opportunities, among others" (Robert Kunzig, October 2016).

This work was funded by the Spanish Ministry of Economy and Competitiveness (MINECO/FEDER),grant reference n. PSI2015-64894-P.

A. Arenas (✉) · D. Di Marco · L. Munduate
University of Seville, Seville, Spain
e-mail: aarenas@us.es

M.C. Euwema
KU Leuven, Louvain, Belgium

A. Arenas et al. (eds.), *Shaping Inclusive Workplaces Through Social Dialogue*,
Industrial Relations & Conflict Management,
DOI 10.1007/978-3-319-66393-7_1

Refugees unable to enter the job market or having major problems to find a job matching their competences is one example of the challenges our societies and organizations face when it comes to inclusion. The negative impact of not having a job is well-established; the impact is large and goes far beyond the effects on income and on access to social security (see, for instance, Deaton 2008; Kunze and Suppa 2014). Financial adversity is only one among many negative outcomes of unemployment, a situation which also results in isolation and psychological stress. Indeed, existing research indicates that a person's employment situation affects his or her social networks, levels of civic engagement, and overall trust in other people, as well as in institutions (for examples from the empirical literature, see Norton and de Haan 2012). Workers who are able to use their skills productively, who perceive that they are treated fairly and are not disadvantaged in their search for jobs, are less likely to disengage from social life (Wietzke and McLeod 2013).

The effects of vulnerable employment—often in the informal sector—and those of insecure and temporary contracts are similar to those of unemployment in that they restrain access "to social protection and sever links with social and political organizations, including unions" (UN 2016a, p. 43). Vulnerable workers, in the sense of access to jobs matching the competences and integrating into the workplace, include also specific categories of people. In many societies, these can be people with physical or mental disabilities, immigrants, lesbians, gay, or transgender people. However, also often relate to the position of women, older workers, or youngsters starting on the labor market.

Our initial example focuses on one of such groups: refugees. Political refugees face many obstacles; language issues, cultural differences, lack of social network in the host country, lack of school and professional skills, but also lengthy administrative procedures when it comes to obtain a permit to exercise a job, or recognition of qualifications from the home country. Not to mention the coping with traumatic experiences from their countries of origin. Social integration and employment can help them rebuild their life histories and those of their families and enable them to find means of survival where they have moved. If employment is fundamental to social integration in all circumstances, it is much more so when it comes to refugees who have fled their homes with little resources. They are highly vulnerable to exclusion from or exploitation at the labor market. For societies striving for social cohesion, it is necessary to guarantee both to help them find new tools for their self-sufficiency and the reconstruction of their lives.

The entry and integration of refugees in the labor market is only one example of today's complexities and diversities. The recognition of women's and social minorities' rights, the aging population, the elimination of spatial barriers, and, consequently, the heterogeneity of society contribute to more diverse workplaces. However, simply being "diverse" is no longer enough (Dobbin and Kalev 2016) and inclusion needs to be fostered. In this sense, inclusion describes the way an organization configures opportunities, interactions, communication, and decision-making to utilize the potential of its diversity (Woods 2002). Inclusive organizations implement practices and goals in which those people, who have different backgrounds, are welcomed and treated equally. Inclusive organizations are focused on values that empower open-mindedness, foster constructive conflict, value new perspectives, and avoid judgmental attitudes, promoting social innovation.

This handbook explores whether and how organizations can be transformed so as to promote equity, voice, participation, and empowerment in the workplace. In doing so, we examine the role that Social Dialogue can play in encouraging organizational change for inclusion. Although organizational change can have different rhythms and be promoted by different stakeholders, shaping inclusive workplaces requires a sustainable change and constant adjustment. This organizational change is connected with the concept of continuous change (Weick and Quinn 1999), which is characterized by the role played by change agents as sense-makers who redirect change. In the path toward inclusive organizations, Human Resource managers are key to play this important role as change agents. We briefly analyze below the theoretical framework of continuous change. Within this framework of change lies the model we propose to outline inclusive organizations, the Circle of Inclusion.

1.1 The Role of Social Dialogue in Organizational Continuous Change

Weick and Quinn (1999) distinguish two different models of organizational change: Change that is continuous, evolving, and incremental; change that is episodic, discontinuous, and intermittent. The basic metaphor of continuous change is that of organizations as emergent and self-organizing, where change is constant, evolving, and cumulative. The idea here is that small continuous adjustments, created simultaneously across units, can cumulate and create substantial change. In contrast, the metaphor of episodic change is of organizations that are inertial and where change is infrequent and discontinuous. The underlying presumption is that episodic change attempts to reach a new equilibrium condition that resolves the grown misalignment between an inertial deep structure and environmental demands. One basic element that clustered the change process into these opposing forms is the kind of innovation pursued—in terms of their radicalism and the level of risk and novelty—and its implementation process (King and Anderson 1995). Thus, radical innovation is distinguished from incremental innovations by a greater level of uncertainty and complexity during its implementation. Tushman and Romanelli (1985) suggest that incremental innovations occur in adaptable periods of continuous change, while radical innovations occur during periods of discontinuous change, with an enormous impact on organizations and within a relatively short time span. Following this perspective, the promotion of inclusive organizations seems to fit better with the objective of an incremental social innovation process, occurring with the involvement of different stakeholders across units and seeking a rather low level of uncertainty in adaptable periods of continuous change.

A characteristic that contrasts continuous change with episodic change refers to the role played by the change agent. As Cheng and Van de Ven (1996) point out, innovation and change have to be understood from the point of view of the actors involved. In episodic change, the change agent's role is that of the prime mover who creates change, while in the continuous change model, this role is characterized as a sense-maker who redirects change. Weick and Quinn (1999) state that to manage change is to tell people what to do (a logic of replacement) but to lead change is to show people how to be (a logic of attraction). The continuous change intervention is characterized by this "logic of attraction" that induces constant adjustments and improvements. From the framework of continuous change, the implementation of an inclusive organization will therefore imply that employers and employees will value diversity because they are attracted to it, inspired by it. The job of Human Resources managers as change agents that lead this process is the thread of the chapters that compose this handbook.

Being inspired by the model of continuous change to shape inclusive organizations means considering the following elements in the implementation process: engage all stakeholders across units, expose them to the holistic view of the strategy to be used, show them how to induce constant adjustment (logic of attraction), and encourage social accountability for a sustainable change. In order to achieve this environment, an organization needs a fully integrated approach driven by the managerial board, facilitated by HR, and implemented at different levels.

In order to lead this process, considering the aforementioned elements, an important strategy for Human Resources managers to use is Social Dialogue. As theorists of continuous change suggest (Schein 1993; Weick and Quinn 1999), the role of the change agent becomes one of managing language, dialogue, and identity. To redirect continuous change is to be sensitive to discourse and dialogue. As Barrett et al. (1995) and Dixon (1997) also argue, the most powerful interventions occur at the level of everyday conversation. This daily dialogue between employees and employers in the organization has been known as Social Dialogue from the perspective of labor relations. This is defined as "all types of negotiation, consultation or simply exchange of information between, or among, representatives of governments, employers, and workers, on issues of common interest relating to economic and social policy" (ILO 2005). The main goal of Social Dialogue is to promote consensus and democratic involvement among the main stakeholders, contributing to a more social and fair world of work (Pender et al. 2017). As an incremental social innovation strategy, Social Dialogue asks for open dialogue and constructive negotiations between management, trade unions, and employee representatives in order to a) promote a change of attitudes, behaviors, and competences on diversity and social inclusion, and b) develop effective organizational responses in terms of policies and procedural aspects to improve inclusion of vulnerable groups at work.

We have seen before that change agents become important for their ability to make sense of change dynamics already under way, to recognize adaptive emergent changes, make them more salient, and reframe them (Weick and Quinn 1999). This is the role to be played by Human Resource managers in a constructive dialogue and creative negotiations with employee representatives. This is essential for inclusion, as this is a social process directly impacting all employees. And too often diversity and inclusion policies fail, because employees do not see any benefit; feel measures are imposed upon them, while they have to face to consequences. Therefore, constructive dialogue is essential and should also focus on benefits of inclusion for the organization, team, and employees. Social Dialogue might be present in each step of the Human Resource Management (HRM) system, promoting a continuous change in order to shape inclusive workplaces. The model of the Circle of Inclusion that we propose later in this introduction is based on this idea of revising the HRM system to create a shared set of meanings and a common thinking process of inclusion at the organizational level.

For Social Dialogue to be effective, previous research (Pender et al. 2017) has shown that it should aim at integrated values, policies, and practices at organizational level. These should be based on sound measures about current states and progress made. The state of the art on Social Dialogue at organizational level has been the aim of two European projects financed by the European Commission on *New European Industrial Relations* (NEIRE). The results of the situation in 11 European countries, and the proposals provided by employers and employees to improve the constructive dialogue in each participating country, have been published in two volumes (Munduate et al. 2012; Euwema et al. 2015).

1.2 A Way to Go: From Diversity Toward Inclusion in the Workplace

Diversity and inclusion are often used interchangeably. As Roberson et al. (2017) pointed out, research to further distinguish the constructs, practices to support each, and their effects on employees and organizations is needed. Previous research has analyzed the effects of differences among members of work units (e.g., van Knippenberg and Schippers 2007). However, there has been relatively scarce attention to the organizational impacts of programs to manage such differences. Most of the research has been focused on how to control for and examine the influences of demographic differences in different HRM practices (e.g., selection, performance evaluation, and training); however, few studies have examined the design, process, and effects of practices specifically aimed to develop more inclusive workplaces (for an exception, see Kalinoski et al. 2013). We do not usually know the best practices to achieve real inclusion, or when programs and policies might lead to negative reactions based on stereotypes and why.

On different continents and different countries, we see quite different frameworks toward diversity. The legal framework in many countries supports diversity management to promote social inclusion and tackle inequalities at work (e.g., European Commission 2014, 2017; ILO 2012; UN 2016a). In fact, these issues are on the mainstream development agenda, because there is now substantial evidence that social exclusion and inequality exacerbate societal conflicts and conflicts at the workplace.

Social and labor exclusion lead to discontent that is often a prelude to violent forms of conflict. Exclusion and the disparities associated with it can be particularly threatening to peace when there is a perception that they are the result of deliberately discriminatory processes (Stewart 2002). Research has shown that when people perceive they have been discriminated against, their physical and psychological health suffer (Jones et al. 2014). It also affects the way people behave and the choices they make, with long-term negative consequences. In turn, conflicts are also often a driver of social exclusion and inequality, as the cases of workplace bullying and harassment, exacerbating existing barriers between people and groups and creating new ones. Conflicts result in deterioration in living standards and employment opportunities and can also undermine transparency, accountability, and trust in organizations (UN 2016b).

To promote equality of opportunity and treatment in the workplace, treating all people in the same way is not enough. For the International Labor Organization (ILO), it is necessary to get "substantive equality." This relates to cope with disadvantage, underrepresentation, and marginalization within the labor market. In this sense, "standard" practices may have to be reconsidered in order to not only manage diversity of the workforce but also promote inclusion at the workplace. Promoting inclusion, therefore, helps people overcome inequalities, but it also requires creating resilience—that is, protecting people against major risks.

Jobs shape the opportunities people have in life. They are likely to be a source of social inclusion and well-being when they provide sufficient earnings to maintain adequate living standards, and particularly when they come with access to social protection, decent working conditions, and prospects for career development. Beyond being an important source of income, employment often confers social identity and brings social acceptance to people's lives, particularly when the workplace enables them to create social and economic ties and build networks. When they promote social dialogue, employment gives workers a voice and therefore enables them to play an active role in making decisions that affect their well-being. Jobs that offer few opportunities for social mobility or voice, in contrast, can lead to the marginalization and exclusion of workers (UN 2016a, b).

"An organization is inclusive when everyone has a sense of belonging, feels respected, valued and seen for who they are as individuals, and experiences a level of supportive energy and commitment from leaders, colleagues and stakeholders so that all people—individually and collectively—can do their best at work" (Miller and Katz 2007, p. 2). For this aim, HRM policies and practices are the formal and informal rules and norms that structure workers' rights, entitlements, opportunities, and voice. They shape most of the working interactions, including among employees, with the supervisors, and with the stakeholders, influencing how organizations develop.

The rights to just and favorable conditions of work, protection against unemployment, equal pay for equal work, access to trade unions and to social security are universal and unalienable (UN 2016a, b). Informal work, however, carries fiscal losses and has potentially negative consequences for competitiveness and growth as well as social cohesion. Recognition that informal work has given opportunities to groups that were formerly excluded from the labor market helps to highlight the positive contribution of informal employment and the need to support informal workers (Harris and Krueger 2015). However, it does not justify the absence of decent work or security safeguards.

In fact, low mobility and persistent wage gaps between informal and formal jobs suggest the presence of a divide between employees in each sector who are, in practice, part of different labor submarkets. A similar divide exists in developed countries between adequately protected workers under open-ended labor contracts and many of those under temporary, as well as other non-standard, labor contracts, among whom young workers, women, migrants, and members of other disadvantaged groups are overrepresented (Harris and Krueger 2015).

In the case of young workers, the first barrier they face is the access to the labor market. High and even growing youth unemployment rates in many societies are coupled with longer job searches and with a surge in the number of discouraged young workers who are not counted among the unemployed because they are not actively seeking employment and are therefore at high risk of the long-term labor market and overall social exclusion. Early unemployment has negative effects not only on the future employability of young people but also on their self-esteem, their role in the society can represent a serious economic burden on governments finances.

Discrimination Suit Alleges Black Applicants Passed by for Temp Jobs (Extracted from Tanzina Vega, December 7, 2016, *CNNMoney*)

In the summer of 2014, Kevin James was trying to find work as a day laborer. He took a city bus from the south side of Chicago to MVP Staffing, an employment agency in Cicero, Illinois, filled out the paperwork and was sent to a local manufacturing plant, where he spent the day packaging cookies in boxes.

That was the only day James, who is African-American, says he was sent on a job assignment.

For the next two months, James says he would make the 35-minute trip to MVP Staffing, a temporary employment agency with 60 offices nationwide, and he would "sit there and wait" for an assignment for hours. None came. So James stopped going. It was "mainly Hispanics" who were getting jobs, according to James. "I didn't see no reason to go down there just to be told to go home," said James, 29, who, despite having worked in various retail jobs, factories and as a dishwasher, remains unemployed.

[…] The complaint includes testimony from several former MVP workers that "African American laborers were marked "Do Not Return" or DNR'd" within hours of their assignments or at the end of their first shift." When black workers were given assignments, the complaint alleges, they were given single assignments and "placed in the worst jobs with the most unpleasant working conditions." Joseph Sellers, chair of the civil rights and employment practice at Cohen Milstein Sellers & Toll who is co-counsel for the plaintiffs said that much of the discrimination was based on "a series of stereotypes about African Americans and Latinos," including that Latinos are immigrants that are less likely to complain about low pay or bad working conditions out of fear.

The lawsuit contains statements from former MVP employees, including Rosa Ceja, who was an on-site manager at one of MVP's client companies in Illinois. "I know that certain clients of MVP do not want African Americans assigned to work at their company and that MVP has a policy of accommodating these requests," Ceja said in her statement. She added that she had been "yelled at" if she assigned black workers to a client.

Ceja's statement includes some of the coded language she says MVP used to describe black and Latino workers. Latino workers were described as "feos" (Spanish for "ugly ones"), she said, while black workers were "guapos" (Spanish for "handsome ones" or, according to the court filings, "pretty boys—ones who don't want to do dirty work.")

"The obstacles in getting a job are among the most difficult to detect," Sellers said. "Most people have no idea if other people are treated differently than they are in applications for jobs."

There is even greater concern about the number of young people, often in emerging and developing countries, who live in poverty despite having a job. Young people struggling to find permanent jobs are inevitable to accept temporary and intern positions. However, training and internships are not always considered by employers as "real" work experience. Moreover, temporary jobs are less protected, often pay less, and do not offer job-related training and social benefits. As a result, underemployed young people are more prone to poverty risk, lower wages, and worst career opportunities.

Through most labor market indicators, there were large disparities between young women and young men, which reinforce and fuel an increase in inequalities during the transition to adulthood (ILO). In 2016, for example, the labor force participation rate for young men stands at 53.9 percent, compared with 37.3 percent for young women, which represents a disparity of 16.6 points. Indeed, women still earn on average between 10 and 30 percent less than men when working full time (OECD 2015).

Equal Pay for Men and Women? Iceland Wants Employers to Prove It (Extracted from Liz Alderman, March 28, 2017, *The New York Times*)

REYKJAVIK, Iceland—On a chilly afternoon in October, Frida Ros Valdimarsdottir, a former home-care worker turned women's rights advocate, left her office at exactly 2:38 p.m. and headed to Reykjavik's main square, where throngs of women were forming a boisterous crowd. It was the time—roughly two and a half hours before the end of the workday—that many protesters reckoned they stopped being paid for equal work.

"For decades, we've said we're going to fix this," said Ms. Valdimarsdottir, the chairwoman of the Icelandic Women's Rights Association and an organizer of the demonstration." But women are still getting lower pay, and that's insane."

The government wants to change that dynamic. Iceland on Tuesday became the first country to introduce legislation requiring employers to prove they are paying men and women equally.

Today, about half of Iceland's Parliament members are women. Nearly 80 percent of women work and, with a gender quota in place, almost half of company board members are women.

Yet many women still have less economic power than men. Top level and intermediate managers are mostly men, and the pay gap is especially persistent for working mothers and women in female-dominated fields.

Such inequalities are not simply due to differences in education and skills among workers. The labor market continues to make socially driven distinctions based on ethnicity, race, sex, age, and other personal attributes that should have no bearing on job opportunities or workers' competencies or ability. For instance, it is the case of lesbian, gay, bisexual, or transgender people. Even when the legal framework is supportive in many countries, overt and subtle discrimination still persist at the workplace.

Lesbian College Coaches Still Face Difficult Atmosphere to Come Out (Extracted from Shannon Ryan, January 17, 2017, *Chicago Tribune*)

Courtney Graham said everything was going smoothly with her assistant coaching job with Drake University's women's basketball team. The Bulldogs were building the program, and Graham said she was handling her recruiting and scouting responsibilities well, resulting in bonuses and positive performance reviews. That changed, she said, when she brought her now-wife to a game to sit in the family section in November 2014. In a federal lawsuit filed in late December, Graham alleges that as a result, head coach Jennie Baranczyk ostracized her from the team, told her she was not acting like herself, diminished her duties and asked her to resign in May 2015. Graham turned in her resignation a month later after, she said, undue pressure from Baranczyk. "She loves coaching," Graham's attorney, Tina Muhammad, told the Tribune. […]

Drake has denied the allegations. A university statement in reply to the suit said the school and Baranczyk "have a strong commitment to diversity, tolerance and non-discrimination." Regardless of the suit's outcome, the case has stirred lingering questions about homophobia in college athletics and the specific challenges lesbian coaches face. Stereotypes about women in sports lead to a don't-ask-don't-tell atmosphere that keeps many closeted, coaches and advocates told the Tribune.

"There is still a lot of fear out there among lesbian coaches about coming out and suffering professional consequences as a result," said Pat Griffin, a Massachusetts Amherst professor who has studied and written about homophobia and sports.

From subtle aspects of coaching such as including family in media guides or inviting the team to their home for a cookout to more significant areas such as recruiting and job security, the culture of college athletics continues to make their sexuality feel like a career risk. [...]

"It's hard when you're hiding part of yourself at work when you're trying to be a role model to 20-year-olds," said Howe, now executive director of the Nashville LGBT chamber of commerce. "There are young people taking their lives. There are young people getting kicked out of their homes and families. I (was) on a daily basis sending this message: It's OK to be gay as long as you don't tell anyone or hide it. Or maybe I (was) sending the message it's not OK".

"It finally became such an internal struggle that it was affecting a lot of parts of my life. It affected how well I was coaching, my happiness, my relationships with friends and my partner. You get tired of lying. I wasn't outright lying, but I wasn't being honest. If you're a person of integrity, you want to be honest."

Another vulnerable group increasingly visible and discriminated at the workplace is transgender people. For example, in the UK's Gender Recognition Act of 2004 and the 2010 Equality Act, discrimination on the basis of gender identity is officially recognized as unacceptable. Even though many organizations worldwide are starting to develop zero-tolerance policies to discrimination, data show that transgender people still cope with many obstacles at the workplace. For example, the last US Transgender Survey (James et al. 2016), with a total of 27,715 participants, reports that one in six (16%) respondents who have ever been employed —or 13% of all respondents in the sample—reported losing a job because of their gender identity. In the past year, 27% of those who held or applied for a job during that year—19% of all respondents—reported being fired, denied a promotion, or not being hired for a job they applied for because of their gender identity. Fifteen percent (15%) of respondents were verbally harassed, physically attacked, and/or sexually assaulted at work because of their gender identity. Nearly one-quarter (23%) reported other forms of mistreatment based on their gender identity, such as being forced to use a restroom that did not match their gender identity, being told to present in the wrong gender in order to keep their job, or having a boss or coworker share private information about their transgender status without their permission. Finally, more than three-quarters (77%) of respondents took steps to avoid mistreatment in the workplace, such as hiding or delaying their gender transition or quitting their job.

Labor market exclusion is also severe among persons with disabilities, who may be employed but unable to fully use their human capital, may not find jobs due to a wide range of barriers, or may have left the labor force in the face of a lack of opportunities. Persons with mental health difficulties or intellectual impairments often have the lowest employment rates (World Bank 2011). People with disabilities face not only physical but also psychological barriers in accessing the workplace. Moreover, there are misconceptions among employers and society at large about the ability of persons with disabilities to work and about their potential productivity (e.g., Nelissen et al. 2016). Thus, open discrimination still exists. Despite legal framework, such as the 2010 Equality Act in the UK, brought into practice to prevent discrimination against disabled people in the workplace, workers with disabilities in many countries are still often treated unfairly.

I'm Disabled and in My 50s—The Fear That I won't Find a Job Is Paralysing (Extracted from *The Guardian*, February 24, 2017)

I have a neurological movement disorder called dystonia which makes the muscles of my face, tongue and larynx spasm uncontrollably. It's a condition most people have never heard of and there is no cure. The good news is it can be managed with regular Botox injections. So six or seven times a year I get injections to numb the muscles in my larynx, face and neck.

I am in my 50s and am fortunate to have a job, but the dystonia affects the clarity of my speech, and it was made it clear to me recently that I would not be progressing any further at work because people find it difficult to understand me. My salary was then arbitrarily cut.

I've started looking for a new job, but it's impossible. One of the problems is the rise of telephone interviews. In a room full of people I can distract and divert, the occasional muscle spasm or slurred S can be missed. On the telephone—and most one-to-one interviews—it is just me and my dodgy diction. There is always that moment: I stumble over a word. They notice. I hesitate. There's a dizzying second of silence and I know the gig is up. I can almost hear them thinking: "Is he drunk? Is his mouth full?"

The fear that I am being coaxed into redundancy and that I won't find another job has become mentally—and physically, because stress makes my spasms worse—paralysing.

The 2008 financial and economic crisis has exacerbated these trends, as employment has become more unstable and precarious for a growing number of workers since the crisis, and those unemployed are at growing risk of long-term exclusion from the labor market (ILO 2014, 2015a). Globally in 2014, two billion people of working age were not participating in the labor force, and the number is projected to continue growing (ILO). For the majority of workers, informal jobs are not a choice but reflect the limited availability of formal, more desirable jobs, as well as workers' limited bargaining power in the businesses that employ them (Harris and Krueger 2015).

Inclusion as business case for organizations

Within the picture delineated before, physical and psychological boundaries among social groups are progressively deeper, increasing not only open but also covert discrimination against vulnerable groups at the workplace. It comes with important economic loss for the societies at large and for organizations which are not profiting from and taking advantages of the business case of diversity and inclusion. Indeed, inclusion is also a business opportunity. As some researchers point out, real inclusion reduces costs associated with turnover, absenteeism, and low productivity; makes greater/new market share as growing diversity of customers; increases sales and profits; and mitigates and minimizes legal risks resulted from grievances (e.g., Lockwood 2005; Özbilgin et al. 2016). When diversity and inclusion come to the organizational agenda, both the moral/values case (the "right thing to do") and the business case (the "smart thing to do") are important and necessary; they do not contradict each other, but rather complement each other. A strong business case for diversity will clearly show that creating a diverse and inclusive workplace will benefit everyone in the organization, by making the organization stronger, more resilient, and more competitive. In this sense, organizations can build the business case for speeding up progress toward diversity and inclusion, developing strategies that engage their stakeholders (Özbilgin et al. 2016). To do so, diversity management and inclusion should be seen as everyone's responsibility where Social Dialogue can help intertwine everyone's needs to achieve a successful continuous change.

Facebook Pushes Outside Law Firms to Become More Diverse (Extracted from Ellen Rosen, April 2, 2017, *The New York Times*)

Like other Silicon Valley giants, Facebook has faced criticism over whether its work force and board are too white and too male. Last year, the social media behemoth started a new push on diversity in hiring and retention.

Now, it is extending its efforts into another corner: the outside lawyers who represent the company in legal matters.

Facebook is requiring that women and ethnic minorities account for at least 33% of law firm teams working on its matters.

Numbers alone, however, are not enough, under a policy that went in effect on Saturday. Law firms must also show that they "actively identify and create clear and measurable leadership opportunities for women and minorities" when they represent the company in litigation and other legal matters.

A holistic view of diversity: The Circle of Inclusion

To date, diversity has been managed through HRM policies like a fixed picture of the work environment. Although it has been one of the core strategies to be successful in the current global market, most organizations have not reached a real inclusion of people belonging to minority or vulnerable groups. Inclusion is not about assimilating and homogenizing differences, it is about valuing difference. It is about the power that an organization can derive from deliberatively nurturing and integrating heterogeneous groups of people so that they fit together (Sposato et al. 2015). This kind of supportive organizational environments can develop policies that promote inclusion more likely to be adopted, embraced, and flourished.

Recent research is wondering how we measure the success of organizational inclusion policies. For example, Adamson et al. (2016) underline the importance of looking at the quality of inclusion in the workplace. In this sense, it becomes more relevant to ask not only "how many," but also "how" and "what types" of protected/vulnerable people are included in an organization. Where are they located? What roles do they occupy? What kind of people are they? Has our organization managed to challenge some of the stereotypes and cultural biases? As these authors show, although there may be a similar number of women and men in employment, more women are employed on a part-time basis, on less favorable contracts, and in jobs for which they are overqualified.

This means that HRM practices can enable or reinforce discrimination through excluding or incorporating in adverse conditions people from vulnerable groups (women, people with disabilities, ethnic minorities, older people, non-heterosexual employees, etc.).

To date, HR processes have been treated separately as well as diversity management interventions. This handbook synthesizes key illustrative evidence in relevant HR areas (recruitment and selection, onboarding and socialization, assessment and remuneration, training and development, career development, workplace design, health, and employee relations) from a holistic approach.

For instance, in the last review about recruitment and selection carried out by Ployhart et al. (2017), authors highlight that many organizations include diversity hiring goals as part of their mission, so it is not surprising that research has been focused on how recruitment can enhance workforce diversity. Much of this work has attempted to identify the recruiting tactics that increase the attraction of diverse candidates (Walker et al. 2009, 2012).

Moreover, Allen et al. (2017) reflect on how globalization and the increasing demographic diversity of the workforce have powered both socialization and mentoring research in order to create an inclusive work environment. Socialization processes and the development of mentoring networks are crucial in terms of preparing employees for new challenges and increasing the success of global and diverse assignments. Diverse mentorships are those in which members differ on the basis of race, ethnicity, gender, sexual orientation, class, religion, disability, and other group membership characteristics (Ragins 1997).

However, as Dobbin and Kalev (2016) point out many diversity programs fail. The problem is that organizations are trying to reduce bias with the same kinds of programs they have been using since the 1960s. And the usual tools—diversity training, hiring tests, performance ratings, grievance systems—tend to make things worse, not better. Authors analyze data from 829 firms over three decades and show that these tools actually *decrease* the proportion of women and minorities in management. Most diversity programs focus on controlling managers' behavior, and as studies show, that approach tends to activate bias rather than cancel it.

In this research, the authors show that the positive effects of diversity training rarely last beyond a day or two, and sometimes can activate bias. Nonetheless, nearly half of midsize companies use it, as do nearly all the Fortune 500. Trainers tell us that people often respond to compulsory courses with anger and resistance—and many participants actually report more animosity toward other groups afterward.

Moreover, some 40% of companies now tries to fight bias with mandatory hiring tests assessing the skills of candidates for frontline jobs. But managers do not like being told that they cannot hire whomever they like, and Dobbin and Kalev's research suggests that they often use the tests selectively. But even managers who test everyone applying for a position may ignore the results. Other companies use performance rating systems trying to prevent biased treatment. However, studies show that raters tend to lower women and minorities in performance reviews. Therefore, ratings do not always boost diversity. Finally, Dobbin and Kalev (2016) refer that when people see that a grievance system does not restrain bad behavior in their organization, they may become less likely to speak up. This leads to another unintended consequence: Managers who receive few complaints conclude that their firms do not have a problem.

In Fig. 1.1, we present the Circle of Inclusion. This model tries to highlight the need to cover each step in the HRM system from a holistic approach in order to create and sustain inclusive organizational environments.

Bearing in mind that diversity and inclusion are key issues to business success in our societies, HRM practices through Human Resource managers as change agents need to show commitment and accountability in achieving the goal that everyone in the organization has the same rights and opportunities and feels valued and respected. In order to ensure everyone, whatever his/her characteristics or background, has equal opportunities in the access to a job position, the organization should develop practices which promote *inclusive recruitment and discrimination-free selection* (see Bozani et al., Chap. 6 and Salgado et al., Chap. 7 in this volume). That means not to focus on any cues which are not relevant for the job using unbiased tools and instruments in the selection process as well as taking into account candidates' perceptions.

Many organizations could think that they would be accomplishing the goal to be diverse, even inclusive, with the previous step. However, when the new employee enters in a new work environment, sometimes she/he needs some kind of accommodations in order to fill in the expectations and job requirements. That is, we need workplaces with *work designs that work* to include people with different characteristics and capabilities (see Zijlstra et al., Chap. 8 in this volume).

Fig. 1.1 Circle of Inclusion through social dialogue

Being and feeling part of the new environment is sometimes difficult and could entail conflicts, isolation, or lack of adjustment. Through *colorful socialization and training*, we emphasize the need for guidelines and training in the new job, where the role of supervisor and coworkers is key to overcome initial barriers and to rule out conscious and unconscious bias (see Medina and Gamero, Chap. 9 and Torres and Hanashiro, Chap. 10 in this volume). Along the employee lifecycle, *performance appraisal and compensation with fairness* become also crucial to have motivated and productive people, who feel identified with the organizational values. To ensure true and constructive performance appraisal and reward accordingly help develop trust and communication.

Healthy and safe workers should be the ideal aim of each organization. However, this is not the case when people do not feel respected or not supported due to any personal feature or trait. Organizations will attain a sustainable development only when *a safe place for all* is promoted, a place where people feel free to be what they are (see Deakin, Chap. 11 and Di Marco, Chap. 12 in this volume). In this sense, to have the possibility of managing your own career is one way to show what everybody is.

Developing multiple careers is the result of taking into account the different roles in life trying to remain employable (see Peters et al., Chap. 14 and Martinez-Corts and Demerouti, Chap. 15 in this volume). It also means promoting the career development of invisible groups in those countries where inclusion is not an important value for organizations (see Obi and Bollen, Chap. 16 in this volume). The final step of this circle is not a real end. Nowadays, there are more diverse ways to stay linked to the organization you were working for. Part-time or mentoring programs, compressed workweek, or job sharing could be some of the key elements to adopt a phased retirement. Therefore, *farewell is not a goodbye.*

All of these steps should be present in a diverse and inclusive HRM system. To do it possible, every organization can start from a different place and in a unique context, but all have room for improvement. In developing a real and complete diversity management which promotes inclusion, it is important to focus on the multiple stakeholders, business environment, and the stage of the process of organizational change. If the conditions of the business environment are supportive, stakeholders have voice and participation; there is a true commitment to diversity and inclusion; and the organization can move toward developing more sophisticated strategies. As Özbilgin et al. (2016) highlight, a strong business case is key in convincing all organizational actors about the importance of diversity management and inclusion, "creating a sense of relevance, urgency, and immediacy."

We have seen in the previous sections the important role that the HRM system can play in the promotion of equity, voice, participation, and empowerment in the process of organizational change. Although some practices can change quickly, organizational change is often a slow and gradual process. In this sense, to be inclusive, it is essential that policies are aligned, both with each other as well as with the broader values, strategy, and priorities of the organization. We need to focus on the employee life cycle to identify diversity gaps in the HRM system and to define how overcoming barriers to diversity can leverage to a successful continuous change.

Once inclusive and participatory organizational policies are in place, they generate virtuous cycles that prevent inequalities and discriminations and tend to support the creation of inclusive organizational environments. Some successful companies have overcome such obstacles applying several basic principles: engage managers, promote Social Dialogue and participation, and encourage social accountability for promoting inclusion. Organizational leaders and other partners commonly present play an important role in setting the tone for the shift toward increased diversity and inclusiveness in an organization. Open, effective communication, as well as clear channels for feedback, optimizes the opportunity for discussion of issues related to inclusion and discrimination.

Changing organizations requires challenging norms and values that evolve slowly and are deeply affected by context, culture, and history. Therefore, there is no only one-size-fits-all template for how organizations can initiate the process of sustainable change, but with concerted effort from all stakeholders involved, they can move forward. Taking initial steps—however modest—toward a more inclusive approach can slowly encourage different group of interest to come together and push for further change.

In doing so, organizations can create an enabling environment for such participation by building capacity, opening spaces for consultation, and forming alliances between social partners, including employers, workers representatives, employees, and unions. These new voices can help to "create momentum" for further change and for those organizations to look beyond the needs of their current agents. While the success of such efforts depends on national and local circumstances as well, it is clear that organizations should lead the way. The continuous change required should be based on Social Dialogue as an incremental social innovation strategy.

This handbook is the fourth volume in Springer series on *Industrial Relations & Conflict Management*. The series takes an interdisciplinary approach; however, it is firmly based on theories about human behavior in relation to work and organizations.

The goal of this handbook is to highlight the connections between theory, research, and practice on diversity and inclusion and how to successfully manage them through Social Dialogue following the HRM system. In doing so, we integrate multiple disciplinary perspectives (e.g., management, business, psychology, law, and sociology) and showcases from different organizational contexts, countries, and cultures. Starting with a conceptual and legislative approach to diversity and inclusion in organizations (see Dovidio et al., Chap. 2 and Demetriades, Chap. 4 in this volume), this handbook teaches how to create and shape inclusive and supportive work environments showing primarily the need for management commitment and organizational code of practices (see Hoel and McBride, Chap. 3 in this volume). The HRM system is covered by empirical research regarding different vulnerable groups. And, finally, the Circle of Inclusion is put into practice through several showcases along the handbook developed in international organizations (see Patricia et al., Chap. 5; Verschueren and Euwema, Chap. 13; Ramirez and Ramirez, Chap. 17 in this volume).

Organizations cannot be considered inclusive if inequalities are high or growing, and decent work opportunities are lacking. Many people remain vulnerable and are "being left behind" (UN 2016a, b). An initial step toward creating more and better work for all, which is the main purpose of this handbook, is to address these inequalities through the whole HRM system, giving voice, and participation with Social Dialogue as incremental innovation strategy, to achieve the successful continuous change needed.

References

Adamson, M., Kelan, E. K., Lewis, P., Rumens, N., & Slíwa, M. (2016). The quality of equality: Thinking differently about gender inclusion in organizations. *Human Resource Management International Digest, 24*(7), 8–11.

Allen, T. D., Eby, L. T., Chao, G. T., & Bauer, T. N. (2017). Taking Stock of two relational aspects of organizational life: Tracing the history and shaping the future of socialization and mentoring research. *Journal of Applied Psychology, 102*(3), 324–337.

Barrett, F. J., Thomas, G. F., & Hocevar, S. P. (1995). The central role of discourse in large-scale change: A social construction perspective. *Journal of Applied Behavioral Science, 31,* 352–372.

Cheng, Y. T., & Van de Ven, A. H. (1996). Learning the innovation journey: order out of chaos? *Organizational Science, 7,* 593–614.

Deaton, A. (2008). Income, health, and well-being around the world: evidence from the Gallup World Poll. *Journal of Economic Perspectives, 22*(2), 53–72.

Dixon, N. M. (1997). The hallways of learning. *Organizational Dynamics, 25,* 23–34.

Dobbin, F., & Kalev, A. (2016). Whay diversity programs fail. *Harvard Business Review, July-August Issue*, 52–60.

European Commission. (2014). *Assessment of progress towards the Europe 2020 social inclusion objectives: Main findings and suggestions on the way forward.* Luxembourg: Publications Office of the European Union.

European Commission. (2017). Commission Recommendation of 26.4.2017 on the European Pillar of Social Rights Brussels, C (2017) 2600 final.

Euwema, M. C., Munduate, L., Elgoibar, P., Pender, E., & García, A. B. (Eds.). (2015). *Promoting social dialogue in European organizations.* The Netherlands: Springer International.

Harris, S. D., & Krueger, A. B. (2015). *A proposal for modernizing labor laws for twenty-first-century work: The "Independent Worker".* Discussion Paper 2015–10. The Hamilton Project

ILO. (2005). *Social dialogue: Finding a common voice. Social dialogue sector.* International Labor Office: Geneva.

ILO. (2012). 101st international labour conference, the youth employment crisis: A call for action. Geneva.

ILO. (2014). *Global employment trends 2014: The risk of a jobless recovery.* Geneva: International Labour Office.

ILO. (2015a). *World employment and social outlook 2015: The changing nature of jobs.* Geneva: International Labour Office.

ILO. (2016). *World employment and social Outlook 2016: Trends for youth.* Geneva: International Labour Office.

James, S. E., Herman, J. L., Rankin, S., Keisling, M., Mottet, L., & Anafi, M. (2016). *The report of the 2015 U.S. Transgender survey.* Washington, DC: National Center for Transgender Equality.

Jones, J. M., Dovidio, J. F., & Vietze, D. L. (2014). *The psychology of diversity: Beyond prejudice and racism.* New York, NY: Wiley.

Kalinoski, Z. T., Steele-Johnson, D., Peyton, E. J., Leas, K. A., Steinke, J., & Bowling, N. A. (2013). A meta-analytic evaluation of diversity training outcomes. *Journal of Organizational Behavior, 34,* 1076–1104.

King, N., & Anderson, N. (1995). *Innovation and change in organization.* New York: Routledge.

Kunze, L., & Suppa, N. (2014). Bowling alone or bowling at all? The effect of unemployment on social participation. Ruhr Economic Papers, No. 510. Dortmund, Germany: Technische Universitat Dortmund.

Lockwood. N. R. (2005, June). Workplace diversity: Leveraging the power of difference for competitive advantage. *Research Quarterly. Society for Human Resource Management*, www.shrm.org/hrresources.

Miller, F.A., & Katz, J.H. (2007). *The path form exclusive club to inclusive organization: A developmental process.* Retrieved from http://blogs.ces.uwex.edu/inclusiveexcellence/files/2011/11/Path-from-Exclusive-Club-to-Inclusive-Organization-Article.pdf.

Nelissen, P. T. J. H., Hülsheger, U. R., van Ruitenbeek, G. M. C., & Zijlstra, F. R. H. (2016). How and when stereotypes relate to inclusive behaviour toward people with disabilities. *The International Journal of Human Resource Management, 27*(14), 1610–1625.

Norton, A., & de Haan, A. (2012). *Social cohesion: Theoretical debates and practical applications with respect to jobs.* Background Paper for the World Development Report 2013. Washington,

D.C.: World Bank. Available from: https://openknowledge.worldbank.org/handle/10986/12147 License: CC BY 3.0 IGO.
Organisation for Economic Co-operation and Development (OECD). (2015). *Indicators of Immigrant integration 2015: Settling in*. Paris: OECD Publishing.
Özbilgin, M., Tatli, A., Ipek, G., & Sameer, M. (2016). Four approaches to accounting for diversity in global organisations. *Critical Perspectives on Accounting, 35,* 88–99.
Pender, E., Elgoibar, P., Munduate, L., Garcia, A., & Euwema, M. (2017). *Improving social dialogue in European organizations: The employers' perspective.* Economic and Labour Relations Review.
Ployhart, R. E., Schmitt, N., & Tippins, N. T. (2017). Solving the supreme problem: 100 years of selection and recruitment at the journal of applied psychology. *Journal of Applied Psychology, 102*(3), 291–304.
Ragins, B. R. (1997). Diversified mentoring relationships in organizations: A power perspective. *Academy of Management Review, 22,* 482–521.
Roberson, Q., Ryan, A. M., & Ragins, B. R. (2017). The evolution and future of diversity at work. *Journal of Applied Psychology, 102*(3), 483–499.
Salikutluk, Z., Giesecke, J., & Kroh, M. (2016). Refugees entered the labor market later than other migrants. *DIW Economic Bulletin, 6*(34/35), 407–413.
Schein, E. H. (1993). On dialogue, culture, and organizational learning. *Organizational Dynamics, 21,* 40–51.
Sposato, M., Feeke, S., Anderson-Walsh, P., & Spencer, L. (2015). Diversity, inclusion and the workplace-equality index: The ingredients for organizational success. *Human Resource Management International Digest, 23*(5), 16–17.
Stewart, F. (2002). Root causes of violent conflict in developing countries. *British Medical Journal, 324*(7333), 342–345.
Tushman, M. L., & Romanelli, E. (1985). Organizational revolution: A metamorphosis model of convergence and reorientation. *Organizational Behavior, 7,* 171–222.
United Nations (UN). (2016a). *Global Initiative on decent jobs for youth: Strategy document page*. New York.
United Nations (UN). (2016b). Leaving no one behind: The imperative of inclusive development. Report on the World Social Situation 2016. United Nations Publication.
van Knippenberg, D., & Schippers, M. C. (2007). Work group diversity. *Annual Review of Psychology, 58,* 515–541.
Walker, H. J., Feild, H. S., Bernerth, J. B., & Becton, J. B. (2012). Diversity cues on recruitment websites: Investigating the effects on job seekers' information processing. *Journal of Applied Psychology, 97,* 214–224.
Walker, H. J., Feild, H. S., Giles, W. F., Armenakis, A. A., & Bernerth, J. B. (2009). Displaying employee testimonials on recruitment web sites: Effects of communication media, employee race, and job seeker race on organizational attraction and information credibility. *Journal of Applied Psychology, 94,* 1354–1364.
Weick, K. E., & Quinn, R. E. (1999). Organizational change and development. *Annual Review of Psychology, 50,* 361–386.
Wietzke, F.B., & McLeod, C. (2013). *Jobs, wellbeing, and social cohe-sion: Evidence from value and perception surveys.* Policy Research Working Paper, No. 6447. Washington, D.C.: World Bank.
Woods, S. (2002). Creating inclusive organizations: Aligning systems with diversity [Electronic version]. *Profiles in Diversity Journal, 4*(1), 38–39. http://digitalcommons.ilr.cornell.edu/articles/57.
World Bank. (2011). *World development report 2012: Gender equality and develop-ment.* Washington, D.C.: World Bank.

Chapter 2
General Concepts About Inclusion in Organizations: A Psychological Approach to Understanding Diversity and Inclusion in Organizations

John F. Dovidio, Silvia Abad-Merino and Carmen Tabernero

2.1 A Psychological Approach to Diversity

Humans evolved as social animals developing groups and social organizations; in this sense, the groups individuals identify with continue to profoundly affect all aspects of social and individual functioning. Social identities delineate those who are members of one's group (ingroup members) and those who are not (outgroup members). Ingroup membership, in turn, defines a bounded community of mutual trust and obligation that delimit mutual interdependence and cooperation. The ingroup provides valuable material benefits (e.g., through reciprocity and support) but also psychological value (e.g., by increasing a sense of security and feelings of esteem). By contrast, when others are defined as outgroup members, they can readily arouse threat and elicit competitive orientations, which often justify their exclusion and exploitation. In complex societies in which people have multiple roles and diverse identities, the dimensions on which people are included or excluded can have significant impact on both individuals and organizations. Diversity can thus either be a valuable resource or a detriment to effective functioning within organizations, depending how it is approached and managed.

In this chapter, we next consider the powerful psychological effects of group identity and categorization—boundaries that define who is included and who is excluded. Then, we discuss the two most dominant approaches to managing diversity in societies and organizations, colorblindness and associated assimilationist strategies compare to multiculturalism. After that, we highlight how understanding the psychological challenges and benefits of diversity is critical for

J.F. Dovidio · S. Abad-Merino
Department of Psychology, Yale University, New Haven, CT, USA

C. Tabernero (✉)
Department of Social Psychology, University of Salamanca, Salamanca, Spain
e-mail: carmen.tabernero@usal.es

A. Arenas et al. (eds.), *Shaping Inclusive Workplaces Through Social Dialogue*, Industrial Relations & Conflict Management,
DOI 10.1007/978-3-319-66393-7_2

managing the dynamic landscape in which diversity operates within organizations and to build more inclusive and effective organizations.

2.2 Social Identity and Categorization

Because of the evolutionary significance of group life, people automatically categorize others as members of the ingroup or the outgroup. This distinction has profound psychological and social consequences (see Dovidio and Gaertner 2010, for a review). When they think about others in terms of their membership in the ingroup or outgroups, people spontaneously value those perceived to be part of the ingroup more (ingroup favoritism) and often devalue those viewed as members of a different group. People process information more deeply and accurately about ingroup than outgroup members (Van Bavel et al. 2008), evaluate them more positively (Otten and Moskowitz 2000), and communicate more effectively with them (Greenaway et al. 2015). Also, people typically behave in a spontaneous cooperative manner in their exchanges with others within their group (Bear and Rand 2016) and display greater loyalty to their group and its members when attractive alternatives are available (Van Vugt and Hart 2004).

While cohesion, cooperation, and commitment represent generally positive organizational qualities, the dynamics of social categorization processes may compromise these benefits as the boundaries defining group membership unfairly exclude individuals because of their social group membership. Because of the social significance of the group distinctions, people automatically—often without conscious intention—categorize others based on gender, race, ethnicity, age, disability, and other socially significant dimensions. This process can create substantial social divides and fissures that undermine coordination, morale, and performance within organizations. Internationally, social diversity is rapidly increasing, and thus understanding the impact of different strategies for managing diversity within organizations is a critical, pressing issue.

2.3 Psychological Theory and Approaches to Managing Diversity

Approaches to managing diversity involve two broad types of diversity ideologies, *colorblindness,* which is a form of assimilation that focuses on de-emphasizing different group memberships (Wolsko et al. 2000), and *multiculturalism,* which focuses on acknowledging and valuing diversity.

2.3.1 Colorblindness and Assimilation

Assimilation of members of other groups into a society can take many forms. One of the most common of such approaches in organizations is colorblindness that emphasizes a shared identity in place of other (e.g., ethnic, gender) group identities. If successfully adopted, it has a number of immediate benefits, particularly with respect to reducing existing intergroup tensions within an organization.

According to the common ingroup identity model (Gaertner and Dovidio 2000; Gaertner et al. 2016), factors that induce members of different groups (e.g., ethnic groups) to recategorize themselves as members of the same more inclusive group (e.g., the particular organization) can reduce intergroup bias through cognitive and motivational processes involving ingroup favoritism (Gaertner and Dovidio 2000; Gaertner et al. 2016). Recategorization changes the conceptual representations of the different groups from an "us" versus "them" orientation to a more encompassing, superordinate "we" connection. Creating a salient common identity thus harnesses the forces of ingroup bias that produce more positive beliefs, feelings, and behaviors usually reserved for ingroup members, but now extends or redirects these forces toward former outgroup members because of their recategorized ingroup status. As a consequence, when members of an organization accept and endorse a common identity they show more positive attitudes toward each other and to the organization and are more trusting and cooperative with each other and more committed to the organization.

However, the effectiveness of colorblindness may be limited both in implementing the approach and in its consequences. Attempts to create a colorblind community may face resistance, particularly among individual with strong allegiance to other identities. Individuals are often reluctant to forsake personally and socially important group identities (e.g., ethnic group identity) to adopt a new shared identity. When attempts are made to forge a common identity, they show resistance and often experience distress (Crisp et al. 2006). Moreover, attempts perceived as imposing a colorblind ideology within an organization are likely to be perceived as communicating disrespect to those who identify with other groups. In intergroup contexts, members of minority and traditionally disadvantaged groups are highly motivated to be respected by majority and advantaged-group members (Bergsieker et al. 2010; Shnabel and Nadler 2005), and the failure to acknowledge their social group identity is perceived as an affront to them and their group (Apfelbaum et al. 2008). In terms of consequences, emphasizing commonality through colorblindness while de-emphasizing others, distinct social identities increase conformity of views and action, narrow the perspectives expressed within an organization, and reduce the organization's ability to consider and respond effectively to the diversity that exists in global markets.

2.3.2 Multiculturalism

To the extent to which multiculturalism makes different group memberships salient, it can activate ingroup-outgroup biases and exacerbate intergroup tensions. For example, emphasizing a multicultural ideology tends to increase stereotyping of members of other groups (Wolsko et al. 2000). Moreover, this heighten salience can increase realistic (material) threat or symbolic threat to traditional values and culture experienced by majority group members and produce social backlash by the majority group to minority groups (Craig and Richeson 2014; Plaut et al. 2011; Yogeeswaran and Dasgupta 2014). For these reasons, members of majority groups support a multicultural ideology less (and a colorblind ideology more) than do members of minority groups.

However, multiculturalism typically involves more than recognizing and accepting group differences; it also highlights the positive interdependence of the various groups. Gaertner and Dovidio (2000), Gaertner et al. (2016) proposed that thinking in terms of a dual identity, different groups within an overarching common identity, permits the recognition of distinctive qualities of members of different groups in ways that support a common identity—conceiving the relationship as "different groups on the same team." Thus, group differences in a dual identity, a form of multiculturalism, are considered a beneficial resource to achieve common goals. As a consequence, members of majority groups attend more closely to the needs and ideas of members of minority groups when they adopt a multicultural perspective than when they endorse a colorblind perspective (Vorauer et al. 2009). This deeper and more individuated processing promotes dialogue and the exchange of personalized information, which in turn facilitates perspective-taking and mitigates the influence of stereotypes within the immediate interaction and undermines that application of stereotypes to the group as a whole (Miller 2002; see also Peters et al., Chap. 12 in this volume). Moreover, dialogue groups, because they recognize the different perspectives, needs, and experiences of members of different groups while fostering interpersonal and intergroup connections, foster the kind of respect between groups that is central to multiculturalism (Gurin et al. 2013).

However, multiculturalism under some circumstances can exacerbate social discord within an organization. To the extent to which members of a majority group believe that their identity is not included and respected in multiculturalism, they respond more negatively to the policy and show greater negativity toward other groups and may be more competitive in their orientation (Plaut et al. 2011). Affirming the importance of the majority group within the organization with a multicultural orientation can also have negative consequences. To the extent that both subgroup (e.g., ethnic) and superordinate group (e.g., organizational) identities are salient, people—mainly members of the ethnic majority group or of the socially dominant in the context—may tend to project the standards of their group as the standards for the superordinate group (i.e., ingroup projection; Mummendey and Wenzel 1999). That is, when a common identity is salient for members of different groups, members of one group or both groups regard their subgroup's characteristics (such as norms, values, and goals) as more prototypical of the common, inclusive category compared with those of the other subgroup. When this occurs, the outgroup is judged as substandard, deviant, or inferior, leading to greater bias between the subgroups (e.g., Waldzus et al. 2004). However, this ingroup projection effect is ameliorated when the superordinate identity is one that is complex, including many facets that are necessary and desirable, rather than simple, in which membership is defined along a singular dimension (Ukes et al. 2012).

2.4 Building XXI Century Inclusive Organizations: Psychological Challenges and Benefits

Not only do the different approaches to managing diversity psychologically—colorblind assimilation and multiculturalism, have different benefits and potential costs, but their effectiveness depends on many different dynamic factors within organizations. Thus, colorblindness and multiculturalism may be viewed as complementary rather than competing strategies for managing diversity and inclusion within organizations. When group tensions within an organization are high, members of different groups tend to be mistrusting of other groups, sensitive to cues of bias, and unwilling to engage in behaviors, such as informal contact or cooperative actions, that can reduce intergroup anxiety and promote organizational cohesion—not simply because of their personal negative feelings but also because they anticipate rejection by members of the other group (Shelton and Richeson 2005). Under such circumstances, emphasizing diversity can create even greater psychological and social divide (Insko et al. 2001). Thus promoting a sense of common identity—a key element of colorblind assimilation—among the members of different groups may be a critical first step to relieve tensions and create a foundation for mutual trust. Organizations and their Human Resource Management System play a key role in developing collective codes (see Hoel and McBride, Chap. 3 in this volume) and learning as an effective answer to promote inclusive leadership and workplaces (Workman-Stark 2017).

Although establishing a sense of common ingroup identity is challenging during periods of intergroup tension and conflict, it is possible. Indeed, the issue of conflict is one that the groups already have in common. Kelman (2005), for example, described the activities and outcomes of a program of workshops for Israeli and Palestinian leaders designed to improve intergroup relations and to contribute to peace in the Middle East. These workshops attempted to create a sense of commonality by emphasizing common fate in terms of the existential interdependence of the groups: The long-term fates of Israeli-Jews and Palestinians in the Middle East are inexorably intertwined, and mutual cooperation is an outcome that is more desirable to both groups than is conflict. After conflict is allayed and opportunities are introduced to induce cooperation between members of different groups to achieve mutually desirable goals (superordinate goals; Sherif et al. 1961) formal acknowledgment of group differences can be reinstated, but in a way that highlights how these differences contribute in essential ways to the successful accomplishment of these goals.

While this emphasis on commonality and colorblindness can have some immediate organizational benefits, harmony achieved through colorblindness can be unstable. One reason is that groups have different orientations toward colorblindness depending on their status (Verkuyten and Martinovic 2012). Members of traditionally advantaged groups tend to prefer colorblindness over multiculturalism. One reason, which may not represent conscious intention, is that colorblindness tends to be system-justifying (Jost et al. 2015)—it reinforces traditional standards, policies, and procedures, which tend to favor members of already advantaged groups. By contrast, members of traditionally disadvantaged groups, within organizations as well as societies, generally favor multicultural approaches and policies, which convey respect (Bergsieker et al. 2010) and affirm and empower (Shnabel and Nadler 2005) their group. Moreover, colorblindness can cloak group-based disparities, for example, in opportunities and achievements, within an organization; to the extent to which group memberships other than the common organizational group identity are de-emphasized, disparities between the subgroups within the organization often go unnoticed or unaddressed (Dovidio et al. 2016). Thus, unless there is salient, concrete evidence that subgroups are appropriately represented in high-status positions within the organization, members of minority groups are suspicious of colorblind policies, which erode their interest in and commitment to the organization (Purdie-Vaughns et al. 2008).

Adopting forms of multiculturalism that acknowledge both difference and commonality may be less comfortable and arouse more intergroup tensions than emphasizing only common identity, colorblindness, and assimilation, but these potentially negative effects may be relieved when diversity is seen as essential to organizational identity. When an overarching organizational identity is represented as one that is more complex and in which different groups are not only included but also integral (e.g., by highlighting the importance of diversity), members of traditionally advantaged groups are less likely to project their group's standards onto the organization, and they are more likely to accept members of other groups within the shared organization identity. As a consequence, they have a more positive orientation to diversity and difference. Members of traditionally disadvantaged groups experience a greater sense of belonging in organizations that espouse a complex identity that they perceive is inclusive of their group. As a result, they experience less stress and less interference with their cognitive functioning, which enhances their personal productivity, as well as their organizational commitment (Cheryan 2012).

In the long term, respecting difference within the context of common connection can reap social and material benefits for both majority- and minority-group members, as well as for the organization as a whole. People show greater integrative complexity (Antonio et al. 2004) and display greater creativity in diverse than homogeneous groups (Crisp and Turner 2011; Leung et al. 2008), and when diversity is acknowledged and respected people are more open and motivated to learn from each other (Migacheva et al. 2011; see also Hahn et al. 2014). Endorsement of a dual identity and the adoption of a multicultural perspective can thus motivate members of majority groups to perceive the value of the distinctive potential contributions of members of different group and communicate the respect that minority-group members seek in their intergroup interactions in ways that promote understanding and acceptance of diversity for common advantage. This collectively generated environment favors social dialogue and facilitates the creation of integrated inclusive values, policies, and practices at organizational level.

2.5 Conclusion

Groups are essential to human existence, both evolutionarily and in contemporary life. Group identity has potent effects psychologically. It can bring individuals together: People automatically value others whom they see as members of their group and willingly cooperate with them to promote the interests of their common group. Group identity can also divide: People value members of other groups less than members of their group, and are more spontaneously competitive and mistrusting toward them. The challenge of diversity in organizations is thus to recognize that diversity is the "social default"—that the world is diverse—and that managing diversity effectively is critical for attracting, retaining, and maximizing the productivity of employees for the organization. However, this management requires a thoughtful and informed balance between stressing commonality—at its extreme colorblindness—and difference within the context of common identity or cooperative relationships among groups. Understanding the psychological dynamics of group identity can thus help leaders respond nimbly and effectively to the social circumstances of their organizations. Intergroup relations are dynamic, often shaped by broad social influences outside the organization, and so assessment of organizational clime and knowledge of psychological process are critical to developing and applying the appropriate policies to cultivate the significant benefits that diversity offers. Social dialogue promotes organizational change to help achieve more inclusive workplaces (Gurin et al. 2013; Munduate et al. 2014). These dialogues, however, require both organizational commitment, reflected in management's inclusive policies and practices, and the reinforcement of positive attitudes and behaviors in the reward structure of the organization. When nurtured and supported, diversity and difference can be valuable resources and can enrich the experiences of both majority- and minority-group members within the organization.

References

Antonio, A. L., Chang, M. J., Hakuta, K., Kenny, D. A., Levin, S., & Milem, J. F. (2004). Effects of racial diversity on complex thinking in college students. *Psychological Science, 15,* 507–510.

Apfelbaum, E. P., Sommers, S. R., & Norton, M. I. (2008). Seeing race and seeming racist? Evaluating strategic colorblindness in social interaction. *Journal of Personality and Social Psychology, 95,* 918–932.

Bear, A., & Rand, D. G. (2016). Intuition, deliberation, and the evolution of cooperation. *Proceedings of the National Academy of Sciences, 113,* 936–941.

Bergsieker, H. B., Shelton, J. N., & Richeson, J. A. (2010). To be liked versus respected: Divergent goals in interracial interactions. *Journal of Personality and Social Psychology, 99,* 248–264.

Cheryan, S. (2012). Understanding the paradox in math-related fields: Why do some gender gaps remain while others do not? *Sex Roles, 66,* 184–190.

Craig, M. A., & Richeson, J. A. (2014). More diverse yet less tolerant? How the increasingly diverse racial landscape affects white Americans' racial attitudes. *Personality and Social Psychology Bulletin, 40*(6), 750–761.

Crisp, R. J., & Turner, R. N. (2011). Cognitive adaptation to the experience of social and cultural diversity. *Psychological Bulletin, 137,* 242–266.

Crisp, R. J., Walsh, J., & Hewstone, M. (2006). Crossed categorization in common ingroup contexts. *Personality and Social Psychology Bulletin, 32,* 1204–1218.

Dovidio, J. F., & Gaertner, S. L. (2010). Intergroup bias. In S. T. Fiske, D. Gilbert, & G. Lindzey (Eds.), *Handbook of social psychology* (Vol. 2, pp. 1084–1121). New York: Wiley.

Dovidio, J. F., Gaertner, S. L., Ufkes, E. G., Saguy, T., & Pearson, A. R. (2016). Included but invisible? Subtle bias, common identity, and the darker side of "we". *Social Issues and Policy Review, 10,* 4–44.

Gaertner, S. L., & Dovidio, J. F. (2000). *Reducing intergroup bias: The Common Ingroup Identity Model.* Philadelphia, PA: Psychology Press.

Gaertner, S. L., Dovidio, J. F., Guerra, R., Hehman, E., & Saguy, T. (2016). A common ingroup identity: A categorization-based approach for reducing intergroup bias. In T. Nelson (Ed.), *Handbook of prejudice, discrimination, and stereotyping* (2nd ed., pp. 433–454). New York: Psychology Press.

Greenaway, K. H., Wright, R. G., Willingham, J., Reynolds, K. J., & Haslam, S. A. (2015). Shared identity is key to effective communication. *Personality and Social Psychology Bulletin, 41,* 171–182.

Gurin, P., Nagda, B. R. A., & Zúñiga, X. (2013). *Dialogue across difference: Practice, theory, and research on intergroup dialogue.* New York, NY: Russell Sage Foundation.

Hahn, A., Nunes, A., Park, B., & Judd, C. M. (2014). Social-psychological recommendations for a diverse work environment. In K. M. Thomas, V. C. Plaut, & M. Tran (Eds.), *Diversity ideologies in organizations* (pp. 236–252). New York, NY: Taylor & Francis.

Insko, C. A., Schopler, J., Gaertner, L., Wildschut, T., Kozar, R., Pinter, B., et al. (2001). Interindividual-intergroup discontinuity reduction through the anticipation of future interaction. *Journal of Personality and Social Psychology, 80,* 95–111.

Jost, J. T., Gaucher, D., & Stern, C. (2015). "The world isn't fair": A system justification perspective on social stratification and inequality. In M. Mikulincer, P. R. Shaver, J. F. Dovidio, & J. A. Simpson (Eds.), *APA handbook of personality and social psychology: Volume 2, Group processes* (pp. 317–340). Washington, DC: American Psychological Association.

Kelman, H. C. (2005). Building trust among enemies: The central challenge for international conflict resolution. *International Journal of Intercultural Relations, 29,* 639–650.

Leung, A. K. Y., Maddux, W. W., Galinsky, A. D., & Chiu, C. Y. (2008). Multicultural experience enhances creativity: The when and how. *American Psychologist, 63*(3), 169–181.

Migacheva, K., Tropp, L. R., & Crocker, J. (2011). Focusing beyond the self: Goal orientations in intergroup relations. In L. R. Tropp & R. K. Mallett (Eds.), *Moving beyond prejudice reduction: Pathways to positive intergroup relations* (pp. 99–115). Washington, DC: American Psychological Association.

Miller, N. (2002). Personalization and the promise of contact theory. *Journal of Social Issues, 58,* 387–410.

Mummendey, A., & Wenzel, M. (1999). Social discrimination and tolerance in intergroup relations: Reactions to intergroup difference. *Personality and Social Psychology Review, 3,* 158–174.

Munduate, L., Di Marco, D., Martínez-Corts, I., Arenas, A., & Gamero, N. (2014). Rebuilding the social dialogue and promoting inclusive organizations. A tool for social innovation in times of crisis. *Papeles del Psicólogo, 35,* 122–129.

Otten, S., & Moskowitz, G. B. (2000). Evidence for implicit evaluative in-group bias: Affect-based spontaneous trait inference in a minimal group paradigm. *Journal of Experimental Social Psychology, 36,* 77–89.

Plaut, V. C., Garnett, F. G., Buffardi, L. E., & Sanchez-Burks, J. (2011). "What about me?" Perceptions of exclusion and whites reactions to multiculturalism. *Journal of Personality and Social Psychology, 101,* 337–353.

Purdie-Vaughns, V., Steele, C. M., Davies, P. G., Ditlmann, R., & Crosby, J. R. (2008). Social identity contingencies: How diversity cues signal threat or safety for African Americans in mainstream institutions. *Journal of Personality and Social Psychology, 94,* 615–630.

Shelton, J. N., & Richeson, J. A. (2005). Intergroup contact and pluralistic ignorance. *Journal of Personality and Social Psychology, 88,* 91–107.

Sherif, M., Harvey, O. J., White, B. J., Hood, W. R., & Sherif, C. W. (1961). *Intergroup conflict and cooperation: The Robbers Cave experiment.* Norman, OK: University of Oklahoma Book Exchange.

Shnabel, N., & Nadler, A. (2005). The role of agency and morality in reconciliation processes: The perspective of the needs-based model. *Current Directions in Psychological Science, 24,* 477–483.

Ukes, E. G., Otten, S., van der Zee, K., Giebels, E., & Dovidio, J. F. (2012). Urban district identity as common ingroup identity: The different role of ingroup prototypicality for minority and majority groups. *European Journal of Social Psychology, 42,* 707–716.

Van Bavel, J. J., Packer, D. J., & Cunningham, W. A. (2008). The neural substrates of in-group bias. *Psychological Science, 19,* 1131–1139.

Van Vugt, M., & Hart, C. M. (2004). Social identity as social glue: The origins of group loyalty. *Journal of Personality and Social Psychology, 86,* 585–598.

Verkuyten, M., & Martinovic, B. (2012). Immigrants' national identification: Meanings, determinants, consequences. *Social Issues and Policy Review, 6,* 82–122.

Vorauer, J. D., Gagnon, A., & Sasaki, S. J. (2009). Salient intergroup ideology and intergroup interaction. *Psychological Science, 20,* 838–845.

Waldzus, S., Mummendey, A., Wenzel, M., & Boettcher, F. (2004). Of bikers, teachers, and Germans: Groups' diverging views about their prototypicality. *British Journal of Social Psychology, 43,* 385–400.

Wolsko, C., Park, B., Judd, C. M., & Wittenbrink, B. (2000). Framing interethnic ideology: Effects of multicultural and color-blind perspectives on judgments of groups and individuals. *Journal of Personality and Social Psychology, 78,* 635–654.

Workman-Stark, A. L. (2017). *Inclusive leadership. In inclusive policing from the inside out* (pp. 167–188). New York: Springer International Publishing.

Yogeeswaran, K., & Dasgupta, N. (2014). Conceptions of national identity in a globalized world: Antecedents and consequences. *European Review of Social Psychology, 25,* 189–227.

Chapter 3
'Getting In,' 'Staying In,' and 'Moving On': Using Standards to Achieve Diversity and Inclusion

Helge Hoel and Anne McBride

3.1 Introduction

The British Standards Institution (BSI) provides standards for UK organizational activity. At their core, standards contain advice about organizational performance and knowledge about how to succeed, in a distilled form. Despite its UK base, the BSI's operation is global in scope, assisting organizations with achieving standards through accreditation and advice. In this, the BSI parallels the work of international standards bodies such as the International Standards Institution (ISO). Whilst standards in connection with organizational activities such as occupational health and safety (BS OHSAS 18001), quality management (ISO 9001), and social responsibility (ISO 26000) are well known to many, the BSI has recently embarked on a process of developing standards for management systems for 'valuing people at work', a process facilitated by the BSI and carried out by means of broad stakeholder involvement. This is new territory for BSI as this is the first British or indeed, first standard altogether which relates directly to the management of people within an organization.

It is a fundamental premise of this new standard (BS 76000) (BSI 2015) that people are inherently valuable—they are an organization's biggest asset and should be treated as such. This standard provides a management system or framework for any organization to put processes in place that will help harness the relationship with their members and assist in realizing people's potential whether in terms of knowledge, skills, experience, behaviors, and attitudes. In line with BSI's adherence to principles of sustainability, it is envisaged that the new standard will also contribute to sustainable operation, ensuring current and future success. The standard was developed using a collaborative, consensus-based approach, drawing on expertise from a range of employers, trade unions, academics, and a variety of

H. Hoel (✉) · A. McBride
Alliance Manchester Business School, University of Manchester, Manchester, UK
e-mail: helge.hoel@manchester.ac.uk

A. Arenas et al. (eds.), *Shaping Inclusive Workplaces Through Social Dialogue*,
Industrial Relations & Conflict Management,
DOI 10.1007/978-3-319-66393-7_3

industry bodies, including the Chartered Institute of Personnel and Development (CIPD), which from the start has played a key role in initiating this undertaking.

To support the practical application of the standard, a new set of management Codes of Practice (CoPs) are currently being developed, themselves free standing standards, the first of which focuses on Diversity and Inclusion, which is the focus of this chapter. The uniqueness of this Code is its focus on people being a value in themselves and is based on the same set of high-level values and principles for valuing people in an organization (BS 76000):

(a) People working on behalf of the organization have intrinsic value in addition to their protections under the law or in regulation, which needs to be respected;
(b) Stakeholders and their interests are integral to the best interests of the organization;
(c) Every organization is part of a wider society and has a responsibility to respect its social contract as a corporate citizen and operate in a manner that is sustainable;
(d) A commitment to valuing people who work on behalf of the organization and meeting the requirements of this standard which are made and supported at the highest level; and
(e) Each principle is of equal importance (BSI 2015).

Together these principles form a holistic approach to valuing diversity and inclusion. They go beyond any legal requirements, engaging with organizations with respect to what they could and should do to improve diversity and inclusion. The language of the code is therefore **normative**, giving directions as to what managers should be doing. The **informative** role of the Code should also be emphasized as it provides information about a wide array of activities necessary to meet its requirements, points in annexes to relevant regulations which organizations must uphold but which themselves do not form part of the standard, and gives details about management systems necessary to ensure its application and uptake. Whilst statutory obligations with respect to equality and diversity focus on the rights of protected groups with the aim of preventing discrimination (e.g., Equality Act 2010), the Code goes further to 'capture individual difference, life experience, and social context.' Furthermore, a unique aspect of this Code is the requirement for communication and dialogue about diversity and inclusion with a broad range of stakeholders within and beyond the organization including customers and clients, communities and supply chains.

To develop the standard, a BSI sponsored fifteen strong working party ensuring broad stakeholder engagement was assembled. The working party encompassed members representing organizations within private industry such as construction and transport industry, the public sector including representatives from universities, key industry bodies such as CIPD, Advisory, Conciliation and Arbitration Service (ACAS) and the Chartered Institute of Management (CIM), as well as private consultancies, all with broad expertise in the area of diversity and social inclusion. To support the development of the CoP and ensure its validity, the development was supported by a broad evidence-based literature review (FairWRC 2015) undertaken by a collective of academics from the University of Manchester's Fairness at Work Research Centre (FairWRC), all acknowledged experts within subjects associated with equality, diversity, and inclusion.

In this chapter, we outline and discuss the dynamic development of the Code of Practice, its scope, and principles on which it rests, assisted by definitions of diversity and inclusion. Although the rationale for the Code resides in the intrinsic value people represent to the organization, its potential benefits are highlighted. As the CoP is set to look beyond the strict confines of the organization with the aim of influencing others and aligning their practices and behaviors with those of the organization, we draw attention to such processes, their objectives, and their prospective impact on diversity and inclusion. To get a clearer picture of the CoP and its normative recommendations, extracts and examples from the Code are provided and discussed under the headings 'getting in,' 'staying in,' and 'moving on' capturing the entire cycle of employment. Where appropriate these are supplemented with comments from the academic debate on the issues. To ensure the CoP's successful implementation and effectiveness, it comes with a set of recommendations in terms of management systems and leadership requirements, some of which we will touch upon. Moreover, with the CoP concerned with continuous development and improvement, particular attention is given to the concept of maturity and the role of benchmarking in achieving this. Finally, in a concluding section we discuss some of the key strengths and potential weaknesses of the approach.

3.2 Developing the Code

The fifteen strong working party or writing panel has since its formation played a key role in developing the CoP. To ensure compatibility with other relevant BSI standards (BS 76000) and adherence to BSI practices, norms, and legal requirements, the panel's work has been facilitated by the BSI secretariat whose representative has acted as panel secretary, including providing minutes of meetings, revising drafts to ensure adherence to BSI linguistic requirements, and providing advice on the process. Moreover, despite the fact that the panel at the outset was given clear instructions with respect to expectations and overall scope of their task, there was considerable freedom in developing the content of the standard as well as its scope. From the start, the panel acted as a collective, gradually developing the Code section by section, through inputs by individuals or groups, and through discussion at and between meetings. Although the resource document (FairWRC 2015) referred to above-provided important insights and guidance, members also relied on their own expertise and insights in offering clarity and innovation to the process. For example, the resources document does not discuss the process of bringing the relationship with the organization to an end, which in the current version of the Code is organized under the heading 'moving on.' In line with this, by arranging the organization's activity to achieve diversity and inclusion under the headings 'getting in,' 'staying in' and 'moving on,' rather than more familiar labels such as recruitment and selection, the panel initially agreed that these labels better captured the totality of activities or responses required (although there were some differences when the panel expanded at a later date). Equally, whilst the scope of the standard at the beginning in its entirety focused its recommendation on the organization itself, the arrival of new panel members with different experiences and outlooks midway through the writing process inserted new ideas and energy into the process, particularly with respect to expanding the scope beyond the organization. Thus, with a focus on influencing others, it was agreed after considerable discussion to expand the scope to address customers and clients, supply chains, and communities. It should be stressed that arriving at an agreed draft is not an easy task as the broad composition of the panel also suggested considerable differences with respect to political views and priorities as far as diversity and inclusion are concerned and the method by which such objectives are best achieved. The application of positive action is one such example where some members consider this as resembling positive discrimination which in most cases is not permitted in the UK, whilst others emphasized that the law clearly allows for positive actions where initiatives primarily are seen to enable people from disadvantaged or disproportionally represented groups to compete for jobs, promotions, etc., on a level playing field. The panel in most cases reached consensus through discussion and negotiation. Where disagreements persisted, for example, the definition of diversity and inclusion (see below) existing BSI definitions were invoked. It should also be noted that as the current draft no doubt will go through further changes and transitions following the public consultation period, any reference to details in the Code in this chapter should not be taken as evidence of the final Code, but seen as examples of the ongoing thinking underpinning the standard.

3.3 Principles and Definitions

In terms of its **scope**, when successfully launched the CoP will represent a holistic approach to diversity and inclusion where people are valued for what they are and where the dignity of everyone at work (and beyond) can be realized. It also rests on the assumption that organizations respect and comply with regulations and statutory requirements to ensure equality of treatment of their members. In this respect, it is worth noting that any requirements that go beyond the organization cannot be legislated for in the first place. As the standard focuses on voluntary requirements over and above the statutory ones, it does not provide or describe any minimum or base-line level of compliance. Instead, it urges organizations to note and internalize the imperative of moving toward a more diverse and inclusive workplace as this is considered as being of self-interest with respect to the success and sustainability of the organization. It sets out an approach which combines recommendations for reviewing, valuing, and undertaking an approach to diversity and inclusion based on a set of principles. It applies to and is intended to be realized in any organization irrespective of size, sector, or degree of development or maturity. It is written to recognize that organizations differ, and it therefore leaves it to employers and decision-makers to decide which path to follow. It should, therefore, not be considered a set of specific actions to be undertaken, but gives normative recommendations in terms of **policies, practices, processes,** and **behaviors**.

Two working definitions were central to the development of the Code: diversity and inclusion (BSI 2016).

"Diversity—recognition of the differences and similarities between people in society such that people are both unique as individuals but may share characteristics that are defined through demographic attributes and/or historical, economic, and cultural exclusion."

This definition amalgamates a view which focuses on individual uniqueness and difference (e.g., Wilson and Iles 1999) with a more traditional equality approach which, to a greater extent, emphasizes social group membership (Hoque and Noon 2004), paying attention to both aspects of diversity.

"Inclusion—this is the approach an organization takes, and the infrastructure it puts in place, to recognize, value, and embed diversity within its operations and relationships with customers/clients, supply chains, and communities, and ensure that everyone has the same chance to do what they can."

The definition highlights that adopting an inclusive approach to diversity would require a relevant organizational framework for its development, implementation and maintenance, and willingness based on internalizing the imperative of the approach to embark upon a long-term journey toward greater diversity and inclusion. By focusing on what people can do rather than necessarily on what they are doing, it draws attention to the need to remove any obstacles to participation and contributions (Robertson 2006). Moreover, by signaling the need to incorporate relationships beyond the confines of the organization, it recognizes the opportunity for organizations to influence others in their mutual striving for diversity and inclusion. This issue will be explored in more depth below.

3.4 Benefits of Adopting This Standard

Whilst the justification for this standard resides in the inherent or intrinsic value of people and what they bring to the organization, implementation of the standard is likely to provide a variety of benefits whilst simultaneously mitigating potential risks. Three levels of benefits can be identified: first, there is a convincing business case for implementing this standard within organizations and their associated supply chains. It could be argued that changing socioeconomic realities makes a diverse workforce an imperative and a necessity rather than a choice. Being diverse and socially inclusive minimizes the risk of being unable to attract prospective employees from a wide pool of talent. A diverse workforce better represents the wider world and the local community within which it is located. It does this by broadening the customer base, assisting businesses in becoming more adaptable and responsive, and addressing their products and services appropriately and encouraging sensitivity to new markets (BIS 2015). A diverse and socially inclusive workforce also assists in enhancing reputation and improves responsiveness to vacancies through recruitment from within local communities (Wilson and Iles 1999). Internally, greater diversity contributes to improved decision-making, problem-solving, creativity, and innovation. It increases the pool of talent and reduces loss of talent due to unwanted levels of attrition through turnover. In this way, it realizes human capital by improving learning opportunities, improving skills utilization, and reducing loss and waste (BIS 2015). Equally, it improves the perception of fairness and dignity with positive implications for productivity and job satisfaction. It improves service provision and reduces the risk of mistakes and accidents affecting customers/clients (e.g., improves accuracy and sensitivity in communications to different stakeholders), thereby lowering potential costs of compensation and liability.

Second, adhering to this standard brings benefits to individuals by better fulfilling their capabilities, needs, opportunities, and personal growth, increasing happiness and contentment in the job, improving wellbeing, job-security, and personal safety. It assists in improving a better balancing of personal life and working life, e.g., fulfilling roles as parents, and enhancing opportunities for participation and social relationships. Such a transparent approach enhances the social role and public perceptions of the management processes and the organization.

Third, greater long-term social value can be achieved through more inclusive policies, procedures, and behaviors. Such policies can increase social mobility, thereby reducing social problems, and health and welfare expenditure as a whole, and make society more cohesive and, therefore, more stable. Furthermore, by strengthening the opportunity to work flexibly and thus maintaining contact with the workplace throughout the various life-stages, labor markets, and the pool of workers can be increased, producing gains for society in terms of productivity as well as expanding the capacity to cater for those in society who require care.

Altogether, whilst adhering to this standard no doubt will represent a cost to organizations, the many potential benefits pointed out above suggest that they are likely to be outweighed by the benefits accrued and the overall reduction of risk.

3.5 Influencing Others: Going Beyond the Organization

It is recognized that for diversity and inclusion to become a reality, it needs to go beyond the organization itself to include relationships with customers/clients, communities, and supply chains which operate at the boundaries of the organization or within which organizations are located, directly, or indirectly. It follows that the nature of this relationship, whether manifest in policies, processes, practices, behavior, or attitudes, would impact on the ability to achieve diversity and inclusion within the organization. For example, different practices and attitudes to flexible working or personal conduct, say workplace bullying, could lead to disagreement and tension at the interface of the organization itself and the contracting organization/supplier, creating conflicts within the respective organizations as well as between their members when occupying the same space. Potential for conflict and tension also applies to interactions with customers where the conduct of either party may be perceived to breach acceptable standards. Consequently, it is considered essential for organizations to influence these relationships where they can as any change or progress would be mutually beneficial. *Vis-à-vis* communities this could mean providing opportunity for work in the locality or support to local activities, at the same time, from the organization's perspective, raising awareness of their products/services as well as any future work opportunities, thus assisting with workforce planning.

Influence can be achieved by means of engaging, consulting, and indeed, when it comes to suppliers, contracting. The exact form this influencing would take would depend on the nature of the relationship and the context within which it takes place. For example, although they depend on market factors, organizations will have considerable opportunity to influence their supplier, whether through dialogue and consultation or more directly via procurement obligations reinforced in contracts. Where relationships are long-term the opportunity to align policy and practices would increase as deeper understanding for the value of diversity and inclusion increases. Similarly, through monitoring of interactions between the organization's service providers and customers/clients, need for improvement in terms of demonstration of inclusive behavior can be identified and expectations expressed through dialogue and consultation. This would apply equally whether the practice or behavior identified in this way resides in the organization or its service providers or indeed is exhibited by customers/clients. Where the customer relationship is ongoing and long-term, there may be a need to involve customers more closely in the development of policy and practices affecting diversity and inclusion. Finally, when it comes to opportunities to influence and engage with communities this would depend upon context and strategic consideration but will involve a combination of exploring the situation, engaging with the community and consulting with regard to policy and practices.

3.6 Implementation: From Principle to Action

To give the reader a feeling for the details or specifics of the standard or CoP, we provide some examples from two of the Code's sections, detailing starting the relationship ('getting in') and continuing the relationship ('staying in'), and discuss how these fit in with the overall approach in achieving diversity and inclusion. (For a comparison see also the Circle of inclusion through social dialogue in this book's introductory chapter.) At the outset, one should note that to address these issues effectively, the advance toward greater diversity and inclusion would combine a set of relevant objectives, policies, practices, and behaviors. Moreover, to highlight the complexity of the issues and address the potential obstacles for the full realization of the Code, we engage with the public debate on these issues. Please also note that the extracts provided here from the Code may diverge from the final CoP due to further revisions following the consultation process.

Getting in.

The objective set out in this part of the Code is to arrive at a fair selection and recruitment process with minimum bias in a way which achieves a 'skilled, talented and more diverse workforce'. The 'getting in' phase would include the following actions or processes:

- Job design
- Candidate requirements and expectations
- Attracting candidates
- Candidate search
- Shortlisting of candidates
- Selection process
- Appointment decision
- Feedback and evaluation.

Here, we will look particularly at some of the normative recommendation associated with **'candidate attraction'**. A smaller group of panel members provided the first draft on this section which has subsequently been changed and revised in plenary panel discussions. As this issue is well covered in the resource document (FairWRC 2015), we draw extensively on this here to provide justifications for the way issues with widening participation are covered in the Code (see below).

Central to this approach is the aim of achieving social mobility through widening participation, acknowledging that 'who you know,' rather than 'what you know' often may impact on recruitment processes (see Salgado et al., Chap. 7 in this volume). The term 'widening participation', thus, refers to fair access to jobs and higher education in order to ensure social mobility. With regard to **jobs**, the term equally applies to attempts to open up entry-level jobs to those who are marginalized and socially excluded (McBride and Mustchin 2013) as well as the opening up of professions or jobs previously considered closed to other than a narrow section of potential recruits (e.g., from a narrow set of elite universities or social backgrounds) (Morley 2007).

Unfortunately, widening participation efforts have often been frustrated by a narrow business case outlook. For example, Ashley's (2010) UK study of law firms' initiatives to widen access to those candidates from non-traditional backgrounds/non-elite universities was thwarted by the business imperative to project a particular type of reputation for clients. Such a strategy was deemed too 'high risk', with managers believing it did not make business sense to employ people who did not fit the Oxbridge mold. This example indicates the need for organization-wide dialogue and agreement and support of senior and line management, if changing norms is not to be problematic.

The importance of an organization-wide approach is further underpinned by the findings of the CIPD report on talent management and diversity, where firms who did try to employ diverse candidates soon found that candidates would leave because they did not feel that they belonged (CIPD 2010). Research also indicates the need for a critical mass of competitor firms to commit to change at a similar pace, as any single organization would fear implementing a new approach to recruitment in case it was only their brand being compromised (Ashley and Empsom 2013).

Exclusion experienced by particular social groups may be facilitated by the greater focus on employability by employers (see Peters et al., Chap. 14 in this volume). For example, with more than a quarter of graduate positions filled by individuals who had previously worked for organizations as interns or through work experience schemes (AGR 2015), the current focus on employability might disadvantage those graduates who cannot afford to work without compensation or who cannot rely on nepotistic processes used to allocate work experience placements (Rolfe and Anderson 2003). Research by Browne (2010) indicates that 69% of interns in financial services are on traditional entry pathways and attended one of the top universities (FairWRC 2015). This issue was also addressed at a break-out session at the launch of the BS 76000, where the extensive use of internships was seen as a key barrier to social mobility with organizations encouraged to find alternative and more democratic ways of filling such posts rather than relying on personal recommendation.

Let us look at how the Code addresses these issues in codified form having explicitly emphasized the importance of using a multitude of avenues to attract talent, and as addressed in the discussion above, acknowledging that each mechanism carries its own strengths and weaknesses.

The following are some of the aspects identified by the panel in an earlier draft as being essential to widening participation:

To broaden outreach and attract candidates from a wider pool of people, organizations should ensure that:
opportunities are promoted broadly and transparently using a range of methods and media private recruitment agencies have a clear understanding of the roles being advertised and the organization's culture and commitment to diversity and inclusion;
private recruitment agencies have a clear commitment to diversity and inclusion and are able to demonstrate this in measurable and transparent ways;
the wording of advertisements accurately describe the purpose and objectives of the role and is inclusive;

Also,

> *Targeted activities should be provided to members of under-represented groups to better prepare them for the process of recruitment and selection. Such action of this kind should be underpinned by statistical analysis of excluded groups and its justification widely communicated within the organization.*

The above list of normative recommendations/requirements emphasizes the complexity of the task and the challenge for the organization. Here, we will particularly draw attention to the issue of targeted actions. This implies that positive action should be applied where it is statistically justified, in other words, where certain groups are disproportionally disadvantaged or where the organization has a particular need to become more diverse.

Staying in—Continuing the relationship

As the subheading implies, this section incorporated a series of activities linked to diversity and inclusion and associated with maintaining and developing the employment relationship. Whilst some of these activities will apply to and affect members of organizations in different ways, e.g., learning and development and compensation/benefits, others by contrast target systems or infrastructure that would apply in a similar way to all employees, e.g., health, safety and wellbeing.

> Overview
>
> - Induction
> - Appearance
> - Job quality
> - Working time
> - Compensation and benefits
> - Promotion
> - Performance appraisal
> - Coaching, mentoring and employee networks
> - Learning and development
> - Relationships
> - Voice and representation
> - Health, safety and wellbeing

Under the heading Relationships (colleagues and supervisors), the Code addresses a number of issues associated with workplace dignity. In terms of behavioral conduct associated with dignified work experience, the CoP acknowledges that boundaries for acceptable/unacceptable behavior need to be discussed, agreed upon and communicated within the organization. A more diverse workplace would also have a greater need for such dialogues to avoid unnecessary conflict and social exclusion. An interesting point associated with this issue was raised at one of the writing panel's meetings, where it was pointed out that for people unfamiliar with work due to long-term unemployment or no previous work experience, such an approach is paramount in order to avoid social exclusion of such workers due to potential norm-breaking behavior. Moreover, as standards for what is considered acceptable behavior will change over time, examples provided in local policies must change accordingly. Following a discussion at another meeting it was agreed to focus more attention on the need for role modeling of behavior, as emphasized by ACAS (2015), with managers perceived to play a particularly important role in setting and reinforcing such standards. However, this may not always be straightforward given that line managers frequently are identified as the alleged perpetrators in bullying scenarios, with accusations of bullying often emerging in response to performance management issues, and these, therefore, may be contested and downplayed by managers (Harrington et al. 2012). Still, for anti-bullying policies (or alternatively Dignity at Work policies) to be effective they would require commitment from senior management, which needs to be demonstrated in deed as well as in writing. This is seemingly often a sticking point with bullying policies often being considered ineffective (ACAS 2015; Rayner and Lewis 2011), mostly due to a lack of real commitment from the top.

In recent years there has been a concerted effort in the UK to seek to shift organizational responses to conflict from formal methods (e.g., disciplinary and grievance) toward a more integrated, strategic and informal approach, e.g., through a greater use of mediation and management training in conflict management skills (see Deakin, Chap. 11 in this volume). As dealing with conflicts can be expensive for organizations, addressing conflict in a more efficient and cost effective way has been on the policy agenda for a number of years (e.g., Gibbons 2007). It is recognized that mediation can help facilitate understanding of the situation and lay the foundation for an improved relationship. However, it is potentially contentious to use workplace mediation and/or other informal mechanisms to deal with issues of harassment and discrimination where an employer may have a legal duty or an employee may have a legal right under current legislation. Moreover, there is also a risk of privatizing and personalizing potential structural and societal problems, e.g., by reclassifying sexual harassment as an interpersonal issue and denying organizations an opportunity to learn and develop (Deakin 2014; see Deakin, Chap. 11 in this volume). This is particularly the case where being in a socially exposed position, or being part of a minority, has been shown to increase the risk of bullying (Einarsen et al. 2011). In this respect UK research has consistently identified disabled workers (those with learning difficulties and social/emotional disabilities in particular), gay, lesbian and bisexual workers as well as younger workers as being at particular risk (e.g., Fevre et al. 2012; Hoel et al. 2014).

The above findings are compelling reasons for organizations to develop systems to deal with complaints of unacceptable behavioral conduct, including bullying and harassment (ACAS 2015; BIS 2011; CIPD 2015). To address such complaints, organizations should have in place a formal procedure which highlights the right to have one's complaint investigated, emphasizes impartiality, gives opportunity for voice for all parties involved and addresses issues of support/representation (ETUC/BUSINESS EUROPE/UEAMPE/CEEP 2007; Hoel and Einarsen 2011). One may also argue that for such processes to be fair they need to make adjustment to the processes which allows for full participation, thus giving real opportunity for voice and involvement.

Below are extracts from an earlier draft of the Code which show how the panel addressed some of the issues discussed above.

The organization should work to ensure that, when at work, staff are treated in a respectful and dignified manner and free from abuse, harassment, bullying and violence from any source.

The organization should have a dialogue about uncivil behavior and what behavior is considered acceptable and what is not conducive to an inclusive environment. Any identified boundaries should be regularly revisited in the light of changing social norms and standards.

Managers should be exemplars or role models and also, in turn, they should encourage their staff to exhibit inclusive behavior, undertake to role model inclusive behavior and challenge unacceptable behavior.

An explicit organizational commitment to adherence to agreed behavioral standards should be expressed in internal policy documents. Policies should emphasize top management commitment to upholding these standards and also managers'/workers' duties to comply, including implications for anyone who fails to uphold and comply with the standards.

A range of alternative routes should be provided for dispute resolution including formal and informal processes, including voluntary mediation where this is available.

There should be opportunities given to any stakeholder to file a formal complaint of breach of policy/standard. In the face of allegations, the organizational response should be to maintain a spirit of curiosity and enquiry to avoid perpetuating a 'blame' or defensive culture or one that results in victimization of the complainant or witnesses.

Necessary adjustments should be made to formal processes (including investigations) in relation to individual circumstances to facilitate access and full participation in the process of investigation.

3.7 Maturity and Benchmarking

The Code recommends that organizations need to assess their own practices in order to measure any progress made with respect to diversity and inclusion. Many organizations may already have implemented some of the requirements of this Code but may still have some way to go before they can be seen to fully comply with the

Code in its entirety, or reach what we here will refer to here as 'maturity' in terms of their involvement with and integration of diversity and inclusion issues within their organization (this is illustrated in Fig. 3.1). Here, maturity is measured across three dimensions: breadth of coverage, depth of coverage, and level of integration. Specifically, breadth of coverage refers to the number of practices utilized in the organization to support diversity and social inclusion. Depth of coverage is indicated by the number of workers and staff groups covered by these practices. Finally, given the holistic nature of the approach set out in the CoP, integration would refer to the ability to connect and link the various activities associated with the full cycle of employment involving the three stages 'getting in,' 'staying in' and 'moving on.' As the current standard goes beyond the organization, requiring organizations to influence others, breadth, depth, and integration would also apply to such practices with the more mature organization more likely to engage in influencing processes. Whilst the figure illustrates clearly the three dimensions of maturity, it is less successful (and therefore not pursued in later drafting) in showing the dynamics of the process, and the role of feedback loops, with successful implementation in some activity areas likely to benefit and encourage progress in others.

When assessing the degree of maturity, it is also necessary to evoke the concept of embeddedness. This would refer to practices, procedures, and behaviors taking hold within the organization to the extent that they become part of its fabric or culture. In other words, they become part of the normal way of thinking and 'doing business' until at some stage one may anticipate that policies will not be needed in

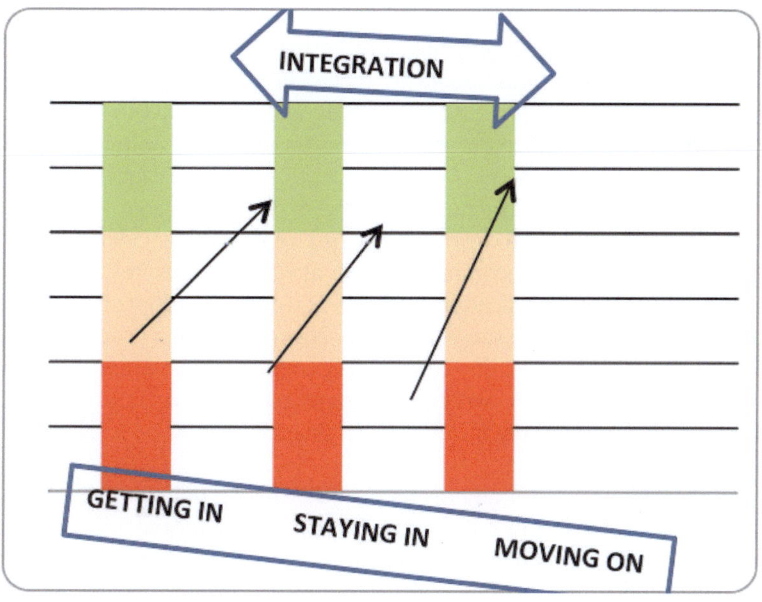

Fig. 3.1 Model of diversity and inclusion maturity

the same way as their activities will be second nature to the organization, or simply 'the way we do things here'.

As with other standards, it is envisaged that at some stage organizations might wish to measure themselves against the success of others as is common for other national or international standards. Such benchmarking, however, requires the establishment of proper auditing systems which in our view are best placed with external providers, who more objectively can assess performance. Organizations which are driven by the conviction that diversity and inclusion are a value in their own right, but also good for business, may have little need for such benchmarking, although they may want to communicate their achievements and success more broadly to their members, customers/clients, suppliers, or the community. But for those who are less convinced, benchmarking might seed the idea and spur interest in diversity and inclusion, setting them on course for gradual compliance and maturity.

3.8 Leadership Commitment: Direct—Resource—Communicate and Monitor

In the previous sections, we have looked in some detail at the processes and activities involved in achieving greater diversity and inclusiveness. Here, we will emphasize the role of leadership which is derived from the overarching standard of Valuing People (BS 76000). It is emphasized that development, implementation, and maturity of approach would rely on senior or top management commitment manifested in behavior and actions taken to ensure the realization of the Code. In practice, this would be brought about by means of a series of integrated policies, practices, objectives, and processes to target and drive forward diversity and inclusion within the organization. Real top management commitment would start with an understanding of the necessity of adopting such an approach, be it economic or social, and the need to integrate this with other organizational policies and processes, including practical ways of ensuring reporting and internal communication. To ensure effective communication, attention needs to be paid to the inclusiveness of the communication channels and formats adopted given the sensitive nature of many of the issues concerned. However, whilst providing clear and unequivocal support and direction to the approach is a precondition for its uptake and gradually embedding it within the organization, providing the necessary resources, whether human, organizational, or financial would be a requirement for its sustainability.

It is acknowledged that for any diversity and inclusion policy to be effective and indeed sustainable, it needs to be relevant and appropriate for the organization itself and the context within which it operates, including its size, resources, labor market, or local community. The policy itself provides a 'framework for setting and renewing objectives for the approach to diversity and inclusion' (BS 76005) and the adoption of the requirement of the CoP as it may apply to the organization. It would emphasize in writing the organization's commitment to diversity and inclusion, highlight rights and opportunities, as well as describing roles and responsibilities. This would include assigning roles and responsibilities with respect to development and integration of policy with other policy frameworks, establishing effective governance and opportunity for involvement in its development, implementation, and governance, for example by establishing an organizational steering group. To give direction, and ensure adaptability, compliance and a continuous steer toward maturity, including influencing others, would require a series of ongoing activities as well as the establishment of feedback loops to senior management for 'reporting on performance'. Practically to ensure senior management accountability, it is acknowledged that the responsibility for the policy's implementation, monitoring its effectiveness, and carrying out any necessary revisions should be allocated to a named senior manager.

Moreover, to ensure its uptake, it should be easily available to any organizational member or stakeholder, posted on the organization's intranet and communicated widely, for example in conjunction with induction or training. Stakeholder awareness and expectations would themselves contribute to put pressure on senior management to live up to its commitments.

3.9 Managing Change

Following on from the previous section, the BS 76000 on Valuing People also sets out in detail the management system needed to ensure that change or maturity with respect to diversity and inclusion can be achieved. It is envisaged that the workforce is involved in this process, and this would also mean giving voice to worker representatives. This comprises the following activities: understand, decide on actions, identify objectives, identify competencies, identify resources, raise awareness, communicate, and control. Here, we will limit ourselves to pointing out the importance of some of these integrated activities all of which are needed for successful implementation.

It can be argued that understanding the nature of the context within which the change would take place is paramount for a successful outcome. In other words, one needs to know what opportunity exists with respect to diversity and inclusion, and equally, what risk there may be in ignoring it. Such a scoping exercise would incorporate understanding the people at work, their jobs, the work environment in which they are located as well as products and services offered. As far as the competences required are concerned, this refers in particular to those in charge who will be introducing, overseeing, and coordinating. As part of such an exercise, competences sought should include behaviors and attitudes necessary to role model, lead, and inspire. Finally, whilst communication is key to raising awareness and ensuring that people are on message, if objectives are to be met, control and monitoring systems are essential, ensuring that the process and its outcomes are documented and any necessary revisions and corrective actions carried out.

3.10 Discussion

In terms of rationale, the links to BS 76000 and its focus on people's intrinsic value rather than justifying its worth to the organization by means of a narrow business case gives this CoP a sound foundation. Furthermore, the holistic approach embarked upon here, captured in a variety of ways including its integration with other organizational policies, practices, and processes, its focus on the full range of the employment cycle, as well as broadening the approach beyond the organization, gives this standard direction, authority, and meaning. The importance given to influencing others through an alignment of approach, whether through contracting or consultation, broadens the overall impact of the approach whilst simultaneously reducing tension and conflict arising where practices, behaviors, and attitudes differ. In terms of strengths, its links to the overarching standard for Valuing People (BS 76000) and other forthcoming related standards, as well as its broad stakeholder support, albeit not emerging from social dialogue in its strictest sense, should increase the possibility of it being adopted by organizations and adhered to by managers. The management system, including details regarding the evidence of senior leadership commitment and actions taken to manage any necessary changes following the adoption of the Code, should equally support its uptake among managers. Although absent from the new Code, the opportunity for benchmarking should, however, be properly addressed in the future as it is likely to broaden the uptake of the Code beyond those who are inclined to do so due to their current commitment to diversity and inclusion.

By contrast, as the success of the approach does require broad commitment from management, line management included, there is some doubt as to whether every line manager would be equipped to play their expected role due to lack of understanding and competence, conflicting priorities or lack of resources. Therefore, only by addressing key concerns that managers may have would it be possible to enable them to carry out their responsibilities within the remit of the CoP. This also acknowledges that the issues line managers are facing may be different or at least perceived differently, than from the perspective of employers.

A further possible limitation of this approach could be associated with its roots within a unitarist approach to management, downplaying any conflict of interest, for example with respect to working time, remuneration as well as potential accusations of bullying against managers associated with failure to meet performance targets. It can also be argued that demands on organizations imposed by their goals, performance expectations and limited resources shape how they practice diversity (Tomlinson and Schwabenland 2010). An example here would be tensions, for example, between organizing flexibility in the interests of employers whilst simultaneously wishing to retain employee commitment (FairWRC 2015).

Equally, in addressing diversity there often appears to be a tendency to individualize difference over and above difference associated with membership of groups already regulated by law, often overlooking or disregarding any difference with respect to historical, cultural, or economic exclusion (including social class).

This also chimes with the resistance often expressed toward the use of positive action to support the fulfillment of the normative recommendations in this Code. However, whilst positive discrimination is often held to have a negative connotation and in many jurisdictions would be deemed illegal, positive action is simply a way of providing a level playing field. As such we would argue that it should be considered a fair and integral part of any organizational effort to achieve diversity and inclusion by compensating historic and cultural disadvantage without putting others at an unfair disadvantage. This also suggests that to ensure fairness a clearer distinction must be made between equity, equality, and need. In this respect, it is our view that in developing and implementing policies for optimal impact on diversity and inclusion, organizations should recognize that, whilst some decisions should be based on strict equality (i.e., treating everyone the same), others, such as pay and promotion, should be based on equity and linked to contribution. But policies, processes, practices, and behaviors should also recognize that ensuring fairness and social inclusion can sometimes necessitate differential treatment of individuals and groups by acknowledging their particular needs beyond what is necessary for compliance with regulation.

Finally, whilst the chapter refers to a specific British approach, there is scope for its replication in other national contexts, particularly as this standard, although part of a broader framework, is free standing and thus could be fully adopted on its own. Whilst there might be national cultural differences impacting on its likely adoption or indeed adaptation, as some countries would have travelled further than others with respect to devising management systems for diversity and inclusion, a recent initiative by the International Standards Organization (ISO) to develop its own standard in this field is encouraging. It is hoped that the thoughts and ideas communicated in this chapter might provide an impetus for discussion and debates with regard to how best to proceed to ensure inclusivity in a globalized world and increasingly diverse workplaces.

References

ACAS. (2015). *Seeking better Solutions: Tackling bullying and ill-treatment in Britain's workplaces*. London: ACAS. http://www.acas.org.uk/media/pdf/e/b/Seeking-better-solutions-tackling-bullying-and-ill-treatment-in-Britains-workplaces.pdf

AGR. (2015). *The AGR Graduate Review Survey 2015—winter review*. London: Association of Graduate Recruiters.

Ashley, L. (2010). Making a difference? The use (and abuse) of diversity management at the UK's elite law firms. *Work, Employment & Society, 24*(4), 711–727.

Ashley, L., & Empson, L. (2013). Differentiation and discrimination: Understanding social class and social exclusion in leading law firms. *Human Relations, 66*(2), 219–244.

BIS. (2011). *Resolving Workplace Disputes: A consultation*. Department of Business, Innovation and Skills. https://www.gov.uk/government/uploads/system/uploads/attachment_data/file/31435/11-511-resolving-workplace-disputes-consultation.pdf.

BIS. (2015). *Evaluation of the employer ownership of skills pilot, round 1: Initial findings*. London: Department for Business, Innovation and Skills.

BSI. (2015). *BS 7600—management system for valuing people in organization—requirements and guidance for use*. London: British Standards Institution.
BSI. (2016). *BS 76005—valuing people through diversity and inclusion-code of practice for organizations*. London: British Standards Institution.
Browne, L. (2010). As UK policy strives to make access to higher education easier for all, is discrimination in employment practice still apparent? *Journal of Vocational Education and Training, 62*(3), 313–326.
CIPD. (2010). *Opening up talent for business success: Integrating talent Management and diversity*. London: Chartered Institute of Personnel and Development.
CIPD. (2015). *Conflict management: a shift in direction?* Research Report. http://www.cipd.co.uk/binaries/conflict-management-shift-direction.pdf
Deakin, R. (2014). *A theoretical framework for exploring the feasibility and fairness of using mediation to address bullying and harassment in UK workplaces.* University of Manchester
Einarsen, S., Hoel, H., Zapf, D., & Cooper, C. L. (2011). Bullying and Harassment in the Workplace: Development in Theory and Practice. (2nd ed.). London/New York: CRC Press—Taylor and Francis Group.
Equality Act. (2010). Elisabeth II. Chapter 15. London: The stationary Office.
ETUC/BUSINESS EUROPE/UEAMPE/CEEP. (2007). Framework Agreement on Harassment and Violence a Work. European Social Dialogue. http://www.ueapme.com/docs/joint_position/2007_Framework_Agreement_Harassment_and_Violence_at_Work.pdf
Fair, W. R. C. (2015). *Diversity and Social Inclusion in the British workplace: An outline of relevant discussions and contributions*. Manchester: University of Manchester Fairness at Work Research Centre (FairWRC).
Fevre, R., Lewis, D., Robinson, A., & Jones, T. (2012). *Trouble at work*. London: Bloomsbury Academic Press.
Gibbons, M. (2007). Better dispute resolution: A review of employment dispute resolution in Great Britain Department of Trade and Industry (London). http://adrresources.com/getdoc-2-2-1113.php
Harrington, S., Rayner, C., & Warren, S. (2012). Too hot to handle? Trust and human resources practitioners' implementation of anti-bullying policy. *Human Resource Management Journal, 22,* 392–408.
Hoel, H., & Einarsen, S. (2011). Investigating complaints of bullying and harassment. In S. Einarsen, H. Hoel, D. Zapf, & C.L. Cooper (Eds.), *Bullying and harassment in the workplace: Development in theory, research, and practice* (2nd ed., pp. 341–357). London/New York: CRC Press—Taylor and Francis Group.
Hoel, H., Lewimitment to diversity and inclusion, highlight rights, D., & Einarsdottír, A. (2014). *The ups and downs of LGBs workplace experiences: Discrimination, bullying and harassment of Lesbian, gay and bisexual employees in Britain*. Research Report, Manchester, UK: Manchester Business School.
Hoque, K., & Noon, M. (2004). Equal opportunities policy and practice in Britain: Evaluating the 'empty shells' hypothesis. *Work, Employment & Society, 18,* 481–506.
McBride, A., & Mustchin, S. (2013). Creating sustainable employment opportunities for the unemployed. *Policy Studies, 34*, 342-359.
Morley, L. (2007). The X factor: Employability, elitism and equity in graduate recruitment. *Twenty-First Century Society*, *2*(2), 191–207.
Rayner, C., & Lewis, D. (2011). Managing workplace bullying: the role of policies. In S. Einarsen, H. Hoel, D. Zapf, & C. L. Cooper (Eds.), *Bullying and harassment in the workplace: Developments in theory, research, and practice* (2nd ed., pp. 327–340). London: CRC Press.
Robertson, Q. M. (2016). Disentangling the Meanings of Diversity and Inclusion in Organizations. *Group & Organization Management, 31*(2), 212–236.
Rolfe, H., & Anderson, T. (2003). A firm choice: law firms preferences in the recruitment of trainee solicitors. *International Journal of the Legal Profession, 10*(3), 315–334.

Tomlinson, F., & Schwabenland, C. (2010). Reconciling competing discourses of diversity? The UK non-profit sector between social justice and the business case. *Organization, 17*(1), 101–121.

Wilson, E., & Iles, P. (1999). Managing diversity: an employment and service delivery challenge. *International Journal of Public Sector Management, 12,* 27–49.

Chapter 4
Social Inclusion on the European Policy Agenda

Stavroula Demetriades

4.1 Introduction

In the context of a modest economic recovery, addressing Europe-wide social challenges is not an easy task. Despite the economic progress, there are still large disparities between Member States, and some are struggling with reducing poverty, income inequality and finding ways to ensure social cohesion across the European Union. Since the beginning of the economic crisis, poverty and income inequality have increased across the European Union. It is notable that between 2009 and 2014, there has been an increase of 1% in the proportion of people whose income is below 60% of the national median (European Commission 2016). Although the proportion of socially excluded people has decreased since 2013, it was estimated that in 2015, there were 119 million people at risk of poverty or social exclusion (European Commission 2016). The crisis slowed down or reversed convergence between Member States. The European Commission considers that countries with well-developed social institutions and reformed social systems have weathered the crisis better than others. Increased investment in social inclusion policies is important for upward convergence in the European Union.

This chapter firstly explores the concept of the social inclusion in the European debate. It continues with some key European (EU)-level initiatives for specific groups of people. The EU-level social partner's work particularly with regard to work-based social inclusion is briefly discussed in the following section. Lastly, the last two sections sketch the work of international organisations, such as ILO, UN, and conclude the chapter.

S. Demetriades (✉)
Eurofound, Dublin, Ireland
e-mail: stavroula.demetriades@eurofound.europa.eu

A. Arenas et al. (eds.), *Shaping Inclusive Workplaces Through Social Dialogue*, Industrial Relations & Conflict Management,
DOI 10.1007/978-3-319-66393-7_4

4.2 The Concept of Inclusion on the European Agenda

The issue of inclusion has been at the heart of several European Union initiatives and actions. To provide with a picture of European policies on social inclusion, this section will highlight the notion of social inclusion as used in the European debate and policy. The role of the European Union on combating social exclusion and supporting and complementing the work of the Member States in that respect was recognised through the Articles 136 and 137 of the Amsterdam Treaty.

The concept of social exclusion was until early 1970s often used interchangeably with poverty. The first European anti-poverty programmes were adopted in 1975 with a focus on material deprivation but since then the concept has evolved and encompassed cultural and social resources. In the joint European Commission's and Council Report on social inclusion is defined quite broadly, reflecting its multidimensional nature as follows:

> Social inclusion is a process which ensures that those at risk of poverty and social exclusion gain the opportunities and resources necessary to participate fully in economic, social and cultural life and to enjoy a standard of living and well-being that is considered normal in the society in which they live. It ensures that they have greater participation in decision making which affects their lives and access to their fundamental rights. (Council, EPSCO, 2004, p. 8)

This definition has been part of the Fundamental Rights of the European Union. Subsequently, indicators to capture social exclusion were developed, and social cohesion became a major priority in European policies.

In the following years, a group-based policy was pursued focusing on individuals and groups who are unable to fully participate in society's activities. Groups at risk of social exclusion (European Commission 2014) received specific attention, including unemployed, people with disabilities, ethnic/language minorities (such as Roma), migrants and those with a migration background, drug abusers, the homeless (disadvantaged), children and youth, the elderly, women, single-parent families and families with a large number of children, and people leaving institutions.

4.3 European Policy Initiatives

Some key initiatives go back to 1990s, with the two White Papers (European Commission 1993, 1994), setting the topic of social exclusion firmly on the European political agenda. Later on, in the context of the Lisbon strategy in 2000 the EU heads of states and governments (European Council 2000) set the objective of making Europe "the most competitive and dynamic knowledge-based economy in the world capable of sustainable economic growth with more and better jobs and greater social cohesion". Social inclusion has been signified as utterly important objective and actions to combat racism and xenophobia, to promote equality of opportunity between men and women and to assist disabled people. It was agreed that Member States should coordinate their policies for combating social exclusion and poverty through an open method. The latter would include common objectives, National Action Plans on inclusion and Community Action Programmes. Having agreed on the common objectives the Member States designed national strategies to fight social exclusion and poverty using an integrated approach. The open method allowed national governments to compare strategies and practices and learn from each other.

In the new start of the Lisbon strategy (European Council 2005), a review of its objectives took place, and the Council of the European Union maintained its determination to preserve the European social model and social cohesion. The multifaceted notion of social inclusion was recognised, and interventions by both the Member states and the European Union were designed, focusing on target groups (for instance the Youth Pact aimed at the full integration of young people).

The Europe 2020 strategy[1] launched in 2010 aims at creating conditions for smart, sustainable and inclusive growth. It sets targets to get people out of poverty and social exclusion with specific actions. A number of flagship initiatives support this strategy, including the Platform against poverty and social exclusion which provides support to EU countries to address their social challenges. Similarly, EU funds such as the European Social Fund and initiatives such as the Social Investment Package can address social exclusion problems in the Member States.

While social inclusion is a shared competence with the Member States, the EU policy developed a "soft law approach" which is part of the EU Semester and the Europe 2020 priorities. In particular, the European Commission works with the Social Protection Committee using the open method of coordination. This process includes a large number of stakeholders (apart from the Member States) including the civil society and the social partners.

4.4 Policy Initiatives for Specific Groups

This section will concentrate on two vulnerable groups that have been a concern for policy makers due to the risks associated with their exclusion from the society and labour market, youth and migrants/refugees.

[1]For more information on the Europe2020 strategy, see https://ec.europa.eu/info/strategy/european-semester_en.

4.4.1 Addressing Challenges of the Youth

A group severely hit by the crisis is that of young people. Evidence demonstrates that protracted periods of unemployment and disengagement from society can have negative consequences on their well-being and future labour market outcomes (Eurofound 2012). It was estimated that 8.7 million young European had difficulties finding a job, and 13.7 million were not in employment, education or training (NEET) (Eurostat 2014) according to the 2015 European Youth report. Poverty rates are higher for young people than the general population which renders them to a precarious situation and is a risk of long-term poverty.

Inclusion of young people at risk has been the focus of several EU initiatives and funding projects, since 2001, when the White Paper "A new impetus for European Youth" (European Commission 2001) set specific priorities for focused action on youth. Several initiatives have been taken in the wake of the economic crisis with a view to support young people. The Europe 2020 flagship initiative Youth On the Move (European Commission 2010) is specifically targeting young people, and the issue has been a priority on the EU agenda. The group not in employment, education or training (NEET) has been considered most at risk already in the 2000s EU debate which also highlighted the heterogeneity of the group. The group consists of young people with different needs such as long-term unemployed, short-term unemployed, youth people with family responsibilities, with disabilities. As their situation exacerbated with the crisis, a separate NEETs indicator was proposed by the Employment Committee (EMCO) group, which allows cross-country comparisons. The situation of the NEETs in the Member States is monitored through this indicator, and a number of initiatives have focused on that group. There are wide variations between Member States regarding the size and composition of the NEETs, as analysis shows. A Eurofound report (2015) found that short-term unemployed are the largest group in Nordic countries whereas long-term unemployed and discouraged are more prevalent in Mediterranean countries. The majority of NEETs in eastern countries are women with family responsibilities.

In 2011, the Youth Opportunity Initiative (European Commission 2011) was launched which required coordinated action between EU institutions and Member States pooling resources (such as national, the European Social Fund (ESF)) to tackle youth unemployment and particularly the NEETs. The initiative takes the form of a broad partnership with different actors, including social partners and different business organisations.

The Youth Guarantee (YG) issue was debated before the economic crisis hit Europe but it was recommended as an action by the European Commission in December 2012 (European Commission 2012). The Council of the European Union finally endorsed the action in April 2013 which was then rolled out in the following year. What the YG guarantees is that young people in the age group of 15–24 not in employment, education or training are provided with a good quality offer of employment, continued education, apprenticeship or traineeship within four months of becoming unemployed or leaving formal education. Financial instruments for the

YG ensure it is actively supported; therefore, ESF funds and other national funds were prioritised for young people and NEETs. Additionally, the Youth Employment Initiative, promoted by the European Commission in 2013, provided additional financial means to support NEETs.

Ensuring quality traineeships in terms of quality of learning and working conditions for trainees has been the concern of the Quality framework for Traineeships as mentioned in the Council Recommendation on a Quality Framework for Traineeships (Council Recommendation (EC), 88/2014). Actions for youth participation in the society and support for intercultural dialogue has been also assisted through the ERASMUS+ programme. Through this programme, four million young people and educators will be assisted in increasing their learning in a different country than their own and with a total budget of 14.7 billion up to 2020. Member states report on the implementation of the framework for European cooperation on education, job and participatory opportunities in inclusive communities.

Monitoring implementation and ensuring that Member States learn from each other, national actions are monitored by the European Commission in the context of the European Semester that takes place every year. Specific country recommendations are then provided to Member States that need to improve certain policy actions. The European Semester takes place in the framework of the European Employment Strategy which also assesses national performance on youth employment and specifically NEETs.

4.4.2 Social Integration of Migrants and Refugees

The recent refugee crisis has been on the EU political agenda in the last few years initially, as a humanitarian response and then as an attempt to integrate the refugees and asylum seekers into the European societies. The majority of those displaced originate from not only Syria but also Africa and South Asia. A World Bank report (2016) estimates the world migrants, refugees and asylum seekers numbers to 60 million which is as many as the population of Italy. With an unprecedented number arriving at European shores in 2015 through Greece and Italy, managing their resettlement and integration became a major political concern. Eurostat data showed that since 2010 there has been a steady increase in the number of migrants; however, 2015 was marked as the year of migrant and refugee crisis in Europe. Eurostat figures for 2014 bring the number of asylum seekers to over 600,000, and the next year, those were increased to 1,322,000. Forced displacement causes enormous human suffering particularly for certain groups such as youth, women and children.

The existing Dublin agreement designed to address occasional and contained migrant flows has proved to be non-sustainable as it put enormous pressure on the receiving countries. Disagreements between the EU Member States regarding the course of action provided a challenge for an early and coordinated response at EU level. However, a number of policy measures have been adopted at EU level: (i) the relocation scheme, (ii) resettlement scheme and (iii) EU–Turkey agreement.

A Eurofound report (2017) highlights challenges faced by Member States in integration of refugees and asylum seekers. Some of the issues raised pertain to housing shortages which often make access to jobs very difficult. Opportunities for self-employment are not always forthcoming. Social security entitlements for asylum seekers vary across countries and may differ for other migrant groups. Furthermore, schools are not always well prepared to receive children of asylum seekers.

Social inclusion of refugees is also linked to their integration in the labour market, and to that end, a number of steps have been taken at EU level. In particular the Reception Conditions Directive (2013/33/EU), which focuses mainly on asylum seekers, covers among others, employment issues.

The European Commission presented in 2016 an Action Plan for the integration of third-country nationals. The Action Plan covers five main policy priorities: (i) Providing support to third-country nationals for pre-departure and pre-arrival measures, as part of the resettlement scheme; (ii) education and training (iii) Labour Market Integration and access to vocational training; (iv) access to basic services (such as housing and health care); (v) active participation and social inclusion, through intercultural dialogue, youth and sport combating discrimination, gender-based violence, etc.

With a view to support policy coordination, the Action Plan suggests to upgrade the existing Network of the National Contact Points on Integration into a European Integration Network with a stronger coordination role. Additionally, a European Integration Forum was set up in 2009 with a view to give voice to civil society and European institutions regarding integration issues. That Forum has since 2015 been evolved into European Migration Forum which will be used to provide further input. Furthermore, inclusive education, non-discrimination, etc., are areas where the European Commission will stress cooperation among Member States for addressing challenges related to migrant integration.

It is important to highlight that Actions without funding would not have any prospects of successful implementation. Funding of migrant integration activities through the Action Plan is foreseen through instruments addressing social and economic cohesion across Member States. The European Integration Fund financed in the previous planning period (2007–13) activities amounting to EUR 825 million. Additionally, funding of further integration actions is foreseen under the structural funds; dedicated funding by ESF (for instance EUR 21 billion for social inclusion) and the European Regional Development Fund (for example, EUR 21.4 billion for social inclusion, housing, education, etc). Another funding mechanism can be provided through the European Agricultural Fund for Rural Development (indicatively, EUR 14.4 billion in the current programming period can cover job creation and provision of basic services and action for social inclusion).

The migration situation is monitored by the European Commission who provides regular reporting and engages with Member states, particularly those falling behind the targets, with a view to find the more suitable ways to implement the Council decisions.

As regards relocation, the European Commission's[2] ninth progress report (European Commission 2017a), issued in February 2017, states that there has been an improvement in action by Member States, and a total of 11,966 people have so far been relocated, very low number compared to those originally anticipated by the Council decisions (approximately 153,000). It is indicative that 13 Member States as well as Norway and Switzerland have provided pledges for relocation during that reporting period while Austria and Hungary have been the only two countries without any pledges or relocation actions at all. Furthermore, Bulgaria and the Czech Republic have not implemented consistently their obligations and others, such as Poland have not followed up their promises, and as a result, no relocations have taken place there.

For the same reporting period, a total of 13,968 people have been resettled while the agreed number was 22,504 following the EU Resettlement scheme. This scheme seems to be working more efficiently as the figures suggest, and the original commitment was more realistic. Under this scheme, Member States should provide "safe and legal avenues" to those people originating from Middle East, North Africa and the Horn of Africa needing international protection. Again, Member States are encouraged to step up their efforts but not all of them have embraced the measures. In the European Commission ninth report, it is reported that most of the Member States participating in the scheme have concentrated efforts (but not exclusively) on Syrians staying in Jordan, Lebanon and Turkey. This also refers to the EU–Turkey agreement to resettle Syrians from Turkey.

The figures above may suggest that the overall outcomes are modest; however, significant efforts at EU level have been taken to coordinate action and convince individual Member States to respond to the challenge. Certain Member States either do not agree to commit themselves to taking action required or do not effectively deliver on commitments, as highlighted in the nineth report (above). Recommendations by the European Commission are regularly provided to Member States for showing solidarity and sharing responsibility with countries mainly affected by migration, such as Greece and Italy.

Lastly, on the occasion of the United Nations' World Refugee Day (20 June), the European Commission launched the "EU Skills Profile Tool for Third-Country Nationals". The tool is an instrument that contributes to the successful integration of migrants. It makes it possible for non-EU nationals to present their skills, qualifications and experiences in a way that is clear and understood by employers, education, training providers and organisations working with migrants across the EU.

[2]The reporting period is for December 2016 to February 2017.

4.5 Social Inclusion at the Workplace Level

With regard to the workplace, the Employment Equality Directive (2000/78/EC) (2000/78/EC) prohibits discrimination based on grounds of religion or belief, disability, age or sexual orientation as regards employment and occupation. Any form of direct (due to the characteristics of a specific group) or indirect discrimination (provisions, criteria or practices that put certain groups in a disadvantageous position) is prohibited. This Directive has already been transposed by all EU Member States. Furthermore, the 2006/54/EC Directive on the implementation of the principle of equal opportunities and equal treatment of men and women in matters of employment and occupation aims to combat discrimination and particularly in relation to (i) access to employment, including promotion, and to vocational training; (ii) working conditions, including pay; and (iii) occupational social security schemes.

Both EU legislation and soft law promote inclusive workplaces, as it is the case for instance with the equal opportunities for women and men, protection against discrimination, ensuring that young people, part-timers or other groups are not deprived of certain rights. Furthermore, social dialogue can also play a major role. Employees and their representatives should be informed about changes in the workplace and the impact those have on different parts of the workforce. The 2002/14/EC Directive sets minimum principles, definitions and arrangements for information and consultation of employees at the enterprise level within each country and plays a key role in promoting social dialogue. According to the Directive, employees should receive information on the employment and economic situation of the company as well as on decisions likely to lead to substantial changes in work organisation or in contractual relations.

The European Commission recently launched a series of consultations on the introduction of a European Pillar of Social Rights, which “takes account of the changing realities of the world of work and which can serve as a compass for the renewed convergence within the euro area”.[3] The principles to be introduced will complement the existing EU “social acquis” rather than replacing them. The “social acquis” is essentially all social legislation; it constitutes part of the acquis communautaire which includes “the body of laws (Treaty provisions, regulations, directives, decisions, European Court of Justice (ECJ) case law and other Union legal measures, binding and non-binding), principles, policy objectives, declarations, resolutions and international agreements defining the social policy of the EU” (Eurofound, Industrial Relations Dictionary).

In April 2017, the European Commission introduced the European Pillar of Social Rights Package. The package contains a Commission Recommendation (European Commission 2017b) containing 20 principles regarding the 20 areas proposed in 2016, prior to the public consultation. This provides some direction

---

[3]For more information on actions, see http://ec.europa.eu/priorities/deeper-and-fairer-economic-and-monetary-union/towards-european-pillar-social-rights_en.

regarding upward convergence and provides a proposal for a joint proclamation (European Commission 2017c) by the Parliament, the Council and the Commission. A social scoreboard[4] is also established to track trends and performance of Member States in 12 areas and to assess progress towards a social "triple A" for the EU as a whole. It is expected that this analysis will feed into the European Semester of economic policy coordination. It also includes a series of documents as part of the consultation of the social partners and other stakeholders on access to social protection—the Written Statement Directive and consultation of social partners. If EU actions are deemed necessary, there will be a second stage of consultation with the social partners on the content of proposals for action. Additionally, a package on the work-life balance of parents and carers was suggested. A staff working document on the **implementation of the Recommendation on Active Inclusion** (European Commission 2013) of people excluded from the labour market was produced and was part of the package.

Another staff working document (European Commission 2017d), the REFIT Evaluation of the "Written Statement Directive" (Directive 91/533/EEC) summarises the findings of this evaluation. Clearly, the Directive has a social role as it intends to provide employees with improved protection against possible infringements of their rights. However, as the labour market has changed significantly over the last 25 years since the Directive was launched, the evaluation assessed the extent to which it still fits its purpose.

The European Social Pillar contains three chapters: (i) Equal opportunities and access to the labour market; (ii) Fair working conditions, and (iii) Social protection and inclusion. It is notable that 10 out of 20 principles refer to the social protection and inclusion, and the areas they cover are the following:

- Childcare and support to children
- Social protection
- Unemployment benefits
- Minimum income
- Old-age income and pensions
- Health care
- Inclusion of people with disabilities
- Long-term care
- Housing and assistance for the homeless
- Access to essential services.

It is expected that the European Pillar will serve as a reference document for the national employment and social policies which will continue to be monitored closely with a view to secure greater convergence between Member States.

[4]https://composite-indicators.jrc.ec.europa.eu/social-scoreboard/.

4.6 European Social Partners

The role of EU-level social dialogue was recognised in the Val Duchesse process in 1985. Building on that the social partners' involvement in shaping and implementing Community social and employment policy was agreed between them in 1991 and then consisted part of the Maastricht Treaty in 1992. Following that, the European social partners developed their own work programme and initiatives as well as an autonomous dialogue. The European-level cross-sector social partners include the following organisations: BusinessEurope,[5] UEAPME,[6] CEEP[7] and ETUC.[8] Social inclusion issues for specific groups of workers were included in various work programmes agreed by the EU-level social partners.

In their 2009–2010 work programme, they agreed to jointly address economic migration issues and promote "the integration of migrant workers in the labour market and at the workplace in order to identify possible joint actions". With Europe at the crossroads, the work programme 2012–14 focused clearly on youth employment and the link between education and work and transitions into the labour market. The social partners committed themselves to provide recommendations to the Member states and EU institutions. Joint actions were also proposed with regard to apprenticeships and integration of migrant workers in the labour market.

The latest 2015–17 work programme promotes an intergenerational approach to the workplace and commits the signatory parties towards considering "joint actions going beyond their regular participation in the Commission's advisory committees linked to free movement of workers". The social partners will also work on the renewal of the EU policy on migration in a mutually beneficial way.

In the context of article 155 of the Treaty, the European-level social partners can sign autonomous European framework agreements,[9] as mentioned above, which commit their members to implement various measures. Those can take place at national, sectoral and/or company levels following the national tradition and industrial relations practice of each Member State (or the European Economic Area state). The agreements also constitute a responsibility of the social partners towards contributing to EU social policies and actions related to the issues tackled in their framework agreements. The signatory parties also invite their member organisations in candidate countries to implement this agreement.

---

[5]BUSINESSEUROPE represent all-sized enterprises at EU and international level.

[6]UEAPME is the employers' organisation representing the interests of European crafts, trades and SMEs at EU level.

[7]CEEP is the **European Centre of Employers and Enterprises providing Public Services and Services of general interest**.

[8]The liaison committee EUROCADRES/CEC is usually represented when framework agreements are concluded.

[9]For a list of the EU-level social partners' framework agreements, see the European Commission web page http://ec.europa.eu/social/main.jsp?catId=329&langId=en.

Several autonomous framework agreements have been concluded by the EU-level social partners, and the one agreed back in 2007 recognised mutual respect for the dignity of all at the workplace and deals with forms of violence and harassment within the competence of the social partners.

The 2015–2017 social partners' autonomous framework agreement on active ageing and an intergenerational approach encourages social partners at the appropriate level to work towards developing a working environment that enables workers of all ages to work together. This is particularly relevant for young workers as the agreement encourages collaboration with education institutions or public employment services to ease transitions into and within the labour market. It also refers to mentoring or tutoring for young workers and actions to enhance their skills so that they can fulfil their potential in the workplace. Both sides are urged to consider the implications of demographic change in the European workplaces. Offering a working environment where workers can stay healthy, safe and productive until legal retirement age and ensuring cooperation for transferring knowledge and experience between different age groups and generations at the workplace are some of the concerns of the agreement. Implementation of the agreement will be within the next 3 years, and the signatory parties will report on implementation to the European Social Dialogue Committee.

Unlike national collective agreements, EU-level framework agreements are not concluded often and have a different scope and mandate. The latest framework agreement "constitutes the social partners' contribution to the European social policies" and the non-discrimination legislation.

4.7 International Initiatives for the Inclusion of Youth, Migrants and Refugees

At the international level, United Nations entities, including ILO, have taken initiatives in support of youth inclusion, migrants or refugees integration in the societies and labour market.

4.7.1 Youth Programmes

The ILO global programme for youth employment has been developed over decades and following different priorities; prior to the 1970s, it focused mainly on the adoption of international labour standards. The following decades were marked with initiatives, such as the Action Programme on Youth Unemployment (1996–97) and the Action Programme to Combat Youth Marginalization and Unemployment (1998–99). More integrated approaches were pursued with the Youth Employment

Programme (YEP) set-up in 2005 and supported by the 2005 and 2007 Resolutions. YEP aimed at coordinated labour market, economic and education and training policies which would better support employment growth and decent jobs.

Later on, the ILO Conference adopted the ILO Declaration on Social Justice for a Fair Globalization (ILO 2008), inviting their members to follow policies that meet the strategic objectives: (i) employment, (ii) social protection and (iii) fundamental principles and rights at work.

At the height of the economic crisis, the ILO adopted a Resolution for immediate, targeted and renewed action to tackle the youth employment crisis (ILO 2012). Measures in the area of macroeconomic policies, employability, labour market policies, youth entrepreneurship and rights were suggested. At the same time, guides were produced for National Action Plans on youth employment.

The United Nations Global Initiative on Decent Jobs for Youth,[10] (United Nations 2016) brings together the United Nations resources and several other key global players. It is in the context of the 2030 Agenda for Sustainable Development. The priority areas addressed are the following:

- Green jobs for young people
- Apprenticeships
- Digital skills and tech hubs to facilitate youth access to digital economy
- Youth in the informal economy, as an attempt to promote their transition to the formal economy
- Activities for young people in rural areas; in fragile states
- Young entrepreneurs
- Action area for youth (15–17 years old) in hazardous jobs and ensuring decent jobs.

The United Nations programme for youth goes back to the mid-1990s with the adoption of the World Programme of Action for Youth (WPAY) with fifteen fields of action covering education, employment, poverty and hunger, girls and women, leisure, environment, substance abuse, juvenile justice, participation in life and society, HIV/AIDS, ICT, globalisation, armed conflict and intergenerational issues. The adoption of the programme means that governments will do their utmost to promote rights and freedoms, protect young people against discrimination within the context of the Action for Youth. To ensure coordination and complementarities of all UN entities' work on youth, the United Nations Inter-Agency Network on Youth Development was set up and has been operating within the context of the WPAY. Built on the Millennium Development Goals, the 2030 Agenda for Sustainable Development with the 17 Sustainable Development Goals came into force in 2016. The Goals related to Quality of education and Decent work and economic growth make specific reference to young people (e.g. reducing the

[10]Different UN entities came together in 2015 to bring this forward: FAO, ILO, ITC, ITU, UNCTAD, UNDESA, UNDP, UNEP, UNESCO, UNFPA, UN-Habitat, UNICEF, UNIDO, UNRWA, UN-WOMEN, UNWTO, WIPO, the World Bank Group and (ex-officio) the Office of the Secretary-General's Envoy on Youth.

number of NEETs, full employment and decent jobs for young people, access to training).

With the development agenda at the heart of its work, the World Bank established the Youth Summit, a platform that connects youth with the development community, researchers, governments, private sector with a view to promote new ideas and debate the future of education. It is the conviction of the Bank that economic growth and human capital accumulation are intertwined and providing better opportunities for education, and skilled youth will assist towards more growth and development. Various programmes in developing countries are aimed towards inclusion of young people through education.

4.7.2 Migrants and Refugees

The issue of migration has been at the heart of the ILO work since its establishment. A number of fundamental rights conventions cover the issue of migration; these are the ILO Conventions No. 97 (migration for employment convention) and 143 (migrant workers convention) on the protection of migrant workers and the governance of labour migration as well as the accompanying Recommendations No. 86 (Migration for employment) and 151 (migrant workers). Furthermore, non-binding principles and guidelines provide a set of good practices on labour migration and incorporated in the Multilateral Framework on Labour Migration (ILO 2006). The Fair Migration Agenda ILO (2014) initiative aims at setting up an agenda for fundamental rights and decent jobs for migrant workers, respecting human rights (including labour rights) and social dialogue, making migration a choice, promoting bilateral agreements for well-regulated and fair migration, etc.

Similarly, the Declaration of the UN General Assembly High-Level Dialogue on International Migration and Development adopted in 2013 (United Nations 2013) recognises the role migration can make towards meeting the Millennium Development Goals. The United Nations Sustainable Development Goals provide for protection of labour rights and promotion of safe and secure working environments for migrant workers, in particular women migrants. They also aim at reducing inequalities through facilitating orderly, safe, regular and responsible migration and mobility of people, including through the implementation of planned and well-managed migration policies.

A number of high-level meetings have taken place under the auspices of the UN to coordinate international efforts with a view to address large movements of refugees and migrants particularly since the Syrian war crisis. The Summit in September 2016 at the Heads of State and Government level concluded with the signature of a Plan for addressing the issue. This was culminated in the New York Declaration which strongly condemns xenophobia against migrants and refugees and includes commitments for securing human rights for refugees and migrants; preventing sexual and gender violence; ensuring education for children of migrant or refugee background; assisting refugee and migrant receiving countries; etc. The

New York Declaration provides for plans for more equitable sharing of the burden for hosting and supporting refugees in 2018.

The World Bank's response to the Syrian refugee crisis has been of humanitarian nature, shoring up public services and institutions in the receiving countries or emergency aid (e.g. in countries such as Lebanon, Jordan). Most of the Bank's operations focus on development with a direct or indirect effect on migration. A number of projects (World Bank 2016) fund activities (lending) and provide technical assistance and advice to governments concerned with management of migration flows and migrant integration.

4.8 Conclusions

European and international efforts towards addressing social inclusion of the most vulnerable groups in societies have been stepped up in the last years, particularly as the economic crisis left a mark on the societal fabric. As the European economy has been recovering (albeit modestly), improvements in the social situation are noticeable in Member States however at different pace. Large social disparities still remain, and economic growth does not lift all boats across the Member States. Therefore, narrowing the divide between Member states and focusing on convergence should be a priority of EU policies. Persistent divergences pose significant risks to social inclusion in the European societies. It is clear that policy interventions have contributed towards containing the negative effects of the crisis but they need to be strengthened in order for them to achieve upward convergence across Europe.

At the time of financial distress as a result of the economic crisis, social policies of the Member States have been under significant strain. Severe youth unemployment has made the situation of young people precarious; many of them are experiencing or threatened by economic and social marginalisation. While the situation in many EU countries has improved, there are still high levels of youth unemployment. Coordinated EU and national policies have gathered pace in the post-crisis era in preventing and addressing youth unemployment and breaking the cycle of disadvantage.

Furthermore, an unprecedented number of migrants and refugees entering the EU in the last few years have put the social infrastructure and social cohesion of the Member states into test. Undoubtedly, migration is a significant challenge for the European Union. With a large demographic problem (at least for some Member States), migration can possibly address some of the EU labour markets' bottlenecks while social policies will have to deal with the social and economic integration of the migrants.

Undoubtedly, EU financial instruments play a key role in encouraging social inclusion policies; implementation of national policies has been supported by the European Structural and Investment Funds, particularly with the ESF priority on social inclusion (including active inclusion) and access to services in the last years (since 2014). These initiatives have certainly helped steering reform processes in the Member States with a strong social inclusion focus. Further developments with the introduction of the European Pillar of Social Rights, the social scoreboard, etc., provide a strong focus on social protection, inclusion and overall social performance. The positive elements provided by the European Pillar of Social Rights could be further strengthened for making a lasting effect. Currently, it constitutes a framework of principles which could be complemented by more binding elements. Further work would need to concentrate on how the principles enshrined in the Pillar will be implemented at national and EU level. Actions resulting from the social scoreboard would need to be complementary to existing monitoring instruments to allow better monitoring of social trends in the European Union. It would be important for the Member States to share ownership of the Pillar with a view to ensure effective implementation, particularly as they have different starting points. Social investment should continue to be a priority at EU level to balance economic policies.

This short overview of key EU initiatives shows that the concept of social inclusion has come a long way since the early days in the 1970s. Moving from poverty to social exclusion and then gradually to social inclusion of different groups, EU-level initiatives complemented and coordinated the Member States' actions in addressing social challenges. The multidimensional character of social inclusion should also be reflected on multidimensional policies. Focusing on one aspect while neglecting others may cancel out the positive effects of the intended policies. Social policies are part of the Europe2020 strategy, and the European Pillar of Social Rights with ten principles focusing on social protection and inclusion aims at meeting the objective of upward convergence for a "fair and truly pan-European labour market" (President Jean-Claude Juncker, State of the Union Address, European Parliament, 9 September 2015).

A key component of the European social model, the European social dialogue can also make a significant contribution to social inclusion through autonomous agreements concluded by the EU-level social partners and other coordinated actions. The recent (March 2017) autonomous agreement is certainly moving towards this direction. The EU social partners' contribution to EU policies through consultations on social policies takes into account impacts of social policies on different groups of workers, such as young workers, migrants, in the Member States.

The debate on the European social model is ongoing, and several questions about the EU social future actions are raised: what actions need to be taken to ensure that the social model is sustainable; how to secure social investments for sustainable growth; how to ensure well-functioning social institutions; how to pursue better social policies for upward convergence; how to shield social policies against future shocks; and eventually, what kind of social Europe do EU citizens want and how to work together? Perhaps it is pertinent to answer these questions in conjunction with the White book on the Future of Europe (European Commission 2017e) presented recently by the President of the European Commission,

Jean-Claude Juncker, which provides some alternative scenarios for the future of the 27 Member States.

References

Council of the European Union. (2004). *Joint report by the Commission and the Council on social inclusion.* Available at http://ec.europa.eu/employment_social/soc-prot/soc-incl/final_joint_inclusion_report_2003_en.pdf. Accessed 20 May 2017.

Eurofound. (nd). *Industrial relations dictionary.* Available at https://www.eurofound.europa.eu/observatories/eurwork/industrial-relations-dictionary/social-acquis. Accessed on 20 May 2017.

Eurofound. (2015). *Exploring the diversity of NEETs.* Luxembourg: Publications Office of the European Union.

Eurofound. (2017). *Approaches to the labour market integration of refugees and asylum seekers.* Luxembourg: Publications Office of the European Union.

European Commission. (1993). *Growth, competitiveness, employment: The challenges and ways forward into the 21st century.* White Paper: Luxembourg, Publications Office of the European Union.

European Commission. (1994). *European social policy—a way forward for the Union, White Paper.* Luxembourg: Publications Office of the European Union.

European Commission. (2001). *White paper—a new impetus for European youth. COM(2001) 681 final*, Brussels.

European Commission. (2010). *Youth on the move: An initiative to unleash the potential of young people to achieve smart, sustainable and inclusive growth in the European Union. COM(2010) 477 final*, Brussels.

European Commission. (2011). *Implementing the youth opportunities initiative: First steps taken, commission staff working document. SWD(2012) 98 final*, Strasbourg.

European Commission. (2012). *Proposal for a council recommendation on establishing a Youth Guarantee. COM(2012) 729 final*, Brussels.

European Commission. (2013). *SWP/2013/039 final.* Available at http://eur-lex.europa.eu/legal-content/EN/ALL/?uri=CELEX:52013SC0039.

European Commission. (2014). *Assessment of progress towards the Europe 2020 social inclusion objectives: Main findings and suggestions on the way forward.* Luxembourg: Publications Office of the European Union.

European Commission. (2016). *Employment and social developments in Europe 2016.* Brussels. Available at http://ec.europa.eu/social/main.jsp?catId=738&langId=en&pubId=7952&visible=0&.

European Commission. (2017a). *Report from the commission to the European Parliament, the European Council and the Council, Ninth report on relocation and resettlement.* COM(2017) 74 final, Brussels.

European Commission. (2017b). *Commission recommendation of 26.4.2017 on the European Pillar of Social Rights, C(2017) 2600 final*, Brussels.

European Commission. (2017c). *Proposal for a interinstitutional proclamation on the European Pillar of Social Rights, COM(2017) 251 final*, Brussels.

European Commission. (2017d). SWD(2017) 205 final, *REFIT Evaluation of the 'Written Statement Directive' (Directive 91/533/EEC), C(2017) 2611 final.* Available at https://www.google.ie/url?sa=t&rct=j&q=&esrc=s&source=web&cd=1&ved=0ahUKEwjS-cb0ydzUAhXFAcAKHYrz-ABAQFggoMAA&url=http%3A%2F%2Fec.europa.eu%2Fsocial%2FBlobServlet%3FdocId%3D17615%26langId%3Den&usg=AFQjCNG2_D9t8w4Upj8FAsLmOqk3x6289g&cad=rja.

European Commission. (2017e). *White paper on the future of Europe: Reflections and scenarios for the EU 27 by 2025, COM(2017)2025 of 1 March 2017*. Brussels.
European Council. (2000). *Presidency conclusions, the Lisbon Special European Council (March 2000): Towards a Europe of innovation and knowledge*. Available at http://eur-lex.europa.eu/legal-content/EN/TXT/?uri=uriserv%3Ac10241.
European Council. (2005). *A new start for the Lisbon strategy*. Brussels. Available at http://eur-lex.europa.eu/legal-content/EN/TXT/?uri=URISERV:c11325.
Eurofound. (2012). *Social inclusion of young people*. Luxembourg: Publications Office of the European Union.
ILO. (2006). *The multilateral framework on labour migration*, Geneva.
ILO. (2008). *105th international labour conference to review the impact of the declaration on social justice for a fair globalization*. Geneva.
ILO. (2012). *101st international labour conference, The youth employment crisis: A call for action*. Geneva.
ILO. (2014). *Fair migration: Setting an ILO agenda, report of the ILO director general to the international labor conference*. Geneva.
United Nations. (2013). *Declaration of the high-level dialogue on international migration and development*. New York. Available at http://www.un.org/ga/search/view_doc.asp?symbol=A/68/L.5.
United Nations. (2016). *Global initiative on decent jobs for youth: Strategy document*. New York.
World Bank. (2016). *Migration and development*. World Bank Group, New York. Available at http://pubdocs.worldbank.org/en/468881473870347506/Migration-and-Development-Report-Sept2016.pdf.

Part II
Following the Circle of Inclusion

Chapter 5
Showcase—"Believe in Diversity and Act Accordingly" Diversity, Inclusion, and Social Dialogue at BNP Paribas

Patricia Elgoibar, Tijs Besieux, Megan McCaffrey and Claire Godding

In this showcase, we aim to describe and analyze the diversity and inclusion (D&I) actions being taken at BNP Paribas Fortis and the impact that social dialogue has in the development, implementation, and monitoring progress in a large company. We link these actions with the circle of inclusion developed by Arenas et al., Chap. 1 in this volume. We start by describing the story of BNP Paribas Fortis in Belgium as an illustration of how social dialogue might promote inclusion and combat discrimination. In that, we enter the specific D&I actions. We finalize the chapter with lessons learned from this case to improve diversity and inclusion.

The information about the company's actions was shared by the two key actors in the diversity and inclusion field at BNP Paribas Fortis, Mr. Bert Van Rompaey—Chief Human Resource Management Officer, and Ms. Claire Godding—Head of Diversity and Inclusion. All the quotes showed in this chapter are coming from them.

*After a master in Law, Claire pursued a career as a Corporate Banker (10 years) and in HR (10 years), heading a Learning & Development international department. She became **Head of Diversity & Inclusion** at BNP Paribas Fortis in 2010. Claire is also **Member of the Board** of Myria, the Federal Center for Migrations (Belgium) and Unia, the Interfederal Center for Equal Chances (Belgium).*

P. Elgoibar (✉)
University of Barcelona, Barcelona, Spain
e-mail: patriciaelgoibar@ub.edu

T. Besieux · M. McCaffrey
KU Leuven, Leuven, Belgium

C. Godding
BNP Paribas Fortis, Brussels, Belgium

A. Arenas et al. (eds.), *Shaping Inclusive Workplaces Through Social Dialogue*, Industrial Relations & Conflict Management,
DOI 10.1007/978-3-319-66393-7_5

Bert holds a master in commercial engineering (KU Leuven). He started his career in banking in 1994. After serving different positions in two banks, Bert joined a consultancy firm for three years. He then returned to banking in 2002. He became Chief Human Resources Officer in 2010. Bert also is a member of the bank's executive committee.

BNP Paribas Fortis is the largest bank in Belgium with 3.5 million private and professional clients, an 800 branch network, and roughly 14,000 employees. BNP Paribas Group, worldwide present, has more than 180,000 employees. At a global level, BNP Paribas considers D&I policies are a high priority in their agendas.

[***Claire Godding***] *There is a global BNP Paribas Group Diversity Committee, which gathers twice a year, once in Paris and once in a different country. We share our latest actions, discoveries, difficulties.*

We decide about common goals and common actions, such as Diversity Week, organized once a year in all countries (see more about this below). Other actions at global level are for example first BNP Paribas Group Multicultural Conference, with more than 150 participants from more than 20 countries, to think together to the multicultural aspects in our company: what goes well, what should be improved, what are the taboos... and to build action plans. Also we check the progress on specific topics, such as senior management, LGBT inclusion, disability policies among others at global level.

[***Claire Godding***] *Our ambition is clearly to help the whole group to progress at the same speed.*

BNP Paribas Fortis (Belgium) received the Brussels Diversity Label 2012–2014 (renewed for 2015–2017), the "Children Welcome" label (Kinderen toegelaten/Enfants admis) and the Disability Matters Award (both received in 2016). Also, in Belgium, no single glass ceiling exists, and in other countries, they are very interested in the methodology and the results obtained. Therefore, we consider relevant to focus on the Belgian example as part of a global action plan.

During the last decade, BNP Paribas Fortis underwent a major change. From a global bank named Fortis employing almost 60,000 people worldwide, the bank became part of the BNP Paribas Group, headquartered in Paris, and now functions primarily as its Belgian daughter bank.

Why did we opt for BNP Paribas Fortis to understand how diversity and inclusion work at the organizational level? As indicated, BNP Paribas Fortis is a large organization in a business context of continuous change. Both the financial crisis—during which clients blamed bankers for their personal financial loss—and the restructuring of the bank affected the stability and resilience of the bank and its employees. In such a dynamic environment, diversity and inclusion issues become especially apparent, because (1) a large workforce brings along the question of how diversity can contribute to the organization's bottom line, and (2) continuous change drives the core question of how each and every stakeholder can remain "on board" of a ship that needs to set new sails every day. And so, we see both theoretical and practice-oriented merit in analyzing the BNP Paribas Fortis case.

5.1 Organizational Social Dialogue at BNP

Social dialogue is institutionalized in all EC member states. The position and functioning of social dialogue in organizations are closely related to the broader context of industrial relations at the national level and sectoral level. In this chapter, we focus on social dialogue at the organizational level and its influence on D&I policies. The impact on D&I policies is mostly developed by workplace employee representation structures or workers councils (WCs).

Homogeneous trends that influence social dialogue at the organizational level are also clear. Here, we highlight four of them. First, the rapidly changing socioeconomic environment leads organizations to high-speed adaptation, jeopardizing traditional industrial relations issues such as national or sectoral collective bargaining negotiation (European Commission 2015). Second, there is the growing diversity of the workforce and the need for inclusion in organizations. Hayter (2015) affirms that inequality and insecurity are the most significant labor problems of our era. At the organizational level, industrial relations agents play a key role in ensuring workers equality and security. To promote diversity and gender equality in industrial relations has become a priority (Gartzia et al. 2016). Third, managing differences between generations and rights of starters have become a major issue in many societies (Farndale et al. 2015). Industrial relations agents face challenges in trying to improve access to the labor market for young people and in offering quality in those positions (European Commission 2015). Older employees protect their rights, however, face a collective layoff in numerous situations, creating social dilemmas between different groups of employees. Fourth, other diversity features such as nationality (De Cieri et al. 2007) and disabilities are also hot-topics in the diversity and inclusion agenda for social actors (Hall and Wilton 2011). How does the social dialogue for diversity and inclusion function at BNP Paribas Fortis?

[***Claire Godding***] *Collaboration with unions is essential. We address diversity very often with our unions. Fortunately, we have several union members that value diversity highly and challenge us continuously. For instance, with the unions we conducted a thorough analysis of pay differences between men and women. We found that the performance scores (directly related to pay level) of part time employees were consistently lower. And we did not manage to eradicate this persistent difference. So, in general, part time employees were paid relatively less compared to full time employees. And more women than men work part time.*

Unions in the bank themselves also face challenges. The first being female/male representation at the union level. The second one is about the next generation. And I do believe this will be the biggest challenge for unions. And thus also for the organization as a whole. Our younger employees do not seem to be highly motivated to join a union. We have to show these young employees that social dialogue can be very constructive. That social dialogue is also important for them.

From the start of the D&I initiative, social dialogue has played a crucial part. We supervise a permanent commission with union members on diversity. We sit together three times a year. At least once a year (usually twice) I [Claire] attend the workers council.

Taking into account the challenges in labor relations, social dialogue is a prerequisite for a fair and competitive social market economy (Thyssen 2016) and this highlighted at BNP Paribas Fortis.

Social dialogue is tremendously important nowadays. Because of the double role on global actions and individual cases, social partners see me as a resource in some difficult cases. Since we started our program, for instance, individual cases of employability issue, for employees with disability or chronic disease have become less frequent. Adaptation to the work environment for employees with disabilities has also become common practice.

In my role, I can bridge different functions. I supervise a permanent commission on diversity, which meets at least three times a year. Also, I am a member of the HR management team. And, during work councils, I participate in meetings on diversity and inclusion. Combining those functions allows me to translate a case that an employee representative has identified to a concrete initiative supported by HR senior leaders. From that perspective, my role allows me to bring closer key stakeholders who can take relevant action for the well-being of our employees.

5.2 Specific Actions Taken at BNP to Promote Diversity and Inclusion

At BNP Paribas Fortis, diversity is understood in its widest sense: gender, ages, cultures, sexual orientation, disabilities, profiles, and experiences. BNP Paribas group has had a consistent diversity policy since 2004, and a Diversity and Inclusion plan started later in 2009, as an indirect consequence of the banks crisis and the absorption by BNP Paribas Group. The crisis had a huge impact on the firm's population, in the sense that there was growing discontent among employees and a palpable need for positive messages and company pride.

After conducting an external audit based on figures and on own perceptions at different levels, five clear goals were identified: (a) Reduction of discrimination risk; (b) Attention to clients' diversity; (c) Attracting and retaining diverse talents; (d) Improving the mix in teams at all levels; and (e) Attention to inclusion. We elaborate on the actions taken to reach these goals.

(a) ***Reduction of discrimination risk***

This goal is closely linked to the practice of "inclusive recruitment and discrimination free selection" from the circle of inclusion.

[***Bert Van Rompaey***] *The Executive Committee (ExCo) has an "ExCo intervention committee" which consists of three people including myself. We screen how managers for instance conduct interviews with candidates. When we ascertain an issue that exceeds the scope of Claire's team, we take responsibility. We seek* *dialogue with the manager in question so we can clarify the firm's perspective on diversity. Because we do this at the ExCo level, we can ask senior executives to take responsibility regarding their specific division. In doing so, we, the ExCo, stays constantly aware about possible issues appearing and can take appropriate action regarding diversity challenges.*

[***Bert Van Rompaey***] *International employees are yet another group targeted for inclusion. The Belgian bank has a strong tradition in employing multinational profiles. At the Group level, I think we can still improve in terms of international representation at the top level. And so, I gladly share my experience with them regarding the Belgian case.*

[***Claire Godding***] *We also manage approximately 10–15 individual cases of "possible discrimination" yearly. These are issues linked to sexism, racism and other types of discrimination, and we report to Top Management on these, in an ad hoc committee.*

On a quarterly basis BNP Paribas controls in detail 40 files, selected at random, of candidates who applied to the bank and were not selected. This is with the purpose of checking objectivity of the selection process.

(b) ***Attention to clients diversity***

For client diversity, a major achievement of BNP Paribas Fortis has been to put "client accessibility" at the top of the priority list and to focus on being the best bank for clients with disabilities. The team member responsible for managing the satisfaction of customers with disabilities is blind himself. Because of his experience, the internal diversity at BNP, and through ongoing dialogue with Belgian associative world on disabilities, BNP fostered innovation and became the best Belgian bank on this client segment (Budget Recht mei-juni 2016).

[***Claire Godding***] *How can we be more sensitive towards client diversity? Age, gender,* etc. *We seek to have marketing pay attention to these aspects. Our diversity plan is not only an HR plan. It is carried out by many different functions within the organization. Ultimately, acting on client diversity throughout the organization also contributes to the success of our HR strategy. The success of HR is only possible by including relevant stakeholders, such as internal/external clients, and marketing to help us in giving voice to our journey.*

(c) ***Attention to inclusion***

This goal is closely linked to the practice of "safe place for all" from the circle of inclusion.

Inclusive workplaces are marked by Mor Barak (2000): pluralistic value frame on the organization level such as open management-employee communication systems and ongoing adjustment of organizational values and norms; acknowledgment of responsibility toward the community including outreach and volunteer involvement; seeing the value and potential contribution of welfare-to-work employees; and collaborative and respectful culture. Pelled and colleagues study (1999) shows empirically that decision-making influence and access to information, among others, are practices that support inclusion in organizations (Roberson 2006).

[**Claire Godding**] *Social partners see me as a resource to combat discrimination. For instance, employability for people with a handicap was a big issue during the past years. Here, unions and I join hands to make a case.*

The social dialogue that encourages the involvement of workers should allow invisible diversities—which are sometimes addressed as taboos—such as educational background, religious, sexual orientation, or mental health—to be managed and discussed openly.

(d) ***Attracting and retaining diverse talents***

This goal is closely linked to the practice of "developing multiple careers" from the circle of inclusion.

[**Claire Godding**] *To make sure that we recruit and retain diverse talents, an important attention group is the young parents. We keep a close dialogue with them. In particular we meet young moms in groups when they come back from maternity leave, and discuss ambitions and hurdles in peer groups. A similar experience was just made for the first time in October 2016 for colleagues (usually less young) having ill parents (i.e. Alzheimer). The need for them to have an exchange group inside the company was high.*

Women in general are another group that is targeted. Recently we started to redefine how we write our job description. We put emphasis on creating a more gender neutral tone of voice. Until now they are sometime vague and abstract, which does not attract women. We focus on masculine words and try to balance them with feminine words. We used the "male words" list from the KU Leuven to create a more balanced way of writing. This is a concrete example of a process based transformation within our organization. We will now measure how these changes lead to more women applying for certain jobs.

[**Claire Godding**] *As an example, between 2011 and 2016, we improved the % of women in Branch managers from 24 to 40%, combining a smart quota (50% of new hires needed to be women—which was easy as the "pipeline" was very balanced) from the top, and local bottom-up initiatives (women managers meeting possible candidates to answer their questions and share their testimonial). Two years of efforts led, successively, to 50% of women in new hires. The 3rd year, no specific initiative was taken regarding this target, and still, at the end of this 3rd year the 50% target was reached as well, showing the essential role of providing more role models, to women of course, but also to HR and Managers, who, when thinking on possible candidates, had now a better mix of examples in mind.*

[**Claire Godding**] *Nobody likes quotas, including myself. However everything depends on why we work on diversity. If you are convinced that you need diversity to boost innovation, then there is a big need. And a big need can only be addressed with quota, to trigger change fast.*

We have experience with quota and results. From 24 to 39% in four years' time of women in charge of a bank branch. In 2011 we changed things. 50% of adjunct bank managers were women. So we wanted to assure that these women could grow to the next level. So we started to organize formal and informal activities, such as meetings between aspiring leaders and current women bank managers. In 2012 we saw that 50% of the appointments were for women. In 2013 we saw, despite not communicating a lot, that still 50% of bank leaders are women. I believe this has a lot to do with role models. Imagine that you differ on three levels with management: female, French speaking, and from different origin. Women who now say they don't want to grow into leadership sometimes say it because they look at a group of people they don't identify with.

Another important point here is to find diverse leaders for the future, in that respect, the ExCo develops a succession planning. Below, Bert talks about diversity as a component of employee's trajectory toward taking on a senior leadership position.

[**Bert Van Rompaey**] *At BNP Paribas Fortis, the "executive committee" (ExCo) performs an exercise in succession planning. We assess whether we have the right people in our organization to support sustainable competitiveness of our business in the long run. When we do the exercise, we look at future leaders from different perspectives. They need to have the right talent. They also need to fit within their division and the entire organization. This is exactly where we value diversity a lot. We do not aim to "copy paste" ourselves in the future. Rather, we proactively look for talent with a diverse profile. And so, the future senior executives represent more than just themselves.*

Thus, our succession planning practice for me is an example of how we work on diversity early on at the top management level.

(e) ***Improving the mix in teams at all levels***

This goal is closely linked to the practice of "colorful socialization" from the circle of inclusion.

BNP defines diversity as a competitive advantage for their organization. This requires integration into organizational structures, strategies, and processes (Cox 2001). Diversity can be considered a source of innovation and creativity, but it can also lead to conflict and inefficient business process (Farndale et al. 2015). This duality is recognized in the bank, and managers are trained to manage tensions related to diversity in teams.

[**Bert Van Rompaey**] *It can seem easier to assemble a homogeneous team. It's a short cut. Nobody in the team asks questions. The team does not reflect on its own actions with a dose of criticism. But, those homogeneous teams no longer suffice in today's constantly changing world. We need people with differences in background, experience, or perspective. Diverse teams look at societal issues differently. A diverse team can be a breeding ground for innovation.*

A diverse workforce is really valuable nowadays for companies, as having heterogeneous teams of bankers can bring higher productivity and "leads to contestation of different ideas, more creativity, and superior solutions to problems. In contrast, homogeneity may lead to greater group cohesion but less adaptability and innovation" (Herring 2009, p. 219). Therefore, BNP focuses on creating diverse and effective groups.

Leaders can create a climate of inclusion by role modeling, and thus inclusive conducts will be copied by followers (Bandura 1977; Theodorakopoulos and Budhwar 2015). In that, BNP considers that leaders need to work on becoming more and more inclusive.

[***Claire Godding***] *Challenging "inclusive leadership" of our Management is also needed, and has seen an improvement in results. A survey conducted in 2015 showed a certain degree of resistance to gender equality among management. This was intertwined with high levels of competitiveness. Also, we learned from the survey that managers are in fact interested in better understanding their unconscious biases. And so, we just launched an "inclusive leadership self-assessment" app for all people managers in our company (2.000 people).*

BNP organized workshops on "inclusion and unconscious bias" for our top management. The scope of these biases expands beyond women and people with a disability. I know that other companies in Belgium work on this topic as well. However, often such initiatives are not welcomed very enthusiastically by top management. The workshops were highly regarded by our senior management.(...) Five years ago I would have never thought that it would be possible to organize such a thing in our organization. And now, we have the majority of senior management on board.

Hyter and Turnock (2006), Mor Barak (2013) conclude that combating discrimination is not possible if managers at all level are not involved seriously in the process and promote the right values and behavior enabling inclusion among the workforce.

[***Bert Van Rompaey***] *"Diversity is a shared responsibility. A responsibility that shapes the future of our firm... Believe in diversity and act accordingly".*

5.3 Other D&I Actions at BNP Paribas Fortis

5.3.1 Diversity Managers

At BNP Paribas, every large entity has a diversity manager. They meet at the international level twice per year to share best practices and define common goals. At the group level, some common requirements are defined together. BNP in Belgium tests easily innovative approaches, which can afterward be extended at the group level.

[***Claire Godding***] *In order to multiply experiences, to share and encourage progression in the corporate world, we created the Diversity Managers Association Belgium (DMAB), involving today more than 20 large companies, representing more than 200,000 workers of all sectors. We meet every two months to share on all aspects of Diversity & Inclusion. This open platform is especially a great* *opportunity to discover totally different realities and efficient actions which can be duplicated, and helps a lot Diversity Managers who have to achieve results in a Diversity part-time role.*

In the diversity managers association we see a pattern. Organization that start with this topic first have to work on diversity before they can address inclusion. So inclusion follows diversity. Inclusion means that everyone feels good at work. If you start with inclusion without diversity, you are making a homogeneous group feel at ease. Today we work both on diversity and inclusion. One of the big elements on inclusion in our bank, although it may seem a bit weird because it's just an event, is our diversity week. During that week we offer a lot of sessions, seminars, etc. for our employees. The topic for this year is "live my life". I believe this adds to our inclusion agenda. We challenge people to address prejudice you might have towards other functions and businesses within our organization.

5.3.2 Diversity as Source of Innovation

[**Claire Godding**] *During the last 3 years innovation has become a clear priority of BNP Paribas Fortis. Several initiatives have been launched in this respect. One of these initiatives is called Home for Innovation, a dedicated team where attention is put into building a diverse team. This team regularly organizes "hackathons" (creative intensive workgroups concentrating during 2–3 days on building new prototypes or concepts) where all employees can decide to participate. The experience of several of these hackathons showed a clear difference in success rate between gender and profile diverse teams and homogeneous teams which are more stuck in ego issues, and are less creative.*

5.3.3 Active Networks

There are certain pivotal networks of the D&I plan at BNP Paribas Fortis. These networks are not always present in diversity approaches, but have proven to be key in the success seen at BNP Paribas Fortis in the past 5 years. Currently, there exist six active voluntary networks by and for employees. One of these is a gender network open to both men and women, which counts more than 1200 members. There is a network for employees above the age of 50, another one for employees below the age of 35, a multicultural network, and an LGBT network that was started in 2016. These are active networks with social partners, meeting three times per year. There are 30 Diversity Coordinators in Businesses and Regions who have taken on this role as an extra responsibility who participate in training once per year.

5.3.4 Diversity Week

[**Claire Godding**] *Since 2014, we have an annual "diversity week." In October 2016 the diversity week took place in a period where media was highly polarized on the European refugee crisis. We decided to host a play in our bank. The play was entitled "Jihad." Needless to say, such an initiative was highly controversial. The venue was completely packed. And the discussion afterwards, which was scheduled to last for about an hour, had to be wrapped up after more than three hours. Such a bold move allows us to create awareness around topical issues that we as an organization need to address as well.*

Also, the ExCo participates in these type of actions.

A while ago we conducted an "ExCo in the dark." During the entire meeting, the ExCo members were blind. For us this was a very valuable lesson to experience life as it is for the many people in our country who are blind. Can you imagine such a session in an organization that is rather traditional?

5.3.5 Global People Survey

Below, Claire talks about the Global People Survey. This is an annual employee survey administered throughout the BNP Paribas Group. A number of topics are surveyed, including: employee satisfaction, leadership, diversity, corporate social responsibility, and mobility. The survey is also used by management to (1) design strategies that focus on core issues and opportunities, (2) evaluate the impact of HR practices on different fields such as mentioned above.

[**Claire Godding**] *BNP Paribas conducts an annual survey, the Global People Survey. Year after year, our employees indicate that they value working with their team, their boss, and other teams as well. For me these results relate back to valuing diversity as an organization, because diversity entails an environment where we collaborate respectfully with each other.*

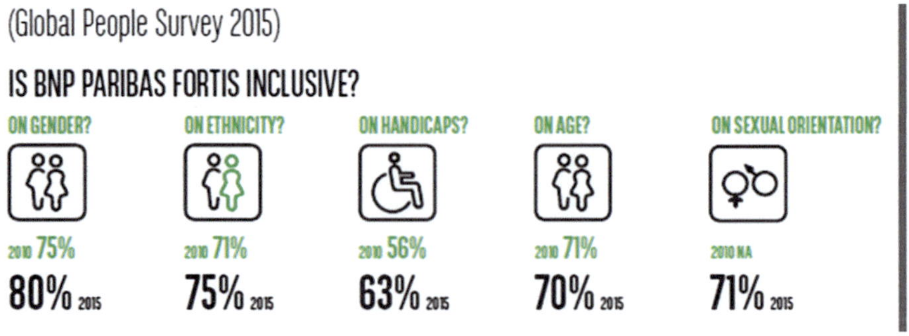

Fig. 5.1 Evolution of perceptions about inclusion inside BNP Paribas Fortis between 2010 and 2015. *Source* Global People Survey, BNP Paribas Fortis

In that, HR and unions through social dialogue agree on fighting against discrimination (Fig. 5.1).

5.4 Challenges for BNP in the Near Future

[***Claire Godding***] *In an effort to advance the business while keeping diversity and inclusion as a central topic, numerous challenges arise. One of these is the glass ceiling, which is experienced quite early on. At the first level of managerial positions in BNP, suddenly the percentage of women drops significantly. Why? Because the organization still operates in a society where, on average, women combine more roles. However, the reversed is really an exception. We must not forget that the firm operates in a broader society, where traditional roles still prevail.*

Another challenge is facilitating successful employment for people with disabilities. Deaf people, for instance, can face immense challenges. To hire a sign language interpreter during a meeting in fact is not very costly and help the inclusiveness and participation of deaf workers. However, there is still a barrier to do so. And so, deaf people are at risk of lagging behind. During high school education, deaf people often have to struggle to get a degree. Not because they are less intelligent. Rather, plenty of practical barriers hold them back. And so, early on when starting a professional career, this population is in fact disadvantaged.

[***Bert Van Rompaey***] *During summer vacation, we aim to hire young non-Western workers for summer work. When I talk to them, they regularly express to me that they never thought a bank would hire them. You see, there is an implicit assumption that a big bank would not hire foreigners. This saddens me, as we explicitly value the input of our diverse workforce to innovate our business.*

These three examples are cases on their own. However, combined, they portray a challenging picture. On the one hand, diversity is the key to innovation. On the other hand, societal issues hold the firm down in an attempt to structurally anchor diversity within the organization.

5.5 Recommendations

Companies aspiring to implement or improve upon existing diversity and inclusion policies are encouraged to take heed of the example of BNP Paribas Fortis:

1. Harness a continuous and constructive social dialogue between key stakeholders. Social dialogue allows to (a) identify issues early on, (b) harness a climate in which employee and employer representatives work on diversity and inclusion from a mutually beneficial perspective, and (c) implement practices that are supported and encouraged throughout the organization.

2. Identify first what the purpose of implementing such an initiative is for your company. Once rationale and targets have been set, start by working on diversity (fighting discrimination, improving the mix, monitoring figures), and then eventually move to initiatives in inclusion. Both are necessary.
3. Medium-sized and large corporations are advised to have one person appointed to Diversity & Inclusion as their only responsibility. Preferably, this is a person with business experience and located within HR to have access to main HR processes which are key to making a difference on diversity, but who also uphold a flexible approach. There are no "one size fits all" solutions for HR; whatever you do needs to fit with the corporate culture and the opinion leaders.
4. The scope of D&I initiatives should be quite broad, from encouraging employees networks, to involving in business with supports and ambassadors in different functions, to demonstrating awareness of clients diversity in customer service and marketing.
5. It should be made clear to all employees that the initiative is supported by top management. A "CEO letter" can help, as well as active participation by top management in D&I initiatives and events.
6. Develop a network of other businesses ready to share their experiences and best practices with D&I. This will be extremely helpful, especially for D&I professionals who maintain other responsibilities.
7. Diversity, inclusion, and social dialogue must be at the forefront of all interactions, initiatives, and decisions for the D&I professional. Particular attention should be given to the interactions and conversations around diversity and inclusion. Recognizing your company's own strengths and limitations will be essential in choosing concrete actions that fit well within the organization (e.g., BNP Paribas Fortis' decision to host the play "Jihad" during a time that this topic was politically potent and timely).

5.6 Conclusions

BNP Paribas Fortis provides a compelling case study to demonstrate how well-integrated policy and practice aimed at diversity and inclusion can have fantastic results, not only for employee experience but also for business as well. Diversity is understood by BNP to be quite broad. It accounts for all variations in gender, age, culture, sexual orientation, (dis)ability, profiles, and experiences, and their initiatives reflect this scope. The Diversity and Inclusion plan at BNP grew from a policy that was implemented in 2004, to a plan put into operation in 2009, to today's fully functional and permanent initiative that pushes for continuous improvement in inclusive hiring, employee management, internal opportunities, and customer experience. This growth, and the strong support by top management, is directly linked to the clear benefits of cultivating a diversity climate and a safe place for all. The case of BNP reinforces the academic literature that diversity is, in fact, a competitive advantage when it is well integrated into organizational structures, strategies, and processes (Cox 2001) as the circle of inclusion proposes (see Arenas et al., Chap. 1 in this volume). It stimulates innovation as well as creativity, productivity, and profitability.

Policies and practices that support diversity can be seen as forming the groundwork for success, while the social dialogue is the platform from which all social actors engage with and promote inclusion. According to BNP, *social dialogue is tremendously important nowadays.*

This chapter examines social dialogue, diversity, and inclusion at the organizational level; however, the sectoral and national levels undoubtedly influence these practices within BNP and other organizations with similar objectives. It is clear that there is growing diversity in the workforce both in Belgium and in European countries more broadly, and that failure to adapt may be fatal for businesses wishing to maintain a competitive edge. But deciding to embrace diversity and work toward inclusive practices and open social dialogue is only the first step. There are several challenges to managing diversity, and having well-integrated policies and practices that are supported by top management and embraced by all employees on a social dialogue level is absolutely essential. Cultivating a diversity climate requires daily effort and almost constant attunement to the environment at the organizational level and beyond. As BNP Paribas Fortis exemplifies, however, it is clear that for the case of diversity, inclusion, and social dialogue in business, the juice is worth the squeeze.

Acknowledgments The authors thank BNP Paribas Fortis and Bert Van Rompaey in particular for providing us information to outline the case and the Fundación Obra Social La Caixa for supporting this research work.

References

Bandura, A. (1977). *Social learning theory*. Englewood Cliffs, NJ: Prentice-Hall.

Cox, T. (2001). *Creating the multicultural organization: A strategy for capturing the power of diversity*. San Francisco, CA: Jossey-Bass.

De Cieri, H., Cox, J. W., & Fenwick, M. (2007). A review of international human resource management: Integration, interrogation, imitation. *International Journal of Management Reviews, 9*(4), 281–302.

European Commission. (2015). *Industrial relations in Europe 2014*. Luxembourg: Publications Office of the European Commission.

Farndale, E., Biron, M., Briscoe, D. R., & Raghuram, S. (2015). A global perspective on diversity and inclusion in work organisations. *The International Journal of Human Resource Management, 26*(6), 677–687.

Gartzia, L., Amillano, A., & Baniandrés, J. (2016). Women in industrial relations: Overcoming gender biases. In P. Elgoibar, L. Munduate, & M. Euwema (Eds.), *Building trust and constructive conflict management in organizations* (pp. 195–211). Switzerland: Springer International Publishing.

Hall, E., & Wilton, R. (2011). Alternative spaces of 'work' and inclusion for disabled people. *Disability & Society, 26*(7), 867–880.

Hayter, S. (2015). Introduction: What future for industrial relations? *International Labour Review, 154*(1), 1–4.

Herring, C. (2009). Does diversity pay? Race, gender, and the business case for diversity. *American Sociological Review, 74*(2), 208–224.

Hyter, M., & Turnock, J. (2006). *The power of inclusion: Unlock the potential and productivity of your workplace*. Canada: Wiley.

Mor Barak, M. E. (2000). The inclusive workplace: An ecosystems approach to diversity management. *Social Work, 45*(4), 339–353.

Mor Barak, M. E. (2013). *Managing diversity. Towards a globally inclusive organization*. Thousand Oaks, CA: Sage Publications.

Pelled, L. H., Eisenhardt, K. M., & Xin, K. R. (1999). Exploring the black box: An analysis of work group diversity, conflict and performance. *Administrative Science Quarterly, 44*(1), 1–28.

Roberson, Q. M. (2006). Disentangling the meanings of diversity and inclusion in organizations. *Group and Organization Management, 31*(2), 212–236.

Theodorakopoulos, N., & Budhwar, P. (2015). Guest editors' introduction: Diversity and inclusion in different work settings: Emerging patterns, challenges, and research agenda. *Human Resource Management, 54*(2), 177–197.

Thyssen, M. (2016). Preface. In P. Elgoibar, M. Euwema, & L. Munduate (Eds.), *Building trust and constructive conflict management in organizations*. Springer International: The Netherlands.

Chapter 6
Inclusive Recruitment? Hiring Discrimination Against Older Workers

Nick Drydakis, Peter MacDonald, Vasiliki Bozani and Vangelis Chiotis

6.1 Introduction

Although the growth in older age groups in national populations around the globe has been well documented, little attention has been given to the policies that will extend opportunities for older workers (Böhm et al. 2013; Posthuma and Guerrero 2013; Naegele and Walker 2011; Van Vianen et al. 2011). According to a 2015 Mercer survey of employers in the UK and Europe, "the vast majority (87%) of the survey respondents have not checked whether their people managers are hiring workers who are older than themselves, and of the remaining 13% of those that do measure it, more than half found that managers do not hire people older than themselves" (Mercer 2015). Also, according to the American Association of Retired Persons (AARP) career study (2014) on older workers, 64% of those surveyed say they have seen or experienced age discrimination in the workplace. The same study suggests that "more than one-third of older workers are not confident that they would find another job right away without having to take a pay cut or move (37%). Of those, about one in five (19%) say the reason they are not confident is due to age discrimination and 21% identify age limitations, such as feeling they are "too old" or limited in some way because of their age." In addition, based on a 2014 global

N. Drydakis (✉) · P. MacDonald · V. Chiotis
Centre for Pluralist Economics, Department of Economics and International Business, Lord Ashcroft International Business School, Anglia Ruskin University, East Road, Cambridge CB1 1PT, UK
e-mail: nick.drydakis@anglia.ac.uk

N. Drydakis
Institute of Labor Economics (IZA), Bonn, Germany

N. Drydakis
Global Labor Organization (GLO), Düsseldorf, Germany

V. Bozani
Economics Research Centre, University of Cyprus, Nicosia, Cyprus

A. Arenas et al. (eds.), *Shaping Inclusive Workplaces Through Social Dialogue*, Industrial Relations & Conflict Management,
DOI 10.1007/978-3-319-66393-7_6

survey (Deloitte 2014) of business and HR leaders, 58% of executives reported that their organizations have "weak capabilities in providing programs for younger, older, and multi-generation workforces." These negative patterns could have a detrimental impact on older workers in the labor market.

Although the target set by the Europe 2020 Strategy to reach 75% employment of all Europeans aged 20–64 (by 2020), a 2011 European Policy Centre study suggests that only 46% of people aged 55–64 are in work; this drops to 11% of 65–69 years-olds and 5% of those aged 70–74 (European Policy Centre 2011). In all developed countries, life expectancy is increasing, fertility is decreasing and people are encouraged to work longer in order pension promises to be sustainable (Age UK 2011). Unfortunately, efforts to extend working lives and to increase participation rates among older people may be undermined by age discrimination in labor markets (Age UK 2011). Discrimination remains a serious issue for older workers because employers' beliefs about the effects of ageing on productivity and workplace performance are influenced by negative stereotypes (George et al. 2015; Age UK 2011; OECD 2004). These stereotypes suggest that older workers are less motivated, less adaptable, less healthy, and more likely to be distracted by family caring responsibilities (Ng and Feldman 2012). However, meta-analyses suggest that the somewhat widespread belief that job performance declines with age is not strongly supported: indeed, many studies point to performance increments with increasing age (Ng and Feldman 2008, 2012; Van Vianen et al. 2011; Sturman 2003; Warr 1994). In addition, according to the literature, emotional resilience has not been shown to be generally related to age (Ng and Feldman 2012; Sturman 2003; Warr 1994) and also, the widespread stereotypical view that older workers are less innovative than younger workers is not supported (Ng and Feldman 2008, 2012; Van Vianen et al. 2011; Sturman 2003; Warr 1994).

In order to eliminate age discrimination in the workplace, the UK implemented European Union legislation in the Employment Equality (Age) Regulations 2006. These were superseded by the Equality Act 2010 which came fully into effect in 2012. This study evaluates whether the legislation has been effective. In the current study, we examine potential demand-side barriers to older UK men and women finding employment by exploring recruitment behavior, specifically invitations to interview, by utilizing an experimental technique; the so-called correspondence test. We focus on recruitment as it is the first stage of the HRM cycle (see the Circle of Inclusion, Arenas et al., Chap. 18 in this volume) and is a critical feature of HR processes in all organizations, regardless of size, structure of location. Decisions made in recruitment are fundamental to how effectively the workforce contributes to organizational objectives. Inclusive recruitment and discrimination free selection are a necessary condition for organizational HRM systems becoming Circles of Inclusion.

Unfortunately, age discrimination is neither overt nor easily measured (Riach and Rich 2002, 2007). Surveys of attitudes toward target groups and employers in the labor market are not likely to produce honest and accurate responses (Riach and Rich 2002). As a result, the lack of direct evidence regarding a recruitment bias against older people might limit our knowledge of the actual extent of the discrimination that such people may face in the initial stage of the recruitment process and discriminatory patterns might remain unchallenged. However, field experiments which minimize bias and catch employers in the act of discrimination provide impressive direct evidence of recruitment bias from a powerful test procedure that enables clear policy adoption (Drydakis 2009).

The current study's results, the first since the Equality Act 2010, suggest that discrimination against older workers remains an important phenomenon. Legislation has not been sufficient to eliminate age discrimination in recruitment. Furthermore, ageism is not gender and occupation-neutral. The results highlight that government should require firms to adopt ageing-at-work policies that explicitly cover all stages of the recruitment process. Social dialogue between employers and employee representatives has a crucial role to play in effectively operationalizing national regulation at an organizational level. Constructive social dialogue has the potential to both promote changes in attitudes toward older workers and in informing effective organizational policies and procedures to eliminate ageism in recruitment. In what follows (Sect. 6.2), we will present the design of the study. The results will be presented (Sect. 6.3) followed by discussion of the implications (Sect. 6.4) and conclusions (Sect. 6.5).

6.2 Design of the Study

Following the methodology of a typical field experiment (Drydakis 2009; Riach and Rich 2002) pairs of matched applications (one from a fictitious 28-year-old male/female applicant and one from a fictitious 50-year-old male/female applicant) were sent to employers with a variety of job openings for restaurant workers, sales assistants, factory workers, and office secretaries. Firms' responses to the applicants, i.e., invitations for interview, were then recorded. As in most field experiments on age discrimination, we suggest that if preferences were found for younger applicants with 19 years less experience, it would indicate a very significant level of bias against older applicants (Riach and Rich 2002, 2007). However, if we were to find preferences for the older applicants in such circumstances, it could be interpreted as an economically rational response to experience superiority, rather than bias against youth (Riach and Rich 2002, 2007).

In the present study, we concentrate on low-skilled jobs in the private sector as this group is expected to be more at risk for age discrimination (Eurobarometer 2007). The labor market demand in these occupations was also sufficiently high. These occupations almost always have fixed pay scales, often advertised with the vacancy, such that potential employers will not perceive older applicants as likely to expect higher wages as younger applicants. It was extremely important to choose job openings where it was realistic to expect that job applications would come from individuals 22 years apart in age range. Hence, jobs with a career hierarchy (i.e., managers, directors) were ruled out of the investigation. The selected occupations allow a further dimension to be investigated (Drydakis 2009) since jobs in industry (i.e., factory/manual workers) are perceived as blue-collar jobs, while jobs in services (such as in restaurant/sales and offices) are perceived as pink-collar and white-collar jobs. Finally, by focusing on both sexes, we can account for how gender might affect access to vacancies (Drydakis 2015).

The current research was administered as part of the Longitudinal Labor Market Discrimination Study (LLMDS) conducted by Anglia Ruskin University (Lord Ashcroft International Business School) in the UK. The LLMDS is an ongoing longitudinal yearly data set beginning in 2012. In this study, we applied for vacancies where there was demand for employment of 8 h a day, 5 days a week. We applied to 1836 available jobs in the selected occupations from July 2013 to May 2015, in the UK. These vacancies were identified through a random sample of advertisements appearing in both leading, as well as local, newspaper websites. We applied only to companies that accepted applications via e-mail. Whenever firms invited the applicants for an interview, it was recorded as a call back (Drydakis 2009). Invitations to interviews were politely declined to minimize the inconvenience to the firms (Drydakis 2009).

As in most EU field experiments, the applications consisted of three parts (Drydakis 2015). Firstly, a message in the e-mail that simply stated that the applicant was applying for the vacant job and that an application letter and a CV were attached. Secondly, an application letter that described the applicant in a narrative form. The letter continued with the applicant stating that he/she had seen the announcement for the job opening and was interested in obtaining the position. The letter contained information about the applicant's age and work experience. It included the applicant's contact information (mail), date of birth, sex (male/female), ethnicity (White-British), marital status (married, one child), previous employment, and education (both applicants had completed school to Year Eleven). The postal addresses were in comparable socioeconomic districts, approximately one mile apart in each region. Thirdly, CVs for waiters, salesmen/saleswomen, factory workers, and office secretaries were prepared, in conjunction with advice from relevant HR departments. Information was carefully matched between the two applications and altered for the four different targeted occupations. Working with HR departments, we conducted internal pretests to ensure that neither the two cover letters nor the CVs that formed a pair would elicit preferences.

The aim of this study was to create pairs of job applicants who were carefully matched in all respects except in the experience inevitably associated with age (Drydakis 2009). The younger applicant was 28 years of age. Also, the letter stated that the younger applicant had 9 years of work experience in the specific occupation. The older applicant was 50 years of age and the letter stated that the older applicant had 28 years of work experience in the specific occupation. As in most field experiments, we controlled for the older applicant's mental and physical capacities (Riach and Rich 2002, 2007). Older applicants were engaged in strenuous physical activity (i.e., cycling, mountain-biking) to demonstrate their current good health and to reduce potential employers perceiving older applicants as at higher risk than younger applicants of future ill health. Their mental flexibility was demonstrated by an up-to-date interest in computers and learning foreign languages (i.e., Spanish) (Riach and Rich 2002, 2007). The reason for so doing is that numerous studies point to negative employer perceptions vis-à-vis older workers, with respect to their productivity, cost, work motivation, current health, future health risks, receptiveness toward training, and ability to cope with technological and organizational change (OECD 2004). Moreover, in this study, we indicated that the applicants were currently in employment so that all applicants had current experience at some form of work, thus diminishing fears that older workers had a longer time for human capital to deteriorate.

For research purposes, we also recorded the characteristics of the firms, such as the existence of HR and written commitments to equal opportunity (Drydakis 2009, 2015). To collect this specific information, we adopted the following process: If a job opening or a firm's official website indicated a job or firm, the information was registered. When limited information was provided, research assistants contacted the firms and collected the relevant data, stating that they were engaged in a university study of the firm environments behind advertised job openings (Drydakis 2009, 2015).

6.3 Results

The primary question we asked was, "What constitutes an outcome that exhibits discrimination?" In a study of majority/minority employment opportunities, an intuitively plausible measure of (the existence of) discrimination is the proportion of times that the two applicants were treated differently by potential employers (Riach and Rich 2002, 2007). Complete results thus necessitate recording when both were rejected or invited and when only the majority or minority applicant was invited to interview (Riach and Rich 2002, 2007).

Table 6.1 summarizes the data and the results of our experiment. We present outcomes of firms who did not respond to either of the applicants (neither invited for interview); firms who responded positively to at least one applicant (at least one invited); firms who responded positively to both of the applicants (both invited); firms who responded positively only to the younger 28-year-old applicant (only the younger was invited), and firms who responded positively to only the older 50-year-old applicant (only the older was invited). The results are presented for the total sample, by occupation, and sex.

Table 6.1, Panel I, presents observations for men. The last row shows the aggregated results and from the second column it can be seen that applications were sent to 894 job openings. The third column shows that in 509 cases, neither individual was invited for interview. In the remaining 385 cases (column four), at least one applicant was invited. In 57 cases (column five), both applicants were invited

Table 6.1 Aggregate outcomes; access to occupations

Panel I: Men									
Outcomes jobs	Jobs	Neither invited	At least one invited (1)	Both invited	Only the younger was invited (2)	Only the older was invited (3)	Net discrimination (2)–(3)	[(2)–(3)]/(1) %	χ^2 test
Factory workers	151	108	43	5	33	5	28	65.1	20.6*
Sales assistants	235	131	104	12	75	17	58	55.7	36.5*
Restaurant workers	245	145	100	13	65	22	43	43.0	21.2*
Office secretaries	263	125	138	27	85	26	59	42.7	31.3*
Total	894	509	385	57	258	70	188	48.8	107.7*
Panel II: Women									
Outcomes occupations	Jobs	Neither invited	At least one invited (1)	Both invited	Only the younger was invited (2)	Only the older was invited (3)	Net discrimination (2)–(3)	[(2)–(3)]/(1) %	$\chi 2$ test
Factory workers	163	132	31	5	25	1	24	77.4	22.1*
Sales assistants	232	163	69	12	49	8	41	59.4	29.4*
Restaurant workers	266	177	89	21	55	13	42	47.1	25.9*
Office secretaries	281	183	98	21	63	14	49	50.0	31.1*
Total	942	655	287	59	192	36	156	54.3	106.7*

Notes 2013–2015 UK Longitudinal Labour Market Discrimination Study data set. The null hypothesis is "Both individuals are treated unfavorably equally often," that is, (2) = (3). The critical value of the χ^2 at the 1% level of significance is 6.635(*)

(equal treatments); in 258 cases (column six) only the younger applicant was invited and in 70 cases (column seven) only the older applicant was invited. Hence, net discrimination (Drydakis 2009) against the older applicant can be read from the last two columns and represents 188 cases (48.8%). The outcome is statistically significant. In other words, the younger male applicant was approximately 3.6 times more likely than the older male applicant (i.e., 258 cases vs. 70 cases) to receive an invitation for a job interview.

In Panel I, it is also observed that older applicants were found to face the highest occupational access constraints for factory/manual jobs, which constitute the lower-status sector (blue-collar) in our sample. To be specific, the net discrimination against the older applicant is 28 cases (65.1%). That is, for factory/manual jobs, the younger male applicant was approximately 6.4 times more likely than the older male applicant (i.e., 33 cases vs. 5 cases) to receive an invitation for a job interview. In Panel I, it is also observed that in office jobs (white-collar occupations), net discrimination against the older applicant is 59 cases (42.7%); in restaurant vacancies net discrimination against the older applicant is 43 cases (43.0%) and in shop sales, net discrimination against the older applicant is 58 cases (55.7%). In all cases, the outcomes are statistically significant.

Panel II presents observations for women. In 192 cases (column six) only the younger applicant was invited and in 36 cases (column seven), only the older applicant was invited. Hence, net discrimination against the older applicant is 156 cases (54.3%). The outcome is statistically significant. The younger female applicant was approximately 5.3 times more likely than the older female applicant (i.e., 192 cases vs. 36 cases) to receive an invitation for a job interview. Furthermore, it is observed that older female applicants were faced with the highest occupational access constraints for factory/manual jobs, that is, net discrimination against the older applicant is 24 cases (77.4%). In Panel II, it is also observed that in office jobs (white-collar occupations), net discrimination against the older applicant is 49 cases (50.0%); in restaurant vacancies net discrimination against the older applicant is 42 cases (47.1%) and in shop sales, net discrimination against the older applicant is 41 cases (59.4%). In all cases, the outcomes are statistically significant.

Interestingly, in Table 6.2 we report the results for the subset of applicants whose resumes were submitted to firms wherein HR departments (a) existed or (b) did not exist. In Table 6.2 Panel I, the net rate of discrimination against the older applicant in the case of the firms having HR was 49.1%. On the other hand, the net rate of discrimination against the older applicant in the case of the firms not having HR was 54.5%. In both cases, the outcomes are statistically significant. In Table 6.3, we also observe that the net rate of discrimination against the older applicant in the case of firms providing written commitments to equal opportunity was 33.0%. The outcome is statistically significant. The patterns suggest that the existence of HR departments, as well as the provision of written commitments to equal opportunities, retain statistically significant discriminatory patterns for the older applicant.

Table 6.2 Aggregate outcomes; access to occupations; men and women

Panel I: Firms having HR									
Outcomes	Jobs	Neither invited	At least one invited (1)	Both invited	Only the younger was invited (2)	Only the older was invited (3)	Net discrimination (2)–(3)	[(2)–(3)]/(1) %	$\chi 2$ test
Total	1157	738	419	77	274	68	206	49.1	124.0*
Panel II: Firms not having HR									
Outcomes	Jobs	Neither invited	At least one invited (1)	Both invited	Only the younger was invited (2)	Only the older was invited (3)	Net discrimination (2)–(3)	[(2)–(3)]/(1) %	$\chi 2$ test
Total	679	426	253	39	176	38	138	54.5	88.9*

Notes 2013–2015 UK Longitudinal Labour Market Discrimination Study data set. The null hypothesis is "Both individuals are treated unfavorably equally often," that is, (2) = (3). The critical value of the χ^2 at the 1% level of significance is 6.635(*)

Table 6.3 Aggregate outcomes; men and women

Firms that provide written commitments to equal opportunities

Outcomes	Jobs	Neither invited	At least one invited (1)	Both invited	Only the younger was invited (2)	Only the older was invited (3)	Net discrimination (2)–(3)	[(2)–(3)]/(1) %	χ2 test
Total	457	265	192	89	84	19	65	33.8	41.0*

Notes 2013–2015 UK Longitudinal Labour Market Discrimination Study data set. The null hypothesis is "Both individuals are treated unfavorably equally often," that is, (2) = (3). The critical value of the χ^2 at the 1% level of significance is 6.635(*)

6.4 Discussion and Implications for Organizations and Social Partners

The results suggest that discrimination in recruitment against older workers in the UK continues at alarming levels. It continues despite the introduction of the Equality Act 2010. Older workers must spend more time and resources finding jobs and firms may lose potential talent through biased recruitment practices. These results support the findings of other field experiments that indicate the existence of ageism in the recruitment process in other countries, such as in the US (Lahey 2008), in Sweden (Ahmed et al. 2012), in France (Riach and Rich 2006) and in Spain (Albert et al. 2011).

In addition, the results suggest that older women are more discriminated against than men (also found by Neumark et al. (2015) for the US) and manual workers more than non-manual workers. These patterns accord with stereotypical beliefs that the physical strengths and job performance of women and manual workers decline earlier than for men and white-collar workers (Böhm et al. 2013; Colin and Loretto 2004). Furthermore, white/pink-collar workers might have clear advantages compared to blue-collar workers (less likely to show signs of exhaustion, more valuable administrative experience, more able to effectively weigh up alternatives). Thus, gender and occupational heterogeneity seem to be factors that moderate ageism and require further attention.

A clear understanding of the nature of age discrimination is essential to derive policies from this analysis. Based on Taste theory of discrimination (Becker 1957), if employers, co-workers and/or consumers have tendencies toward discrimination and can distinguish older workers from younger, the result may be discriminatory treatment. In addition, based on the Statistical discrimination (Arrow 1973) if, in general, it is true that there is a systematic differential between the older and younger applicants in their productivity, this is sufficient to create a permanent differential in occupational access. In this situation, discrimination is not the consequence of exogenous preferences (distastes) but of profit-maximizing behavior of risk-averse employers. In practice, if Taste-based discrimination (Becker 1957) accounts for lower occupational access for older people, then anti-discrimination legislation may be the appropriate response. However, if Statistical discrimination is important (Arrow 1973), then a better means of assessing workers' productivity (i.e., through diagnostic tests) may contribute to the reduction of discrimination at the individual or group level. Importantly, in the current study, we have controlled for the older applicants' mental and physical capacities. Hence, it might be that firms may not invite older applicants to be interviewed, thus equalizing the unit costs of labor after factoring the distaste toward older people. Thus, in this study, evidence was found to support Taste-based discrimination as a reason for ageism and not Statistical discrimination, despite anti-discrimination legislation having been introduced.

6.4.1 Inclusive HR Policies Begin at the Recruitment Stage

Much of the existing work into the effects of ageing workforces has focused on adapting HR processes and policies for organizations' existing workforces. For example: The effect of job-related health problems on age/performance relations suggests adapting management of workers physical, mental, and social health should be a critical priority (Posthuma and Guerrero 2013; Naegele and Walker 2011); offering older workers renewed stimulation at key points in their careers may help to maintain high levels of commitment and skills (Ng and Feldman 2008; Sturman 2003); introducing flexible working-time arrangements to avoid demotivation and early exit from the workforce, especially for women (Posthuma and Guerrero 2013).

A clear focus on anti-discrimination policies and inclusion would result in a circle in which unbiased recruitments would promote inclusive practices, which, in turn, would promote a greater diversity of people drawn to join the workforce. If efforts to extend working lives and to increase participation rates among older people are to be successful, adapting HR policies to accommodate the aging of only existing workers is not sufficient. Older workers must also have equal access to vacancies in the recruitment process. Despite the existence of anti-discriminatory legislation, there remains widespread discrimination against older workers at an early stage of the recruitment process. HR policies can create behaviors in organizations and the right practices can encourage more inclusive behaviors. These practices should be focused on recruitment, career development, work design, etc.

As the results in Table 6.2 show, the existence of an HR department is not sufficient to eliminate age discrimination in recruitment. Even in firms with HR departments, younger applicants are four times as likely to receive an interview as older applicants (i.e., 274 cases vs. 68). These results reinforce previous findings that workforce ageing is often viewed negatively by HR practitioners, focusing on difficulties and conflicts instead of potential and opportunities (Naegele and Walker 2011). Interestingly, while firms with written commitments to equal opportunities (Table 6.3) still showed statistically significant rates of net discrimination against older applicants, the level of net discrimination was reduced. Net discrimination was reduced because, if any applicant was invited to interview, firms with written commitments to equality were far more likely to invite both applicants than firms without written commitments. Where at least one applicant was invited for interview, firms with written commitments invited both in 46.4% of cases against 17.3% of cases for firms without written commitments.

Our results show that current HR recruitment policies fail to prevent discrimination against older applicants. Inclusive HR policies must begin at the recruitment stage. Firms should not only actively solicit applications from older applicants (Lievens et al. 2012) but also ensure that they are fairly considered once received (see Salgado et al., Chap.7 in this volume).

Age discrimination in recruitment should not be considered in isolation. It should be seen in the context of other characteristics such as race, gender, socioeconomic background, ethnicity, and disability that may be discriminated against in recruitment. As we show for the case of gender, these characteristics are likely to moderate the effects of ageism. It is those firms with written commitments to equality (and across all characteristics rather than just age) who display the lowest levels of net discrimination. Firms need to ensure that shared values and beliefs, as well as policies, practices, and procedures are not age-discriminatory but recognize the strengths and potentials of workers from different age groups (Naegele and Walker 2011). The government should require firms to have ageing-at-work policies (Naegele and Walker 2011) but such policies need to explicitly address all stages of the recruitment process.

Inclusive HR policies must recognize both that older workers may maintain (or improve) productivity across their working lives in a way that compensate for reduced physical ability (Ng and Feldman 2012) and that there exists, on average, (perhaps unconscious) taste-based bias against older workers among recruiters which is unrelated applicants' productivities. There must be less reliance on chronological age and greater use of intrinsic predictors of job performance, such as use of job analysis and specific performance tests (Naegele and Walker 2011; see Salgado et al., Chap. 7 in this volume). Clearly, those conducting interviews need to be trained to carry out age-sensitive selection processes. Our results show that discrimination occurs prior to this, when selecting which applicants are interviewed. Similar training is necessary for those involved in selecting interviewees though there is little evidence yet as to the effectiveness of such training relating to age discrimination (Lievens et al. 2012). Avoiding revealing age at the application stage (or details from which age might be inferred such as extensive experience, dates of qualifications) would reduce opportunities for recruiters to discriminate against older applicants.

6.4.2 Social Dialogue to Promote Fair Recruitment

The results of this study show how much work needs to be done to address age discrimination in the labor market. We found evidence strongly suggestive of discrimination taste-based age discrimination, despite European and national regulation aimed making such practice unlawful. Eliminating such age discrimination in recruitment requires not only a fundamental change in attitudes and behaviors toward older workers by recruiters, but also recruiting organizations designing and implementing effective policies and procedures (Collin 2005). This suggests a key role for constructive and informed social dialogue in improving recruitment practices. Its importance lies in ensuring that within organizations both sides (employers and workers) can represent their interests and, through discussion, arrive at practices beneficial for all. It is only through social dialogue and cooperation between both parties in workplaces that recruitment issues such as age discrimination can be highlighted and resolved.

Social dialogue should be an integral part of the process of changing attitudes and establishing more inclusive workplaces, as it gives the opportunity for parties to raise issues and negotiate solutions. Cooperative social dialogue between employers and employee representatives offers the greatest opportunities for developing HR policies at the organizational level to confront and eliminate age discrimination in recruitment (Bryson et al. 2012). Effective social dialogue requires effective representation of both employers and workers. The UK is distinct from other European countries in having much lower levels of formal employee representation at the organizational level (Martinez-Lucio and Keizer 2015). This lack of effective employee representation is especially acute for the low-skilled occupations, private sector roles that form our sample. These have notably low levels of union membership, and the UK has traditionally relied solely on unions as the channel for employee representation (Euwema et al. 2015).

Developing inclusive recruitment policies is in the interests of both employers, who may otherwise overlook the most productive applicants to vacancies and increasingly so as workforces age, and employees, who will become older applicants in the future. On the issue of age discrimination, there exist incentives, recognizing their shared interests, to develop cooperatively orientated relations between employers and employee representatives. Developing cooperative relations require investments by both parties (Euwema et al. 2015). The primary challenge, especially in the UK, but more generally across Europe is cultivating effective employee representation at the level of the organization. If mechanisms can be developed to ensure effective, competent, and trustworthy employee representation, whether through the unions or not, cooperative social dialogue offers the opportunity to employers, employees and potential employees put forward their claims for a fairer, more inclusive and more efficient recruitment practices. Developing inclusive recruitment policies to address age discrimination will not only protect older workers and job candidates. As our results show, age discrimination is moderated by characteristics such as gender. Recruitment policies that are inclusive for one characteristic are likely to be more inclusive for all characteristics. Hence, social dialogue is an essential condition for an inclusive work environment as it allows arguments for special cases within the workforce to be presented, and solutions developed, within each organization's environment (Collin 2005).

Of course, relations and dialogue between employers and employees are affected and defined by society-wide beliefs and norms. Norms in the workplace follow society-wide ethical norms and as such there can be delay in adoption and application. Ageism and age discrimination has only recently become part of the ethical discourse and, notwithstanding regulatory changes, our results suggest that informal workplace behavior is yet to adapt. As norms evolve, discrimination against older workers in the labor market will reduce over time. However, such adaptation can take decades as, for example in the case of gender discrimination (Phillips 1998). The pressures of population aging make swift adaptation imperative. An active older population enjoying equal treatments in the labor market will be better able to help build the social and economic capital of their countries (Age UK 2011).

6.5 Conclusions

This study has provided strong evidence of age bias due to distastes against older applicants at the first stage of the recruitment process in the UK for the 2013–2015 period. The results, based on a sample of low-skilled occupations, suggest that, despite the introduction of the Equality Act 2010, many employers reject applications from individuals because they have reached the age of 50. Furthermore, the results indicate that women and those in blue-collar occupations are at greater disadvantage compared to men and those in white/pink-collar occupations. The results of this study highlight that a history of discrimination is not reversed overnight by passing legislation. Nor do the existence of HR departments or written commitments to equal opportunities by firms eliminate discrimination against older people. As the baby boom cohort reaches retirement age, social programs face looming funding crises (Lahey 2008; OECD 2004). One often-suggested solution is to encourage older workers to remain in the labor force, so that benefits can be cut without compromising living standards. Simply encouraging older people to reenter the labor force may not guarantee that they will be able to find jobs in a timely manner, if at all. Our study has shown that older people must spend more time, effort, and resources than younger people to obtain an interview.

Social dialogue between social planners and trade unions can play an important role in effectively operationalizing national regulation at an organizational level. Social dialogue should ask for open dialogue and constructive negotiations between management, trade unions, and employee representatives in order to promote a change of attitudes, behaviors, and competences on diversity and social inclusion, and develop effective organizational responses in terms of policies and procedural aspects to improve inclusion of older people at workplaces.

Finally, it is important to consider that the study's results should be evaluated while considering the characteristics of the experiment and data set. Our study has focused on the recruitment stage and has ignored potential discrimination that could arise later on. We have focused on only a few low-skilled occupations, applicant profiles, and regions. Consequently, firm generalizations are not possible. One may need to consider additional occupations, applicants with heterogeneous human capital and demographic characteristics and countries. These should be interesting new studies.

References

Age UK. (2011). *Grey matters: A survey of ageism across Europe*. London: Age UK.

Ahmed, A. M., Anderssona, L., & Hammarstedt, M. (2012). Does age matter for employability? A field experiment on ageism in the Swedish labor market. *Applied Economics Letters, 19*(4), 403–406.

Albert, R., Escot, L., & Fernandez-Cornejo, J. A. (2011). A field experiment to study sex and age discrimination in the Madrid labor market. *International Journal of Human Resource Management, 22*(2), 351–375.

American Association of Retired Person. (2014). *Staying ahead of the curve 2013: AARP Multicultural work and career study. Older workers in an uneasy job market*. Washington, DC: AARP.

Arrow, K. J. (1973). The theory of discrimination. In A. Orley & R. Albert (Eds.), *Discrimination in labor markets* (pp. 3–33). NJ: Princeton University Press.

Becker, G. S. (1957). *The economics of discrimination*. Chicago: University of Chicago Press.

Böhm, S. A., Schröder, H. S., & Kunze, F. (2013). Comparative age management: Theoretical perspective and practical implications. In J. Field, R. J. Burke, & C. L. Cooper (Eds.), *The SAGE handbook on work, aging, and society* (pp. 211–237). CA: Thousand Oakes, Sage.

Bryson, A., Forth, J., & George, A. (2012). *Workplace social dialogue in Europe: An analysis of the European Company Survey 2009*. Dublin: Eurofound.

Colin, D., & Loretto, W. (2004). Never the right age? Gender and age-based discrimination in employment. *Gender, Work and Organization., 11*(1), 95–115.

Collin, A. (2005). *Age discrimination and social partners: a comparative study of France and the United Kingdom*. Warwick Papers in Industrial Relations No. 75. Coventry: University of Warwick.

Deloitte, L. L. P. (2014). *Global human capital trends 2014: Engaging the 21st-century workforce*. Texas: Deloitte University Press.

Drydakis, N. (2009). Sexual orientation discrimination in the labor market. *Labour Economics, 16* (4), 364–372.

Drydakis, N. (2015). Measuring sexual orientation discrimination in the UK's labor market. *A Field experiment. Human Relations, 68*(11), 1769–1796.

Eurobarometer. (2007). *Discrimination in the European Union. Wave 263 65.4*. Brussels: EU.

European Policy Centre. (2011). *Working away at the cost of ageing: The labor market adjusted dependency ratio*. EPC Issue Paper No. 64. Belgium: European Policy Centre.

Euwema, M. C., Garcia, A. B., Munduate, L., Elgoibar, P., & Pender, E. (2015). Employee representatives in European organizations. In M. C. Euwema et al. (Eds.), *Promoting social dialogue in European Organizations* (pp. 1–17). Cham: Springer.

George, A., Metcalf, H., Tufekci, L., & Wilkinson, D. (2015). *Understanding age and the labor market*. York: Joseph Rowntree Foundation.

Lahey, J. N. (2008). Age, women, and hiring: An experimental study. *The Journal of Human Resources, 43*(1), 30–56.

Lievens, F., Van Hoye, G., & Zacher, H. (2012). Recruiting/hiring of older workers. In W. C. Borman & J. W. Hedge (Eds.), *The Oxford handbook of work and aging* (pp. 380–391). Oxford: Oxford University Press.

Martinez-Lucio, M., & Keizer, A. B. (2015). Employee representatives and participation in the United Kingdom. In M. C. Euwema et al. (Eds.), *Promoting social dialogue in European organizations* (pp. 1–17). Cham: Springer.

Mercer, U. K. (2015). *Age-friendly employer research*. London: Mercer.

Naegele, G., & Walker, A. (2011). Age management in organizations in the European Union. In M. Malloch, B. N. O'Connor, K. Evans, & L. Cairns (Eds.), *The SAGE handbook of workplace learning* (pp. 251–267). CA: Thousand Oakes, Sage.

Neumark, D., Burn, I., & Button, P. (2015). *Is it harder for older workers to find jobs? New and improved evidence from a field experiment*. NBER Working Paper No. 21669. Cambridge, MA: National Bureau of Economic Research.

Ng, T. W. H., & Feldman, D. C. (2008). The relationship of age to ten dimensions of job performance. *Journal of Applied Psychology, 93*(2), 392–423.

Ng, T. W. H., & Feldman, D. C. (2012). Evaluating six common stereotypes about older workers with meta-analytical data. *Personnel Psychology, 65*(4), 821–858.

OECD. (2004). *Ageing and employment policy, United Kingdom*. Paris: OECD.

Phillips, A. (1998). *Feminism and politics*. Oxford: Oxford University Press.

Riach, P. A., & Rich, J. (2002). Field experiments of discrimination in the market place. *The Economic Journal, 112*(483), 480–518.

Riach, P. A., & Rich, J. (2006). *An experimental investigation of age discrimination in the French labor market*. IZA Discussion Paper No. 2522. Bonn: Institute for the Study of Labor.

Riach, P. A., & Rich, J. (2007). *An experimental investigation of age discrimination in the Spanish labor market*. IZA Discussion Paper No. 2654. Bonn: Institute for the Study of Labor.

Posthuma, R. A., & Guerrero, L. (2013). Age stereotypes in the workplace: Multidimensionality, cross-cultural applications, and directions for future research. In J. Field, R. J. Burke, & C. L. Cooper (Eds.), *The SAGE handbook of aging, work and society* (pp. 250–265). CA: Thousand Oaks, Sage.

Sturman, M. C. (2003). Searching for the inverted U-shaped relationship between time and performance: Meta-analyses of the experience/performance, tenure/performance, and age/performance relationships. *Journal of Management, 29*(5), 609–640.

Van Vianen, A. E., Dalhoeven, B. A., & De Pater, I. E. (2011). Aging and training and development willingness: Employee and supervisor mind-sets. *Journal of Organizational Behavior, 32*(2), 226–247.

Warr, P. (1994). Age and job performance. In J. Snel & R. Cremer (Eds.), *Work and aging: A European perspective* (pp. 309–322). London: Taylor and Francis.

Chapter 7
Inclusive and Discrimination-Free Personnel Selection

Jesús F. Salgado, Silvia Moscoso, Antonio L. García-Izquierdo and Neil R. Anderson

7.1 Introduction

In recent years, changes in society in general and in the labor market in particular have led to a greater diversity in the work force. For instance, the number of women is increasing at top organizational levels (Bastida and Moscoso 2015), the percentage of the population which is aging is remarkably higher, and the variety of ethnic groups is larger than at any time in the past (van Knippenberg and Schippers 2007). In addition, globalization has, since the end of the last century, been accelerating dramatic changes in relation to several work issues. Such changes are also taking place in the nature of work. Jobs are more complex in terms of information processing and dealing with others, demanding higher cognitive abilities and better emotion management in the workplace.

Inclusive organizations must know how to manage the diversity not only to succeed, but also to make fair decisions, to respect and value all the different people and groups inside organizations, to promote social dialogue and active participation of all stakeholders involved (e.g., employees, managers, trade unions, employee

---

This chapter was partially supported by Grant PSI2014-56615-P from the Spanish Ministry of Economy and Competitiveness to Silvia Moscoso and Jesús F. Salgado and by Grant PSI2013-44584-R to Antonio García-Izquierdo.

J.F. Salgado · S. Moscoso (✉)
University of Santiago de Compostela, Santiago de Compostela, Spain
e-mail: silvia.moscoso@usc.es

A.L. García-Izquierdo
University of Oviedo, Asturias, Spain

N.R. Anderson
Brunel University London, London, UK

A. Arenas et al. (eds.), *Shaping Inclusive Workplaces Through Social Dialogue*, Industrial Relations & Conflict Management,
DOI 10.1007/978-3-319-66393-7_7

representatives) in the organizational dynamics, and to behave in a nondiscriminatory way toward their employees.

Legislation in some countries in Europe defines discrimination as an unlawful different treatment based on prohibited criteria, mainly on grounds of sex. Directive 2010/41/EU deals with equal employment opportunities between women and men, avoiding discrimination on grounds of sex in the public or private sectors either directly or indirectly. Most countries in Europe have developed employment laws that distinguish between direct and indirect discrimination after some Directives (e.g., Directives (2000a) 2000/43/EC, (2000b) 2000/78/EC, (2006) 2006/54/EC). *Direct discrimination* consists of treating someone differently, solely on the basis of age, sex, skin color, national origin, or disability, among other factors. If we focus, for example, on sex discrimination, this would take place where one person is treated less favorably on the grounds of sex than another is, has been, or would be treated in a comparable situation. *Indirect discrimination* takes place where an apparently neutral procedure, criterion, or practice would put persons of a protected group at a particular disadvantage compared with persons of the majority group, unless that procedure, criterion, or practice is objectively justified. Organizations can carry out different types of so-called affirmative action measures (AAMs) in order to reduce and avoid discrimination, which can be classified into various categories. One of them is the positive discrimination actions, such as quotas, preferential treatment on equal merit, and merit exemption for the focal group. However, the implementation of positive discrimination actions is a controversial issue, and the legislation varies across the countries (Crosby et al. 2006; Moscoso et al. 2012).

Beyond countries legislation, Human Resource Management (HRM) policies are fundamental to achieving an inclusive workplace. Right practices in recruitment and selection, training and development, performance, promotion, or remuneration through social dialogue are directly related to effective management of diversity, attitude and behavior change, and organizational justice. The Circle of Inclusion (see Arenas et al., Chap. 1 in this volume) represents these best practices in HRM where the first step is the hiring process, known in this context as inclusive and discrimination-free personnel selection (IPS).

IPS is, therefore, one of the most critical processes in the study of human behavior in inclusive organizations because it determines the efficiency of other elements of management practices represented in the Circle of Inclusion (e.g., performance appraisal, training, or compensation). IPS is used by inclusive organizations to decide which of the applicants shows the best fit to the job and company, but simultaneously conducts a process that respects diversity and is discrimination-free. In this sense, IPS, like all personnel selection processes (see Drydakis et al., Chap. 6 in this volume), represents a kind of "barrier to entry" for individuals to any work organization (Moscoso et al. 2017). But equally in the context of workplace diversity (e.g., gender, race, ethnic group, age, personality, tenure), justice, impartiality, fair treatment, and nondiscrimination in personnel procedures are a necessity and a growing social demand (García-Izquierdo and

García-Izquierdo 2007), which affects not only evaluators and organization, but which should also actively involve both applicants and all other social actors.

The first and fundamental point that must be taken into account in any IPS process is to use appropriate procedures (e.g., cognitive tests, structured interviews, and personality inventories) with strong psychometric properties (i.e., reliability and criterion-oriented validity), as this is what will permit the making of correct predictions about the person-organization fit and person-job fit to support an inclusive and fair process. However, reliability and criterion-oriented validity alone are what could be described as "necessary but not sufficient conditions" to ensure fairness overall. Other factors, described subsequently in this chapter, will also have to be present to guarantee an IPS process.

Additionally, it should be taken into account that the candidates also make decisions. In other words, the candidate perspective regarding the inclusive selection process (e.g., the applicant reactions and perceptions) must also be considered (Anderson et al. 2010; McCarthy et al. 2017; Truxillo et al. 2016). In connection with this, Anderson and his colleagues (Anderson et al. 2004; Moscoso et al. 2017), Schuler (1993) identified two main perspectives in personnel selection. The first perspective is the predictivist one, the essence of which is to establish the *person-job fit*. According to this perspective, the selection procedures are predictors of future job performance and the candidates are seen as "subjects" to the selection procedures. The second is the constructivist perspective, which emphasizes that the candidates, as well as organizations, also make decisions in personnel selection processes. According to Anderson and his colleagues, this perspective sees selection as an opportunity for information exchange and to explore if a future working relation would be viable. Therefore, from the constructivist perspective, personnel selection focuses not only on ensuring person-job fit but also *person-organization fit* and *team-organization fit*. In this context, person-organization fit is conceptualized as the adjustment between the candidate's values and the organizational values and culture, and person-team fit is conceptualized as the adjustment between the candidate's competencies and attitudes and the abilities and climate of the immediate working group.

7.2 Procedures and Techniques for Inclusive Personnel Selection

Regardless of whether the approach used in selection is the predictivist perspective or the constructivist perspective, the appropriateness of the selection decision will depend upon the psychometric properties (reliability and criterion-related validity) of the procedures used for making the decision. A selection process can never be fair and ensure equal opportunities in employment if the instruments do not predict future interest criteria. Job performance ratings are the most widely used organizational criterion in personnel selection, followed by measures of training proficiency (Salgado et al. 2016). In this sense, the first aspect to take into account, within the IPS, is that the procedures must be valid; otherwise, we would be making arbitrary selection decisions that would affect the processes of organizational justice. Thus, from the point of view of social dialogue in inclusive organizations, trade unions and employee representatives should ensure that the psychometric principles of the procedures used in recruitment are met. In this case, we would be talking about indirect participation (Nauta 2015) in the selection processes.

Some of the most commonly used selection procedures are briefly described below and, in Table 7.1, we summarize succinctly the meta-analytic evidence of their criterion-oriented validity[1] for predicting job performance and the coefficients refer to the operational validity.[2] The greater the coefficient of validity of an instrument, the greater its predictive capacity and therefore the greater is the likelihood of making correct decisions.

(*a*) ***Selection Interview***: The interview is probably the most used procedure for personnel selection, and applicants tend to rate the interview highly (Salgado et al. 2001; Kehoe et al. 2017).

Salgado and Moscoso (2002) classified employment interviews into three main types: unstructured interviews, conventional structured interviews, and behavioral structured interviews in function of the degree of structure and the content of the questions. Unstructured interviews have no fixed format regarding the content of the questions and the assessment of the answers. Conventional structured interviews ask the same questions to the candidates and can rate the answers using the same form. Behavioral structured interviews (BSI) possess the following characteristics: (a) the questions are based on a job analysis, using typically the critical incident technique; (b) the job analysis also serves to identify the main job dimensions that should be assessed with the interview; (c) the same questions are asked to all the candidates; (d) the same procedure is used for all candidates; (e) in many cases, the candidate replies are assessed using behavioral anchoring rating scales; (f) the interviewer is previously trained in this method to ensure that all interviewers understand the standardized format; (g) the decision is made only when all the candidates have been interviewed. Structured interviews are more valid and reliable than unstructured interviews, and BSI shows an excellent validity coefficient.

Recently, the meta-analysis of Alonso et al. (2017) found that structured behavioral interviews are a very robust technique for ensuring equal employment

[1]In personnel selection, coefficients of less than .15 are usually considered to be scarcely valid; The validity between .16 and .30 is usually considered small; Moderately valid coefficients between .31 and .40 and of appreciable validity the coefficients greater than .40. From .50, it is understood that the validity is excellent. However, it is also necessary to take into account the type of criterion being predicted and that some instruments that show little validity may, however, be interesting, since such validity could increase that achieved by other instruments.

[2]Operational validity is the correlation between an assessment method (e.g., interview) and job performance after correction for job performance reliability and any range restriction in the measure used.

Table 7.1 Operative validity of techniques for inclusive personnel selection

Techniques	Operational corrected validity
Unstructured interview	.20[a]
Conventional structured interview	.35[a]
Structured behavioral interview	.62[b]
Work sample test	.33[c]
Job knowledge test	.48[d]
Situational judgment test	.26[e]
Assessment center	.36[f]
General mental ability test	.62[g]
Numerical ability test	.52[g]
Verbal ability test	.62[g]
Memory test	.56[g]
Conscientiousness—SS	.22[h]
Emotional stability—SS	.11[h]
Openness to experience—SS	.05[h]
Agreeableness—SS	.08[h]
Extroversion—SS	.12[h]
Conscientiousness—quasi-ipsative FC	.38[h]
Emotional stability—quasi-ipsative FC	.20[h]
Openness to experience—quasi-ipsative FC	.22[h]
Agreeableness—quasi-ipsative FC	.16[h]
Extroversion—quasi-ipsative FC	.12[h]

Note [a]From Huffcutt et al. (1996); [b]From Salgado and Moscoso (2006); [c]From Roth et al. (2005); [d]From Hunter and Hunter (1984); [e]From McDaniel et al. (2007); [f]From Gaugler et al. (1987); [g]From Salgado et al. (2003a, b); [h]From Salgado et al. (2015); *SS* single stimulus personality inventories; *FC* forced-choice personality inventories

opportunities for women. The results of this meta-analysis showed that the difference of the SBI scores of women and men is very small but favorable to women.

(*b*) ***General and Specific Cognitive Ability Tests***: General mental ability (GMA) can be defined as the capacity of an individual to learn rapidly and accurately in optimal conditions of instruction (Schmidt and Hunter 1998). In addition, there are a number of specific cognitive abilities, including verbal, numerical, spatial, memory, perceptual, and reasoning, among others (Salgado and Anderson 2002). Typically, general and specific cognitive abilities are assessed with psychometric tests, and these have been found to be highly predictively valid for different job occupations.

(*c*) ***Personality Inventories***: Personality measures (also called personality tests or personality inventories) are widely used in personnel selection processes across the world. Recent advances in the domain of personality at work have been due, to a great extent, to the use of the five factor model (FFM). The FFM of the structure of personality posits that there are five basic personality dimensions or factors

("The Big Five"), hierarchically organized (Judge et al. 2013): (a) emotional stability, (b) extroversion, (c) openness to experience, (d) agreeableness, and (e) conscientiousness.

Some of the most relevant results of research on the FFM in the last years are as follows (Salgado 2017): (1) The taxonomy of personality traits derived from the FFM has proved to be a very useful framework for organizing various single measures; (2) conscientiousness is the best personality predictor of job performance and counterproductive behaviors, and it has shown validity generalization across samples, occupations, and countries; (3) emotional stability was the second most relevant personality predictor of job performance and counterproductive work behaviors; (4) the format of the personality inventory is an important moderator of the criterion-related validity of the Big Five dimensions, so that the validity increases dramatically when quasi-ipsative forced-choice formats[3] are used.

(*d*) ***Assessment Centers***: Assessment centers involve a combination of selection methods, commonly, in-basket tests, leaderless group discussions, case analysis, role play, and other simulations, but also cognitive ability tests, personality tests, and interviews. Candidates' behaviors are rated along identified selection dimensions (e.g., leadership, problem-solving, interpersonal behavior). Another important characteristic of the assessment center method is that different raters assess the candidates. Overall, applicants tend to favor assessment centers (Anderson et al. 2010).

(*e*) ***Work Sample Tests***: Work samples involve identifying tasks representative of the job and using these to develop a representative short test resembling actual components of the job. These tests have been used typically for selecting skilled workers, and they have the limitation that they can be used only with candidates who already know the job. Applicants rate work sample tests very positively, perceiving them as fair, valid, and job related (Anderson et al. 2010).

(*f*) ***Job Knowledge Tests and Situational Judgment Tests***: *Job knowledge tests* are techniques for assessing the degree to which the applicants have the knowledge needed for a specific job. *Situational judgment tests* are a type of job knowledge test which present the individual with hypothetical job scenarios and ask the candidates to identify the most appropriate answer for effective job performance.

[3]Forced choice (FC) is a specific format of rating procedures. The FC method gives the individual (e.g., the applicant) a number of words or phrases, along with instructions to select the ones he or she most or least likes. The number of words or phrases may be, for instance, pairs, triads, or tetrads, which are paired in terms of an index of preference and discrimination (e.g., social desirability). Three types of scores can be obtained from a FC personality inventory (ipsative, quasi-ipsative, and normative). Quasi-ipsative inventories include measures that do not totally meet the criterion of pure ipsativity, because, for example, not all alternatives ranked by respondents are scored or the scales have different numbers of items.

7.3 Applicant Reactions

The previous section showed that selection techniques with strong psychometric properties are a compulsory requirement for making correct-and-inclusive personnel selection decisions. On the other hand, the inclusiveness of the selection process also implies the necessity of considering the candidate perspective, i.e., the applicant reactions and perceptions (Anderson et al. 2010; Truxillo et al. 2016). This necessity is linked to the overall objective of making fair decisions, to promote social dialogue and active participation of all stakeholders, and to behave in a nondiscriminatory way toward their employees.

The term "applicant reactions" has been defined by Ryan and Ployhart (2000) as "attitudes, affect, or cognitions an individual might have about the hiring process" (p. 566). Organizations should allow candidates to directly voice their reactions and perceptions, because, as we will see below, these can have important consequences for the selection process and for other organizational areas. Anderson (2004) and Hausknecht et al. (2004) indicate that there are several reasons for the importance of the applicant reactions. In first place, if candidates find that some aspects of the selection process are invasive, they could discard the organization or consider this organization to be less attractive for a jobseeker. The loss of candidates means an additional cost for the company and, consequently, it is important that it maintains a positive image during the hiring process. A second reason is that candidates with a negative image of the organization can dissuade other potential candidates from seeking employment in this company. A third reason is that the experiences of candidates during the selection processes can affect other relevant areas such as attitudes to this organization, the image of the company that they will project to the outside world, and the experiences may affect even the consumption behavior toward products and services of the company. A fourth reason is that the applicant reactions can be related to legal complaints because it is more than probable that the candidates who perceive a specific selection technique to be discriminatory or invasive may allege that such procedures are unfair. A fifth reason is that all selection processes are an information exchange and a bidirectional decision making in which both parties make a decision. Therefore, it is less probable that the selected applicants will accept a job offer from an organization in which the personnel selection procedures are considered to be negative or discriminatory.

In recent years, several frameworks for examining the social issues involved in selection have emerged, providing more detailed insight into the etiology of the applicants' perspective (McCarthy et al. 2017). An important body of research has centered on studying the topic from a justice perspective (e.g., Gilliland 1993; Hausknecht et al. 2004; Ryan and Ployhart 2000); other authors have analyzed the applicant reactions from the point of view of social impact, psychological contract, or social identity (Anderson 2001; Schuler 1993). Also, recently the attribution theory has been analyzed in this context (Ployhart and Harold 2004). We explore some of these issues below.

One of the first theoretical accounts of applicant reactions was developed by Gilliland (1993). This author used organizational justice theories (OJT) to develop a model of applicant reactions to selection procedures. OJT distinguishes between *distributive justice* and *procedural justice*. The former refers to the perceived fairness in decisions on resource assignment (perceived fairness in the outcome allocation). The latter refers to the perceived fairness in the ways used to determine the outcomes within the decision-making process (perceived fairness in the way outcomes is determined).

Gilliland (1993) distinguished ten procedural justice rules in personnel selection issues that he classified in three categories. The first category is referred to formal characteristics. It includes job relatedness of measurement instruments, the opportunity to give a display of knowledge, skills and abilities, opportunity to check tests scores, and the consistency of test administration that relates to the standardization of administrative procedures for people and techniques. The second category is information provided, including the supply of timely and informative feedback regarding selection performance and its outcome, the adequacy of information provided to applicants regarding the selection process and the organization's integrity during the selection process. Finally, the last category is interpersonal treatment, regarding the interpersonal effectiveness and interest of the recruiter, the extent to which conversation flows in a normal pattern and applicants are given the opportunity to ask questions and the appropriateness of the questions asked. Consistent with OJT, Gilliland suggested that it is the combined satisfaction or violation of specific rules that produces overall evaluations of procedural and distributive fairness.

Research indicates that candidates' reactions to selection justice can have an impact on three important outcomes (Truxillo et al. 2016). First, perceptions of justice influence applicants' reactions and decisions during hiring, for example, the extent to which the candidate will recommend the organization to others, and their intention to withdraw from the procedure. Second, perceptions of fairness impinge upon candidates' attitudes and behaviors after being hired or rejected, for example, organizational commitment, intention to leave and work performance in the case of being hired, and the decision of whether to pursue discrimination cases if rejected. Third, perceived fairness influences applicants' well-being and self-perceptions, such as self-esteem and self-efficacy.

Anderson (2001), Anderson and Ostroff (1997) has developed a model of the "socialization impact" of selection methods. Anderson proposed an empirically testable model whose fundamental postulates suggest that all selection procedures have a socialization impact. According to the model, socialization impact is articulated across five constituent domains: information provision, preference impact, expectational impact, attitudinal impact, and behavioral impact. Schuler (1993) developed a theory explaining applicant reactions to selection techniques, and he named these reactions "social validity." Schuler hypothesizes that these reactions depend on four factors: (1) The information applicants receive about task requirements and the characteristics of the organization; (2) direct or representative (e.g., unions) participation that applicants have in the development and execution of the selection process; (3) the transparency of the selection procedure (situation, the assessment tools, and the judgmental evaluation); and (4) the form and content of feedback given to applicants regarding their results.

Ployhart and Harold (2004) basing their work on the attribution theory proposed a new one called the Applicant Attribution-Reaction Theory (AART).The authors suggest that attributions are the first step in the applicant's reaction to selection procedures. Specifically, the theory proposes that applicant's affective, behavioral, and cognitive reactions, with respect to fairness, test perceptions, test performance, and motivation, are fundamentally driven by attributional processes. In a selection situation, for instance, applicants who receive a rejection decision may not react negatively toward the organization if they believe the decision is based on their own substandard performance during testing. However, if a rejected applicant perceives the rejection as unfair, he or she might react more negatively. A third possibility is that the applicant perceives the negative decision as being caused by an external and uncontrollable factor, for example, an extremely low selection ratio. AART also explains the occurrence of a self-serving bias in applicant reactions: Applicants who are hired by an organization generally perceive the procedure and organization as fair, while those who are rejected arrive at the opposite conclusion. Thus, in keeping their self-perceptions intact, rejected applicants lower their positive perceptions of an organization. To reduce the chances of this bias, organizations could provide applicants with clear information about the selection procedure and decision (Ployhart and Harold 2004).

In addition to theoretical models, empirical research about applicant reactions has centered on different aspects of this topic. For example, some studies have analyzed perceptions about face validity, fairness, job relevancy, or the invasiveness of different techniques and selection instruments in different countries and cultures. Thus, the meta-analysis carried out by Anderson et al. (2010) examined applicant perceptions and reactions using studies conducted in 17 countries in Europe, North America, Asia, and Africa. Findings showed a great deal of similarity in the favorability reactions between countries. With small exceptions, interviews and work sample tests were the most preferred instruments; resumes, cognitive tests, personality inventories, biodata, and reference checks were perceived quite favorably. Finally, honesty tests, personal contacts, and graphology were the least preferred and perceived unfavorably. These authors also examined the relationship between applicant reactions and the validity of the selection procedures. They found strong positive correlations (over .60) between the validity of the procedures and the perceptions of favorability, scientific evidence, face validity, and opportunity to perform.

Other studies have researched some variables that can affect perceptions such as demographic variables, individual differences, job characteristics, or feedback about test performance. For example, Hausknecht et al. (2004) found that variables such as gender, age, and ethnic background were not related with applicant reactions. They also found that when applicants have positive perceptions about the selection process, they perceive the organization more favorably, have more intention of accepting the job, and recommend the organization to others. More recently,

Truxillo et al. (2009) found that providing explanations to applicants on the selection process had a positive effect on fairness perceptions, test-taking motivation, performance on cognitive ability tests, and organizational attractiveness.

7.4 Justice Principles for an Inclusive and Discrimination-Free Personnel Selection Procedure

IPS, as already indicated in the introduction of this chapter, is deeply related with equality, diversity, and nondiscrimination. Avoiding discrimination is a laudable but difficult task. The Equal Employment Opportunity (EEO) is a well-accepted social movement pushing for a diverse and egalitarian workforce. The EEO is mainly concerned with equality, which is a fundamental right and *a common principle in some EU fundamental directives*. Moreover, equality is a necessary condition for the welfare state, in terms of employment and social cohesion. The EEO frames measures directed toward *giving a voice* to all people involved in organizations (Folger 1977), that is, the possibility to give one's own opinion and arguments on organizational processes. The EEO is directly related, therefore, to the model of the circle of inclusion proposed in this book. The EEO ensures impartiality and equality, and when applied to IPS, facilitates access to the labor market for all collectives and social groups, especially for those which are underrepresented.

In this context, collective bargaining and the role of employees' representatives can be useful for reducing discrimination and reaching an agreement on equality measures and plans within organizations. Based on Gilliland's (1993) rules, Bauer et al.'s (2001, 2012) Social Validity Theory (Schuler 1993), and the International Test Commission Guidelines, we have elaborated Table 7.2, where we can find several justice principles and some associate recommendations which allow social agents to evaluate to what extent a personnel selection procedure is inclusive and discrimination-free. In the left-hand row, we can see the justice principles, and in the right-hand row we can see the recommendations to fulfill those principles. It should be advisable social agents to inform previously the personnel selection board about what they are going to check out in order to develop a real fair process. Having this in mind, every company can produce its own procedures and a checklist, and consequently evaluate the quality of the personnel selection and promotion process. All the justice principles are relevant and consequently should be taken into account simultaneously. These principles aim to unveil implicit concepts under consideration and respect to applicants needs during the evaluation process, and giving them voice in the procedure as well. Privacy, fairness, communication, merit and efficacy, and equality are the basis of the justice principles we develop in the table.

Table 7.2 Justice criteria and recommendations list for an inclusive and discrimination-free personnel selection procedure

Justice principle	Recommendation
1. *Opportunity to perform*: Having the opportunity to demonstrate one's competences and abilities during the assessment process	– The selection system should be comprised of multiple components—(interview, standardized tests, work samples, etc.) for assessing competences and other characteristics related with the task and duties of that job – Pay enough attention to the methods so that they are long enough for a full and detailed evaluation. – The selection process should be updated in line with the evolution of findings over time
2. *Job relatedness*: Establish the relationship of the measurements with the content of the job	– The selection system should be based on job analysis, and/or organizational matching – Take into account the merit system principles – The selection system must be based on scientific evidence – If the selection method is not obviously job related to candidates, candidates deserve an explanation – The selection process must be updated with tools and new scientific findings
3. *Validity*: Measuring job-related constructs with scientific instruments	– It is important to assure the use of standardized tests and interviews – Measurements must have scientific characteristics: reliability and validity (apparent, construct, and content) – Variables must have a well-demonstrated relationship with criteria
4. *Consistency*: Uniformity of content across test settings, scoring, and administration of the tests	– Develop and use standardized tests and interviews based on extensive job analysis – Ask the same questions of each candidate – Scoring procedures must be also standardized – Certified adequate training of administrators to guarantee consistent standard procedures for all candidates across people and over time – All materials (online and elsewhere) may give consistent messages regarding your organization
5. *Congruency*: The extent to which the job is really in accordance with candidates expectations	– Present to all applicants a Realistic Job Preview (RJP) – Avoid giving false expectations to candidates, especially those who may have little chance of getting the job

(continued)

Table 7.2 (continued)

Justice principle	Recommendation
6. *Communication*: Information given and interaction during the selection process 6.1. *Feedback*: Providing candidates with accurate and timely information on aspects of the decision-making process and/or the performance 6.2. *Explanations & Justification*: The provision of justification for a selection decision and/or procedure 6.3. *Two-way Communication*: The interpersonal interaction between candidate and test administrator that allows candidates the opportunity to give their views or have their views considered in the selection process 6.4. *Accessibility and usability:* The degree to which information regarding the selection process should be easy for all the candidates	– The information provided through all the selection process should be accurate, timely, and helpful from the very moment after people are evaluated – The use of a computerized application system whereby the candidate can track their progress and view results of the decision-making process is advisable. Make timely feedback a priority and track time to feedback for each selection hurdle – Give candidates as much information as possible – Put the information in context such as the number of applicants. Provide candidates with information regarding future job applications – Give solid and well-evidence-based explanations when required – Interviewers have been trained to be good listeners – Include open-ended questions as part of the standardized test process that allows candidates to ask questions at various points during the selection process – To give the chance to applicants to express concerns (voice) – Accessibility in Web and ads: Recruitment advertising and information in the Web site must be easy to read and to interpret, facilitating disabled people the access – Also use paper communication to avoid digital divide – Be sure to disseminate information through different sources
7. *Treatment*: The degree to which candidates feel they are treated with warmth and respect by the test administrator	– Check if candidates are treated with respect. – Administrators must demonstrate competence in interpersonal relations – Highlight the importance of ensuring that the organization is perceived in a positive light
8. *Privacy*: The extent to which questions are not illegal in terms of intimacy invasion	– Ensure data about the candidates are not shared with those outside the selection process – Most of the information shared while (or learned through) the interviewing process needs to be strictly confidential – Evaluators must not express personal preferences to others during the selection process and not be tempted to learn about

(continued)

Table 7.2 (continued)

Justice principle	Recommendation
	an applicant's protected status or aside irrelevant information while making conversation during "downtime" – Information recording and filing after the evaluation must be properly protected
9. *Ethics*: The importance of honesty and truthfulness when communicating with candidates, and in particular, in instances when either candidness or deception would likely be particularly salient in the selection procedure	– Ensure that the process is transparent – Deliver training to administrators to be honest with candidates and reward administrators for honesty – If providing negative results, focus on the facts and not personal characteristics. Do not make it personal and keep it simple – Ensure all materials (online and elsewhere) are accurate messages regarding your organization
10. *Free of Bias/Stereotyping*: Assurance that decision-making procedures are fair	– Be aware of bias, heuristics, and stereotyping in decision making. When a panel scores candidates, revise high discrepancies between the members – Avoid making a general assumption that individuals with disabilities will always require an accommodation – The constructs being assessed must be meaningful in each of the groups represented – Evidence must be available on possible group differences in performance on the test

7.5 Conclusions

The objective of this chapter was to review recent advances in personnel selection from the point of view of inclusive organizations. Inclusive organizations establish the human resources management policy through social dialogue and, personnel selection is the first step within the Circle of Inclusion (see Arenas et al., Chap. 1 in this volume). Thus, this chapter on inclusive and discrimination-free personnel selection has focused on three fundamental aspects: validity of the instruments, the perspective of candidates, and equality and nondiscrimination in access to employment. With regard to the first and fundamental aspect, meta-analytic studies have made it possible to know the validity of the instruments most used in IPS. In this way, we can conclude that there are currently a large number of valid assessment procedures that will allow us to make correct and fair hiring decisions, and employee representatives should ensure that these procedures are used correctly within organizations.

With regard to the second aspect, the significant changes that have occurred in organizations due to the phenomena of globalization and diversity at work, among others, have given greater relevance to the *constructivist perspective* in IPS, where applicants, as well as organizations, come to decisions about their experiences during selection. That is, applicants have voice to express their perceptions about the selection processes in which they are participating. In this respect, our conclusion is that the perceptions and reactions of the candidates in the selection process influence not only in the hiring decisions, but have an effect on other processes and areas of the organization.

Third, we showed that ensuring equality, fair treatment, and nondiscrimination in personnel procedures are crucial goals in inclusive organizations. We include a series of measures related to justice and nondiscrimination in selection processes. With regard to this, our conclusion is that measures against discrimination at work should be one of the priorities within inclusive organizations, and not only in order to meet legal obligations, but also because justice and nondiscrimination in the workplace should be part of the essence and culture of organizations.

We can summarize these conclusions, recommending four specific goals: (1) using valid and bias-free procedures, based on accurate information, and upholding ethical standards in accordance with workers' expectations; (2) maintaining consistently the procedures; (3) allowing that stakeholders (e.g., workers) can express their views and feelings during the procedures; and (4) ensuring that employees have voice during the processes of organizational entry. Inclusive personnel selection will be reached if organizations finally are able to achieve these four goals.

Finally, it is important to indicate that inclusive and discrimination-free personnel selection procedures are a good investment for organizations. Studies on this topic show that these measures are beneficial for both organizations and applicants, as those procedures considered fair are related to individual satisfaction and attachment to the company. Furthermore, they contribute to job offers being accepted (Anderson 2003); may convey a better organizational image of a potential employer (Bauer et al. 2001; Schmitt and Gilliland 1992); may even have a possible impact upon the attitudes, motivation, and job performance of candidates accepted into an organization (Ryan and Ployhart 2000; McCarthy et al. 2017); the economic utility of these procedures in terms of profit and savings for organizations has been demonstrated (e.g., Salgado 2007). Therefore, organizations should be increasingly aware of the benefits of IPS to their interests.

References

Alonso, P., Moscoso, S., & Salgado, J. F. (2017). Structured behavioral interview as a legal guarantee for ensuring equal employment opportunities for women: A meta-analysis. *The European Journal of Psychology Applied to Legal Context, 9,* 1–14. doi:10.1016/j.ejpal.2016.03.002.

Anderson, N. R. (2001). Towards a theory of socialization impact: Selection and pre-entry socialization. *International Journal of Selection and Assessment, 9,* 84–91. doi:10.1111/1468-2389.00165.

Anderson, N. R. (2003). Applicant and recruiter reactions to new technology in selection: A critical review and agenda for future research. *International Journal of Selection and Assessment, 11,* 121–136. doi:10.1111/1468-2389.00235.

Anderson, N. R. (2004). The dark side of the moon: applicant perspectives, negative psychological effects (NPEs), and candidate decision making in selection. *International Journal of Selection and Assessment, 12,* 1–8. doi:10.1111/j.0965-075X.2004.00259.x.

Anderson, N. R., Lievens, F., van Dam, K., & Ryan, A. M. (2004). Future perspectives on employee selection: Key directions for future research and practice. *Applied Psychology: An International Review, 53,* 487–501. doi:10.1111/j.1464-0597.2004.00183.x.

Anderson, N. R., & Ostroff, C. (1997). Selection as socialization. In N. Anderson & P. Herriott (Eds.), *International handbook of selection and assessment* (pp. 413–440). London, UK: Wiley.

Anderson, N. R., Salgado, J. F., & Hülsheger, U. R. (2010). Applicant reactions in selection: Comprehensive meta-analysis into reaction generalization versus situational specificity. *International Journal of Selection and Assessment, 18,* 291–304. doi:10.1111/j.1468-2389.2010.00512.x.

Bastida, M., & Moscoso, S. (2015). Steel barrier: Legal implications from a gender equal opportunity perspective. *European Journal of Psychology Applied to Legal Context, 7,* 13–22. doi:10.1016/j.ejpal.2014.11.004.

Bauer, T. N., Truxillo, D. M., Sanchez, R. J., Craig, J., Ferrara, P., & Campion, M. A. (2001). Applicant reactions to selection: Development of the selection procedural justice scale (SPJS). *Personnel Psychology, 54,* 387–419. doi:10.1111/j.1744-6570.2001.tb00097.

Bauer, T. N., McCarthy, J., Anderson, N., Truxillo, D. M., & Salgado, J. F. (2012). *What we know about applicant reactions on attitudes and behavior: Research summary and best practices.* Bowling Green, OH: Society for Industrial and Organizational Psychology.

Council Directive. (2000a). 2000/43/EC of 29 June 2000 implementing the principle of equal treatment between persons irrespective of racial or ethnic origin.

Council Directive. (2000b). 2000/78/EC of 27 November 2000 establishing a general framework for equal treatment in employment and occupation.

Crosby, F. J., Iyer, A., & Sincharoen, S. (2006). Understanding affirmative action. *Annual Review of Psychology, 57,* 585–611.

Directive. (2006). 2006/54/EC of the European Parliament and of the Council of 5 July 2006 on the implementation of the principle of equal opportunities and equal treatment of men and women in matters of employment and occupation.

Folger, R. (1977). Distributive and procedural justice: Combined impact of 'voice' and improvement on experienced inequity. *Journal of Personality and Social Psychology, 35,* 108–119. doi:10.1037/0022-3514.35.2.108.

García-Izquierdo, A. L., & García-Izquierdo, M. (2007). Discriminación, igualdad de oportunidades en el empleo y selección de personal en España [Discrimination, equal employment opportunities and personnel selection in Spain]. *Revista de Psicología del Trabajo y de las Organizaciones, 23,* 111–138.

Gilliland, S. W. (1993). The perceived fairness of selection systems: An organizational justice perspective. *Academy of Management Review, 18,* 694–734. doi:10.5465/AMR.1993.9402210155.

Gaugler, B. B., Rosenthal, D. B., Thorton, G. C., & Bentson, C. (1987). Meta-analysis of assessment center validity. *Journal of Applied Psychology, 72,* 493–511. doi:10.1037/0021-9010.72.3.493.

Hausknecht, J. P., Day, D. V., & Thomas, S. C. (2004). Applicant reactions to selection procedures: An updated model and meta-analysis. *Personnel Psychology, 57,* 639–683. doi:10.1111/j.1744-6570.2004.00003.x.

Huffcutt, A. I., Roth, P. L., & McDaniel, M. (1996). A meta-analytic investigation of cognitive ability in employment interview evaluations: Moderating characteristics and implications for incremental validity. *Journal of Applied Psychology, 81,* 459–473. doi:10.1037/0021-9010.81.5.459.

Hunter, J. E., & Hunter, R. F. (1984). Validity and utility of alternative predictors of job performance. *Psychological Bulletin, 96,* 72–98. doi:10.1037/0033-2909.96.1.72.

Judge, T. A., Rodell, J. B., Klinger, E. R., Simon, L. S., & Crawford, E. R. (2013). Hierarchical representations of the five-factor model of personality in predicting job performance: Integrating three organizing frameworks with two theoretical perspectives. *Journal of Applied Psychology, 98,* 875–925. doi:10.1037/a0033901.

Kehoe, J., Mol, S., & Anderson, N. R. (2017). Managing sustainable selection programs. In J. L. Farr & N. T. Tippins (Eds.), *Handbook of personnel selection* (2nd ed.). New York: Routledge.

McCarthy, J. M., Bauer T. N., Truxillo, D. M., Anderson N. R., Costa A. C., & Ahmed, S. (2017). Applicant perspectives during selection: A review addressing "So What?", "What's New?" and "Where to Next?". *Journal of Management, 43,*1693–1725. doi:10.1177/0149206316681846.

McDaniel, M. A., Hartman, N. S., Whetzel, D. L., & Grubb, W. (2007). Situational judgment tests, response instructions, and validity: A meta-analysis. *Personnel Psychology, 60,* 201–210. doi:10.1111/j.1744-6570.2007.00065.

Moscoso, S., García-Izquierdo, A. L., & Bastida, M. (2012). A mediation model of individual differences in attitudes toward affirmative actions for women. *Psychological Reports, 110*(3), 764–780. doi:10.2466/01.07.17.PR0.110.3.764-780.

Moscoso, S., Salgado, J., & Anderson, N. R. (2017). How do I get a job, what are they looking for? Personnel Selection and Assessment. In N. Chmiel, F. Fraccaroli, & S. Magnus (Eds.), *An introduction to work and organizational psychology: An international perspective* (3rd ed.). Chichester, UK: Wiley.

Nauta, A. (2015). Industrial Relations and works councils in the Netherlands. Results from interviews and a survey among HR managers. In M. Euwema, L. Munduate, P. Elgoibar, E. Pender, & A.B. García. (Eds.), *Promoting social dialogue in European Organizations.* London: Springer Open.

Ployhart, R. E., & Harold, C. M. (2004). The applicant attribution-reaction theory (AART): An integrative theory of applicant attributional processing. *International Journal of Selection and Assessment, 12,* 84–98. doi:10.1111/j.0965-075X.2004.00266.x.

Roth, P. L., Bobko, P., & McFarland, L. A. (2005). A meta-analysis of work sample test validity: Updating and integrating some classical literature. *Personnel Psychology, 58,* 1009–1037. doi:10.1111/j.1744-6570.2005.00714.x.

Ryan, A. M., & Ployhart, R. E. (2000). Applicants' perceptions of selection procedures and decisions: A critical review and agenda for the future. *Journal of Management, 26,* 565–606. doi:10.1177/014920630002600308.

Salgado, J. F. (2007). Análisis de la utilidad económica de la entrevista conductual estructurada en la selección de personal de la Administración General del Pais Vasco. *Revista de Psicología del Trabajo y las Organizaciones, 23,* 139–154.

Salgado, J. F. (2017). *Personnel selection. Encyclopedia of psychology.* Oxford, UK: Oxford University Press.

Salgado, J. F., & Anderson, N. (2002). Cognitive and GMA testing in the European Community: Issues and evidence. *Human Performance, 15,* 75–96. doi:10.1080/08959285.2002.9668084.

Salgado, J. F., & Anderson, N. (2003). Validity generalization of GMA tests across countries in the European Community. *European Journal of Work and Organizational Psychology, 12,* 1–17. doi:10.1080/13594320244000292.

Salgado, J. F., Anderson, N., Moscoso, S., Bertua, C., De Fruyt, F., & Rolland, J. P. (2003). A meta-analytic study of general mental ability validity for different occupations in the European Community. *Journal of Applied Psychology, 88,* 1068–1081. doi:10.1037/0021-9010.88.6.1068.

Salgado, J. F., Anderson, N., & Tauriz, G. (2015). The validity of ipsative and quasi-ipsative forced-choice personality inventories for different occupational groups: A comprehensive meta-analysis. *Journal of Occupational and Organizational Psychology, 88,* 797–834. doi:10.1111/joop.12098.

Salgado, J. F., & Moscoso, S. (1996). Meta-analysis of interrater reliability of job performance ratings in validity studies of personnel selection. *Perceptual and Motor Skills, 83,* 1195–1201. doi:10.2466/pms.1996.83.3f.1195.

Salgado, J. F., & Moscoso, S. (2002). Comprehensive meta-analysis of the construct validity of the employment interview. *European Journal of Work and Organizational Psychology, 11,* 299–324. doi:10.1080/13594320244000184.

Salgado, J. F., Moscoso, S., & Anderson, N. (2016). Corrections for criterion reliability in validity generalization: The consistency of Hermes, the utility of Midas. *Revista de Psicología del Trabajo y de las Organizaciones, 32,* 17–23. doi:10.1016/j.rpto.2015.12.001.

Salgado, J. F., Viswesvaran, C., & Ones, D. S. (2001). Predictors used for personnel selection: An overview of constructs, method and techniques. In N. Anderson, D. S. Ones, H. K. Sinangil, & C. Viswesvaran (Eds.), *Handbook of industrial, work, & organizational psychology, Vol. 1. Personnel psychology* (pp. 165–199). London, UK: Sage.

Schmitt, N., & Gilliland, S. W. (1992). Beyond differential prediction: Fairness in selection. In D.M. Saunders (Ed.),*New approaches to employee management: Fairness in employee selection* (Vol. 1, pp. 21–46). Greenwich, CT: JAI Press.

Schmidt, F. L., & Hunter, J. E. (1998). The validity and utility of selection methods in personnel psychology: Practical and theoretical implications of 85 years of research findings. *Psychological Bulletin, 124,* 262–274. doi:10.1037/0033-2909.124.2.262.

Schuler, H. (1993). Social validity of selection situations: A concept and some empirical results. In H. Schuler, J. L. Farr, & N. Schmitt (Eds.), *Personnel selection and assessment: Individual and organizational perspectives* (pp. 11–26). Mahaw, NJ: Erlbaum.

Truxillo, D. M., Bodner, T. E., Bertolino, M. B., Bauer, T. N., & Yonce, C. A. (2009). Effects of explanations on applicant reactions: A meta-analytic review. *International Journal of Selection and Assessment, 17,* 346–359.

Truxillo, D., Bauer, T., McCarthy, J., Anderson, N. R., & Ahmed, S. (2016). Applicant perspectives on employee selection systems. In D. S. Ones, N. R. Anderson, C. Viswesvaran, & H. K. Sinangil (Eds.), *Handbook of industrial, work and organizational psychology* (2nd ed.). London, UK: Sage.

Van Knippenberg, D., & Schippers, M. C. (2007). Work group diversity. *Annual Review of Psychology, 58,* 515–541. doi:10.1146/annurev.psych.58.110405.085546.

Chapter 8
Designing Work for Inclusiveness

Fred Zijlstra, Gemma van Ruitenbeek, Henny Mulders and Brigitte van Lierop

8.1 Introduction

In our modern society it is expected that everybody participates, this is one of the central policy goals of the European Commission. Participation is generally operationalized by having a paid job. And most people want a decent job. However, for an increasing group of people this seems to be unachievable. One of the reasons is that work has changed enormously: It has become quite complex and demanding over the past decades. As a consequence the threshold to entering the labor market has increased, causing a large (and growing) group of people to be at a 'distance to the labor market'. These people are qualified as having a distance to the labor market because they lack the adequate skills and competences that are needed to function in a 'regular' job, and often they also lack the capacity to master these skills and competences.

Capacity, in particular intellectual capacity, is increasingly important to survive in our ever more complex society. Diversity on the labor market generally focuses on differences in gender, ethnicity, but much less on differences in capacity. We argue that the diversity discourse should be extended to include 'diversity in capacity' as well, as this has to be an important element of the social dialogue in our society in the coming years.

In this chapter we will present a method (based on Redesigning Work) that will allow organizations to create jobs for people with limited capacities and thus become an 'Inclusive Organization'. First we will describe some background

F. Zijlstra (✉) · G. van Ruitenbeek
Maastricht University, Maastricht, The Netherlands
e-mail: fred.zijlstra@maastrichtuniversity.nl

H. Mulders · B. van Lierop
Centre of Expertise for Inclusive Organizations, Maastricht, The Netherlands

A. Arenas et al. (eds.), *Shaping Inclusive Workplaces Through Social Dialogue*,
Industrial Relations & Conflict Management,
DOI 10.1007/978-3-319-66393-7_8

information as to why work has become so complex, and subsequently we will present the underlying principles of our method.

8.2 Developments in the Labor Market

The domain of work and organizations has changed considerably over the past decades. Jobs that existed 50 years ago are now extinct, and have been replaced by new type of jobs (like Information and Communication Technology (ICT) related jobs). As a consequence many employees of previous generations would now be *unqualified* for most jobs, and often also practically *unfit* to work. The type and level of qualifications have changed, but also the required functional and health capacities of employees have changed. These changes have particularly impacted the lower educated people, and this change is expected to be on-going (Josten 2010).

Over the years we have seen our economies change from a manufacturing and production type of economy into a 'service economy'. Through ongoing development of technology machines could take over most parts of production work: this has been labelled 'automatization' and 'robotization' (cf. Zijlstra and Nyssen 2017). Other manufacturing work has been outsourced to low wage countries. The consequence was that this production work, which often was lower qualified work, was no longer available for employees. At the same time new type of jobs have emerged, like application programmers, website designers, database managers, whereas existing jobs also have developed and changed. Introduction of technology has generally led to upgrading jobs to a higher level of required qualifications, whereas the lower qualified employees saw their jobs being downgraded or disappearing (Aronsson 1989). For instance, when word processors and personal computers were introduced in offices, typing pools were dismantled and the job of secretary changed considerably. The typists were made redundant, because everyone started to write their memo's, manuscripts and letters on computers and secretaries were upgraded to 'office managers', or 'assistant to the manager'. Evidently similar developments took place in many other sectors, and are taking place again at this point in time. At this moment we see again that jobs are disappearing and people are made redundant because their jobs are being taken over by technology, now primary in the financial and administrative sector. This is sometimes referred to as 'Industry 4.0' (cf. Kagermann et al. 2011).

One of the results of the developments at that time is that the majority of employment is now in the service industry, up to 75% of all employment in western economies. This means that 'services' are provided to other companies and people (clients, customers, patients, students, etc.), which means that employees are in contact with these groups. Concepts like 'client centered', or 'customer satisfaction' have become important and are relevant to assess the performance and skills of employees. This illustrates that work in the service sector is different than the manufacturing industry (often a factory). In the service industry 'social skills' are very important; in particular when dealing with a customer, client or patient. In fact, this is part of the behavior that employee's display when dealing with customers, and thus *behavior* at the workplace is part of their work *performance*.

Technology itself is also a factor that has changed the demands of the job and the skills that are required. There are hardly any jobs left in which people do not have to work with computers. And working with computers places high demands on people's cognitive capabilities: one has to understand what the computer does, or can do, how it should be operated. In order to fully understand the functionality of a system requires a level of abstract thinking. Furthermore, an operator needs to have a mental model of the functionalities of the system, and adequate information processing capacity. For these reasons it is acknowledged that the introduction of ICT has led to an increase of complexity of work (Parent-Thirion et al. 2012; Zijlstra and Nyssen 2017). ICT has also made factors like 'time' and 'place' less relevant in relation to work: people can work anywhere and at any time whilst using mobile technology to be connected to the workplace. Employees can work from home, during the day or evening, or when travelling. As a consequence the traditional boundaries between the work domain and the private domain have faded. Although this has contributed to greater flexibility, it also implies higher demands because there is increased 'availability' for work, and less opportunity for rest (Zijlstra and Sonnentag 2006).

Organizations have changed as well, in order to be more flexible many organizations have become flatter and 'lean'. In order to be leaner they adopted the 'self-steering teams' concept, in which members of a team are responsible for planning and organizing their own work (cf. Dankbaar 1997). This is generally a consequence of the Sociotechnical Systems Approach (Emery 1959) that was introduced in the 60s and became popular in the 90s. The consequences for employees are huge: employees need (again) good social skills in order to maintain their position in the group, and to negotiate or discuss their planning and actions with colleagues. In addition one needs planning skills, and adequate psychological awareness of one's capacities, strengths and weaknesses to function in a group. And these skills are on top of the traditional skills that belong to the craftsmanship of the job.

And because efficiency and production are high on the agenda of most managers, they have adopted techniques and methods that are aimed at facilitating these aspects. 'Goal setting' is often translated into 'setting targets for individuals', which implies that individuals are held accountable for reaching predefined targets. But since employees generally do not control most of the environmental conditions and factors that are important for achieving those targets, this becomes another source of stress.

All together the above makes clear that the demands of work have changed and generally also have increased over the past decades. This corresponds with findings of the *European Foundation for the Improvement of Living and Working Conditions* (Eurofound) in Dublin. They monitor the development of trends in the European Union, and their surveys of 2011 and 2015 signalize a steady trend of increasing complaints of work pressure and intensity of work (Parent-Thirion et al.

2012, 2016). The prevalence of psychological complaints regarding mental health has also increased over the past years (OECD 2014). In fact, mental health complaints have become the main cause for disability for work in the Netherlands, according the Dutch Centre for Professional Diseases in their annual report of 2013.

The economic and cultural necessity to have a job has increased in our society. The European Commission has formulated as one of their main aims to strive for an inclusive society. Due to the developments described above this has increasingly become problematic for a growing group of people. The demands of work have increased to an extent that they are difficult to fulfil for a group of people that is increasing. When the threshold of entering the labor market is made higher, the consequence is that a large group will not be able to overcome this threshold without support (see Hoel et al., Chap. 3 in this volume).

8.3 The Need for Inclusive Organizations

Organizations need to be competitive and thus are always looking for the 'most suitable' employees. This term 'most suitable' generally translates into: people that are 'flexible', 'well-educated', 'stress resistant', and are 'excellent team players'. And besides this, in order to meet the current demands regarding workload and work intensity, people have to be healthy and fit. Whereas we have outlined above, not everybody in our society can meet those criteria. Since the threshold of entering the labor market is getting higher, the consequence is that the group below the threshold is increasing. Although the general level of education in society has increased, there is also a large (and increasing) group of people that doesn't have the right education, either because they didn't finish school, or 'dropped out' early. Another group consists of people that have been unemployed for a long time, which also, according to Human Capital Theory, deteriorates the relevant skills to be employed (Arulampalam et al. 2001). In addition Europe has currently to deal with a large group of refugees and asylum seekers that need to be integrated in our society and that need to find a job. They also lack the right skills and knowledge to function adequately in the Western European labor market. However, for some of these groups education and training can help, but for a large part this is not a solution, since they lack the capacity to be educated (in our current system).

In addition, as the average age of the current working population is increasing, and since people are stimulated to work longer, we will find that increasingly employees will have health issues, both physical and mental. Increasingly we will be confronted with employees with a chronic disease, just simply because elderly people have more health issues than younger people. This, of course, does not imply that all elderly workers have health issues; also many younger people have chronic diseases. Notwithstanding those health issues, these people still have a capacity to work, and most of them would like to work and be independent rather than living from social benefits. In many cases the health complaints do not affect the capacity to work; this is also dependent on the type of complaints, and the type of work (Zijlstra and Nijhuis 2014).

Nevertheless, it is also clear that when work demands are increasing, and thus making it increasingly more difficult to participate in the labor market for particular groups of people because work is exceeding their capacity to work, this calls for new solutions. In order to create an ‘inclusive society’, that allows people with a large variety of capabilities to participate via paid work; we have the obligation to find solutions that also allow people with limitations to work. Moreover, also from a perspective of sustainability of employment we need to address this tendency of ever increasing demands.

In this respect it is worthwhile to examine the recently introduced concept of ‘inclusive organizations’ (Zijlstra et al. 2012). Inclusive organizations aim to enhance diversity in organizations, in particular diversity in terms of employees’ capacity. This means that there is a need to have work for people with limited capacities, and in particular when the limitations concern cognitive, or social, or emotional capacities this can be challenging since we have indicated earlier that work demands are currently primarily of a cognitive, social, and/or emotional nature. In fact this means that work for this group of people has to be created, or rather designed (Zijlstra 2009). Hereto a method was developed that aims to create jobs for people with a distance to the labor market, and which makes use of principles of Job Re-Design (cf. Zijlstra et al. 2009; Van Ruitenbeek et al. 2013). The underlying principle is ‘task differentiation’, i.e. designing tasks of different levels of complexity for people with various levels of capacities, or in other words: by creating or designing ‘simple jobs’ again.

Jobs generally consist of several tasks, and those tasks are in fact agreements between people about how to divide the work in an organization (cf. Roe and Zijlstra 1991). Although those agreements have been formalized in job descriptions, they are not cut in stone. In fact tasks and jobs have evolved over the course of years, mainly in relation to the introduction of new technology. In fact the approach of Business Process Redesign, which was quite popular in the 90s, is an illustration of the fact that those agreements concerning ‘who does what’ in an organization are changeable (cf. Earl 1994). Job design and job redesign are core elements of the discipline of Work & Organizational Psychology, and always have focused on establishing a fit between person and task, but with a focus on enhancing well-being and performance. However, an alternative would be to design tasks that take the capability of employees into account, and particular when it is evident that employees have limitations. This is a different way of creating a fit between the human and the work. In fact, to do so one needs to analyze the work processes in an organization or department and need to find a division of tasks that allows to create tasks that are in fact ‘simple’, or at least in accordance with a number of criteria. Business Process Redesign is based on a similar approach: analyzing the work processes and trying to find a different arrangement for the processes. In principle this means that a variety of tasks can be created taking into account various criteria that can be derived from theoretical considerations (cf. Hacker 1978; Hackman and Oldham 1980; Roe and Zijlstra 1991). Thus tasks can be created that consist primarily of routine activities that require only cognitive regulation at the lowest level, or tasks that require to a large extent intellectual regulation (or problem solving activities) and are thus more complex tasks. Combining a number of routine activities or tasks can form a 'simple' job, and a compilation of activities (tasks) that require problem solving (or intellectual regulation) generally forms a 'complex' job. Normally one would design jobs that contain a mixture of the three regulation levels ('intellectual regulation', 'rule-based regulation', or 'skill based regulation'—see Hacker 1978; Rasmussen 1983; Roe and Zijlstra 1991). However, the more 'intellectual regulation' (or problem solving behavior) is required the more complex skills are required, and thus the more 'complex' the job is. At the same time 'skill-based regulation' consists primarily of routine activities, and thus generally constitutes a fairly 'simple' task.

Furthermore not only the types of the tasks need to be considered, but also the conditions under which these tasks need to be executed. As highlighted above, work pressure and work intensity are serious complaints in organizations, and this can, to some extent, be attributed to the management style in the organization. It is evident that when work pressure is a serious problem for regular and healthy employees, it is even more a problem for the vulnerable employees. Therefore work pressure is another design criterion that needs to be taken into account. Generally this can (and should) be dealt with on the managerial level, with planning and organization. Similarly, the social conditions need to be taken into account. Colleagues and management need to be aware of the constraints (and opportunities) that are related to the presence of more vulnerable employees.

8.4 The Approach: Redesigning Work to Create New Jobs

Various attempts have been developed to help people with 'a distance to the labor market' to find a job. An approach developed in the USA and Canada is 'job carving' (Griffin and Hammis 2003), where elements (tasks) are 'carved out' of existing jobs in order to let these be executed by people with a disability (for instance, making photocopies). This approach appears to have limited effectiveness since it (a) is based on a bilateral exchange relationship between two people, which means that as soon one of the two leaves the exchange relationship will be terminated, and (b) job carving focuses on a particular person with particular limitations, and neglects organizational circumstances and the work processes in the organization. This makes it an individually based intervention rather than a structural approach to create jobs on a larger scale.

The approach we propagate starts with describing and charting the work processes in an organization or department. A good understanding of the work processes, and how the work is currently divided, helps to find alternative ways of organizing those processes, and thus dividing the work. This allows creating tasks of various levels of complexity. And when at the same time 'human centered' criteria are taken into account this helps to ensure that the resulting tasks are of acceptable quality, which is important to make the newly created positions sustainable. Evidently, when these new jobs are created for people with a distance to the labor market, this will also have consequences for the other employees in the organization/department. Their tasks will also be affected and probably the climate in the group will change. Therefore these aspects need to be looked at as well, and one should also think about how such a project should be introduced in the organization.

Therefore the main ingredients of the *Inclusive Redesign of Work* method are: (1) starting with a comprehensive analysis of the work processes, and then (2) making an inventory of the various redesign options (taking into account various work psychological criteria; see Roe and Zijlstra 1991), (3) including an assessment of work capability of potential candidates, and (4) organizing social support from colleagues. These main ingredients are represented by 9 steps, which are graphically depicted in Fig. 8.1.

The steps will be elaborated below:

Evidently the process starts with *commitment of the organization*, and in particular of the management of the organization. At this stage the process of *Social Dialogue* should be started in the organization. Management and the Works Council need to be open to the idea of scrutinizing the organization for potential workplaces of people from the target group. And of course, this support needs to be communicated throughout the organization, to make sure that the next step can take place. *Analysis of work processes* is the actual starting point of the redesign phase. The analysis should focus primarily on entire work processes with a department or organization, rather than on activities within individual jobs. These individual jobs

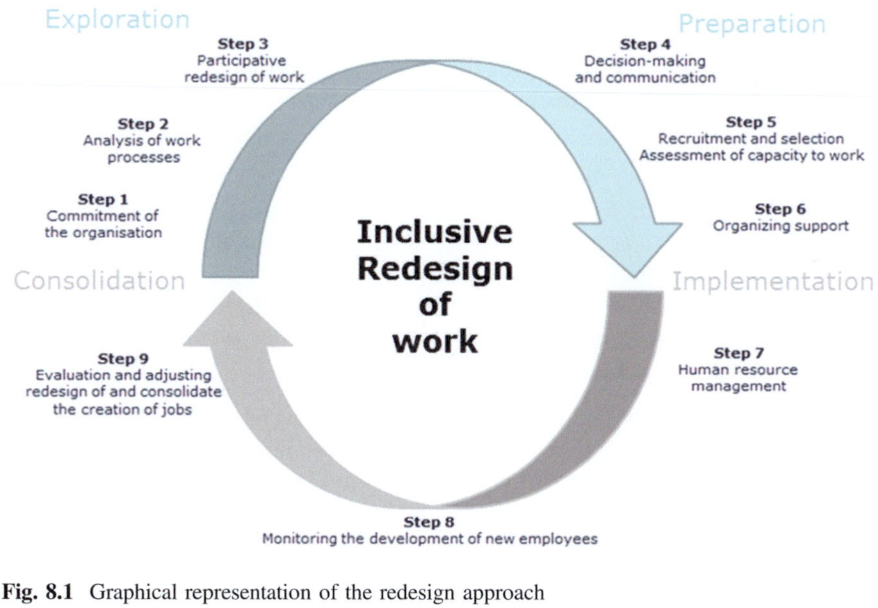

Fig. 8.1 Graphical representation of the redesign approach

are the consequence of dividing the work within the organization. And with the analysis these work processes should be described and chartered in order to find options for new or alternative ways, of dividing the work. Redesigning tasks is a joint process in which analysts present options for redesign and employees indicate the feasibility of those options (and thus making it *participative redesign of work*) as part of the dialogue process. In line with the literature on job analysis (cf. Algera and Greuter 1998; Morgeson and Humphrey 2006; Wilson et al. 2012) five main themes can be distinguished that need to be addressed within the analysis: (1) the goals of the organization and the tasks within the organization; (2) the structure of the organization and the work processes; (3) the type of task, or rather the task content, (4) demands of the tasks, and (5) the context of the task (social and physical). What is particularly relevant here is that one should look at the design of the 'prospective task' (cf. Roe and Zijlstra 1991), so, how will the new task look like? What kind of characteristics will this new task have?

(1) *Goals of the organization*: the tasks and jobs reflect the goals of the organization and together form the production processes. In fact tasks are the formalized agreements concerning the division of work within the organization: who does what (cf. Roe and Zijlstra 1991). And evidently agreements between people can be changed. This means that tasks and jobs are changeable. Therefore they need to be the starting point for the analysis, and need to be described in their interdependencies.
(2) *Structure of the organization and the work processes*: the structure of the organization reflects the interdependencies of the tasks, and jobs: who works with whom. Generally an organogram illustrates the structure of the organization. This can either be the formal structure or the functional structure of the organization (ideally they are identical). Analysis of the functional structure provides insight in how the work is actually divided, in particular the activities that are related to the routing of the product (or service) through the organization (Jones 2007). In principle three different types of work processes can be distinguished:

    - *primary* (or main) processes: these are focused on achieving the main goals of the organization, the primary production process;
    - *secondary* (or support) processes: they ensure that the main production processes can proceed undisturbedly;
    - *tertiary* (or additional) processes: are not directly related to the main goal of the organization, but are generally present in an organization, such as 'cleaning', or 'catering'.

'Process mapping' can be used to describe the various processes (Biazzo 2002). This technique provides a good visualized map of the interdependencies of tasks, jobs and technology, and is therefore a good starting point for redesign.

Description of the work processes provides information that goes beyond the job descriptions, and might reveal activities that indeed take place, but are not formally described. These activities can be essential when considering options for re-designing the processes.

(3) After the work processes have been defined and described, the translation needs to be made to what activities are involved in the work processes. It needs to be very clear what the content of these activities are, and what kind of demands they constitute for the worker. This is also important when considering redesign options. Therefore a few questions need to be answered: The first question is what *Type of task* (work content) is this? This should provide a detailed description of the specific activities that belong to a task or job. In fact it should describe what, how, when and where the task is executed as it currently is, by whom it is executed, how frequently the activities need to be executed and how long the execution takes. This will lead to answering the next question: what are the demands of the task?
(4) *Demands of the task*: in particular to what extent cognitive, emotional, physical and psychomotor capacities are required to execute a task or activity. In addition to specific expertise and knowledge of a task it is important to know to what extent coordination activities are involved as these require communication and social skills, and a level of autonomy, independence and conscientiousness.
(5) *The context of the task*: does not immediately refer to the task itself, but refers to the conditions under which the tasks have to be executed. The physical conditions (outdoor or inside) are important, but the social conditions (colleagues, the supervisor, and the social climate) are often much more important. The support and awareness of supervisor and colleagues are crucial for the success of integrating people with limitations in the work place (Lammerts and Stavenuiter 2010; Nelissen et al. 2016). This includes issues like supervisory style, the way feedback is provided (if at all), and how work pressure and deadlines are handled, and so on (see Van Ruitenbeek et al. 2013).

The *Inclusive Redesign of Work* approach contains 9 steps as depicted in Fig. 8.1. The first 3 steps have been described in detail above; the remaining steps will be briefly mentioned in the following part. The *Inclusive Redesign of Work* approach is based on an extensive hierarchical analysis of work; this implies that all aspects of the organization are included in the analysis. The results of these analyses form the basis for finding options to rearrange the activities and thus redesigning the tasks. Important is that the various activities are assessed with respect to whether they require intellectual regulation, or only motoric regulation, or in other words, whether they require 'problem solving' behavior, or that they consist of routine activities, and of course what other kind of skills are required. Redesigning means finding alternative arrangements and ways to group the various activities in such a way that meaningful tasks can be created that are of various levels of complexity. A set of tasks together will form a new 'job', and the complexity of the most difficult task will determine the level of complexity of the new job. Evidently functional (ergonomic) and human (well-being) criteria need to be taken into account to ensure that the newly designed tasks are of acceptable quality (cf. Hacker 1978; Hackman and Oldham 1980; Roe and Zijlstra 1991). But it is important to keep in mind that criteria are dissimilar for various groups. Where limitations are limiting the capacities, the requirements of the task should also be limited. This often implies that routine (or motoric regulated) or skill based activities should be overrepresented as these activities are generally well-structured and contain few or no elements that require coordination or adjustment/synchronization activities. The latter activities generally require communication and problem solving behavior. When the options are clear a *decision should be made* by the organization *and communicated* throughout the organization to the stakeholders (including workers council).

Recruitment and selection; Assessment of capacity to work. Organizations are focusing on selecting people that are best qualified for a particular job. However, for the group with a distance to the labor market selection is not feasible, because they cannot compete on the labor market for regular jobs. Many of them have never worked before, or have never finished a school. For this group the challenge is trying to assess what their capacities actually are. This particular angle has been underdeveloped in W&O psychology. Assessment instruments that are available have been developed from a medical (and income insurance) perspective and focus primarily on assessing the limitations and degree of *in*capacity (Nijhuis 2011). While in fact it is, from the current perspective, more important to focus on what people actually *can* do, rather than what they can*not* do.

Capacity to work should be defined as: "the set of personal qualifications that allow a person to meet the demands of a (set of) task(s) in a sustainable way" (see Groothoff et al. 2008). Work & Organizational psychology does not have many instruments that take this perspective. And, as indicated above, general mental capacity (intelligence and knowledge) is the most important predictor for performance and development of personnel (Schmidt and Hunter 1998), this is also one of the important limitations of people with a distant to the labor market. Furthermore, as indicated above, in a service oriented economy concepts like emotional stability, conscientiousness, and agreeability (friendliness) are important. And for people with low levels of self-efficacy, and who have little or no work experience, these aspects are difficult to assess. In particular, because having been out of work or unemployed has a negative effect on work-related skills (Van Kalken et al. 2012). It is an important task to fill this void of instruments that allow assessing capacity and *potential to develop the capacity* to work.

Organizing support. The lack of work experience of this group means that these people also lack basic employees' skills, like 'adhere to working procedures', 'accepting and dealing with authority', and 'having a cooperative attitude'. Various studies have demonstrated some level of support from a colleague is most effective to facilitate integration and socialization in the workplace. This applies to regular employees, and is certainly applicable for this group of employees. However, for this particular group it is recommended that colleagues are informed about their new colleague, and often they should receive some kind of instruction. Colleagues need to know what to expect, and how work performance of their new colleague may be affected, and how they can be of assistance (if needed). There is empirical evidence indicating that when a few employees pick up this attitude of 'helping behavior' this has a positive effect on the other employees in the group and department and might result in, what is called, an 'inclusive climate' (Nelissen et al. 2016).

Contextual aspects. As the aim of the *Inclusive Work Design approach*, as described in this chapter, is to create structural workplaces in organizations for people with a distance to the labor market it should be acknowledged that this implies a structural embedding within organizations. This means that this is an organizational change (or development) process, and should be treated as such. Like every organizational change process it starts with acknowledging that there is a need for change (or adaptation) by management (Daft and Noe 2001). And they should be committed to the goals of the change process (i.e. including people with a distance to the labor market). Subsequently they need to inform and involve the employees of the organization of the goals and potential implications for their own work. As the *Inclusive Work Design approach* should results in a redistribution of activities and tasks within an organization, or rather 'task differentiation', the method will also affect the set of tasks (i.e. job) of other employees. This needs to be discussed and agreed with the employees in the organization. Ignoring this aspect can lead to resistance and can contribute to failure of the project (cf. Lammerts and Stavenuiter 2010). In that sense the *Inclusive Work Design approach* should be seen as a 'participative approach' in which the participation of employees is actively sought by discussing (and deciding about) the various redesign options with them. The *Inclusive Work Design approach* should be considered as a 'cyclic process' (see Roe and Zijlstra 1991) in which presenting redesign options, and evaluating and adjusting these options are not activities that take place only at the start and end of the cycle, but should be part of a continuous process. And in fact should be implemented as part of Human Resources Management procedures (Steps 7, 8 and 9 of Fig. 8.1).

8.5 Inclusive Work Design in Practice

At the time of writing this chapter numerous organizations, both profit and non-for-profit organizations have embarked on an organizational change process involving the *Inclusive Work Design approach*. Evidently Management and Works Council have discussed this issue and have concluded that this project could start, which concerns the analysis. Generally a next 'decision making moment' is scheduled when the decision *to implement* has to be made. Works councils are generally concerned with the consequences for employment opportunities for current staff, but when they can be convinced that none of the current staff will be made redundant and/or replaced by someone from the target group, the Works Council approves. And this has resulted in the creation of a considerable number of jobs for people from the 'target group'. Examples are: in a hospital a combination was made from cleaning and food assistant into'assistant to the nurse' (helping with feeding patients, and cleaning during the day); or 'logistic assistants' (helping in transporting hospital beds; and changing beds); in a penitentiary institution a job was created in the safety department for checking the serial numbers of keys and inspecting the fire extinguishers. Other examples concern a company that delivers services and goods in the field of industrial automation (panel construction). See box:

Example Box:

Company X delivers goods and services in the field of industrial automation: panel construction. From the perspective of 'Corporate Social Responsibility' (CSR) the company would like to have an inventory made whether jobs could be created in the construction department for 'people with a distance to the labour market'.

The construction department builds fuse boxes for electricity supply. The mechanics need to build such a fuse box according specifications provided by a technical drawing. The company experiences difficulties in hiring qualified technicians.

In order to determine whether there are opportunities to create jobs for the target population the (flow of) work processes were analysed and described. Hereto managers and technicians were interviewed in addition to observations in the organisation. The goal of the analysis is to answer a number of questions:

(1) What is/are the flow of the work processes?
(2) What activities are required in the various work processes?
(3) What are the demands of the various activities (i.e. what level of education or training, skills: decision making, coordination, socials skills are required)?
(4) Are there activities that are 'simple' (indicating that the activity requires no special training and can be performed by a person from the target group, now or in the future, and does not require decision making skills, coordination skills, or extensive communication skills, and so on)?
(5) Could it have added value when the technicians don't have to do these activities themselves? (i.e. help them focus on their core activities, help them work more effectively or reduce overtime?)

Results:

Together with the technicians a number of activities in their work package were identified that can also be carried out by someone with a lower level of education, and at lower speed. They also indicated that they would like to have some 'extra hands' when building the panels that need to be placed in the housing of the fuse box. According to observations many activities involve repetitive movements.

Subsequently a flowchart was made comprising the main actions of the technicians while building the fuse box, consisting of 28 steps. The first schema describes the process and the routing of the fuse box (Fig. 8.2).

Based on the analysis and interviews a proposal was made to redesign the work process. The old situation was based on building a fuse box at one station, while the technician walked to the various stations. The new situation (second schema) is more 'zone-oriented' in which fuse boxes are built in different stages. The work

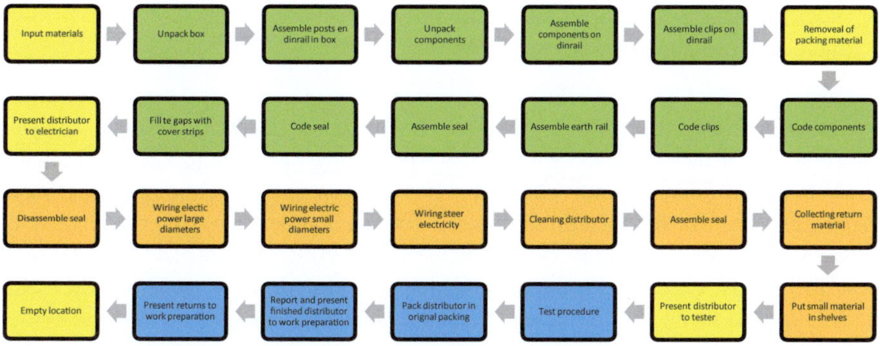

Fig. 8.2 *Yellow* Logistics operations; *Green* Assembly operations; *Orange* Wiring the fuse box; *Blue* Testing, and preparing the fuse box for shipping

process has improved because walking distances for the technicians are reduced, and they now have a few 'extra hands' which has increased the effectiveness of the technicians. In the old situation technicians could build, on average, one fuse box per day. In the new situation it is estimated that they build approx. three fuse boxes per day. The new situation is presented below (Fig. 8.3).

Moreover, the company is growing and is not only relying on recruiting technicians anymore. A number of jobs have been created for people with a disability.

This was a clear 'win-win situation' both for Company X and for the people with disabilities:

- The company was seen as Corporate Social Responsible with the inclusion of 5 positions (full-time) for people with limited capacities
- Less recruitment problems

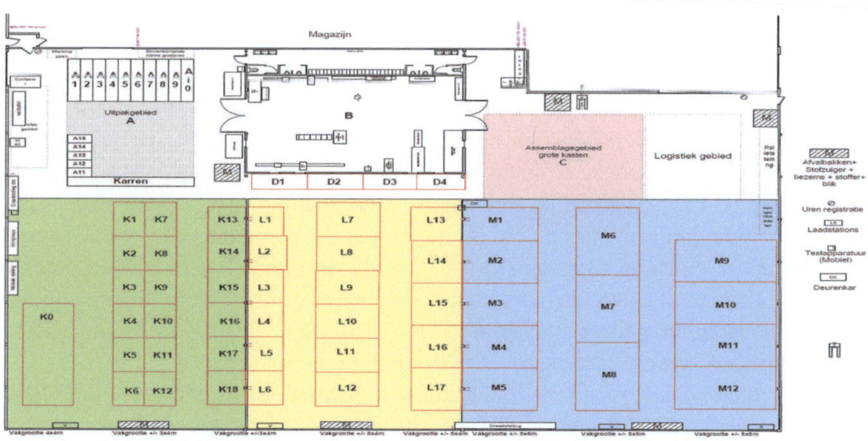

Fig. 8.3 It is important to notice that the *colours* (representing various operations) are now neatly organized; this implies saving of time for the technicians (less walking)

- Reduced salary costs per unit of output
- Increased productivity (approx. 200%).

These cases have been evaluated, which has resulted in several 'lessons learned' concerning this approach. An important lesson to be learned from the analysis phase is that a thorough analysis of the *work processes* is required, while many analysts tend to focus on individual jobs. For this approach it is important that work *processes*, i.e. the organization of work (which includes the interdependencies between employees, required communication and collaboration) are analyzed and described. It is important to understand that 'job descriptions' generally lack this information, because the job descriptions are generally focusing on those activities that are relevant for determining the salary level. As a consequence the activities that have a less 'high profile' are generally not mentioned, while these are very important from the perspective of 'inclusive redesign'. A rearrangement of tasks generally focuses on these kinds of activities. Furthermore, work processes also reveal activities related to the routing of products or services that cut across the functional structure of an organization. Another lesson to be learned is that the so-called 'contextual factors' should be included in the analysis as well, these are indications of the organization's climate, style of leadership, communication style among team members, and so on. These factors are important factors as they determine to what extent the climate in the organization is 'inclusive' (as opposed to 'competitive') and these factors determine whether the process will be successful, or not. As a consequence attention should be given to the consequences for the current staff, as they will be affected when tasks are rearranged. For that reason we recommend that redesign options are discussed within the organization and that this should be an important aspect of the social dialogue within the organizations.

8.6 Conclusion

The result of the various changes in the domain of work and organization is that work has become quite complex and meeting the work demands has become very challenging. For an increasing group of people these demands have become too challenging. A consequence is that a large group of people cannot find a job in the current labor market. While at the same time many organizations are facing shortages on the labor market due to demographic developments. In several sectors (like education, care and technology) it is already becoming a problem. In order to address labor market challenges organizations may have to resort to unconventional approaches: becoming more 'inclusive'. This is also a societal goal, as our society cannot afford to leave a large part of the population side-lined in society.

Trying to create jobs that take into account the variety of capabilities in the labor market is a new approach and might be fruitful to help overcome these issues. The Dutch Parliament has accepted the *Participation Act* that should facilitate the inclusion of people with limitations, and indicated that if organizations are not cooperating on a voluntary basis, then a Quota will be issued. So far, many organizations are responding to the challenge, and the *Inclusive Work Design approach* appears to be a very fruitful approach to facilitate the sustainable uptake of people with limitations in regular organizations. One of the important aspects is that it helps to create structural jobs in organizations, and it also draws the attention to other relevant organizational factors that influences the acceptance of people with limitations in organizations.

At the same time many of the factors that determine the inclusiveness of the organizational climate seem to relate to sustainability of employment of other employees as well (cf. Fleuren et al. 2016; van der Klink et al. 2016).

In this chapter we have argued that inclusion of people with limitations in organizations is a societal obligation: everyone has the right to participate in society. And this can only be achieved through a process of social dialogue: At societal level a dialogue between Government and employers is required, and within organizations a dialogue between management and Works Council should take place (assisted by analysts who can provide the redesign options).

References

Algera, J., & Greuter, M. (1998). Job analysis. In P. J. D. Drenth, H. Thierry, & Ch. De Wolff (Eds.), *Handbook of work and organizational psychology: Volume 3: Personnel psychology*. Hove, UK: Psychology Press (Taylor & Francis).

Aronsson, G. (1989). Changed qualification demands in computer-mediated work. *Applied Psychology: An International Review, 38*(1), 57–71.

Arulampalam, W., Gregg, P., & Gregory, M. (2001, November). Unemployment scarring. *The Economic Journal, 111*(475), 577–584. doi:10.1111/1468-0297.00663.

Biazzo, S. (2002). Process mapping techniques and organisational analysis: Lessons from sociotechnical system theory. *Business Process Management Journal, 8*, 42–52.

Daft, R. L., & Noe, R. A. (2001). Organisational learning and change. In R. L. Daft & R. A. Noe (Eds.), *Organisational behaviour* (pp. 618–650). Orlando, FL: Harcourt College Publishers.

Dankbaar, B. (1997). Lean production: Denial, confirmation or extension of sociotechnical systems design? *Human Relations, 50*(5), 567–583. doi:10.1177/001872679705000505.

Earl, M. J. (1994). The new and old of business process redesign. *The Journal of Strategic Information Systems, 3*(1), 5–22.

Emery, F. E. (1959). *The characteristics of sociotechnical systems*. Londen: Tavistock Institute.

Fleuren, B. P. I., de Grip, A., Jansen, N. W., Kant, I. J., & Zijlstra, F. R. H. (2016). Critical reflections on the currently leading definition of sustainable employability. *Scandinavian Journal of Work, Environment & Health, 42*(3), 34–42. doi:10.5271/sjweh.3585.

Griffin, C., & Hammis, D. (2003). *Making self-employment work for people with disabilities*. Baltimore: Brookes Publishing.

Groothoff, J., Brouwer, S., Bakker, R., Overweg, K., Schellekens, J., Abma, F., et al. (2008). *Bimra: Beoordelen van interventies en meetinstrumenten bij reintegratie naar arbeid*. Groningen: RUG.

Hacker, W. (1978). *Allgemeine Arbeits- und Ingenieurspsychologie, Psychische Struktur und Regulation van Arbeitstätigkeiten*. Bern: Huber Verlag.

Hackman, J. R., & Oldham, G. R. (1980). Approaches to change: The work itself. In J. R. Hackman & G. R. Oldham (Eds.), *Work redesign* (pp. 44–68). Reading: Addison-Wesley Publishing.

Jones, G. R. (2007). Types and forms of organisational change. In G. R. Jones (Ed.), *Organisational theory, design and change* (pp. 269–299). Upper Saddle River, NJ: Prentice Hall.

Josten, E. (2010). *Minder werk voor laagopgeleiden? Ontwikkelingen in baanbezit en baankwaliteit 1992–2008*. Den Haag: Sociaal en Cultureel Planbureau.

Kagermann, H., Lukas, W., & Wahlster, W. (2011). Industrie 4.0: Mit dem Internet der Dinge auf dem Weg zur 4. industriellen Revolution. *VDI Nachrichten Nr. 13*/2011.

Lammerts, R., & Stavenuiter, M. (2010). *Wajongers op de werkvloer*. Amsterdam: RWI.

Morgeson, F. P., & Humphrey, S. E. (2006). The Work Design Questionnaire (WDQ): Developing and validating a comprehensive measure for assessing job design and the nature of work. *Journal of Applied Psychology, 91,* 1321–1399.

Nelissen, P. T. J. H, Hülsheger, U. R., van Ruitenbeek, G. M. C., & Zijlstra, F. R. H. (2016). How and when stereotypes relate to inclusive behaviour toward people with disabilities. *The International Journal of Human Resource Management, 27*(14), 1610–1625. Published online: 18 Sep 2015. doi:10.1080/09585192.2015.1072105.

Nijhuis, F. J. N. (2011). *Werken naar vermogen: vermogen om te werken*. Inaugural lecture: Maastricht University.

OECD. (2014). *Mental health and work: Netherlands, mental health and work*. OECD Publishing. http://dx.doi.org/10.1787/9789264223301-en.

Parent-Thirion, A., Biletta, I., Cabrita, J., Vargas, O., Vermeylen, G., Wilcynska, A., et al. (2016). *Sixth European Working Conditions Survey (EWCS)—Overview report*. Dublin: Eurofound. doi:10.2806/518312.

Parent-Thirion, A., Vermeylen, G., van Houten, G., Lyly-Yrjänäinen, M., Biletta, I., & Cabrita, J. (2012). *Fifth European Working Conditions Survey (EWCS)—Overview report*. Dublin: Eurofound. doi:10.2806/34660.

Rasmussen, J. (1983). Skills, rules, and knowledge; signals, signs, and symbols, and other distinctions in human performance models. *IEEE Transactions on Systems, Man, and Cybernetics, 13*(3), 257–266. doi:10.1109/TSMC.1983.6313160.

Roe, R. A., & Zijlstra, F. R. H. (1991). Arbeidsanalyse ten behoeve van (her)ontwerp van functies: een handelingstheoretische invalshoek. In J. A. Algera (red.), *Analyse van Arbeid vanuit Verschillende Perspectieven* (pp. 179–243). Lisse: Swets & Zeitlinger. ISBN 90 265 1136 1.

Schmidt, F. L., & Hunter, J. E. (1998). The validity and utility of selection methods in personnel psychology: Practical and theoretical implications of 85 years of research findings. *Psychological Bulletin, 124,* 262–274.

Van der Klink, J. J. L., Bültmann, U., Burdorf, A., Schaufeli, W. B., Zijlstra, F. R. H., Abma, F. I., et al. (2016). Sustainable employability—Definition, conceptualization, and implications: A perspective based on the capability approach. *Scandinavian Journal of Work, Environment & Health, 42*(1), 71–79. doi:10.5271/sjweh.3531.

Van Kalken, M., Brouwer, S., & Schellekens, J. (2012). Effect van een reactiveringsprogramma op arbeidsmarktafstand bij mensen met een arbeidsongeschikt-heidsuitkering. *Tijdschrift voor Bedrijfs- en Verzekeringsgeneeskunde, 20,* 8–16.

Van Ruitenbeek, G. M. C., Mulder, M. J. G. P., Zijlstra, F. R. H., Nijhuis, F. J. N., & Mulders, H. P. G. (2013). Een alternatieve benadering van voor herontwerp van werk. Ervaringen met de methode Inclusief Herontwerp Werkprocessen. *Gedrag & Organisatie, 26*(1), 104–122.

Wilson, M. A., Bennet, W., Gibson, S. G., & Alliger, G. M. (2012). *The handbook of work analysis: Methods, systems, applications and science of work measurement in organizations*. New York: Routledge, Taylor & Francis Group.

Zijlstra, F. R. H. (2009). Taken voor laag-gekwalificeerden: op weg naar een parallelle arbeidsmarkt? In Projectgroep SMBA (Eds.), *Innovatieve voorstellen voor Sociaal-Medische Beoordeling van Arbeidsvermogen* (pp. 177–191). Uitgave: UWV, Amsterdam.

Zijlstra, F. R. H., Mulders, H. P. G., & Nijhuis, F. J. N. (2009). Speciale taken voor speciale groepen. *Tijdschrift voor Bedrijfs- en Verzekeringsgeneeskunde., 17*(7), 298–301.

Zijlstra, F. R. H., Mulders, H. P. G., & Nijhuis, F. J. (2012). Inclusieve Organisaties - Op weg naar duurzame arbeidsparticipatie. *Tijdschrift Voor Arbeidsvraagstukken, 28*(1), 21–29.

Zijlstra, F. R. H., & Nijhuis, F. J. N. (2014). Return to work for long-term absentees: An undervalued topic in (psychological) research. In M. Kröll (Ed.), *European labour market strategies put to test*. Book series: Bildung und Arbeitswelt, LIT-Verlag. ISBN 978-3-643-12481-4.

Zijlstra, F. R. H., & Nyssen, A.-S. (2017). How do we handle computer-based technology? In N. Chmiel, F. Fraccaroli, & M. Sverke (Eds.), *An introduction to work and organizational psychology: An international perspective*. London: Wiley Blackwell.

Zijlstra, F. R. H., & Sonnentag, S. (2006). After work is done: Psychological perspectives on recovery from work. *European Journal of Work and Organizational Psychology, 15*(2), 129–138. doi:10.1080/13594320500513855.

Chapter 9
The Socialization Process: Helping Organizations Integrate People with Disabilities into the Workplace

Francisco J. Medina and Nuria Gamero

9.1 Workplace Accommodation of People with Different Capabilities

> A multinational insurance company based in Seville (Spain) with over 450 employees decided to launch a program entitled *Experiencias Profesionales para el Empleo* (*Work Experience for Employment*). The program, developed in partnership with an NGO working on this sector, is aimed at people with physical disabilities and seeks to facilitate their integration into the labor market through paid work placements covering a two-month period. Once the participants had been selected, the NGO specialists met with the interns individually to inform them about the company they had been assigned to, their position, and duties. For their part, the insurance company held two welcome sessions for all staff letting them know about the program, where each person would be going, and the types of tasks they would be expected to undertake. The aim was to introduce the newcomers to the current workforce and help to facilitate their integration. When the work placements were over, one of the mentors made the following comment: '*She is very intelligent and has a great attitude. She is willing to take on new challenges and shows initiative. It's been a pleasure having her on the team.*'

This is just one example of many successful stories involving people with disabilities and their positive inclusion into the new work environment. Interventions associated with the employment, accommodation, and effective workplace integration of people with disabilities require multiple actors and policies (Meyer

This work was funded by the Spanish Ministry of Economy and Competitiveness (MINECO/FEDER), grant reference n. PSI2015-64894-P.

F.J. Medina (✉) · N. Gamero
University of Seville, Seville, Spain
e-mail: fjmedina@us.es

A. Arenas et al. (eds.), *Shaping Inclusive Workplaces Through Social Dialogue*,
Industrial Relations & Conflict Management,
DOI 10.1007/978-3-319-66393-7_9

2001), as evidenced in the example given at the start of this chapter: human resource managers, occupational health professionals (Coole et al. 2012), line managers (Haafkens et al. 2011), disability advocacy organizations, NGOs, and families (Nesbitt 2000). The presence of different stakeholders implies the need for collaboration and social dialogue among all agents to facilitate this group's integration and inclusion.

People with disabilities are particularly vulnerable in the labor market, where achieving social integration and inclusion within organizations is a constant challenge. This vulnerability is especially pronounced in the current economic context. Most studies on people with disabilities at work have focused on labor market access and workplace accommodation to their individual needs. Consequently, organizations have introduced policies, programs, and interventions directed to helping employees with disabilities to overcome these barriers. However, research about how to facilitate integration into ordinary jobs, and how to work inside organizations with people with disabilities is anecdotal (Gensby et al. 2014).

The aim of this chapter is to understand how to work with people with disabilities in an organizational setting to ensure effective integration. We focus on socialization as a process through which newcomers acquire knowledge about their work and adjustment to the new workplace, thus becoming 'contributing' organizational members (Korte et al. 2015). We also engage in an in-depth analysis of the importance of social dialogue when it comes to integrate people with disabilities.

9.2 Socialization Processes for Workers with Disabilities

Medina and Munduate (2012) conducted research alongside large, leading organizations in Spain to analyze the integration processes of people with disabilities. They asked workers (with and without disabilities) how the organizational entry process went, what kinds of tactics were employed by the companies, and how the information was acquired.

This study revealed no differences between workers with and without disabilities in socialization tactics (Fig. 9.1). For the most part, organizations used serial and investiture tactics. Lesser-used tactics were the formal kind (Table 9.1).

The main differences between both groups (workers with disabilities and workers without disabilities) were found in the type of information passed on by the organization to the new employee (Fig. 9.2). In general, organizations are required to provide information about the job and the role, interpersonal and group relationships, and the nature of organizations as a whole. Knowing the technical and social aspects specific to both the company and the job is essential to performing well in a new environment. However, the information obtained by workers with disabilities, especially with regard to the organization, was perceived as poorer than that of their peers without disabilities, thereby hindering the integration process.

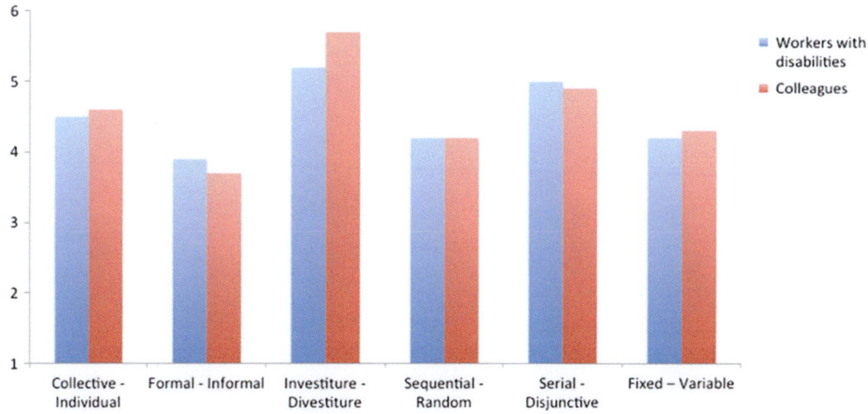

Fig. 9.1 Socialization tactics employed by organizations

Table 9.1 Socialization tactics

Tactics of socialization	Definition
Collective (vs. *individual*) tactic	This tactic involves grouping newcomers so that they share a common learning
Formal (vs. *informal*) tactic	This tactic involves transmitting information to newcomers off the workplace. Newcomers are separated from organizational insiders, for a limited period, through activities such as training and orientation classes
Sequential (vs. *random*) tactic	This tactic entails structuring learning experiences through a lock-step series or sequences
Fixed (vs. *variable*) tactic	This tactic involves setting a timetable for moving from one learning experience to another
Serial (vs. *disjunctive*) tactic	This involves providing newcomers with a role model, such as a mentor, supervisor, or experienced peer, to help them learn the ropes
Investiture (vs. *divestiture*) tactic	This involves affirming the incoming identities, attributes, and competencies of newcomers when hired based on their training and/or experience

Source Van Maanen and Schein (1979)

More specifically, the main differences revolved around three information domains: *background* (learning about organizational traditions, habits, and legends); *language* (acquiring technical language and organization-specific jargon); and *policies* (obtaining political information about formal and informal work relationships and the distribution of power within the organization). According to the literature mentioned, we assume that the ignorance of these domains is the first warning sign of a poor integration process (Benzinger 2016).

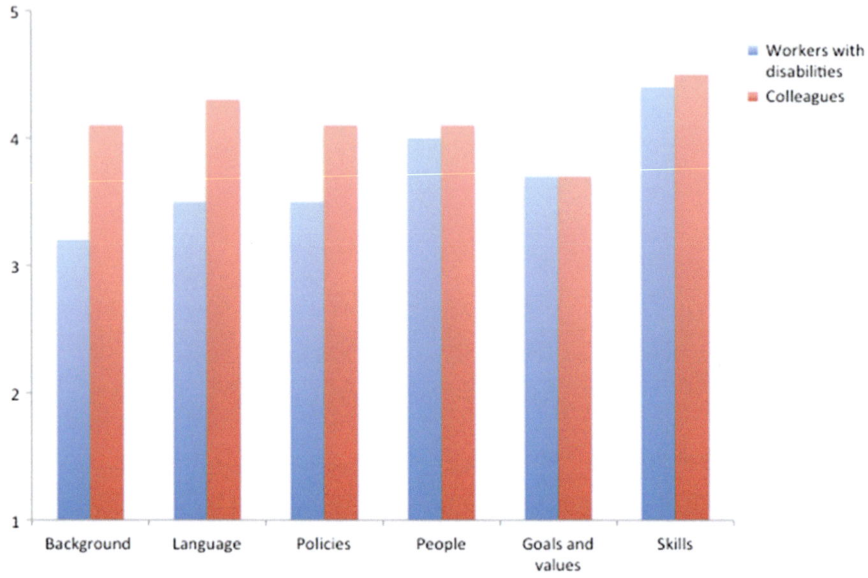

Fig. 9.2 Information passed on to workers with disabilities and colleagues about the organization

9.3 Key Points to Designing Inclusive Socialization Processes

9.3.1 Preparing Newcomers with Disabilities and Adjusting Expectations

Before entering an organization, people with disabilities have preconceived expectations about the organization in question, their new workplace, and the job involved. These expectations come from different sources. One such source is the organization itself, where information is exchanged through interaction between people with disabilities and managers or recruiters during the recruitment and selection processes (Delobbe et al. 2015).

Early socialization experiences have an influence on the success or failure of newcomers with disabilities adjustment. People with disabilities should arrive with realistic expectations and receive clear-cut, honest information from the organization regarding what constitutes organizational reality (Kulkarni and Lengnick-Hall 2011). However, workers with disabilities generally have unrealistic expectations about their new job and the organization. First, this group expects the job to be tailored to their personal circumstances and particular needs (e.g., Smith 2002); and second, they come with negative expectations about how the rest will interact with them (Colella 1994; Goffman 1963). Workers with disabilities usually perceive other people's treatment of them as being based on their disabilities rather than as peers. According to Goffman (1963), this is because, generally speaking, the group has had unsatisfactory work-related experiences in the past, which led them to believe that working relations with new colleagues will not be positive. There is evidence that workers who have negative expectations about the job will tend to perceive it in a more negative light than those who have more positive expectations. Similarly, overly optimistic expectations held by people with disabilities about the level of complexity behind the tasks to be performed, the opportunities for career development, and interpersonal relationships in the workplace can also lead to distrust and frustration (Colella and Varma 1999).

One way of getting involved in the preparation and adjustment of expectations at this pre-entry stage is to promote social dialogue with other agents, actively engaged in helping people with disabilities, to become integrated and included (Kulkarni 2013). Companies especially need to maintain continuous dialogue with associations supporting people with disabilities. These associations play their part in pre-entry preparations; they also provide training, promote the acquisition of skills, competencies and attitudes, and adjust expectations. The work carried out by associations for people with disabilities entails guidance and counseling, improvements in knowledge and skills, and shifts in attitudes toward the job. They open the way for experiences in a pre-employment setting, resembling what one can expect to find at future, receiving organizations. Moreover, some of these associations provide internships that enable candidates to gain professional experience in preparation for the job market, offering mentoring that gives people with disabilities a glimpse into the world of work (Medina and Munduate 2012). These actions support the subsequent adjustment and integration of this group, allowing for the development of skills and habits and adjusting expectations that may be too positive or too negative.

Furthermore, associations are in a position to provide specific information and advice and meet the demands of companies in terms of guidance, training, awareness-raising activities, and accompanying the various groups with disabilities in the insertion process. The dialogue and collaboration with these specialists, who act helping newcomers to effectively adjust to the new job, should occur naturally, given that this support constitutes complementary and coordinated actions that help to facilitate organizational integration and socialization among workers with disabilities (Colella 1994).

From this perspective, the majority of Spanish organizations under study in Medina and Munduate's research (2012) worked alongside NGOs in several different ways: (a) together they analyzed the job vacancies and skills required; (b) they jointly developed work experience programs for people with disabilities; and (c) together they devised a follow-up program specifically for new employees. As a result of this collaboration, a better adjustment of the job conditions is achieved. The internships aimed at preparing this group for the world of work are particularly important, whether organized by the company itself or in partnership with associations or NGOs. Organizations should be prepared internally to facilitate the participation of NGO in human resource practices in relation to people with disability, where social dialogue between employers and unions is absolutely necessary.

9.3.2 Preparing Organizations for the Successful Integration of People with Disabilities

A number of measures can be implemented to improve the integration of people with disabilities into organizations. These organizational measures are structured around two main lines of action: introducing equality in organizational policies and practices and increasing psychological safety.

First, the implementation of practices for the integration of people with disabilities in HRM policies is of primordial importance in the current organizational climate. It has been shown that fair and responsive work environments are especially beneficial for people with disabilities (Schur et al. 2009). Inclusive organizations that strive to achieve a diverse workforce are advised to include corporate sustainability and responsibility in their mission statements. An active implementation of the values that foster belonging is key to achieving sustainable employment for people with disabilities (Schur et al. 2009). Particularly in the case of larger organizations and the public sector, practices for an effective integration of people with disabilities are influenced by collective negotiation processes, in which trade unions play an important role, having had some success in getting disability onto organizational agendas (Bacon and Hoque 2015; Foster and Fosh 2010). In this regard, social dialogue between social agents (unions and companies) could be seen as a key skill to harness when developing integration processes within organizations.

Second, it is also necessary to promote a climate of psychological safety, respect, and acceptance, thus creating a suitable environment in which people with disabilities feel welcome and accepted. A psychologically safe work environment is characterized by feelings of safety, interpersonal trust, and mutual respect (Nembhard and Edmondson 2006). Organizations can enhance psychological safety: (a) reducing the leaders' dysfunctional use of power that, as a consequence, decreases toxic work behaviors such as bullying or harassment (Shain 2009); (b) promoting disability awareness training programs for supervisors (McLellan et al. 2001); or (c) improving a clear, robust policy that comprehensively addresses issues of diversity.

Via their social responsibility programs, organizations put into practice measures that fall under the aforementioned lines of action. These include: institutional statements of respect and support for diversity addressed to the organization itself as well as to organizational partners (suppliers, clients, etc.); integration schemes for people with disabilities; preferential hiring policies; and 'Planes Familia' (Family Schemes) to support the relatives of workers with disabilities (Medina and Munduate 2012).

These organizational policies are also reflected in social dialogue processes via certain mechanisms such as the introduction of integration policies in collective bargaining; negotiations with unions concerning the jobs that best suit these candidates; the joint development of integration schemes using job banks and other systems; and joint negotiations on Respect for Diversity schemes (Medina and Munduate 2012).

9.3.3 Working with Socialization Agents

Organizations call upon various socialization agents during the socialization process (e.g., supervisors, peers, and mentors) to help newcomers with disabilities adjust effectively. Beyond formal orientation programs and employee handbooks designed by organizations, newcomers with disabilities find these organizational insiders the most useful source of knowledge and support (Saks and Gruman 2014). These organizational agents help them to adjust by providing information, feedback, role models, social validation, social relationships, appreciation, and support, as well as access to broader networks and other work-relevant resources (Nifadkar and Bauer 2016). In this regard, organizations use manuals specifically designed for working with people with disabilities and implement mentoring programs to facilitate integration (Medina and Munduate 2012).

9.3.3.1 How to Work with Supervisors

Two HRM theories can help us understand the role that supervisors play in the socialization process of workers with disabilities: transformational leadership (TFL) theory and leader–member exchange (LMX) theory. A transformational leader motivates followers to pursue high-level goals, encouraging experiences of meaningfulness and moral purpose in their work (Kark et al. 2003). TFL has four components: inspirational motivation, idealized influence, intellectual stimulation, and individualized consideration, all of which have been shown to positively influence various follower outcomes that are crucial to organizational functioning, including job performance, job satisfaction, and motivation (see Judge and Piccolo 2004). TFL can be considered a key approach that particularly meets the requirements of people with disabilities, given that it positively influences their self-concept and consequentially enhances their job performance while preventing emotional exhaustion (Kensbock and Boehm 2016). Transformational leaders also act as role models to their followers, thus increasing their identification with and acceptance of the leaders' values and beliefs (Kark et al. 2003). Furthermore, they display empowering behaviors by delegating responsibility, encouraging followers to think on their own, and coming up with new and creative ideas. As a consequence, followers feel trusted, challenged, and valued by their supervisors (Kark et al. 2003).

In addition, supervisors are found to establish different exchange relationships with their subordinates, where we see an overlap of a personal and working relationship. Dienesch and Liden (1986) identified three dimensions in these supervisor–subordinate exchange relationships: first, the perceived contribution to the exchange in relation to work-oriented activities, that is, the employer has specific expectations about how subordinates will perform at work and how their performance will impact on the company; second is loyalty, namely an employer who maintains good working relations with subordinate staff will express support, treat them fairly, keep them informed, and show an active interest in their professional development and future careers; and the third is mutual affection, in which interpersonal attraction comes into play, adding to a purely working relationship.

The nature of this leader–member dynamic will determine whether the latter group will have a successful relationship. It is widely known that relationships established between supervisor–subordinate dyads are formed quickly and remain stable over time, meaning that if good relationships are successfully forged, we are likely to find a great deal of support from the supervisor to guide the subordinate's work, high satisfaction levels from subordinates, good performance levels, and low staff turnover rates (Liden et al. 1993).

There are reasons to suggest that disabilities may affect these supervisor–subordinate relationships. Regarding the first dimension (employees' contribution), we know that future expectations concerning employee performance are better predictors of these relationships than the worker's current performance. From this perspective, we can identify stereotypes against people with disabilities which include competence attributions; for example, they will show a lack of skills in terms of work and demonstrate a certain degree of dependency, which in turn can affect the workers' own performance (Fichten and Amstel 1986). As for the second dimension, their disabilities can have a negative impact on these relationships, given that supervisors may display less affection toward these employees due to the perception that they are different from the rest.

Moreover, the expectations that a superior casts upon the newcomer's performance are also a determining factor when predicting their performance, namely through a *self-fulfilling prophecy process* (Eden 1990; Peters et al., Chap. 14 in this volume). In other words, the supervisor's low expectations predict the employee's subsequent failure to adjust to the labor landscape. In the case of people with disabilities, organizations are shown to hold very low expectations in terms of this group's performance capabilities depending on the limitations specific to the person's condition and the corresponding special healthcare needs (e.g., Smith 2002). As a consequence, this group's opportunities for career development are more limited. In contrast, people with disabilities expect to be assigned tasks with the same degree of responsibility and complexity as their peers without disabilities (Colella et al. 1993), resulting in a mismatch between the expectations of this group and of the organization.

Given the importance of middle management in the integration process of people with disabilities, some organizations run specific programs tailored to this group. These may include experiential workshops where managers experience the integration difficulties faced by these individuals; specific awareness-raising workshops for middle management and human resource managers; and team building days at special employment centers, where middle management has the opportunity to learn first-hand about the work of people with disabilities at centers in which this group accounts for more than 70% of the workforce (Medina and Munduate 2012).

9.3.3.2 How to Work with Coworkers and Work Groups

One of the key factors behind the successful integration of employees with disabilities is the way in which they are received and accepted by their colleagues (Saks and Ashforth 1997). The role that coworkers play is important, owing to the fact that many workplace adaptations call upon the cooperation and support of others. The possible changes that people with disabilities require, whether referring to job duties (reassigning tasks); accommodations (longer work breaks, excused absences); tools for the job (e.g., bigger, better quality screens); available resources (money spent on workstation adaptation); and place of work (possibility of working from home) may be viewed by the rest of the team as the result of unfair preferential treatment, leading to an integration process that falls short of what is expected (Colella and Varma 2001).

Furthermore, negative reactions from coworkers are likely to affect the rights of workers in some work-related adaptations. If people with disabilities feel that their colleagues will not understand their particular circumstances, they may choose to decline a claim for any adaptation or modification to the job in question. In addition, the fear of receiving negative feedback from work colleagues may convince certain senior staff that necessary work-related adaptations are not worth implementing (Cleveland et al. 1997).

There are two overriding social obstacles for people with disabilities at work (Ferro and Boyle 2013): the first is that this group is particularly prone to stigma attributions (Stone and Colella 1996), and the second is stereotyping (Colella and Bruyère 2011).

On the one hand, the internalization of stigma by the stigmatized person makes this worker feel deviant, limited, spoiled, or generally undesirable (Jones 2002). Stigma perceptions have negative implications for a person's self-esteem (McGonagle and Barnes-Farrell 2013). On the other hand, in the work environment, people with disabilities belong to a minority group, which is often confronted with stereotypes and negative attitudes on the part of coworkers and supervisors (Lengnick-Hall et al. 2008; Nelissen et al. 2016).

Stigma and stereotyping can elicit negative reactions among staff:

- Workers without disabilities can have mixed feelings about people with disabilities: aversion and hostility on the one hand and sympathy and compassion on the other (Katz and Glass 1979). This ambivalence creates an inner conflict in the person who feels this way, leading to extremes of behavior toward the stigmatized. From this perspective, the context will determine how far the behavior goes and in which direction: A favorable context involving people with disabilities may result in very positive responses, whereas a highly unfavorable context can determine very negative responses.
- Thus, many workers may come across as reluctant to interact with people with disabilities, especially those with physical or intellectual disabilities (Ruiz and Moya 2007). This ultimately results in fewer interactions with this group and a lengthy, problematic work-entry process, which in turn elicits feelings of

distrust and exclusion. Workers with disabilities do not have the same capacity as their peers without disabilities to obtain the necessary information that enables them to learn the habits and ways of doing things within the new organization, as this information is usually shared in casual conversations (Bowman 1987). Consequently, it will take them longer to obtain the keys to organizational success needed to ensure quality work and full integration.
- There may also be a strong tendency to be overly friendly toward people with disabilities. To achieve successful organizational socialization processes, it is important that the worker receives systematic and ongoing information from both the organization and their colleagues. In other words, they should receive realistic feedback that dispels the misconceptions workers normally bring to the organization. If no realistic feedback is given to these employees with disabilities, this hinders their socialization process (Hastorf et al. 1979).

To break stigma and stereotyping, Hunt and Hunt (2004) identified the main challenge as changing people's beliefs. They introduced an educational intervention that increased knowledge on and yielded positive attitudes toward people with disabilities in the workplace. Stone and Colella (1996) argued that organizations should develop training programs that counter the misleading information that may have been engendered by stereotypes, on norms of day-to-day interaction and on reducing feelings of anxiety while working with people with disabilities.

The information-sharing actions aimed at all members of the company, in particular the members of the work groups which include newcomers with disabilities, contribute toward breaking stereotypes and negative beliefs, revealing the real picture and their personal and working capabilities. It is advisable to carry out awareness-raising campaigns on diversity so that this becomes a transversal theme within the company's culture. The way in which this is conveyed to all other members of the organization is key. For this reason, it should be a planned and researched project, where associations can be called on to assist during the different stages of the process. In the workplace setting, people must be informed when a person with a disability is scheduled to enter the company in order to help the adaptation process, especially the team the person is set to join (Medina and Munduate 2012).

9.3.4 Encouraging Serial Socialization Tactics

Serial tactics, among others, are key to fostering the integration of newcomers with disabilities. These specific tactics involve assigning newcomers a mentor to help them learn the new job (Benzinger 2016).

Inclusion processes cannot be configured homogeneously; rather, they have to adapt to the general characteristics of the group and the specificities of each individual (Kulkarni 2012). Every disability has its own characteristics and challenges. A person with both general and specific training, and who is a qualified partner in dialogue with associations, enables the integration process to be brought to fruition. Furthermore, interventions involving people with disabilities are not one-off programs. They constitute ongoing work, especially when it relates to certain types of disabilities, such as intellectual disabilities, autism spectrum disorders and, on occasions, hearing impairments. In view of their permanent and unique nature, they require support at all stages of Circle of Inclusion (see Arenas et al., Chap. 18 in this volume). To enable the individual's adaptation to the job and to ensure effective integration, having a mentor is necessary (Kulkarni 2013). The ideal profile is someone from the organization itself, predisposed to offering support to the new recruit, with guidance training, awareness and knowledge of the disability and, more specifically, someone who knows how to deal with the different situations that may arise at work affecting the person with disability. It is necessary that individuals with a disability have a referent person, who acts as a counselor, helping to clear up any doubts or needs they have.

9.4 Conclusions to Facilitate Inclusive Socialization Processes

To summarize, best practices for the successful socialization of newcomers with disabilities can be broken down into six main actions:

1. Working with associations supporting this group to guarantee the necessary preparations and to create realistic expectations in the new recruits. Cooperation between both agents prior to and during the incorporation process is key. The activities carried out by associations in partnership with the organization may include the following: (a) informing companies to help them gain real knowledge about the different disabilities; (b) collaborating on the design of awareness-raising programs that address the social environment in which the new member with a disability is set to join; and (c) accompanying the people with disabilities in the insertion process from the outset of their organizational working life. On occasions, on-the-job learning is an ongoing process, and associations should continue their supporting role in the workplace to achieve the highest level of adjustment to the proposed performance objectives.
2. Introducing equality in organizational politics and including corporate sustainability and responsibility in organizational mission statements. Social dialogue established between trade unions and companies is also especially important. In large companies and those in the public sector, disability action plans are influenced by group negotiation processes, in which trade unions play an important role.
3. Promoting a climate of psychological safety, respect, and acceptance, thus creating a suitable environment for the welcome and integration of people with disabilities. From this perspective, the process would benefit from a clear, robust policy that comprehensively addresses issues of diversity, is well-informed and

is shared among the entire workforce. The receiving work group should also be informed of the person with disabilities set to join the team in order to help the adaptation process along.

4. Designing training programs for supervisors. The content of these programs should include information on how people with disabilities want to be treated, the problems and issues related to newcomers with disabilities, the impact of socialization on individual integration, and the potential obstacles to socialization for new employees with disabilities. Supervisors must also learn what they can truly expect from an employee with a given disability, what the capabilities of applicants with disabilities are, and what type of accommodations are required.
5. Highlighting the decisive role of work colleagues. Developing awareness-raising campaigns alongside the work group colleagues of the individual with disabilities, making them aware of the specific needs of the person joining the team, their competencies, the various duties they may perform, and the support they may need. These programs should also provide guidelines on how to interact with people with disabilities, in turn avoiding overprotective and permissive attitudes that jeopardize their chances of fully integrating in the organization.
6. Developing the role of mentor. Given that every disability has its own characteristics and challenges, a person with both general and specific training, and who is a qualified partner in dialogue with associations, enables the integration process to succeed.

To sum up, integrating people with disabilities into organizations is more than introducing a series of concrete actions; it implies a different approach of organizational policy about diversity, where all stakeholders are needed, and the social dialogue between them is absolutely fundamental. To sum up, integration implies to develop an organizational culture friendly to the workers with different capabilities. This culture has to be reflected in formal documents and HRM practices.

Acknowledgement This work was funded by the Spanish Ministry of Economy and Competitiveness (MINECO/FEDER), grant reference n. PSI2015-64894-P.

References

Bacon, N., & Hoque, K. (2015). The influence of trade union disability champions on employer disability policy and practice. *Human Resource Management Journal, 25,* 233–249.

Benzinger, D. (2016). Organizational socialization tactics and newcomer information seeking in the contingent workforce. *Personnel Review, 45,* 743–763. doi:10.1108/PR-06-2014-0131.

Bowman, J. (1987). Attitudes towards disabled persons: Social distance and work competence. *Journal of Rehabilitation, 53,* 41–44.

Cleveland, J. N., Barnes-Farrell, J., & Ratz, J. M. (1997). Accommodation in the workplace. *Human Resource Management Review, 7,* 77–108.

Colella, A. (1994). Organizational socialization of employees with disabilities: critical issues and implications for workplace interventions. *Journal of Occupational Rehabilitation, 4,* 87–106. doi:10.1007/BF02110048.

Colella, A., & Bruyère, S. (2011). Disability and employment. In S. Zedeck (Ed.), *APA handbook of industrial and organizational psychology* (Vol. 1: Building and developing the organization, pp. 473–504). Washington, DC: American Psychological Association.

Colella, A., DeNisi, A. S., & Lund, M. (1993). *The job socialization of employees with disabilities: The role of expectations.* Paper presented at the Academy of Management National Meetings, Atlanta, Georgia.

Colella, A., & Varma, A. (1999). Disability-job fit stereotypes and the evaluation of persons with disabilities at work. *Journal of Occupational Rehabilitation, 9,* 79–95.

Colella, A., & Varma, A. (2001). The impact of subordinate disability on leader-member exchange relationships. *Academy of Management Journal, 44,* 304–315.

Coole, C., Radford, K., Grant, M., & Terry, J. (2012, December). Returning to work after stroke: Perspectives of employer stakeholders, a qualitative study. *Journal of Occupational Rehabilitation, 23,* 406–418.

Delobbe, N., Cooper-Thomas, H. D., & De Hoe, R. (2015). A new look at the psychological contract during organizational socialization: The role of newcomers' obligations at entry. *Journal of Organizational Behavior.* doi:10.1002/job.2078.

Dienesch, R. M. S., & Liden, R. G. (1986). Leader-member exchange model of leadership: A critique and further development. *Academy of Management Review, 11,* 618–634.

Eden, D. (1990). *Pygmalion in management: Productivity as a self-fulfilling prophecy.* Lexington, Massachussets: Lexington Books.

Ferro, M. A., & Boyle, M. H. (2013). Longitudinal invariance of measurement and structure of global self-concept: A population-based study examining trajectories among adolescents with and without chronic illness. *Journal of Pediatric Psychology, 38,* 425–437.

Fichten, C. S., & Amstel, R. (1986). Trait Attributions about college students with a physical disability: Circumplex analysis and methodological issues. *Journal of Applied Social Psychology, 16,* 410–427.

Foster, D., & Fosh, P. (2010). Negotiating 'difference': Representing disabled employees in the British workplace. *British Journal of Industrial Relations, 48,* 560–582.

Gensby, U., Labriola, M., Irvin, E., Amick, B. C., & Lund, T. (2014). A classification of components of workplace disability management programs: Results from a systematic review. *Journal of Occupational Rehabilitation, 24*(2), 220–241. doi:10.1007/s10926-013-9437-x.

Goffman, E. (1963). *Stigma: Notes on the management of spoiled identity.* Englewood Cliffs, NJ: Prentice Hall.

Haafkens, J., Kopnina, H., Meerman, M., & van Dijk, F. (2011). Facilitating job retention for chronically ill employees: Perspectives of line managers and human resource managers. *BMC Health Services Research, 11,* 104–110.

Hastorf, A., Northcraft, G., & Picciotto, S. (1979). Helping the handicapped: How realistic is the performance feedback received by the physically handicapped? *Personality and Social Psychology Bulletin, 5,* 373–376.

Hunt, C. S., & Hunt, B. (2004). Changing attitudes toward people with disabilities: Experimenting with an educational intervention. *Journal of Managerial Issues, 16,* 266–280.

Jones, M. (2002). *Social psychology of prejudice.* Upper Saddle River, NJ: Prentice-Hall.

Judge, T. A., & Piccolo, R. F. (2004). Transformational and transactional leadership: A meta-analytic test of their relative validity. *Journal of Applied Psychology, 89,* 755–768.

Kark, R., Shamir, B., & Chen, G. (2003). The two faces of transformational leadership: Empowerment and dependency. *Journal of Applied Psychology, 88,* 246–255.

Katz, D., & Glass, D. C. (1979). An ambivalence-amplification theory of behavior toward the stigmatized. In W. G. Austin & S. Worchel (Eds.), *The social psychology of intergroup relations* (pp. 55–84). Monterey, CA: Brooks/Cole.

Kensbock, J. M., & Boehm, S. A. (2016). The role of transformational leadership in the mental health and job performance of employees with disabilities. *The International Journal of Human Resource Management, 27,* 1580–1609. doi:10.1080/09585192.2015.1079231.
Korte, R., Brunhaver, S., & Sheppard, S. (2015). (Mis)interpretations of organizational socialization: The expectations and experiences of newcomers and managers. *Human Resource Development Quarterly, 26,* 185–208. doi:10.1002/hrdq.21206.
Kulkarni, M. (2012). Social networks and career advancement of people with disabilities. *Human Resource Development Review, 11,* 138–155. doi:10.1177/1534484312438216.
Kulkarni, M. (2013). Help-seeking behaviors of people with disabilities in the workplace. *Employee Responsibilities and Rights Journal, 25,* 41–57. doi:10.1007/s10672-012-9202-x.
Kulkarni, M., & Lengnick-Hall, M. L. (2011). Socialization of people with disabilities in the workplace. *Human Resource Management, 50,* 521–540. doi:10.1002/hrm.20436.
Lengnick-Hall, M. L., Gaunt, P. M., & Kulkarni, M. (2008). Overlooked and underutilized: People with disabilities are an untapped human resource. *Human Resource Management, 47,* 255–273.
Liden, R. G., Wayne, S. J., & Stilwell, D. (1993). A longitudinal study on the early development of leader-member exchanges. *Journal of Applied Psychology, 78,* 662–674.
McGonagle, A. K., & Barnes-Farrell, J. L. (2013). Chronic illness in the workplace: Stigma, identity threat and strain. *Stress and Health, 30,* 310–321.
McLellan, R. K., Pransky, G., & Shaw, W. S. (2001). Disability management training for supervisors: A pilot intervention program. *Journal of Occupational Rehabilitation, 11,* 33–41.
Medina, F. J., & Munduate, L. (2012). *Breaking walls in the integration of disability workers [Rompiendo barreras en la integración laboral de las personas con discapacidad].* Madrid: Servimedia.
Meyer, R. (2001). *Asperger syndrome employment workbook: An employment workbook for adults with Asperger syndrome.* London: JKP.
Nelissen, P. T. J. H., Hülsheger, U. R., van Ruitenbeek, G. M. C., & Zijlstra, F. R. H. (2016). How and when stereotypes relate to inclusive behavior toward people with disabilities. *The International Journal of Human Resource Management, 27,* 1610–1625. doi:10.1080/09585192.2015.1072105.
Nembhard, I. M., & Edmondson, A. C. (2006). Making it safe: The effects of leader inclusiveness and professional status on psychological safety and improvement efforts in health care teams. *Journal of Organizational Behavior, 27,* 941–966.
Nesbitt, S. (2000). Why and why not? Factors influencing employment for individuals with Asperger syndrome. *Autism, 4,* 357–369.
Nifadkar, S. S., & Bauer, T. N. (2016). Breach of belongingness: Newcomer relationship conflict, information, and task-related outcomes during organizational socialization. *Journal of Applied Psychology, 101,* 1–13. doi:10.1037/apl0000035.
Ruiz, J., & Moya, M. (2007). El estudio de la discapacidad física desde la Psicología Social. *Revista de Psicología Social, 22,* 177–198.
Saks, A. M., & Ashforth, B. E. (1997). Socialization tactics and newcomer information acquisition. *International Journal of Selection and Assessment, 5,* 48–61.
Saks, A., & Gruman, J. (2014). Making organizations more effective through organizational socialization. *Journal of Organizational Effectiveness: People and Performance, 1,* 261–280.
Schur, L., Kruse, D., Blasi, J., & Blanck, P. (2009). Is disability disabling in all workplaces? Workplace disparities and corporate culture. *Industrial Relations: A Journal of Economy and Society, 48,* 381–410.
Shain, M. (2009). Psychological safety at work: Emergence of a corporate and social agenda in Canada. *International Journal of Mental Health Promotion, 11,* 42–48.
Smith, T. (2002). Diversity and disability: Exploring the experiences of vision impaired people in the workplace. *Equal Opportunities International, 21,* 59–72.
Stone, D. L., & Colella, A. (1996). A model of factors affecting the treatment of disabled individuals in organizations. *Academy of Management Review, 21,* 352–401.
Van Maanen, J., & Schein, E. H. (1979). Toward a theory of organizational socialization. In B. M. Staw (Ed.), *Research in organizational behavior* (pp. 209–264). Greenwich, CT: JAI Press.

Chapter 10
Cultural Diversity and Inclusion in Brazilian Organizations: Challenges for Training of Minorities Groups

Cláudio V. Torres and Darcy Mitiko Mori Hanashiro

10.1 Introduction

Little is known in Brazil about the impact of cultural diversity and inclusion in organizations. Systematically, cultural diversity has been defined as the representation, in a social system, of people with different group identities and that have different cultural meanings (e.g. Roberson 2006). There is already a consensus that organizations need to go beyond the mere concern with diversity and also consider inclusion in its context (e.g. Qin et al. 2014; Shemla et al. 2014; Thomas and Ely 1996). In organizations with a culture of inclusion, all identity groups have the opportunity to be present, so that their voices are heard, appreciated and can perform core activities on behalf of the community (Ferdman 2014; Pless and Maak 2004).

This chapter has the initial objective to identify and explore the Brazilian academic production between the years 2010–2015, pinpointing some practical experiences in training aimed at diversity. Then, we point out some already established practices in diversity management and inclusion in organizations, which may contribute to the growth of companies beyond the effects of traditional affirmative action programs. These practices typically encompass training and monitoring diversity and inclusion aimed at minority groups, among others. In short, what is expected, above all, it is that this chapter can help to expand knowledge and debate on diversity and inclusion in organizations, serving as a reference for future projects, and for the formulation of organizational practices regarding the theme.

C.V. Torres (✉)
University of Brasilia, Brasilia, Brazil
e-mail: claudio.v.torres@gmail.com

D.M.M. Hanashiro
Presbyterian University Mackenzie, São Paulo, Brazil

A. Arenas et al. (eds.), *Shaping Inclusive Workplaces Through Social Dialogue*, Industrial Relations & Conflict Management,
DOI 10.1007/978-3-319-66393-7_10

10.2 Brazilian Literature on Diversity and Inclusion

To draw a picture of Brazilian literature on the theme, a search of the studies was done in SPELL (Scientific Periodicals Electronic Library), a Brazilian scientific articles repository in the area of Administration, Economy and Accounting, SciELo (Scientific Electronic Library Online) which covers a selected collection of Brazilian scientific journals. The searches were conducted by the combination of the key words "diversity" and/or "inclusion" and "management of organizational diversity", for the period of 2010 and 2015. To ensure that most studies in the field would be identified, the "snowball" technique was used, which consisted in checking the references of all initially selected studies, so that in the end, studies could reference each other and no studies would be ignored. In total, 54 studies were identified, which were then analyzed according to the following criteria: (a) the context of publications; (b) methodological characteristics; and (c) results found. A large number of publications were actually reviews of international literature, its theoretical applications to the Brazilian context, or essays with no empirical findings. These studies were afterwards reduced to a list of 18 publications (Table 10.1). Most highlight the connections between theory, empirical research and practice. Nevertheless, only few of them are directly connected to the HRM system and Circle of Inclusion already discussed in the book (see Arenas et al., Chap. 1 in this volume).

It should be noticed that in none of the 54 Brazilian publications the theme of Social Dialogue was identified, or discussed. Social dialogue, in Brazil, is understood in terms of collaborative and social networks that facilitate the diversity management and real inclusion of employees (Pulignano 2011). For the author, such practices are sustained by new forms of direct support of the State, at the supranational level, highlighting the intra-organizational difference. This lack of reference to Social Dialogue, or even of a discussion regarding its idea and meaning, is probably related to the fact that the concept of social dialogue is yet largely neglected by the national scientific production, and equally important, to the practice of diversity and inclusion in Brazilian organizations, as the brief review of its intervention will show. For the International Labor Office (ILO), Social Dialogue includes all types of negotiation, consultation or simply exchange of information between, or among, representatives of governments, employers and workers on issues of common interest relating to economic and social policy. The Social Dialogue is a tool of good governance and its relevance is not just related to promote more performing and competitive economy but to make society in general more stable and more equitable (ILO 2015). In the context of ILO, Social Dialogue takes many different forms. In *stricto* sensu it can exist as a tripartite process, with the government as an official party in the dialogue, along with workers and employers through their independent representative organizations on issues of common interest. Whereas in Europe trade unions and labor associations exert substantial influence on the decisions in economic and social policy construction, in many Latin American countries Social Dialogue with a functioning institutionalized

Table 10.1 Bibliographic survey on diversity and inclusion in Brazilian scientific journals—2010–2015

Article	Title	Author	Year	Sample	Method	CI
1	Human resource practices for diversity management: the inclusion of intellectual disabilities in a public federation of Brazil	Maccali, N. et al.	2015	1 female managers; 6 employees; 5 intellectually disabled people and 1 external collaborator	Qualitative	C
2	The identity dynamics of people with Disabilities: a study in Brazil and In the United States	Moreira, L.B. et al.	2015	12 PwDs in Brazil; 8 in the United States	Qualitative	E
3	The social representations of gay executive secretariat: gender and diversity at work	Souza, E.C.P.; Martins, C.B.; Souza, R.B.	2015	6 executive secretariat gay men	Qualitative	No
4	Case study on the integration of people with disabilities on a large organization	Silva, A. M.; Carvalho-Freitas, M.N.	2014	291 PwD; 198 managers; 1 HR professional	Quantitative Qualitative	B
5	Sexual diversity in organizations: a study on coming out	Caproni Neto, H.L.; Saraiva, L.A.S.; Bicalho, R.A.	2014	11 homosexual (6 males and 5 females)	Qualitative (Oral history)	E
6	Meaning of work and diversity: a study with gay men	Silva, A. et al.	2013	6 gay men	Qualitative	E
7	The meaning of work for persons With disability	Lima, M.P. et al.	2013	10 disabled people PwD	Qualitative	E
8	Inclusion of people with disabilities in a company: case study of a Brazilian multinational	CAMPOS; VASCONCELLOS; KRUGLIANSKAS	2013	2 HR managers; 2 direct supervisors of professionals with disabilities	Qualitative	A
9	Management of diversity and buying consumer behavior	Pereira et al.	2012	35 (qualitative research); 182 (quantitative research)	Quantitative Qualitative	No

(continued)

Table 10.1 (continued)

Article	Title	Author	Year	Sample	Method	CI
10	Selective Placement of Mentally Challenged People in Organizations	Mourao, l.; Sampaio, S.; Duarte, M.H.	2012	23 intellectually disabled people, their families, and employers	Qualitative	A
11	The perception of organizational distributive justice in the face of actions that provide resources for diversity	Pereira et al.	2012	253 individuals (52% women, 84% Caucasian and 94% without disabilities)	Quantitative	No
12	Diversity on the Board of Directors and firm performance: an empirical research	Fraga, J.J.; SILVA, V.A.B.	2012	Composition of the Board of Directors of Brazilian companies listed on BM & FBOVESPA	Quantitative	No
13	Readings from the formal discourse of project managers regarding diversity in teams	Rocha-Pinto, S.R.; DIAS, P.D.G.	2012	15 project managers	Qualitative	No
14	The time as a dimension of research on diversity policy and labor relations	Irigaray, H.A.; Vergara, S.C.	2011	49 individuals (RH and Marketing professionals, people with and without disabilities)	Qualitative	No
15	The disabled person (dp) and the manager: reflections on learning and competencies in the construction of diversity in organizations	Serrano, C.; Brunstein, J.	2011	12 individuals (6 PwD and their direct supervisors)	Qualitative	No
16	Insertion of people with disabilities in Brazilian enterprise	Carcalho-Freitas.M.N.; Marques, A.L.	2010	163 individuals (HR professionals, health and safety's at work professionals, PwD supervisor)	Quantitative	No

(continued)

Table 10.1 (continued)

Article	Title	Author	Year	Sample	Method	CI
17	The inclusion of disabled people in business: responsibilities, practices and pathways	Bahia, M.S.; Schommer, P.C.	2010	16 (PwD, supervisors, managers)	Qualitative	No
18	Ways people with disability are seen: an empirical study of the construct of conceptions of disability in work situations	Carvalho-Freitas, M.N.; Marques, A. L.	2010	227 MBA (Master in Business Administration) students	Quantitative	No

PwD People with Disability
CI Some connection with Circle of Inclusion: *A* (Inclusive Recruitment & Discrimination Selection; *C* (Colorful Socialization & Training); *E* (A safe place for all); *NO* (any connection)

framework for social partnership is still at an early stage (Schrey 2007). This is the case of Brazilian Trade Union model that limits and constrains the true Social Dialogue.

The Brazilian Trade Union model is not governed by freedom of association, since Brazil has not ratified Convention N. 87, established by ILO. This fundamental convention sets forth the right for workers and employers to establish and join organizations of their own choosing without previous authorization. Workers' and employers' organizations will organize freely and not be liable to be dissolved or suspended by administrative authority. Consequently, in Brazil there is a lack of respect for the right of freedom of association and incipient collective bargaining, due to a industrial relations system deeply rooted in a political and historical context, which was consolidated in a "social protection model", as opposed to a more liberal, flexible one (Cardoso 2004). Thus, the Trade Union model in Brazil prevents the full development of Social Dialogue (Godoy 2010). In this context, social inclusion of minority groups in private organizations has been done 'by top down public policies without a broad discussion with representatives of employer and workers, such as the Law for People with Disabilities (Law No. 13,146), for instance.

Although scarce and recent, the studies in Brazil discuss, in general, the representation of different groups in organizations, and organizational practices for an effective inclusion. Another trend of investigation studies the feelings and experiences of minorities, and organizations' quota policies targets. We can also highlight studies that address specific discrimination processes with respect to race/ethnicity, gender or age, or racism, sexism and ageism, as the main sources of *isms*. It is worth noticing that these studies point how such *isms* mean that prejudice (i.e., attitude) or discrimination (i.e., behavior) do exist in the organization. They refer to the organization's own institutionalized oppression system in its context, which creates, implements and maintains phenomena such as lack of equal opportunity for growth within the organization, biases in recruitment, segregationist organizational policies, among others (Cox 1994). Being institutionalized, they need little or no participation of individuals to their continuity, hence being kept for their own purposes, forming a vicious cycle.

In the following paragraphs we will briefly describe the findings of the reviewed studies, following the steps of the Circle of Inclusion in the human resource management system, introduced in Chap. 1 (please see Arenas et al., Chap. 1 in this volume). Presotti (2011) investigated the visions and practices of diversity management and their effects on inclusion, using as main reference the paradigms of diversity management by Thomas and Ely (1996). Clearly referring to *Inclusive Recruitment and Discrimination-free Selection* step, the author identified a tendency in organizations to manage their diversity from the discrimination and justice perspective (i.e., quotas as a way of promoting justice). Nevertheless, organizations seem to have built in its discourse the *Learning and Effectiveness* paradigm (Thomas and Ely 1996), which includes diversity as a source of learning and effectiveness in the organization.

Within the theme of *isms*, some relevant work deserve attention. Zauli et al. (2012) investigated the attitude of the Brazilian House of Representatives in relation to equal opportunities and career advancement of Women.[1] Referring to *Performance Appraisal and Compensation* step, they observed that opportunities to engage in leadership positions in the House of Representatives is lower for Women when compared to Men. The same relationship was found by Zidório (2012) in hospitals, which is also consistent with the surveys of the ILO, which shows that the female presence is only 5% in high-rank positions in Brazil (ILO 2015).

Sexual discrimination was investigated by Irigaray et al. (2010), who identified the use of humor as a legitimate way of ensuring discrimination against Homosexuals in organizations. As for ageism, Nascimento (2010) observed evidence of discrimination (by age) within police organizations. Other studies present an overview of age discrimination in recruitment and selection practices, specifically aimed at the elderly and retirement (França and Stepansky 2012). Pereira and Hanashiro (2014) also studied the practice of discrimination in organizations, and noticed that professionals unemployed aged over 45 did use several strategies in order not to reveal the true age. Once again, these studies can be understood as representatives of the *Inclusive Recruitment and Discrimination-free Selection* step, when the Circle of Inclusion is referred to.

Cerqueira and Pérez-Nebra (2013) and Oliveira and Pérez-Nebra (2012) conducted a series of in-depth interviews with cleaning employees, identifying mechanisms of exclusion and discrimination that operate in their work environments. Clearly connected with the *A Safe Place to All* step, the authors observed

[1]It is common in the diversity and inclusion literature the use of the terms that define groups with first capital letters. We adopt this practice here to highlight and recognize the cultural significance of these group identities.

that different forms of discrimination ranged from subcontracting (i.e., outsourcing), to the relationship between peers (i.e., ignoring the employee's name). Such mechanisms impact the organization in terms of its turnover and employees' relations, considering the social invisibility of these employees and their consequent social devaluation. This study also identified correlations with the gender, since this professional category is typically made up of Women in the country.

Most studies that deal with diversity and inclusion practices in Brazilian organizations are focused on People with Disabilities (PwD), as shown in a survey conducted in the years of 2010 and 2015, in the electronic library SPELL®. As such, in almost their entirety, these studies deal with Inclusive Recruitment and Discrimination-free Selection processes, a clear recurrent theme in Brazil. The reason for this is that Brazil enforced quotas for PwD and for youngsters, the latter being commonly hired as apprentices or interns. However, after more than 20 years since the publication of the PwD's Law, there are continuing difficulties of organizations in adapting their practices to the laws and to the needs of these people (Campos et al. 2013; Carvalho-Freitas and Marques 2010; iSocial 2015; Presotti 2011).

Two antagonistic positions are present when it comes to enforcement of quotas for PwD's. On the one hand, managers state as a reason for non-compliance of the law the lack of people with compatible skills with the position, and the lack of government support (Presotti 2011; Campos et al. 2013). On the other hand, HR professionals indicate that the qualification of persons with disabilities is average or above average when compared to persons without disabilities (iSocial 2015), although few are the references made to the steps *Colorful Socialization and Training* and *Work designs that work*. These two positions reveal an important contradiction that must be deepened. From the point of view of PwD, there is the recognition of quotas as a facilitator of access to the labor market. However, they realize that there is distrust of their skills and capabilities, and difficulties in accessibility and promotion within the company (Vianna et al. 2012), in contrast to the perception of themselves as positive and not limited by disability (Coelho 2012). These data are consistent with research conducted by Leão and Silva (2012) that identified the excess of suffering over pleasure at work, by PwD due to physical and mental exhaustion and lack of recognition at work.

Similarly, a survey conducted with 1519 HR professionals in Brazil, revealed that only 3% said that the reason for hiring PwD is due their working potential, while 86% say that hire the PwD only to comply with the quotas law, and finally, only 2% do so because they value diversity (iSocial 2015). Thus, there are indications that there is still prejudice against this group, and it is possible that this is impacting on both their exclusion *from* work and *at* work.

As discussed by Presotti (2011) and previously by Saraiva and Irigaray (2009), it is remarkable the internalization of a politically correct speech in diversity, which is not necessarily accompanied by the application of this speech. Themes such as *Developing Multiple Careers* and *Termination* are not even discussed, while others such as *Inclusive Recruitment* are emphasized, what per se draws a picture regarding Inclusion in Brazilian organizations. In order for the practice to be increasingly closer to the theory, we must invest in policies and management tools, making efforts for the accomplishment of inclusion as practice.

10.3 Diversity and Inclusion in Brazil

10.3.1 What's the Scenario?

In recent years, Brazil begins to dawn a timid attention to the issue of diversity and inclusion (Hanashiro et al. 2011). As noticed elsewhere, "we do not address the intellectual debate in academia regarding the concept of inclusion, neither the tension regarding its conceptual breakthrough" (Hanashiro 2016, p. 86). The international studies have been used in Brazil more as a theoretical reference, than a possibility for immediate application. This is due to historical, cultural and social differences, which give different contexts for businesses, and especially to the access to goods and power for different social groups. Even so, Brazilian cultural diversity is visible, which places its discussion at a compulsory level and, above all, a promising one. The status of the implementation of inclusion in the Brazilian reality is the same of the classic studies on diversity of the 80s and 90s. Still, most recent studies can serve as a horizon for which to aim.

10.3.2 Main Practices in Brazilian Organizations: Affirmative Action and Diversity Training

Affirmative action programs, themselves, do result in making organizational demographics more diverse with the compulsory insertion of historically under-represented groups. However, inclusion is more difficult to be achieved than diversity (Winter 2014). Policies and practices of training are welcome to create an inclusive culture. To talk about inclusion in Brazilian organizations means, largely, to understand the impacts of the Law for People with Disabilities (Law No. 13,146), due to its scope and impact on management. Some affirmative action policies aimed at different social groups do contribute to the expansion, directly or indirectly, of diversity and inclusion in Brazilian organizations.

10.3.2.1 Affirmative Action in the Public and Private Sectors

The United Nations Development Programme (UNDP) has assumed an important role as a network for the development of cultural diversity, social inclusion and quality of life. Its concern with human development has seeded affirmative action programs at different levels and countries, aiming the social and economic inclusion of historically excluded populations. In Brazil, the idea of affirmative action programs (AAP) is based on the understanding that social phenomena are not natural, but a result of the various social interactions (Presotti 2011), hence the need for political intervention in reversing the inequality in a given society (Alves and Galeão-Silva 2004). One of the landmarks of policies against discrimination and in favor of equal treatment was given in 1948 with the Universal Declaration of Human Rights (UN 1948).

Studying AAP, Menezes (2003) discussed the Brazilian Public Policies for Social Inclusion, and claimed the importance of the participation of the private sector for the implementation and success of these policies. According to the authors, almost all of Public Policies for Social Inclusion in Brazil, especially in the economic field (generation of employment and income), depend on the public and private sectors in order to promote social inclusion. A good example is the Law 10,097/2000 (known as Apprentice Law) which plays the role of a professional training tool, to generate income and employment for under aged (especially lower income) through training and internship in companies. To improve access of youngsters to the labor market, the Law requires of the company to hire a percentage of young employees. In the same vein, the Law 8,213/1991 requires companies with more than 100 employees to have in their workforce from 2 to 5% rehabilitated people or people with physical or intellectual disabilities. Thus, it appears that companies have a strategic role in the success of inclusive public policies that are organized by the Brazilian government, whether at the Federal, State or Municipal levels (Menezes 2003).

Also seeking a greater social inclusion the government programs 'Education for All' and the 'All the School' point to the fact that the formal education problem in Brazil is not limited to the inclusion of PwD, once there is a large percentage of people without learning difficulties still outside the room of class. As discussed by Glat and Nogueira (2002), in the past decade about 3.8 million children and young people (4–17 years) were out of school, which was reflected in actions that were taken in both the public and private sectors, in order to minimize this gap. With regard to higher education, Almeida and Ernica (2015) indicate that during the 2000s there was a significant expansion of this educational group in Brazil, from the perspective of social inclusion.

Regarding the public higher education, AAP have been around longer than its private counterpart, and have played an important role for the expansion of social inclusion. Feres Jr. and Daflon (2015) point out that more than 70% of State and Federal public universities practice some kind of affirmative action since 2011, mainly through quotas systems and student finance systems. In 2012, the government introduced an ambitious measure to expand social inclusion and equity of opportunity, by the Law 12,711/2012. This law states that at least 50% of students of federal universities and institutes are those who have completed high school in public schools. In filling in these vacancies, 50% will be reserved for students from families with low income (at or below 1.5 minimum salaries per capita). This program still has a racial perspective (based on self-declaration), and vary according to the proportion of Blacks, Brown and Natives in the state's population of Brazil where the institution is located.

The same can be observed in civil society. According to Lima (2010) significant changes in the society regarding the racial theme can already be perceived due to the adoption of AAP. Although, according to the author, the debate has strongly focused on the quota system for public universities, the actions of past governments and civil society have similar programs in other areas. However, AAP are still scarce in the country if we consider all excluded groups in organizations. And there are still operational problems when it comes to those AAP that have been implemented, such as difficulties for recruiting skilled workers, discrimination regarding the programs themselves, and cultural barriers, such as that of the myth that in Brazil we live in "a country without prejudices." Although it can be considered as a way to move political responsibilities from the public to the private sphere (Presotti 2011), AAP in the country are still insufficient, and those in place remain with little or no impact assessed.

An affirmative action program that has been going in the opposite direction of the social inclusion of low-income people is Bill 112/2010. The Bill states that the board of directors of public companies, as well as other companies controlled by the federal government must have a minimum of 40% Women in its composition by the year 2024. The proposition for the implementation of quotas on the board derives from a Brazilian reality that remains almost unchanged: the presence of Women on board of directors represents only 8% of the 2647 effective positions in 2011 (IBGC 2009).

10.3.2.2 From Diversity to Inclusion: Training

Public policies aimed at social inclusion are fulfilling its role in the democratization of higher education. However, some evidences (Aranha Neto 2014) show that the institutions involved have yet not developed initiatives for the permanence of these students in the university and their integration in environments that do not reflect the profile of quota students. This reality highlights the importance of socialization practices in order to integrate groups of different social identities in the academic environment. Similarly, we can argue that employees from different cultural identities in Brazil still need actions oriented towards their socialization to the working group. Organizational socialization refers to "the way in which the learning experiences of people who assume new positions, status, or roles in organizations are structured by others within the organization" (Van Maanen 1989, p. 45). These people, according to Van Maanen, acquire a social knowledge and experience required to perform a specific activity in the organization. Regarding its feasibility—to make the individual an effective member of the organization—organizational socialization reflects "the individual's integration process with the organization in the exercise of certain office" (Borges and Albuquerque 2004, p. 333).

Organizational socialization, thus, is so important for all employees in transition (of office, job, business etc.), as well as it seems exceptionally relevant to the effectiveness of diversity policies (see also Medina and Gamero, Chap. 9 in this volume). It is assumed that, in the case of minority (historically underrepresented groups) the primary socialization (the one learned in family) and secondary (learned in other settings) may have been different from the dominant group. Thus, regarding PwD employees, who are facing a reality still little experienced by most of them, data from a survey conducted by Carvalho-Freitas and Marques (2010) with PwD managers showed that few actions are carried out by the Human Resources sector for their integration in Brazilian organizations. The reason, according to respondents, is based on the fact that they consider PwD equal to other employees, denying any special needs (Carvalho-Freitas and Marques 2010, p. 269). Surveys conducted in two Brazilian companies (Maia and Carvalho-Freitas 2015) revealed that workers with disabilities are subjected to an integration training when joining the company that do not use systematic methodological strategies that ensure equal opportunities for PwD. Preferably, companies performed on-the-job training, i.e., learning is done informally in the routine work, with monitoring and the help of their colleagues, who were not previously prepared for such task.

The practices developed by successful private companies (mainly global) in Brazil point to a more promising reality for effective diversity management. A survey conducted by the authors for this chapter on institutional sites of a sample of these companies—*Serasa/Expirian, PriceWaterhouse Cooper (PWC)s, Ernst & Young (EY), Natura and Ericsson*—showed that the best practices of diversity are aimed at training, development and education. In a nut shell, the focus of such policies is directed especially to Women and PwD. These companies develop various practices to promote diversity and inclusion, and have formal area within its organizational structure responsible for these issues. All have training programs, formal or informal, mandatory or voluntary. Among the training strategies stand out: events for promotion of inclusive culture (Serasa/Expirian), mentoring programs, coaching or sponsorship to support the construction of social networks and accelerate Women's career to achieve strategic positions (PWC, EY and Ericsson), portals for specific topics (PWC and Ericsson), release films (Ericsson), among other minor initiatives.

On the top of these specific programs, some companies go beyond the organizational wall when it comes to diversity. For example, Ericsson and PWC are engaged in the HeforShe solidarity movement. This is an international campaign of United Nations for gender equality and Women empowerment. It aims to engage Men and Boys to new gender relations without attitudes and sexist behaviors. Natura is inserted in one association named "movement Woman 360". This association is a Brazilian Non-Governmental Organizations made up of 12 companies. Its purpose is to stimulate the engagement of business communities on the issue of gender equality and address ways to incorporate this discussion in their business strategy. PWC provides racial equality training through partnership with Zumbi of

Palmares, a Brazilian Black college. Ericsson participates in the international program Girls in the Information and Communication Technologies day. These socially responsible initiatives express an incipient concern for an education for (and towards) diversity.

The way diversity training is faced in Brazil reflects the way diversity is understood in its organizational context. The way diversity is perceived is a broad question, and the expression diversity in organizations can refer to any features that make people different from each other. When organizations deal with the issue of diversity only from the perspective of avoiding discrimination, they seek to work through justice and compliance with laws. Thus, it is expected that all are treated equally and respected. Some examples of this approach are the Brazilian affirmative action programs and quotas for minorities. Yet, the Straight White Man still has the largest market wage, sometimes while playing the same organizational role of a Woman. For these reasons there are affirmative action programs and quotas for minorities; it is an attempt to include them. When the organization uses this type of strategy to deal with diversity, it can be said that the workforce is diverse, but the company does not take advantage of people with different stories who, in turn, cannot add to the organization in terms of different forms of vision, and performance of tasks. More broadly the issue of diversity is based on the understanding that Women, Blacks, Natives, Homosexuals and many other groups can bring knowledge and different views, which are important and competitively relevant to how the work can be done, enabling new and innovative ways to design processes, achieve goals, create teams, communicate ideas and lead. Most of private institutions in Brazil have no direct concern to inclusion issues. Bearing in mind that the main approach of these companies is the pursuit of profit, inclusion seems to be a question of merely complying with the legislation.

10.4 Conclusions and Agenda

Cultural diversity in organizations also means the inclusion of different people from Men, White, Heterosexual, married and with an average of 1.7 children—the "normal" Brazilian. And what is more important: diversity and inclusion recognize, reinforce and value the differences and similarities between people, which will help to achieve organizational and individual goals, on a win-win focus (Torres and Pérez-Nebra 2014). Culturally diverse organizations have both the potential for strong competitive advantages, as well as to be dysfunctional. In a simple illustration of this idea, we see that the practice of pointing racial groups through nicknames is considered in Brazil a friendly and caring practice (Rothblatt 2003), contributing to the notion of "racial democracy" in Brazil. However, this racial consciousness is pluralistic in symbolism, including race, social class and social position simultaneously, which creates a particularly virulent form of racism: the silent racism (Mikulak 2011).

However, diversity and inclusion have become part of social and organizational policies recently. The culture of racism, sexism, ageism and many other *isms* is still very present both in society as a whole, and in public and private institutions and organizations in particular. Much still has to be done in research terms and, more than that, much needs to be done to society and working organizations in order for them to realize the importance of these constructs, resulting in less prejudiced attitudes and more acceptance of diversity (Torres and Pérez-Nebra 2014). To accept individually, socially and historically significant differences is to develop attitudes in society that bring together actions that minimize, or even ban behaviors of discrimination and privilege within and outside organizations. It is expected that members of all groups are treated fairly in order to feel genuinely included, with equal opportunities in organizations and outside them. Fortunately, the themes of cultural diversity and inclusion are gaining an increasing space on the agenda of many organizations, however there is still much to be done to inclusive diversity management in organizations.

The fact that in none of the 54 Brazilian publications revised for this chapter the theme of Social Dialogue was identified or discussed may also reflect a serious agenda, both for scholars and practitioners. More incentives and efforts should be directed towards collaborative and social and organizational networks in order to smooth the progress of the diversity management and inclusion in Brazilian organizations. Further, we suggest that official organizational policies should move from a paternalist perspective, to one that brings together the participation of the State, employers' and workers' representatives in an economic and social policy-making in a variety of contexts, aiming at inclusion and diversity. Changes should start in the current instances, for instance, in the often rather confrontational Brazilian government-union-employer relations, when the State, unions and companies tend to only schedule discussions at the time of the yearly collective bargaining negotiation sessions.

A fair management of diversity and inclusion goes beyond the implementation of a set of practices to minimize the diversity mix in the organization. It refers to an environment that people may feel that they are accepted by the working group, authentic, and respected as a member of a given identity group. More than the demographic insertion through public policies or voluntary initiatives, inclusion requires training strategies towards historically excluded social groups. These are critical, since the corporate environment can be perceived as unfavorable and unfriendly by members of minority groups in general. It has been said that people search and aim to live with similar others, in the light of the Attraction and Similarity paradigm (Byrne 1971), and with a tendency to associate with and connect with people similar to themselves (McPherson and Smith-Lovin 2001). Due to that, diversity training initiatives are imperative, both for preparing the minority group members and their managers, so that they can live, share, value and create an opening environment to all.

References

Almeida, A. M. F., & Ernica, M. (2015). Inclusão e segmentação social no Ensino Superior público no Estado de São Paulo (1990–2012). *Educação e Sociedade, 36*(130), 63–83.

Alves, M. A., & Galeão-Silva, L. G. (2004). A crítica da gestão da diversidade nas organizações. *Revista de Administração de Empresas, 44*(3), 20–29.

Aranha Neto, M. O. (2014). Compreendendo a dinâmica de inclusão e/ou exclusão de alunos bolsistas do PROUNI. Dissertação, Universidade Presbiteriana Mackenzie.

Bill No. 112/2010, of April 6th, 2012. Defines the minimum attendance of women in public services. *Brazilian Federal Senate*.

Borges, L. O., & Albuquerque, F. J. B. (2004). Socialização Organizacional. In J. C. Zanelli, J. E. Borges-Andrade, & A. V. B. Bastos (Orgs.), *Psicologia, Organizações e Trabalho no Brasil* (pp. 331–356). Porto Alegre: Artmed.

Byrne, D. (1971). *The attraction paradigm*. New York: Academic Press.

Campos, J. G. F., Vasconcelos, E. P. G., & Kuglianskas, G. (2013). Incluindo pessoas com deficiência na empresa: estudo de caso de uma multinacional brasileira. *Revista de Administração (São Paulo), 48*(3), 560–573.

Cardoso, A. (2004). *Industrial relations, social dialogue and employment in Argentina, Brazil and Mexico*. Prepared for the ILO as part of the studies for the Global Employment Agenda.

Carvalho-Freitas, M. N., & Marques, A. L. (2010). Inserção de pessoas com deficiência em organizações brasileiras: um estudo com empresas socialmente responsáveis. *Gestão.Org – Revista Eletrônica de Gestão Organizacional, 8*(3), 483–502.

Cerqueira, F. B. P., & Pérez-Nebra, A. R. (2013). Significado do trabalho para mulheres de serviços terceirizados de limpeza e conservação. Trabalho apresentado no XXXIV Congresso Interamericano de Psicologia, Centro Universitário de Brasília, Brasília.

Coelho, M. R. (2012). A inserção da pessoa com deficiência no mercado de trabalho sob o ponto de vista da pessoa com deficiência. Relatório Final de Estágio Supervisionado apresentado como requisito para o grau de bacharel em Administração Empresarial pela Universidade do Estado de Santa Catarina – UDESC.

Cox, J. R. T. (1994). *Cultural diversity in organizations: Theory, research and practice*. San Francisco, CA: Berrett-Koehler Publishers.

Ferdman, B. M. (2014). The practice of inclusion in diverse organizations. In B. M. Ferdman & B. Dease (Eds.), *Diversity at work: The practice of inclusion* (pp. 3–54). San Francisco, CA: Jossey-Bass.

Feres, J., Jr., & Daflon, V. T. (2015). Ação afirmativa na Índia e no Brasil: um estudo sobre a retórica acadêmica. *Sociologias (UFRGS), 17*(40), 92–123.

França, L. H. F. P., & Stepansky, D. V. (2012). Voices from the front: the view from Brazil. *Global Aging: Issues and Action, 8,* 40–42.

Glat, R., & Nogueira, M. L. L. (2002). Políticas educacionais e a formação de professores para a educação inclusiva no Brasil. *Revista Integração, 24*(14), 22–27.

Godoy, D. (2010). Desafios e perspectivas para o diálogo social no brasil: o modelo sindical brasileiro e a reforma sindical. *Revista* do *Tribunal Superior do Trabalho (TST), 76*(4), 110–115.

Hanashiro, D. M. M. (2016). A dinâmica da in(ex)clusão no ambiente organizacional. In B. R. E. Saeta & J. M. C. Ferreira (Orgs.), *A diversidade humana e o contexto laboral* (pp. 84–114). São Paulo: Editora Mackenzie.

Hanashiro, D. M. M., Torres, C. V., Ferdman, B. M., & D'Amario, E. Q. (2011). *Medindo Inclusão no Ambiente Organizacional: Uma Visão "Emic" da Escala de Comportamento Inclusivo.* Trabalho apresentado no XXXV Encontro da Associação Nacional de Pós-Graduação e Pesquisa em Administração, Rio de Janeiro, RJ.

IBGC. (2009). Mulheres nos Conselhos. http://www.ibgc.org.br/Pesquisas.aspx. Accessed October 2, 2016.

ILO—International Labour Organization. (2015). *Women in business and management: Gaining momentum*. http://www.ilo.org/wcmsp5/groups/public/—dgreports/—dcomm/—publ/documents/publication/wcms_334882.pdf. Accessed January 4, 2016.

Irigaray, H. A. R., Saraiva, L. A. S., & Carrieri, A. P. (2010). Humor e discriminação por orientação sexual no ambiente organizacional. *Revista de Administração Contemporânea, 14*(5), 890–906.

iSocial. (2015). *Profissionais de Recursos Humanos: Expectativas e percepções sobre a inclusão de pessoas com deficiência no mercado de trabalho* (2nd ed.). São Paulo: Autor.

Law No. 10,097, of December 19th, 2000. Regulates about Consolidation of Brazilian Labor Laws regarding working age limit for minors. *Amendment to the Brazilian Constitution 1988.*

Law No. 12,711, of August, 29th, 2012. Regulates about the equality of opportunity of access to universities and public institutions. *Amendment to the Brazilian Constitution 1988.*

Law No. 13,146, of July 5th, 2015. Regulates about the inclusion of people with disabilities (Policy of People of Deficiencies). *Amendment to the Brazilian Constitution 1988.*

Law No. 8,213, of July 24th, 1991. Regulates about the workers social security. *Amendment to the Brazilian Constitution 1988.*

Leão, M. A. B. G., & Silva, L. S. (2012). Vivências de trabalhadores com deficiência: uma análise à luz da Psicodinâmica do Trabalho. *Revista Brasileira de Saúde Ocupacional, 37,* 159–169.

Lima, M. (2010). Desigualdades Raciais e Políticas Públicas: Ações Afirmativas no Governo Lula. *Novos Estudos-CEBRAP, 87,* 77–95.

Maia, A. M. C., & Carvalho-Freitas, M. N. (2015). O trabalhador com deficiência na organização: um estudo sobre o treinamento e desenvolvimento e a adequação das condições de trabalho. *REAd, 82*(3), 689–718.

McPherson, M., & Smith-Lovin, L. (2001). Birds of a feather: Homophily in social networks. *Annual Review of Sociology, 27,* 415–444.

Menezes, P. L. (2003). *A Ação Afirmativa no Direito Norte Americano*. São Paulo: Editora Revista dos Tribunais.

Mikulak, M. (2011). The symbolic power of color: Constructions of race, skin color and identity in Brazil. *Humanity and Society, 35,* 62–99.

Nascimento, T. G. (2010). *Polícia: uma identidade em discussão: construção, validação e aplicação de um Instrumento*. Dissertação: Universidade de Brasília.

Oliveira, M. K., & Pérez-Nebra, A. R. (2012). Quando sair é a única saída: Uma análise do sentido do trabalho e a da rotatividade na função de servente de limpeza. Trabalho apresentado no *V Congresso Brasileiro de Psicologia Organizacional e do Trabalho,* Universidade Estadual do Rio de Janeiro, Rio de Janeiro.

Pereira, M. F. M. W. M., & Hanashiro, D. M. M. (2014). Etarismo em Seleção: a dura realidade para quem tem acima de 45 anos no Brasil. Trabalho apresentado no XXXVIII Encontro da Associação Nacional de Pós-Graduação e Pesquisa em Administração, Rio de Janeiro, RJ.

Pless, N. M., & Maak, T. (2004). Building an inclusive diversity culture: Principles, processes and practice. *Journal of Business Ethics, 54,* 129–147.

Presotti, L. (2011). *Gerenciar a diversidade cultural nas organizações: caminhos para a inclusão.* Dissertação de Mestrado: Universidade de Brasília.

Pulignano, V. (2011). The EU and industrial relations modernization: Supranational state support for trade union and social partner modernization and social dialogue. *The International Journal of Human Resource Management, 22*(18), 3775–3793.

Qin, J., Muenjohn, N., & Chhetri, P. (2014). A review of diversity conceptualizations: Variety, trends, and a framework. *Human Resource Development Review, 13*(2), 133–157.

Roberson, Q. M. (2006). Disentangling the meanings of diversity and inclusion in organizations. *Group and Organization Management, 31*(2), 212–236.

Rothblatt, J. (2003). Ó Crioulo! Addressee terms that address race relations in Brasil. Unpublished paper. Recuperado em 02/06/2013 de:http://www.udc.es/dep/ix/cac/aa1998/rothblatt.htm.

Saraiva, L. A. S., & Irigaray, H. A. R. (2009). Políticas de diversidade nas organizações: uma questão de discurso? *Revista de Administração de Empresas, 49*(3), 337–348.

Schrey, D. (2007). *The role of labour unions in Latin America in the process of globalization*. Belgium: The Konrad-Adenauer-Stiftung (KAS).
Shemla, M., Meyer, B., Greer, L., & Jehn, K. A. (2014). A review of perceived diversity in teams: Does how members perceive their team's composition affect team processes and outcomes? *Journal of Organizational Behavior*. doi:10.1002/job.1957.
Thomas, D. A., & Ely, R. J. (1996). Making differences matter: A new paradigm for managing diversity. *Harvard Business Review, 74*(5), 79–90.
Torres, C. V. & Pérez-Nebra, A. R. (2014). Diversidade e Inclusão nas Organizações. In J. C. Zanelli, J. E. Borges-Andrade, & A. V. B. Bastos (Orgs), *Psicologia, Organizações e Trabalho no Brasil* (2 Ed., pp. 526–546). Porto Alegre: Artmed.
UN—Organização das Nações Unidas (1948). *Declaração Universal dos Direitos Humanos*. New York: Autor.
Van Maanen, J. (1989). People processing: Strategies of organizational socialization. *Organizational Dynamics, 7*(1), 18–36.
Vianna, L. M. B. P., Tardelli, P. G. A. S., & Almeida, L. I. R. (2012). Inclusão e mercado de trabalho: uma análise das dificuldades enfrentadas por pessoas com deficiência em ingressar no mercado de trabalho da Grande Vitória (ES). *Destarte, 2*(2), 95–109.
Winter, M. F. (2014). From diversity to inclusion: An inclusion equation. In B. M. Ferdman & B. R. Deane (Eds.), *Diversity at work: The practice of inclusion* (pp. 3–54). San Francisco, CA: Jossey-Bass.
Zauli, A., Torrres, C. V., & Galinkin, A. L. (2012). Câmara dos Deputados: democracia e igualdade de oportunidades entre mulheres e homens? *Cadernos de Psicologia Social do Trabalho, 15*(1), 49–64.
Zidório, A. P. C. (2012). Desenvolvimento da carreira de executivas do Hospital Universitário de Brasília-HUB. *Participação*, 42–51.

Companies' Websites

Ericsson. (2016, September 9). Retrieved from https://www.ericsson.com/br/article/diversity-po_732377866_c.
Ernest & Young. (2016, September 9). Retrieved from http://www.ey.com/br/pt/about-us/our-people-and-culture/diversity-and-inclusiveness.
Natura. (2016, September 9). Retrieved from http://www.natura.com.br/relatorio-anual/2015/nossa-cultura/promocao-da-diversidade.
PriceWaterhouse Cooper. (2016, September 9). Retrieved from http://www.pwc.com.br/pt/quem-somos/diversidade-inclusao.html.
PriceWaterhouse Cooper. (2016, September 9). Retrieved from http://www.pwc.com.br/pt/publicacoes/setores-atividade/financeiro/2016/women-world-aligning-gender-diversity-international-mobility-financial-services.html.
Serasa/Experian. (2016, September 9). Retrieved from http://noticias.serasaexperian.com.br/blog/2015/06/03/rede-empresarial-de-inclusao-lanca-guia-para-melhorar-o-processo-de-contratacao-de-pessoas-com-deficiencia-no-mercado-de-trabalho/.

Chapter 11
A Safe Place for All: Social Dialogue and Workplace Harassment

Ria Deakin

11.1 Introduction

Increased diversity in the workplace is to be welcomed. Inclusive workplaces increase the opportunities for members of marginalized groups to participate in the labor market and, where managed effectively, a diverse workforce can lead to innovation and to increased performance (Roberge and van Dick 2010). Increases in cultural diversity, however, may also lead to increased levels of conflict (Chua 2013). This is not necessarily a bad thing, and conflict, where based on task, or differences in experience or knowledge, may result in positive organizational outcomes (Jehn et al. 1999). However, conflict on the grounds of social group membership is problematic. Aside from possible negative impacts on productivity, failure to deal with such conflict may expose an organization to legal liability due to violations of anti-discrimination law. Further, negative treatment based on social characteristics can have severe implications for individual health (Raver and Nishii 2010) and threatens collective notions of social justice (Fredman 2011). An inclusive employer must therefore ensure that the work environment is safe for all. For the purposes of this chapter, a safe workplace is to be understood as one where every individual is treated in a way which respects their dignity and does not harm their physical or mental health and well-being. The question, however, of how to effectively manage diversity in order to create safe and inclusive workplaces is not a straightforward one.

Social dialogue through the coordination and joint (bipartite) action of the social partners can potentially play a crucial role in creating and sustaining safe and inclusive workplaces. The social partners represent both sides of the employment relationship, i.e., employers (and their representative associations) and trade unions and/or employee representatives. The State may also play an important role in

R. Deakin (✉)
University of Huddersfield, Huddersfield, UK
e-mail: r.deakin@hud.ac.uk

A. Arenas et al. (eds.), *Shaping Inclusive Workplaces Through Social Dialogue*, Industrial Relations & Conflict Management,
DOI 10.1007/978-3-319-66393-7_11

social dialogue, leading to tripartite action. Here, the discussion will primarily focus on bipartite social dialogue and the extent of cooperation and coordination between the social partners.

In this chapter, the role of bipartite social dialogue in navigating diverse workplaces will be considered in relation to workplace harassment. Examples of social dialogue in this context are varied and include trade union and employer collaboration over training, and the inclusion of harassment protection through collective bargaining. Although the points may also apply to general forms of harassment, the discussion will focus on harassment on social demographic ('social group') grounds, e.g., race, sex, and sexual orientation, since these most explicitly engage with the tensions in managing socially diverse workforces. Focusing on harassment and social dialogue also helps to expand the discussion around social dialogue and equality. In comparison with the attention given to tackling direct and indirect discrimination in relation to access to employment and benefits (e.g., equal pay) (Dickens 1999; Hoque and Bacon 2014), preventing and dealing with harassment appears to have received little attention.

It will be argued that social dialogue can, and should, play two interrelated roles. The first concerns the setting of standards of behavior to prevent harassment, and the second concerns the enforcement of those standards. It will, however, be suggested that the scope for social dialogue is greater in the case of the former, since traditional adversarial structures and the increasing push toward the informalization of workplace resolution limits opportunities in the latter. The role of the social partners and of HRM policies in shaping these roles will be highlighted. The operation of social dialogue at regional and national levels will be considered, but the focus will primarily be on the possibilities at company level. Comparative examples will be introduced but the focus is on the UK context. Finally, to conclude, theoretical and practical implications for diversity management will be offered. Firstly, however, the importance of addressing harassment will be outlined.

11.2 Positioning Harassment as a Legal, Moral, and Business Issue

Harassment may take many forms, and may, or may not be linked with social characteristics. Regardless of form taken, in the context of creating safe workplaces for all, it is vital to note that harassment should never be tolerated. The need to distinguish harassment from other forms of negative conflict, such as bullying, is beyond the scope of this chapter, save to acknowledge the differences in legislative protection across countries. For example, in the UK, there are no specific anti-bullying laws, but there are for harassment (Equality Act 2010, and through judicial extension the Protection from Harassment Act 1997); while a number of other countries (e.g., France and Australia) provide legal protection from both. Of particular interest to the creation of inclusive workplaces are forms of harassment related to social group or status characteristics, i.e., sexual or racial harassment. The need to address problems of harassment may be justified on a number of interrelated grounds: legal, moral, and business.

11.2.1 The Legal Case

Social and institutional shifts, particularly over the past few decades, have led to workplace changes—both in the organization of work, and the composition of the workforce. Workplaces have become increasingly diverse with participation in the labor market of historically disadvantaged groups such as woman and black and minority ethnic groups rising. This increased participation has been facilitated by anti-discrimination legislation, grounded in most instances, in the principle of equal treatment (Hepple 2013). Certainly across EU member states, Directives at the European-level have influenced the development of domestic law across a number of demographic characteristics. Such legislation was traditionally concerned with removing barriers to participation and progression in the workforce (Fredman 2011). However, it became apparent that prohibiting unequal treatment—either directly or indirectly—was not sufficient and that presence in the workplace may expose individuals to negative treatment beyond access to opportunities and resources. This resulted in the recognition of harassment as a distinct form of discrimination in many jurisdictions.

Failure to adequately deal with problems of harassment in the workplace can, therefore potentially expose employers, to legal liability. The presence and effective enforcement of Dignity at Work and/or grievance and disciplinary policies and procedures reflecting national legal frameworks are thus an important tool for addressing harassment and developing safe workplaces.

11.2.2 The Moral Case

Fredman (2011) suggests that it is the notion of 'dignity' that should be seen as underlying regulation around harassment. Treatment which violates dignity is explicitly included in the definition of harassment in the Equality Act 2010 (s26). This is also reflected in the frequent accommodation of anti-bullying, harassment, and discrimination guidance and protection in workplace Dignity at Work policies. For Fredman, dignity should be understood as 'the value attached to individuals simply by virtue of humanity' meaning 'that all are entitled to equal concern and respect' (2011: 20). This is interesting because it helps to explain why, aside from legal compliance, organizations should be seen to have a moral duty to respect and protect the dignity of their employees).

Taking the notion of dignity as the starting point for the need to address harassment also has important consequences for situating harassment on social group grounds as a collective and not a solely interpersonal or individualized issue. Divorcing disadvantage from an individual's own group membership, it explains why, as a society, individuals who are not a member of a disadvantaged group may object to the sexist, racist, or homophobic behavior of others. Collective recognition of the relative social disadvantage of certain groups, regardless of whether or not an individual is a member of those groups thus recognizes the socially embedded and contextualized nature of harassment. Approaching harassment in this way should be distinguished from the more micro-level understandings of diversity and inclusive approaches which characterize managing diversity arguments.

In these approaches, individuals are treated solely as individuals, with social group membership becoming just one of a number of potentially relevant personal characteristics, and in which questions of equality and disadvantage are marginalized or overlooked (Healy et al. 2011). This contextualized approach also necessitates an extension of the discussion about creating inclusive workplaces beyond the psychologically grounded social identity theory and in-group/out-group classification utilized in some research into diversity and conflict (e.g., Guillaume et al. 2017). Both managing diversity and social identity approaches are insufficient to explain why conflict based on demographic differences is collectively objectionable, regardless of group membership.

11.2.3 The Business Case

In both the managing diversity and social identity and diversity discourses, the desire to create an inclusive workplace, manage difference, and minimize conflict arising from demographic difference predominantly is motivated by a business case (e.g., Noon 2007). The focus on the bottom line characterizes the shift from the social justice case in equal opportunities to the business case in managing diversity, and most recently in inclusion (Oswick 2011). Organizational failure to manage diverse groups, for example by neglecting to address sources of contention and/or address sexual harassment, can have an adverse impact of the health and well-being of the target, as well as other members of the work group (Benavides-Espinoza and Cunningham 2010); these may then result in decreased productivity. Conversely, diversity properly managed, i.e., where to bring insight from varied experiences and skills may lead to innovation and access to wider customer bases and markets (Noon 2007). Empirical evidence to support the business case for diversity is varied (Riley et al. 2013) but it does, nevertheless persist as the dominant discourse for encouraging the creation of inclusive, yet diverse workplaces.

Positioned within the business case, harassment can be seen as a cost which needs to be minimized. While this recognition is important in understanding how the need to address problems of harassment may be sold to employers—and indeed how it may shape the nature of the interaction between the social partners—focusing solely on the business case should be avoided as it risks decollectivizing and decontextualizing societal problems.

It is proposed in this chapter, therefore, that any consideration of how to deal with harassment must be contextualized within social, as well as organizational conditions, and therefore needs to account for the legal, moral, and business dimensions of social group harassment. Having set out the conditions under which harassment may arise, and why it is important to address it, the discussion will now turn to what may be considered as the dual role of social dialogue in creating safe workplaces: setting standards against harassment (1) and ensuring those standards are upheld and enforced (2).

11.3 Standard Setting and the Role of Social Dialogue

Simply accepting that harassment at work should not be tolerated is not sufficient. HR policies, procedures, and practices also need to be put in place to ensure this rejection of intolerance is realized in practice (see Hoel and McBride, Chap. 3 in this volume).

11.3.1 The Source of Standards of Around Harassment

Protection from harassment on social grounds may come from a number of sources, including international agreements and law, national activism, and/or a combination of influences.

For example, the development of sexual harassment in the USA is an interesting case of national activism translating into legal and public policy changes. Of particular relevance to discussions of the role of the social partners is the initial reluctance of some male-dominated unions to support the push for action on sexual harassment by the minority number of female members (Baker 2008). Overtime, however, strikes and actions designed to raise awareness around sexual harassment and how to deal with it led to greater union and employee association involvement in the cause. Some unions, for example the United Auto Workers in 1979, negotiated specific clauses in contracts with Ford and Chrysler to make sexual harassment complaints subject to grievance procedures (Baker 2008). Activism from unions, other collective associations and a series of law suits led to the development of federal legislation against sexual harassment.

However, the development of protection in other countries has not necessarily been quite so insular. The European Union, for example, has been instrumental in developing normative and practical obligations and guidance for all Member States.

11.3.2 *European-Level Standards*

For Member States of the European Union, the guiding force for protection against harassment on social grounds now largely comes from European-level Directives, for example Directive 2000/78/EC establishing a general framework for equal treatment in employment and occupation. This extended protection on grounds of religion or belief, disability, age, and sexual orientation. However, in some instances, for example the UK, protection predates EU legislation, with sexual harassment being recognized by judicial interpretation of the discrimination provisions in the predecessor to the Equality Act 2010, the Sex Discrimination Act 1975 (Fredman 2011).

Harassment in various directives related to equal treatment is 'deemed to be a form of discrimination…when unwanted conduct related to any of the grounds… takes place with the purpose or effect of violating the dignity of a person and of creating an intimidating, hostile, degrading, humiliating or offensive environment' (Art 2 (3), 2000 Directive). Definition of the concept is to be 'in accordance with the national laws and practice of the Member States'. This latter qualification has led to differences in implementation across Member States.

Regulation at the EU level attaches to Member States to ensure provisions are reflected in domestic law. However, the legislation itself charges employers with the responsibility to protect workers. It is therefore crucial to look at the interaction between normative standards expressed at international level and the way they are transferred to, and implemented at, the national and workplace level, and the role trade unions and/or employee representatives can play in this.

11.3.2.1 Autonomous Framework Agreement on Harassment and Violence at Work

The 'Framework agreement on harassment and violence at work' was entered into by the European Social Partners in 2007 (Monks et al. 2008). The framework agreement aimed to raise understanding and awareness around harassment at work, as well as 'provide employers, workers, and their representatives at all levels with an action-oriented framework' (Monks et al. 2008). While acknowledging the responsibility placed on employers under EU law, it positions harassment and violence at work as shared and joint problems, thus requiring collaborative solutions and actions. The need to respect dignity and avoid economic and social costs is identified in the opening paragraph.

Unlike this chapter, the agreement is not limited to social group harassment but harassment and violence more generally. Harassment is accordingly described as occurring 'when one or more worker or manager are repeatedly and deliberatively abused, threatened and/or humiliated in circumstances relating to work'. This is a potentially controversial definition and differs from the Directive in two key respects (aside from the reference to protected groups): the reference to repetition of behavior and the requirement for the behavior to be deliberate.

The framework agreement also moves beyond a relatively normative description to include an indication of the forms behavior considered to be harassment may take. Harassment may be physical, psychological, and/or sexual. When seeking to explain how organizations may appropriately manage diversity and address harassment, understanding the content to be assigned to broad definitions is fundamental. Including possible examples not just of the form the behavior may take, but also specific examples of behavior that will be considered harassment is helpful for guiding behavior. The framework agreement also sets out guidance on what was agreed to be the appropriate steps to be taken when dealing with a complaint of harassment. These included investigating complaints and ensuring all parties involved get an impartial hearing and are treated fairly.

11.3.2.2 Implementation of Standards—National, Sectoral, and Company Action

The flexibility afforded by the agreement was reflected in the way it was utilized across Member States. The results of a review published in 2011 on the initial application of the framework agreement indicated different responses in different national contexts (ETUC et al. 2011). The responses varied in relation to the depth in which the social partners may be seen to have influenced, or at least sought to influence, national and company-level policy and practices.

In ten of the countries who responded to the call for evidence for the review, an assessment of national legislation had been triggered (ETUC et al. 2011). Social partners in seven countries, including Denmark, France, Latvia, and the Netherlands, had entered into overarching agreements. Protection had been included in collective agreements in the hospital sector in Portugal and had been the subject of collective bargaining in Spain, and had been incorporated in the form of behavioral rules in Codes of Conduct at the company level in some German companies (ETUC et al. 2011).

The most common action was concerned with increasing awareness and understanding, broadly grouped under 'complementary activities'. Examples included undertaking research into the prevalence of harassment (e.g., the Netherlands), the design and delivery of training courses at cross-national (ETUC) and national level (e.g., Austria). Perhaps unsurprisingly given the traditions in the UK around social partnership (Stuart et al. 2011), action was limited to the production of joint guidance on the framework agreement. The guidance document is hosted on a dedicated Web site but has not been updated to reflect changes in the legislative framework around harassment, and still provides an option to be contacted in 2010 to participate in the European-level review of the framework. It should suffice to say that while the guidance itself may still broadly stand, there appears to have been little momentum to ensure its continued use in practice.

The review was conducted several years ago now so it is difficult to determine whether the framework agreement has continued to have an impact, or whether the initial actions have led to longer term improvements—a line of inquiry certainly worthy of future exploration. Some recent insight is offered by a Eurofound report published in 2015 (Eurofound 2015). The report offers examples of social dialogue in unilateral, bilateral, and tripartite forms, operating at various levels across Member States. For example, in 2013, the European social partners (the European Transport Workers' Federation—ETF and the European Community Shipowners' Associations—ECSA) launched a project to tackle harassment and bullying in the maritime industry.

At a national level, the extent of coordination between social partners varied. A decentralized, largely company-level, approach was adopted in a number of countries, including Bulgaria, Croatia, and the Czech Republic. There was evidence of some weakly coordinated national and/or inter-sectoral level in places such as Austria, Cyprus, and Luxembourg. Such initiatives were largely focused on prevention, for example the establishment of an anti-mobbing procedure by a social partner joint group in Poland which employers and trade unions are encouraged to apply at company level (Eurofound 2015: 40, 44). There was a greater degree of coordination in countries such as Germany, where institutions for social dialogue are stronger.

The findings in the Eurofound report reflect the conclusions of the 2011 report reviewing the agreement; the 2011 review concluded by identifying national context as the biggest constraint on the potential for social partner action and influence on harassment and violence at work. As may be seen by the nature of the approaches adopted, the structures and processes—formal and informal—around social dialogue in the different Member States indicate the difficulties in transposing cross-national social dialogue to lower levels in any uniform way.

Nevertheless, the responses demonstrate a range of possibilities for social partners to work together—at national, sectoral, and workplace level—to help to improve the safety of workplaces by raising awareness of harassment as a problem and in recommending and instituting practices to deal with it should it arise.

Before moving away from the influence and possible lessons to be learnt from the EU-level framework, in the context of diversity and inclusion, it is useful to note that though there is an explicit aim to ensure workplaces are safe for all, this is not approached from an equality agenda. The agenda is grounded in health and safety, consistent with an EU-level social dialogue focus on psychosocial risks at work (Ertel et al. 2010). This may help to explain the focus on general harassment. From a managing diversity perspective, it is interesting to note that 'sexual' is the only characteristic-related form of harassment explicitly identified. Collaboration in a number of Member States (e.g., Finland) was concentrated on the involvement of health and safety representatives—these may or may not have been attached to a trade union. To accommodate this approach within diversity and inclusion, the involvement of equality representatives from the social partners should be encouraged. For example, trade union equality representatives in the UK have been involved with championing the agenda for equality (Bennett 2010). Ensuring equality representatives are consulted in organizational development and review of standards and procedures could help to encourage social dialogue in the area of harassment.

11.3.3 Standard Setting—Social Dialogue or Unilateral Action?

Aside from those examples reported in the context of the 2007 framework agreement it appears to be difficult to find examples of where social dialogue—i.e., a collaboration between the social partners—has been used to address harassment in any systematic way. This may be because it is rare in practice, or perhaps more likely, because it is not explicitly or adequately isolated from other equality issues in reporting on, for example, collective bargaining; it may also be because campaigns and actions around 'harassment' at work do not distinguish between social group and more general forms of harassment. Neither of these approaches is inherently problematic if they result in improved awareness and conditions at work, although it does present issues if clarity around the treatment of social group harassment specifically is sought (as is, of course, the case here).

While collective bargaining as a form of social dialogue is to be encouraged, its scope and impact are arguably limited. Bargaining appears to focus around the inclusion of anti-harassment provisions in policies and establishing appropriate responses (Hoque and Bacon 2014). These are certainly of importance for sending the message that harassment should not be tolerated and for setting standards of acceptable behavior. However, without further and continued attention to ensure that those standards are realized and enforced in practice, the potential for creating safe workplaces may be limited. Further, depending on national context, the scope and coverage for collective bargaining may be severely constrained (e.g., Marginson 2015).

Aside from a relatively small number of examples of the use of bipartite and tripartite social dialogue, there is a plethora of examples across countries where the social partners (frequently trade unions) have acted unilaterally to address issues of harassment at work (Eurofound 2015). An example of this is the Irish Business and Employers Confederation (IBEC) issuing guidance to its members on the issue of bullying, harassment, and sexual harassment.

Interestingly against a concern for safety for all, campaigns and actions seem to have focused only on certain characteristics—e.g., sexual and/or racial harassment (including the framework agreement which singled out sexual harassment), and more recently homophobic and transphobic behavior. Unfortunately, space does not permit a detailed consideration of the reasons for the focus on these groups, but it would certainly be interesting to explore further. It would also be interesting to see what impact the apparent prioritization of certain characteristics has on attempts to manage diverse workplaces.

The first aspect of the dual role of social dialogue (standard setting) has been given a lengthier treatment than the second will have, chiefly because this is arguably where the greatest potential for social dialogue lies—even if realizing that potential requires overcoming a number of barriers. The second role relates to the role of social dialogue in ensuring the policies and practices around harassment are adequately implemented and enforced.

11.4 Enforcement and the Role of Social Dialogue

Introducing anti-harassment policies in workplaces is undoubtedly a crucial first step in seeking to manage diverse workplaces and in indicating that negative and unwanted conflict will not be tolerated. It is, nevertheless, just the first step, and the mere presence of policy statements and associated practices is not sufficient. It may serve to help guide individuals in their behavior, but the examples included in employee handbooks and supporting documents cannot be exhaustive, meaning there will always be areas where it is not clear whether behavior amounts to harassment or not. Even where examples are given, the culture and/or practice in an organization may mean that problematic behavior is not dealt with (e.g., Harrington et al. 2012). In organizations where policies are in place but there is a culture where no, or inadequate, action is taken to add function to the policy, it is not possible to say that adequate steps are being taken to create a safe and inclusive workplace. What is needed, therefore, are supportive practices that are consistently and adequately employed.

These supportive practices may be proactive or reactive and include those evident in the social partner responses in some countries to the 2007 framework agreement, e.g., training programs to increase awareness and knowledge (proactive), and/or the development of communication systems, such as the introduction of harassment advisors (reactive). Again, however, these practices, though useful, need to accompany appropriate practices for dealing with complaints of harassment once they arise.

11.4.1 Collectivism, Individualization, and Arguments for Dealing with Harassment

When moving from questions of standard setting to enforcement, there is a problematic shift away from the treatment of harassment as a collective concern and toward an individualization of the problem. This shift is particularly difficult to reconcile with the moral case which treats both the responsibility and interest in dealing with harassment as a collective endeavor, an approach which sits comfortably with calls for the involvement of social dialogue in managing diversity issues. This approach, however, stands at odds with the requirement in many countries (including the UK) for complaints of harassment to be dealt with on an individual basis.

The move away from collectivism toward individualization is necessitated by the legal framework for harassment which treats it as an individual right, requiring an individual to bring a claim, and removing opportunities for collective enforcement (Colling 2006). As the content of HR policies likely mirror legal requirements (legal case), where complaint procedures associated with harassment are accommodated within grievance and disciplinary procedures, the individual right in law is translated into organizational practices. This problem is not isolated to harassment but is typical of the trend in many countries (and in EU law) to increase the number of individual rights, with a consequent marginalization of scope for collective activity (Colvin 2016).

A weakening in trade union power may constrain the opportunities for social dialogue, perhaps because there may be no union presence, or because there is insufficient motivation for employers to collaborate. Colling (2006) suggested that this is not necessarily the case. Drawing on examples in relation to health and safety and parental leave, he suggests that individual rights could be extended through collective bargaining. This is an interesting proposition but again, in the context of managing diverse workplaces, is perhaps limited to standard setting, rather than enforcement.

In relation to enforcement, the legal treatment of harassment seemingly compartmentalizes the collective interest in prohibiting harassment from the responsibility to do so—placing the responsibility to prevent harassment on an organization, and the responsibility to ensure organizations do this on individual complainants. Of course in practice it is not necessarily that clear cut. Trade unions and/or employee representatives may have a role but it may be limited to providing advice, support, and representation on an individual basis (e.g., see Van Wanrooy et al. 2014).

11.4.2 Enforcement—Antagonism, Marginalization, or Cooperation?

The guidance for dealing with harassment given in the 2007 framework agreement was outlined above. It recognizes the potential for both formal and informal routes, although there is far more detail in relation to the former. The steps given reflect those established as good HR practice in relation to harassment e.g., Acas Code of Practice on Discipline and Grievance (UK). One of the initial steps is investigating a complaint.

11.4.2.1 Formal Antagonism

Conducting an investigation serves an important function in retaining the societal element in complaints of harassment since it evaluates the behavior(s) complained of against objective criteria and standards of reasonableness and is not solely reliant on individual perception (Hoel and Einarsen 2011; Hoel and McBride, Chap. 3 in this volume). In terms of managing a diverse range of characteristics, using a shared point of reference, rather than relying on perception can be a helpful tool in balancing individual sensitivities and in facilitating inclusive environments. Indeed there is a 'reasonable' requirement in the Equality Act 2010. Investigations can, therefore, play a crucial role in channeling complaints and determining what the appropriate steps to take are. For example, if a complaint is upheld, the perpetrator should be disciplined accordingly.

Investigations and formal procedures are, however, often (and increasingly), criticized for being too bureaucratic and resource intensive (e.g., Roche and Teague 2012). Of particular relevance to the current discussion, they are also criticized for being too adversarial in nature, forcing an organization into a defensive position (e.g., Bingham 2004). Thus, in principle, this approach positions the social partners on opposing sides, rather than as partners, and potentially inhibits any opportunities to cooperate to contemplate and deliver wider changes which may arise out of individual complaints, for example better diversity training for all or increased awareness campaigns.

11.4.2.2 Informal Resolution and Risks of Marginalization

To address these perceived limitations and move away from an antagonistic approach, the use of informal mechanisms is encouraged. This encouragement is, however, often qualified with a rather vague and somewhat unhelpful statement of 'where appropriate' (or something to that effect) (e.g., Bennett 2014)—quite when this will be appropriate in respect of allegations of harassment is open to debate. The term informal refers to a range of responses, beginning at a 'quiet word' with the parties involved, through to structured processes such as mediation.

There are interesting, though largely unexplored parallels between the business case arguments in diversity and inclusion literature and those deployed in favor of an increased use of alternative (informal) approaches in conflict literature. This is particularly true in relation to arguments for the use of workplace mediation. In both instances, there is a concern with minimizing the costs associated with conflict, a decontextualization of issues, and a use of the language of individual empowerment and cooperation (for example see Bennett 2014). On the face of it, these similarities may allow for synergies facilitating the management of diverse workplaces; a more critical approach would doubt this. In this chapter, workplace mediation is to be understood as a voluntary, confidential, and informal but structured process where two or more parties to a dispute seek a mutually agreed outcome in the presence of an impartial third party. There are differences in national structures and practices around mediation (e.g., see Bollen et al. 2016). At the workplace level, it may explicitly be incorporated into HR procedures or it may sit outside them and be used in a more ad hoc way. In places where mediation is well-established, e.g., the USA, it may be used strategically (see Lipsky et al. 2016).

Workplace mediation is not concerned with evidence or with establishing 'rights' which poses questions about its appropriateness in relation to harassment where legal rights do exist. The benefit of this is allowing individuals to determine for themselves what an appropriate resolution to their situation is, and thus more inclusive teams may be developed on the basis of these agreements. What this feature of mediation may also serve to do, however, is circumvent agreed standards of acceptable behavior and allow organizations to shift both the blame for the behavior and the responsibility for addressing it onto the individuals involved (Keashly and Nowell 2011). This reasoning is evident in some trade union opposition to mediation (Bleiman 2008), and takes the concern over the individualization of problems one step further since it leads not only to an individualization but also a personalization, i.e., it risks treating problems of organizational (and societal) significance as purely interpersonal ones. This amounts to a further decontextualization of social group harassment.

In addition to the impact on the moral, and possibly legal, arguments for dealing with harassment, from a social dialogue perspective, an increased use of mediation may serve to marginalize both employers and trade unions/employee representatives in the enforcement process. This marginalization may prohibit opportunities for a sharing of insight between an employer and trade union representatives, as well as limiting, or even excluding unilateral action of either partner. For example, though HR and a line manager may be aware that mediation is taking place, the confidential nature means they have no control over the outcome and may only receive information confirming whether an agreement has been reached, with little or no information as to the detail of the dispute, or the resolution. The use of representatives in mediation may well be discouraged (as is the case in the UK) which positions employee representatives in a predominantly advisory function (Branney 2016). This marginalization or even exclusion—compounded by the requirement for confidentiality may preclude the identification of systemic problems in an organization and may also prevent an organization from sending the right messages out to its workforce that diversity is valued and intolerance is not.

11.4.2.3 Informal Resolution and Opportunities for Cooperation

Though they do raise questions about the role of employers and trade unions/employee representatives in enforcing standards, the problems associated with mediation as a tool for inclusion do not render social dialogue redundant in relation to harassment. The decision to utilize more informal approaches, and to introduce (or review) the use of mediation should be a joint one—with both employer and employee interests represented (Branney 2016; Saundry et al. 2013). Cooperation in this way, particularly in relation to addressing the 'where appropriate' qualification potentially allows for a balancing of the business case with other concerns. It allows social dialogue to work not only to set the standards around acceptable behavior but also around how alternative approaches are used, meaning there may be additional scope for employee representatives and employers to ensure standards are sufficiently enforced, thus helping to create a safe and inclusive environment.

11.5 Implications for Research and Practice

This chapter has argued for the need to ensure that discussions and actions around the treatment of harassment on the grounds of social group characteristics are sufficiently contextualized since its prohibition serves a collective societal, as well as individual and organizational purpose—a consequence which is overlooked or ignored in some approaches to diversity and inclusion. The role of social dialogue in relation to harassment generally, and social group harassment more specifically, and in the context of creating inclusive workplaces, is a surprisingly underdeveloped area. In light of these two observations, the discussion in this chapter has two main implications for future research and practice aimed at creating safe and inclusive workplaces.

The first is the need for more research into the role of social dialogue in relation to social group harassment. The focus placed on social dialogue and harassment by the 2007 framework agreement was an important step, but almost a decade later, the composition of the workforce continues to change and problems persist, indicating the need for a renewed effort. Rather than a focus on measuring the prevalence of the problem, an inquiry into the qualitative experiences of harassment would help to improve understandings of how diverse characteristics are being used to create divisive and hostile environments. This would provide an insight to develop and deliver nuanced and targeted training and guidance, helping to add substance to the normative standards. It would also help to provide justification for the moral case for dealing with harassment.

Structuring future discussions around the dual role suggested here will also help with identifying areas of strength and weakness and thus help to inform efforts. Distinguishing between standard setting and ensuring those standards are enforced exposed a limitation for the operation of social dialogue. While it is important to ensure that organizations provide protection from harassment and procedures associated with that, this, by itself is not sufficient. A combination of proactive and reactive steps need to be taken. Proactive steps may include the provision of training and guidance as suggested above. Reactive steps require the fair application of procedures and ensuring adequate action is taken to deal with complaints of harassment when they arise. This is where scope for social dialogue may be most constrained.

Challenges are posed both in respect of formal responses, and informal responses —challenges which are worthy of greater attention if social dialogue is to be able to deliver on both standard setting and enforcement. One of the key challenges is seeking to overcome the individualization, and potential personalization, of harassment, and ensure that collective interests are adequately respected. This may, for example, simply involve employer and employee representatives debriefing following a harassment complaint to ensure any wider problems and/or opportunities for learning are identified.

The need to balance individual and collective aspects forms the basis of the second implication: the need to challenge the dominance of the business case in diversity and inclusion discourses. This is obviously easier said than done, but is, nevertheless an important task. By ensuring discourse around diversity remains tied to concerns for morality, dignity, and equality, the social contextualization of the issues is retained; causes and consequences of harassment do not exist in a vacuum and therefore activities to prevent and address these should acknowledge this. A focus on the impact on the bottom line may lead to underlying issues—for example a lack of understanding of what is acceptable language or behavior and why—not being addressed. The in-group/out-group focus in literature around conflict and diversity also risks decontextualizing issues. While it is understandable that an employer may wish to focus on the business case, ensuring that the social and moral aspects are considered could fall to trade unions and/or employee representatives.

As a closing remark, it is necessary to acknowledge that though social dialogue provides potential for creating safe and inclusive workplaces, this potential is necessarily limited to those workplaces, sectors, and/or countries where cooperative relationships between the social partners exist or can be fostered. However, where this is not the case, opportunities for unilateral action by the social partners may exist and are also worthy of further exploration (e.g., O'Sullivan et al. 2015).

References

Baker, C. N. (2008). *The women's movement against sexual harassment*. Cambridge University Press.

Benavides-Espinoza, C., & Cunningham, G. B. (2010). Bystanders' reactions to sexual harassment. *Sex Roles, 63*(3–4), 201–213.

Bennett, T. (2010). Exploring the potential of the union equality representative. *Employee Relations, 32*(5), 509–525.

Bennett, T. (2014). The role of workplace mediation: A critical assessment. *Personnel Review, 43*(5), 764–779.

Bingham, L. B. (2004). Employment dispute resolution: The case for mediation. *Conflict Resolution Quarterly, 22*(1–2), 145–174.

Bleiman, D. (2008). Should I try mediation? A discussion paper for trade union members.

Bollen, K., Euwema, M., & Munduate, L. (Eds.). (2016). *Advancing workplace mediation through integration of theory and practice*. Springer International Publishing.

Branney, V. (2016). Workplace mediation and UK trade unions: The missing link? In R. Saundry, P. Latreille, & I. Ashman (Eds.), *Reframing resolution: Innovation and change in the management of workplace conflict* (pp. 191–214). London: Palgrave Macmillan.

Chua, R. Y. (2013). The costs of ambient cultural disharmony: Indirect intercultural conflicts in social environment undermine creativity. *Academy of Management Journal, 56*(6), 1545–1577.
Colling, T. (2006). What space for unions on the floor of rights? Trade unions and the enforcement of statutory individual employment rights. *Industrial Law Journal, 35*(2), 140–160.
Colvin, A. (2016). Conflict and employment relations in the individual rights era. In D. Lipsky, A. Avgar, & R. Lamare (Eds.), *Managing and resolving workplace conflict (Advances in Industrial and Labor Relations)* (Vol. 22, pp. 1–30). Bingley: Emerald Group Publishing Limited.
Dickens, L. (1999). Beyond the business case: A three-pronged approach to equality action. *Human Resource Management Journal, 9*(1), 9–19.
Ertel, M., Stilijanow, U., Iavicoli, S., Natali, E., Jain, A., & Leka, S. (2010). European social dialogue on psychosocial risks at work: Benefits and challenges. *European Journal of Industrial Relations, 16*(2), 169–183.
ETUC, BUSINESSEUROPE, UEAPME, & CEEP. (2007). *Framework agreement on harassment and violence at work.* Signed by the European Social Partners on 26 April 2007.
Eurofound. (2015). *Violence and harassment in European workplaces: Causes, impacts and policies.* Dublin.
Fredman, S. (2011). *Discrimination law* (2nd ed.). Oxford: Oxford University Press.
Guillaume, Y. R., Dawson, J. F., Otaye-Ebede, L., Woods, S. A., & West, M. A. (2017). Harnessing demographic differences in organizations: What moderates the effects of workplace diversity? *Journal of Organizational Behavior, 38*(2), 276–303.
Harrington, S., Rayner, C., & Warren, S. (2012). Too hot to handle? Trust and human resource practitioners' implementation of anti-bullying policy. *Human Resource Management Journal, 22*(4), 392–408.
Healy, G., Kirton, G., & Noon, M. (2011). Inequalities, intersectionality and equality and diversity initiatives. The conundrums and challenges of researching equality, inequalities and diversity. In G. Healy, G. Kirton and M. Noon (Eds.) *Equality, Inequalities and Diversity. Contemporary Challenges and Strategies* (pp. 1–17). Basingstoke: Palgrave Macmillan.
Hepple, B. (2013). Back to the future: Employment law under the Coalition government. *Industrial Law Journal, 42*(3), 203–223.
Hoel, H., & Einarsen, S. (2011). Investigating complaints of bullying and harassment. In S. Einarsen, H. Hoel, D. Zapf, & C. Cooper (Eds.), *Bullying and harassment in the workplace: Developments in theory, research and practice* (2nd Ed., pp. 341–357). Florida: CRC Press, Taylor and Francis.
Hoque, K., & Bacon, N. (2014). Unions, joint regulation and workplace equality policy and practice in Britain: Evidence from the 2004 Workplace Employment Relations Survey. *Work, Employment & Society, 28*(2), 265–284.
Jehn, K. A., Northcraft, G. B., & Neale, M. A. (1999). Why differences make a difference: A field study of diversity, conflict and performance in workgroups. *Administrative Science Quarterly, 44*(4), 741–763.
Keashly, L., & Nowell, B. (2011). Conflict, conflict resolution and bullying. In S. Einarsen, H. Hoel, D. Zapf, & C. Cooper (Eds.), *Bullying and harassment in the workplace: Developments in theory, research and practice* (2nd ed., pp. 423–446). Florida: CRC Press, Taylor and Francis.
Lipsky, D., Avgar, A., & Lamare, J. (2016). The evolution of conflict management policies in US corporations: From reactive to strategic. In R. Saundry, P. Latreille, & I. Ashman (Eds), *Reframing resolution: Innovation and change in the management of workplace conflict* (pp. 219–314). London: Palgrave Macmillan.
Marginson, P. (2015). Coordinated bargaining in Europe: From incremental corrosion to frontal assault? *European Journal of Industrial Relations, 21*(2), 97–114.
Monks, J., de Buck, P., Benassi, A., & Plassmann, R. (2008). Implementation of the European autonomous framework agreement on work-related stress. *Report by European social partners adopted at the Social Dialogue Committee on June 18*, 2008.

Noon, M. (2007). The fatal flaws of diversity and the business case for ethnic minorities. *Work, Employment & Society, 21*(4), 773–784.

O'Sullivan, M., Turner, T., Kennedy, M., & Wallace, J. (2015). Is individual employment law displacing the role of trade unions? *Industrial Law Journal, 44*(2), 222–245.

Oswick, C. (2011). The social construction of diversity, equality and inclusion. An exploration of academic and public discourses. In G. Healy, G. Kirton, & M. Noon (Eds.), *Equality, inequalities and diversity. Contemporary challenges and strategies* (pp. 18–36). Basingstoke: Palgrave Macmillan.

Raver, J. L., & Nishii, L. H. (2010). Once, twice, or three times as harmful? Ethnic harassment, gender harassment, and generalized workplace harassment. *Journal of Applied Psychology, 95*(2), 236.

Riley, R., Metcalf, H., & Forth, J. (2013). The business case for equal opportunities. *Industrial Relations Journal, 44*(3), 216–239.

Roberge, M. É., & Van Dick, R. (2010). Recognizing the benefits of diversity: When and how does diversity increase group performance? *Human Resource Management Review, 20*(4), 295–308.

Roche, W. K., & Teague, P. (2012). The growing importance of workplace ADR. *The International Journal of Human Resource Management, 23*(3), 447–458.

Saundry, R., McArdle, L., & Thomas, P. (2013). Reframing workplace relations? Conflict resolution and mediation in a primary care trust. *Work, Employment & Society, 27*(2), 213–231.

Stuart, M., Martínez Lucio, M., & Robinson, A. (2011). 'Soft regulation' and the modernisation of employment relations under the British Labour Government (1997–2010): Partnership, workplace facilitation and trade union change. *The International Journal of Human Resource Management, 22*(18), 3794–3812.

Van Wanrooy, B., Bewley, H., Bryson, A., Forth, J., Freeth, S., Stokes, L., et al. (2014). *The 2011 workplace employment relations study. First findings* (4th ed.). London: Palgrave Macmillan.

Chapter 12
Unlocking Closets at Organizations

Donatella Di Marco

> I was working there one year, I lasted one year. I was not able to last anymore. I thought "[now] I am young, but if I spend the next ten years here [...] they will realize that I am lesbian and they will destroy me [...]". Actually, I wanted to leave the job because I perceived discrimination there, it was bad there. There was a moment that I could not get up to go to work in the morning, because I was afraid. (Andreina, lesbian woman)
>
> When I arrive at [organization name] for the training, I receive a notebook with a cover about respecting diversity. In each sheet of the notebook, there was a drawing which represented a diversity trait. For example, in one sheet there were two man shoes, or two woman shoes, or three chairs, and one of them was a wheelchair. In another sheet, there were two couples: a man and a woman and two women, or two men. When I saw that there I said "Wow, here it is..." [gasp]. A few weeks later, after knowing people, [coming out] was natural, I don't remember how I came out, it was quite spontaneous. (Carlos, gay man)

Inclusion at the workplace is becoming a strategic pillar for organizations. Due to the multifaceted composition of the workforce and the changing nature of societies, practitioners, and academics have focused their attention on those dynamics that characterized the encounter of diverse people at work, and how organizations have incorporated such changes in their daily life. Gender, ethnic origin, disability, gender identity, sexuality, and age are just some of those identity traits that have been recognized in diversity management. The struggle against discrimination and the effort for fostering inclusion entail several meanings, according to the historical moment and the protected group considered. It includes eliminating obstacles that preclude the entrance of such protected groups into the workplace, removing barriers that do not provide equal opportunities for everybody, guaranteeing a fair treatment at work and decent work conditions, recognizing, and valuing individual differences as a strategic resource for organizations. And the list might continue. In some cases, we can say that we have experienced an evolution of the content and the meaning of diversity management: Nowadays, fighting against discrimination

This work was funded by the Spanish Ministry of Economy and Competitiveness (MINECO/FEDER), grant reference n. PSI2015-64894-P.

D. Di Marco (✉)
University of Seville, Seville, Spain
e-mail: ddimarco@us.es

A. Arenas et al. (eds.), *Shaping Inclusive Workplaces Through Social Dialogue*, Industrial Relations & Conflict Management,
DOI 10.1007/978-3-319-66393-7_12

and providing equal opportunities is not enough if organization does not promote inclusion at the same time.

Thinking that discrimination is an obsolete issue is a mistake: If it is true that western legislation and societies have rejected many discriminatory behaviors, other subtle forms of discrimination still exist (Jones et al. 2015).

The case of lesbian, gay, and bisexual (LGB) people represents one example of what has been said before. Nowadays in many countries, discrimination against LGB people is banned due to both LGB rights movements and the social shift that have led to LGB people inclusion in all the spheres of life, including the labor one. However, in many other parts of the world, non-heterosexual people and transgender people are victimized at legal and social level, being impossible for them to live their sexual orientation or identity without severe consequences (International Lesbian, Gay, Bisexual, Trans, and Intersex Association and Carroll 2016).

Moreover, international studies report that discrimination on the basis of sexual orientation is still present also in those countries where it is considered a crime (*Eurobarometer*, European Commission 2015; International Labour Organization 2015). Despite the progress in terms of acquisition of legal rights, Andreina and Carlos's stories, both Spanish workers, clearly represent the multifaceted experience of LGB people at work. Positive experiences intersect with open and subtle discriminations, provoking negative consequences for people and organizations (e.g., Di Marco et al. 2015b; Ragins 2004) and showing that Diversity Management policies have still not reached their goal.

12.1 LGB People at Organizations

Due to the range of consequences both discriminatory behaviors and the lack of inclusion entail, researchers have tried to find out the causes and solutions to reach inclusive workplaces for LGB people. Consequently, the scientists' interest has been focused on several aspects concerning the experience of LGB people at work and the issues analyzed have been numerous: The income imbalance faced by LGB employees, the presence of prejudice and negative stereotypes at an explicit and implicit level; their manifestation through discriminatory behaviors; consequences of discrimination at personal, interpersonal, and organizational level; and how the existence of supportive policies shape and influence the experience of LGB groups at work (e.g., Bryson 2016; Hatzenbuehler 2009; Ragins 2004). However, to our knowledge, little has been done in order to underline how to promote the inclusion of LGB employees through Social Dialogue, allowing and fostering participation of all the actors involved in the decision processes (e.g., Unions or Work Councils, human resource managers, government/administrations, employees, and LGB networks) which affect such protected groups (Bryson et al. 2012; Euwema et al. 2015; Nauta 2015). Following this approach, we try to identify how to improve instruments and practices that organizations might apply in order to shape a real Circle of Inclusion (Arenas et al., Chap. 1 in this volume) which includes LGB employees through Social Dialogue.

Before that, given the alarming international data on discrimination of LGB people at work (European Commission 2015, 2016; International Labour Organization 2015), we are going to focus on two aspects that still characterize the experience of such groups at work: Firstly, we will briefly analyze the disclosure process, focusing on the actors involved and roles played by organizations during this process. Secondly, we will shed light on "disrespectful" behaviors against LGB employees that, in some circumstances, might be interpreted as subtle discrimination. In fact, although in many countries the prevalence and impact of open discrimination have decreased (e.g., physical attacks, insults), there exist other incipient forms of discriminatory behaviors. Their effects harm people and organizations together with open discrimination (Jones et al. 2015). These two aspects affect the experience of LGB people at work (Di Marco et al. 2015a, b), and both have been widely studied by academia (Herek and McLemore 2013; Ragins 2008). Rather than revising all the existing studies in these fields, the goal of this chapter is to reflect on the role that organizations play when these issues arise within the work context. Moreover, we will try to highlight how Social Dialogue might intervene in such process, fostering the inclusion of LGB people at work.

12.2 Disclosing Sexual Orientation: Do Organizational Actors Play a Role?

Disclosure (or coming out) is the process by which LGB people reveal their sexual orientation. In the last few years, researchers have explored questions connected to this process within the inner circle (e.g., family, friends) and the organizational context. In the workplace, factors analyzed have been several: How people carry out such a process, strategies used by LGB people, causes, and consequences of revealing or covering sexual orientation at work (e.g., Clair et al. 2005; Croteau et al. 2008; Lidderdale et.al. 2007; Ragins 2004, 2008).

All these studies have shown the complex nature of this process and the dynamics that it entails. According to them, LGB people "decide" if they will disclose sexual orientation at work after "testing the waters" (Day and Schoenrade 1997; Ragins et al. 2003), that is, after studying to what extent context and colleagues tolerate and respect sexual and gender minorities. In others words, when a new LGB employee enters at an organization, she/he analyzes the context and people who live in it; She/he tries to discover colleagues' values (conservative vs. liberal ones) and attitudes toward LGB people. Finally, she/he decides to reveal sexual orientation or cover it, and the strategies that best fit that situation. Several studies have shown that this process is not linear (Ragins 2004). On the contrary, LGB people might decide to be open with some colleagues and cover their sexual orientation with others; or maybe they might give indirect information in order to disclose their sexual orientation to few or some colleagues.

Beyond the strategies, LGB employees use and the consequences of them, just recently researchers have started to conceive the disclosure process as an interpersonal process, of which results depend on LGB employees and the people who surround them (e.g., Di Marco et al. 2014). Consequently, two premises have to be considered. Firstly, for many LGB people, disclosing sexual orientation is not a "declaration" or "choice" but an issue of their personal domain that enters into the daily conversations, such as many other aspects of their personal life. Third parties might play a role in terms of being receptive or ignoring the information received. Secondly, it is necessary to consider to what extent LGB employees desire to share their personal life with their colleagues or create a barrier between the domains of their life.

Therefore, if we consider the disclosure process as the result of the interaction between LGB workers and their colleagues, we can consider such process as an issue of the employee's life which is involved in the construction of boundaries between the personal and the work domain. In fact, according to past studies (e.g., Anderson et al. 2001; Button 2004; Ragins 2008), people disclose (or cover) their sexual orientation giving (or hiding) information that indirectly can convey they are LGB. Both heterosexual and non-heterosexual people, indirectly, speak about their own sexual orientation, talking about their own partner, activities carried out during free time, etc. Therefore, people might wish to either disclose their sexual orientation at work, creating weak frontiers between personal and work domain, or to cover it, creating strong frontiers between both domains. However, the initial desire to disclose or cover sexual orientation at work might be violated by colleagues, who might ignore the information given, or openly suggest avoiding issues related to the personal life, guided by their own prejudice and negative stereotypes. On the contrary, the initial desire to cover sexual orientation at work (due to people's preference for not sharing information connected with the personal domain at the workplace) might be ignored, and LGB employees might be the target of continuous questions and rumors.

Both violations might be the cause of conflictive situations and negative consequences at individual (lower well-being, motivation, etc.) and organizational level (higher rate of turnout, absenteeism, etc.) (Di Marco et al. 2015a; Ragins 2004; Ueno et al. 2013).

At this point, several questions arise: Should organizations recognize this issue in order to create an inclusive workplace? Or does the disclosure of sexual orientation belong to the employees' private life? To what extent should organizations intervene?

12.3 The Subtle Power of Workplace Incivility

The disclosure process is not a unique issue that researchers have analyzed to understand the experience of LGB employees. It is just one piece of a more complex image that involved their reality at work. In fact, another important aspect widely studied is open discrimination against them (e.g., Herek 2009). Nowadays, while the focus on open discrimination has taken a second place, thanks to a legislative and societal shift, cover (or subtle) discrimination has captured the attention of many researchers, due to its consequences and scarce visibility. The covering of discrimination is difficult to identify because it is connected to prejudice and negative stereotypes that are often situated at an unconscious level. Consequently, negative attitudes and beliefs toward LGB people have not disappeared (Dovidio 2001; Herek and McLemore 2013), but are transmitted in a different way. Past studies have already shown how the presence of unconscious prejudice and negative stereotypes affect the experience of protected groups, such as women, black people, and immigrants (e.g., Cortina et al. 2001, 2013; Krings et al. 2014). In a context where negative attitudes against protected groups are not allowed by law and considered politically incorrect, they might be exteriorized through uncivil acts (e.g., Andersson and Pearson 1999), which are defined as ambiguous behaviors that break the established norms of respect in a certain context. Therefore, when these acts are mainly directed against protected groups, they might be an expression of unconscious (and sometimes conscious) prejudice and stereotypes.

Some studies (e.g., Di Marco et al. 2015b) have demonstrated that LG employees are still victims of uncivil acts, which are perceived as covered discrimination. The most widespread behaviors identified within organizations are as follows:

- Disrespectful language. It includes uncivil jokes and expressions, such as "poof," which enters in the daily and accepted language. Many times these expressions are not directed to LGB colleagues, but they are used in their presence and often refer to something negative.
- Subtle devaluation of non-heterosexuality. Also in this case, language is involved in cover discrimination. This group of behaviors refers to those comments that indirectly devaluate non-heteronormativity without being perceived as discriminatory by speakers (e.g., "He is very smart, even though he's gay").
- Stereotyping. Stereotypes represent people's beliefs about social groups. It is information that allows us to simplify the world where we live in, because it represents generalized beliefs. However, many times, such beliefs are wrong and attribute to a social group a set of negative features, behaviors. Stereotypes can lead to uncivil behaviors during social interactions.
- Intrusive questions. These refer to questions connected to sexual or private life that, usually, are not permitted at the workplace. In the study above mentioned, lesbian employees receive such type of questions more often, experiencing uncomfortable situations.
- Isolation. Involuntary ostracism is also a demonstration of negative attitudes. Forgetting to invite only a colleague who is LGB, when it is a repeated action, might be a sign of discrimination. Moreover, recent studies have shown that ignoring might be more harmful than direct discrimination (O'Reilly et al. 2014).
- Incivility related to the workplace. Finally, behaviors connected with the work domain (such as the level of workload received and lack of promotions) are a group of acts that even if it is not possible to define as uncivil, are still connected to prejudice and stereotypes.

These groups of behaviors are just an example of unconscious prejudice and stereotypes communicated in an ambiguous way. They are difficult to recognize for people who bring them. Organizations might want to look away, justified by the limited power they might have in unmasking subtle negative attitudes. Consequently, other questions arise: Should organizations intercede in order to make such processes visible? To what extent can organizations modify prejudice and negative stereotypes?

12.4 Is a Discrimination-Free Workplace Enough?

We have seen how unconscious prejudice and stereotypes are responsible for negative interpersonal dynamics at the workplace which involved LGB employees and their colleagues. Such dynamics affect the extent LGB people disclose or cover their sexual orientation at work and in turn, are also influenced by the perception of discrimination and workplace incivility. Although the legislation shifts have promoted the elimination of open discrimination in many countries, we have seen that other subtle processes might affect LGB workers' well-being and the real inclusion.

Reflecting briefly on issues such as disclosure process and workplace incivility against LGB employees led us to several questions of which answers are difficult to identify because a high number of factors intervene. However, despite the sensitiveness of the issues being handled, organizations cannot remain silent in the face of daily dynamics that involve LGB employees, especially when such dynamics become prejudicial for them (Fig. 12.1).

Starting with the disclosure process, several dilemmas are presented. The beginning point is probably related to the domain into which the disclosure of sexual orientation falls: Is it an issue that has to be relegated to the private life? Or can it enter into the public conversation? The answer is probably connected with another question: What does disclosing the sexual orientation mean? In fact, although it apparently seems like an issue that pertains to the private life, our daily conversations are continuously full of information that transmits our sexual orientation: Talking about a partner or free time is probably the easier form to convey this kind of information. Both heterosexual and non-heterosexual employees are involved in disclosing interactional dynamics, but often only the latter group realizes it (European Commission 2016).

Consequently, the domain into which sexual orientation falls is established by two other factors, regardless of if we are talking about LGB or heterosexual people. The first is set at an individual level, and it is linked to the desire of employees to segment or integrate their personal life at work. In fact, LGB or heterosexual people might prefer not to talk about their personal issues with colleagues, and in this case, their desire should be respected. However, we have to take into account that often the desire to cover sexual orientation is due to a perception of an unsafe and discriminatory climate in the organization. As shown in Fig. 12.1, the perception of overt and covert discriminations might affect the construction of boundaries between personal and work (thus public) domains. Therefore, LGB employees might fear the negative consequences of the disclosure process at work or at a personal level.

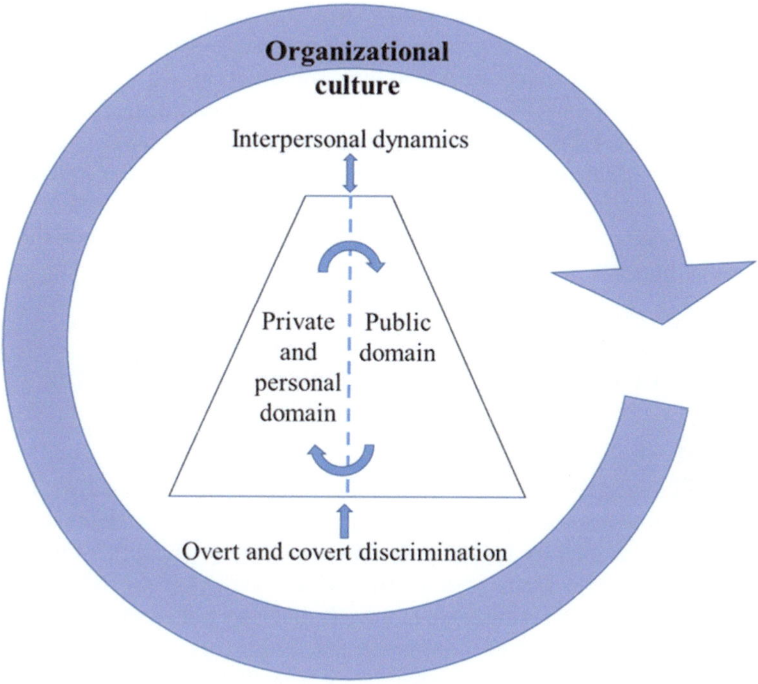

Fig. 12.1 Boundaries construction and disclosure dynamics in the workplace

On the contrary, LGB or heterosexual people might desire to integrate their personal life at the workplace. In that case, a second organizational factor has to be considered: The norms and policies established by the organization regarding to what extent it is possible to share or show information and elements that speak about workers' personal life at work (e.g., family photos), thus the organizational culture (Fig. 12.1). In that sense, policies such as "lean office," which require to remove all those objects that are not necessary to work from the workplace (Harford 2016; Knight and Haslam 2010), have to be applied to everyone. The problem arises when such policies do not exist but are applied informally only to LGB workers and are transmitted as a "kindly advice", in order to avoid problems of other nature, such as rumors, embarrassing questions, and discriminatory behaviors (Di Marco et al. 2015b). Therefore, such advice is intent to avoid those conversations related to LGB people's sexual orientation, thus a form of covert discrimination. When such situations happen, organizations have to intervene, clarifying which are the norms of respect established, unmasking behaviors that are perpetrating both subtle forms of discrimination and ingrained prejudice and stereotypes, and shaping an inclusive organizational culture. Work Councils or Employees Representatives, according to the labor relations system applied (Euwema et al. 2015), should be vigilant and sensitive to such processes. Equity (in terms of guaranteeing a similar treatment to people who are in similar circumstances) is a condition that organizations have to make sure they have (Budd and Colvin 2008).

Hence, the questions are connected to the issue of workplace incivility as a form of subtle discrimination. Because of the long time required to change people's prejudices and stereotypes, human resources managers need to make them visible at least, offering instruments and strategies to recognize them. In the following section, we are going to analyze how the diversity management system has tried to foster the inclusion of non-heterosexual employees, and how it is possible to get better results through Social Dialogue.

12.5 New Frontiers of Diversity Management Through Social Dialogue

In the last few decades, Diversity Management has become a must for organizations. Firstly, motivated by legislative reforms on diversity, organizations have seen a new source of benefits by fostering diverse workplaces, creating a business case for diversity (European Commission 2016; Olsen and Martins 2012; Sabharwal 2014). Starting from this premise, several LGB diversity policies have been applied in order to eliminate negative bias presented within organizations. Among the policies implemented, pro-diversity statements at organizational level, training, and grievance procedures are ones of those most applied (Dobbin and Kalev 2016). Over time, however, it has been possible to recognize those measures that work and those that do not.

According to previous research, the outcomes of pro-diversity statements within the organizational policies, training, and other measures are controversial. While some studies highlight the beneficial effects they have on shaping inclusive workplaces (under certain conditions), others doubt about it (Dobbin and Kalev 2016; Kalinoski et al. 2013). For example, according to a meta-analysis on the evaluation of the diversity training outcomes (Kalinoski et al. 2013), it can help employees to recognize their prejudice and negative stereotypes. However, it might not be enough, due to the uncertain effect that diversity training has on negative attitudes, specially internal or subtle ones, which might be resistant to this type of instruments (Dobbin and Kalev 2016). However, training has a stronger effect on skills and beliefs, even if its effectiveness depends on several factors (e.g., trainees' motivation, how training is carried out, etc.) (Kalinoski et al. 2013).

Diversity policies and diversity measures also help employees to understand the position of the organization regarding discrimination and protected groups. Moreover, they seem useful in order to help people to realize and manage their prejudice and negative stereotypes (Dobbin and Kalev 2016; Kalinoski et al. 2013). In other terms, diversity policies might be a powerful organizational instrument to the extent to which they define borders between what is considered acceptable and what is not functioning as a regulator of conscious employees' behaviors.

The case of LGB Diversity Management has often been associated with hiring, retention, and promotion (Sabharwal 2014), which are obviously important organizational processes of employees' careers, as the Circle of Inclusion showed (Arenas et al., Chap. 1 in this volume). Nevertheless, not going beyond these steps might be even prejudicial for organizations, because employees who are not involved in such measures might feel discriminated against, and conflict may arise (Bendick et al. 2010). To obtain significant outcomes for people and organizations, it is necessary to shape a real and trusting climate of inclusion shared by all the stakeholders and the employees within the organization. Moreover, it has to be created taking into account the specific needs and dynamics in which LGB people are involved, and the sociohistorical and cultural context. And to do it, overcoming the business case is required (Kalinoski et al. 2013; Knights and Omanovic 2016). The Circle of Inclusion might be an inspiring starting point in order to shape inclusive organizations for LGB people (Arenas et al., Chap. 1 in this volume).

12.5.1 Unlocking Closets Through Social Dialogue

Social Dialogue represents a powerful instrument to reach the aims above described. In the last few years, Work Councils/Unions/Labor Movements (according to the labor relations system of the country considered) have worked in order to keep the debate on LGB(TI[1]) inclusion alive (Kelly and Lubitow 2015). However, past studies have pointed out that Work Councils/Unions/Labor Movements might have failed to represent the interests of some protected groups, misunderstanding their needs (Martínez Lucio and Perrett 2009). To avoid that the debate on relevant issues should include such groups, rather than starting at an institutional level, as it was highlighted in the case of migrant and black workers (Martínez Lucio and Perrett 2009).

Work Councils/Unions/Labor Movements should take in mind the features of LGBTI people (as well as the features of all the other protected groups) when they arrive at the bargaining table. Issues, such as family leaves, languages allowed at work, the inclusion of LGBTI-phobia within the group of psychosocial risks, and measures to take when LGBTI staff is moved abroad (where they might be not protected by a legal framework), should be discussed from the point of view of inclusive organizations, taking into account LGBTI workers' perceptions.

Moreover, Work Councils/Unions/Labor Movements should be vigilant and act as a wake-up call when LGTBI workers' rights are threatened. Beyond the traditional issues treated, they should point out those subtle dynamics that keep locked closets at the organization. In order to reach such goal, they should embrace a

[1]Although this chapter has focused on the experience of LGB people, an inclusive organization will include also transgender and intersexual workers, as well as all those people who do not fit the heteronormative discourse.

cooperative attitude, working close to all the actors involved, such as LGBTI workers and LGBTI networks, if present at the organization.

Until now, organizational LGBTI networks have represented the interests of non-heterosexual employees, supporting and representing LGBTI workers' right within and outside the organization (European Commission 2016). However, the mere presence of LGBTI networks cannot guarantee the inclusion and the creation of a safe workplace for them. Networks have to be connected with management and participate in the decision-making process (European Commission 2016). For doing that, they must be able to count on management's commitment at all organizational levels (Hoel and McBride, Chap. 3 in this volume). Work Councils/Unions/Labor Movements, LGBTI networks, and managers have to be allies, in order to guarantee that the voice of LGBTI groups is heard, as explained in the following section.

12.5.2 Direct Participation to Foster LGTBI Inclusion at Work

Work Councils/Unions/Labor Movements, and LGBTI networks are not the unique actors in shaping inclusive workplaces for LGBTI people. Inclusive workplaces should facilitate the direct participation of actors involved. However, this might represent a controversial issue, specially when an inclusive climate is not perceived and LGBTI people fear of disclosing their sexual identity, reporting having been victim of discriminatory acts or speaking up to defend their rights. To avoid it, a respectful climate has to be shaped at all levels of the organization. How to do it? Probably one of the first steps is to commit management with this mission, as said before (Dobbin and Kalev 2016; Hoel and McBride, Chap. 3 in this volume). In fact, a recent study showed that LGBTI human diversity policies are not successful if there is no trust in management and organization (Capell 2013). Managers, at all levels, can foster LGBTI people trust by applying several measures and policies: through mentoring, by showing interest in the experience of those LGBTI workers who are out, promoting an optimal contact between diverse people, and fostering the interchange of experience between LGBTI people and other workers (Capell 2013; Davidi 2015; Dobbin and Kalev 2016). Managers, with their example, help to clarify organizational norms which guide workers' behaviors and, in doing so, spread a culture of inclusion. In fact, when organizational rules are not clear, people's personal attitudes might overcome and an informal and discriminatory behavioral code might affect LGBTI colleagues or other social categories (Ward and Winstanley 2006). It is the case of the normalization of "jokes" whose protagonists are LGBTI people.

To sum up, managers have to be the main promoters of the LGBTI voice, helping to shape what is often called a "LGBTI-friendly workplace," and fostering a respectful climate at individual, group, and organizational level, aiming to reach a safe environment, where people feel included and free to speak up their voice;

where co-workers accept differences and behave in line with the norms of respect established by the organization; and where a culture of diversity becomes a strategic pillar of the organization and a sense of accountability for the well-being of LGBTI people is spread across it.

12.6 Conclusion

In the previous sections, we have discussed some issues related to the inclusion of LGB people at work, taking into account the main challenges they face at the workplace, although our revision does not aim to be exhaustive. Disclosure processes and subtle discrimination are just two general issues that LGB employees' experience entails. Moreover, we have explored Diversity Management limits and challenges, shedding light on the new horizons that Social Dialogue and direct participation might open in order to shape an inclusive workplace.

Shaping inclusive organizations for LGBTI people goes beyond banning discrimination against LGBTI employees. It also goes beyond creating an equal context for all workers. It means building a safe workplace, where diversity is valued and is considered a strategic resource. Therefore, an inclusive organization acknowledges and accepts diversity. It does not try to create a homogeneous group of workers, but it respects their diversity recognizing the value of being different (Sposato et al. 2015). This process has ethical implications (Deakin, Chap. 11 in this volume), beyond the effects that it can produce at economic level (it decreases the level of absenteeism, talented employees are retained, productivity increases, etc.) (Hoel and McBride, Chap. 3 in this volume). Creating a respectful and safe climate allows actors involved to speak up their voice and trust into the organization.

Not all Diversity Management measures have the same effect in fostering inclusion. Many times, their presence at organizational level just covers a culture that keeps close LGB people within glass closets (Di Marco et al. 2014). Moreover, in order to obtain an effective result, it is necessary to consider the social and the historical features that characterized each protected group, in this case LGBTI people (Knights and Omanovic 2016). Human resource management should work with LGBTI networks, Unions/Work Councils/Labor Movements, in order to give voice to all the actors involved, and promoting their participation in this process.

All the organizational actors are involved in, and responsible for, this process. LGBTI people, other protected groups, supervisors, and colleagues: All of them play a role. A respectful workplace is the result of a series of interactions which are realized at group and organizational level.

This work does not consider features and challenges transgender and intersexual people have to cope with at the workplace and within society. In the last few years, organizational psychologists and practitioners have started to take into account the dynamics in which they are involved, as well as the specific biases, prejudices, and stereotypes that surround them (e.g., Law et al. 2011). However, transgender and intersexual people are still the most discriminated against. Future efforts from practitioners and academics should be made in order to guarantee a safe work environment for these groups.

Moreover, in the future, we should consider instruments to value workers' satisfaction with the diversity climate, and measures able to recognize the presence of subtle biases and the effectiveness diversity policies applied for changing them.

A big challenge for human resource managers and for all the organizational actors involved is helping workers to recognize the role each worker plays in, and the personal accountability for, shaping a safe and inclusive workplace.

References

Anderson, M. Z., Croteau, J. M., Chung, Y. B., & DiStefano, T. M. (2001). Developing an assessment of sexual identity management for lesbian and gay workers. *Journal of Career Assessment, 9,* 243–260.

Andersson, L. M., & Pearson, C. M. (1999). Tit for tat? The spiraling effect of incivility in the workplace. *Academy of Management Review, 24,* 452–471.

Bendick, M., Egan, M. L., & Lanier, L. L. (2010). The business case for diversity and the perverse practice of matching employees to customers. *Personnel Review, 39,* 468–486.

Bryson, A. (2016). Pay equity after the Equality Act 2010: Does sexual orientation still matter? *Work, Employment and Society*. doi:10.1177/0950017016664678.

Bryson, A., Forth, J., & George, A. (2012). *Workplace social dialogue in Europe: An analysis of the European Company Survey 2009*. Dublin: Eurofound.

Budd, J. W., & Colvin, A. J. S. (2008). Improved metrics for workplace dispute resolution procedures: Efficiency, equity, and voice. *Industrial Relations, 47,* 460–479.

Button, S. B. (2004). Identity management strategies utilized by lesbian and gay employees: A quantitative explanation. *Group and Organization Management, 29,* 470–494.

Capell, B. (2013). *A Question of Trust: LGBT Visibility in the workplace*. Amsterdam: Workplace Pride Foundation.

Clair, J. A., Beatty, J. E., & MacLean, T. L. (2005). Out of sight but not out of mind: Managing invisible social identities in the workplace. *Academy of Management Review, 30,* 78–95.

Cortina, L. M., Kabat-Farr, D., Leskinen, E. A., Huerta, M., & Magley, V. J. (2013). Selective incivility as modern discrimination in organizations: Evidence and impact. *Journal of Management, 39,* 1579–1605.

Cortina, L. M., Magley, V. J., Williams, J. H., & Langhout, R. D. (2001). Incivility in the workplace: Incidence and impact. *Journal of Occupational Health Psychology, 6,* 64–80.

Croteau, J. M., Anderson, M. Z., & VanderWal, B. L. (2008). Models of workplace sexual identity disclosure and management: Reviewing and extending concepts. *Group and Organization Management, 33,* 532–565.

Davidi (2015, April 29). *Lord Browne: LGBT networks are fine, but CEOs must set the tone on inclusion.* The Guardian. Retrieved from https://www.theguardian.com/media-network/2015/apr/29/lord-browne-bp-lgbt-networks-inclusion.

Day, N. E., & Schoenrade, P. (1997). Staying in the closet versus coming out: Relationships between communication about sexual orientation and work attitudes. *Personnel Psychology, 50,* 147–163.

Di Marco, D., Arenas, A., Munduate, L., & Hoel, H. (2015a). Coming out strategies of lesbians and gays at work. *International Journal of Social Psychology, 30*, 122–135.

Di Marco, D., Hoel, H., Arenas., A., & Munduate, L. (2015b). Workplace incivility as modern sexual prejudice. *Journal of Interpersonal Violence.* doi:10.1177/0886260515621083.

Di Marco, D., Hoel, H., Arenas, A., & Munduate, L. (2014). *Identity management strategies applied by Spanish Lesbian and Gay employees.* Paper presented at the 6th Equality, Diversity and Inclusion International Conference, Munich, Germany.

Dobbin, F., & Kalev, A. (2016). Why diversity programs fail. *Harvard Business Review, July-August issue*, 52–60.

Dovidio, J. F. (2001). On the nature of contemporary prejudice: The third wave. *Journal of Social Issues, 57,* 829–849.

European Commission. (2015). *Special Eurobarometer 437. Discrimination in the UE in 2015.* Retrieved from http://ec.europa.eu/COMMFrontOffice/publicopinion/index.cfm/Survey/getSurveyDetail/instruments/SPECIAL/surveyKy/2077.

European Commission. (2016). *The business case for diversity in the workplace: Sexual orientation and gender identity. Report on good practices.* Luxembourg: Publications Office of the European Union.

Euwema, M., García, A. B., Munduate, L., Elgoibar, P., & Pender, E. (2015). Employee Representatives in European Organizations. In M. Euwema, L. Munduate, P. Elgoibar, E. Pender, & A. B. García (Eds.), *Promoting Social Dialogue in European Organizations* (pp. 1–17). The Netherlands: Springer International.

Harford, T. (2016). *Why every office should scrap its clean desk policy.* Available on: http://ideas.ted.com/why-every-office-should-scrap-its-clean-desk-policy.

Hatzenbuehler, M. L. (2009). How does sexual minority stigma "get under the skin"? A psychological mediation framework. *Psychological Bulletin, 135,* 707–730.

Herek, G. M. (2009). Hate crimes and stigma-related experiences among sexual minority adults in the United States. Prevalence estimates from a national probability sample. *Journal of Interpersonal Violence, 24,* 54–74.

Herek, G. M., & McLemore, K. A. (2013). Sexual prejudice. *Annual Review of Psychology, 64,* 309–333.

International Labour Organization. (2015). *Discrimination at work on the basis of sexual orientation and gender identity: Results of the ILO's PRIDE Project.* Available on: http://www.ilo.org/gender/Informationresources/Publications/WCMS_368962/lang–en/index.htm.

International Lesbian, Gay, Bisexual, Trans and Intersex Association, & Carroll, A. (2016). *State Sponsored Homophobia 2016: A world survey of sexual orientation laws: Criminalisation, protection and recognition.* Geneva: ILGA.

Jones, K. P., Peddie, C. I., Gilrane, V. L., King, E. B., & Gray, A. L. (2015). Not so subtle: A meta-analytic investigation of the correlates of subtle and overt discrimination. *Journal of Management, 42,* 1–26.

Kalinoski, Z. T., Steele-Johnson, D., Peyton, E. J., Leas, K. A., Steinke, J., & Bowling, N. A. (2013). A meta-analytic evaluation of diversity training outcomes. *Journal of Organizational Behavior, 34,* 1076–1104.

Kelly, M., & Lubitow, A. (2015). Pride at work: Organizing at the intersection of the labor and LGBT movements. *Labor Studies Journal, 39,* 257–277.

Knight, C., & Haslam, S. A. (2010). The relative merits of lean, enriched, and empowered offices: An experimental examination of the impact of workspace management strategies on well-being and productivity. *Journal of Experimental Psychology: Applied, 16,* 158–172.

Knights, D., & Omanovic, V. (2016). (Mis)managing diversity: Exploring the dangers of diversity management orthodoxy. *Equality, Diversity and Inclusion: An International Journal, 35,* 5–16.

Krings, F., Johnston, C., Binggeli, S., & Maggiori, C. (2014). Selective incivility: Immigrant groups experience subtle workplace discrimination at different rates. *Cultural Diversity and Ethnic Minority Psychology, 20,* 491–498.

Law, C. L., Martinez, L. R., Ruggs, E. N., Hebl, M. R., & Akers, E. (2011). Trans-parency in the workplace: How the experiences of transsexual employees can be improved. *Journal of Vocational Behavior, 79,* 710–723.

Lidderdale, M. A., Croteau, J. M., Anderson, M. Z., Tovar-Murray, D., & Davis, J. M. (2007). Building LGB vocational psychology: A theoretical model of workplace sexual identity management. In K. Bieschke, R. Perez, & K. DeBord (Eds.), *Handbook of counseling and psychotherapy with lesbian, gay, and bisexual clients* (2nd ed., pp. 245–270). Washington, DC: American Psychological Association.

Martínez Lucio, M., & Perrett, R. (2009). The diversity and politics of trade unions' responses to minority ethnic and migrant workers: The context of the UK. *Economic and Industrial Democracy, 30,* 324–347.

Nauta, A. (2015). Industrial relations and works councils in the Netherlands—Results from interviews and a survey among HR managers. In M. Euwema, L. Munduate, P. Elgoibar, E. Pender, & A. B. García (Eds.), *Promoting social dialogue in European organizations* (pp. 105–122). The Netherlands: Springer International.

Olsen, J. E., & Martins, L. L. (2012). Understanding organizational diversity management programs: A theoretical framework and directions for future research. *Journal of Organizational Behavior 33*(8), 1168-1187.

O'Reilly, J., Robinson, S. L., Berdahl, J. L., & Banki, S. (2014). Is negative attention better than no attention? The comparative effects of ostracism and harassment at work. *Organization Science, 26,* 774–793.

Ragins, B. R. (2004). Sexual orientation in the workplace: The unique work and career experiences of gay, lesbian and bisexual workers. *Research in Personnel and Human Resources Management, 23,* 35–129.

Ragins, B. R. (2008). Disclosure disconnects: Antecedents and consequences of disclosing invisible stigmas across life domains. *Academy of Management Review, 33,* 194–215.

Ragins, B. R., Cornwell, J. M., & Miller, J. S. (2003). Heterosexism in the workplace. Do race and gender matter? *Group and Organization Management, 28,* 45–74.

Sabharwal, M. (2014). Is diversity management sufficient? Organizational inclusion to further performance. *Public Personnel Management, 43,* 197–217.

Sposato, M., Feeke, S., Anderson-Walsh, P., & Spencer, L. (2015). Diversity, inclusion and workplace-equality index: The ingredients for organizational success. *Human Resource Management International Digest, 23,* 16–17.

Ueno, K., Peña-Talamantes, A. E., & Roach, T. A. (2013). Sexual orientation and occupational attainment. *Work and Occupations, 40,* 3–36.

Ward, J., & Winstanley, D. (2006). Watching the watch: The UK fire service and its impact on sexual minorities in the workplace. *Gender, Work and Organization, 13,* 193–219.

Chapter 13
Showcase: Inclusive HR Policy in Times of Change

Marc Verschueren and Martin C. Euwema

13.1 Introduction

In this case study, we discuss how the management of Saint Barbara Hospital in Belgium consciously opted for an inclusive HR policy on the occasion of a radical and comprehensive change. First, we explain what exactly included the change. Then we describe the guiding principles used by the management with regard to inclusion as well as the initiatives they took to make the policy concrete. The manager of Saint Barbara defined inclusion as the intentions he and his team had, as well as the actions they took, to make coworkers and their representatives, whatever their age, ethnicity or gender, as much partner of their policy as possible. Finally, we see what lessons can be drawn from this case.

13.2 Description of the Situation: Major Change

Saint Barbara Hospital is one of the 5 hospitals which together form UZ Leuven, a 1900-bed academic hospital with a total of 8000 employees. Saint Barbara Hospital was built in the 50s as a sanatorium. The sanatoria were then constructed to allow people with tuberculosis to take an extensive health cure. Bed rest and fresh air were the main remedies for this serious infectious disease because there were no tuberculosis drugs. Later, the original sanatorium was transformed into a hospital for pulmonary diseases and lung surgery, rheumatology and orthopedics, and one rehabilitation unit, more specifically neuromotor rehabilitation.

However, the diagnostic and therapeutic options for patients with lung diseases evolved very quickly, which meant that the infrastructure of Saint Barbara Hospital

M. Verschueren (✉) · M.C. Euwema
KU Leuven, Louvain, Belgium
e-mail: marc.verschueren@uzleuven.be

A. Arenas et al. (eds.), *Shaping Inclusive Workplaces Through Social Dialogue*,
Industrial Relations & Conflict Management,
DOI 10.1007/978-3-319-66393-7_13

became inadequate and that almost daily patients had to be carried in an ambulance to the main campus of UZ Leuven, situated 15 km away. It was therefore that it was decided to move the entire department of pulmonary diseases to the main campus; this included: three major hospital wards, a consultation unit, an operating theater, an intensive care unit, an examination unit, and a lung function laboratory.

It was also decided to recondition the vacant infrastructure and to further develop there the rehabilitation clinic. The existing neuromotor rehabilitation ward had to be supplemented with a unit from another campus and another two units for three new programs: one unit for psychosomatic rehabilitation and pain rehabilitation and another one for geriatric rehabilitation.

Saint Barbara therefore faced two large change projects at the same time: reallocation of the department of pulmonary diseases on the one hand and further development of the department of rehabilitation on the other.

The time between the final decision and transfer of pulmonary diseases was exactly one year. The time between the transfer and the start of the extended rehabilitation center was three months.

These changes included major logistical transformations such as renovations but mainly had an impact on more than 200 staff: mainly doctors, nurses, and paramedics.

The changes were led by the nursing manager, who had the daily management of Saint Barbara and further reported directly to the top management of UZ Leuven.

13.3 Guiding Principles for an Inclusive Policy

The manager who guided this major change operation, decided, in consultation with the executives of the hospital and consultation in the social dialogue, for the following operating principles:

1. In the entire operation, no people would be laid off, everyone was promised that no contract changes would occur.
2. The objective was to create an optimal situation for each involved employee with respect for everyone's personal situation and taking into account their experience and competence.
3. For this impactful change, they opted for the model of social dialogue: Trade union delegates were given a central role; although Saint Barbara is part of the large teaching hospital UZ Leuven, there is a separate Works Council and also a separate Committee for Prevention and Protection at Work (CPPW) at Saint Barbara. These were the main partners in the social dialogue.
4. Given that multidisciplinarity is a key success factor in rehabilitation medicine, it was decided to develop the project from the outset in a multidisciplinary way.

13.4 Inclusive Approach of the Change

Here, we describe the major initiatives that were taken to successfully execute the change in an inclusive way. It was the personal conviction of the manager of Saint Barbara that the two major changes, how radically too, entailed the opportunity to build a culture of involvement.

- *Cooperation with the members of the Works Council and the Committee for Prevention and Protection at Work*

Saint Barbara was once an autonomous sanatorium, later it became legally part of the major teaching hospital, UZ Leuven, but it retained its own Council and Private Committee. In Belgium, any organization that employs 100 workers has to set up a Works Council and a Committee for Prevention and Protection at Work (CPPW). Both bodies are jointly composed by representatives of the employer and representatives of the employees. They are elected every four years by the employees of the organization on the basis of lists of candidates nominated by the organizations of workers and executives. Both bodies meet monthly and are chaired by the head of the organization. The Works Council discusses and negotiates labor regulations, human resources, economic situation, and future prospects of the organization. The CPPW treats themes such as psychosocial well-being, ergonomics, environment, and unacceptable behavior.

The social dialogue in Saint Barbara was positively encouraged by two factors:

- There was already an effective consultative model; employee delegation always stood constructively critical in a positive rapport with the management and always showed also great concern for the reputation of the hospital and the well-being of both patients and staff.
- The scale of the hospital made that everyone knew everyone and that both employer and employee delegations could handle the problems of certain employees on a nominative way.

From the start of the change project, the manager decided to involve the members of the Works Council and the CPPW very actively in his approach. A joint information session was organized for all employees impacted by the departure of lung diseases. The head of the workers' delegation was involved in preparing this session. For all further steps, such as the reallocation of staff and the relocation operation in itself, members of the Works Council and the CPPW were engaged. The manager gave them explicitly the mission to serve as 'a sensor': the accessibility of the union delegates would probably help the employees to tell them without any hesitation their concerns and resistances with regard to the change. After all, the union delegates themselves were nurse, housekeeper, laboratory, and physiotherapist.

Everybody worked in high transparency, the situation was monitored closely, not only on the formal consultation moments but also on the informal contacts between the union representatives and the manager. By doing so, they could optimally take into account everyone's interests.

- *Reallocation of staff of the department of pulmonary diseases*

The manager organized for all the employees, over 200 persons, an individual, personal consultation meeting, where also the HR manager was present. The employee could then tell what desirable was for him or her with regard to the new situation. After all, the teams as they functioned in Saint Barbara could not be retained in the new situation. The operating theater of lung surgery would be included in the large cluster of thoracic surgery, consultation would be included in the larger consultation of internal medicine, etc.

During the individual interview, employees were asked about their concerns. Most common was the impact of the move on mobility and daily routine of the people. Many lived near the hospital, even did not possess a car, which would be necessary for the relocation to their new workplace in the main campus of UZ Leuven. There, the walking distance from parking to changing rooms and then to the departments was greater than in Saint Barbara, which meant that people had to leave home earlier for work and that they had to organize their families in another way.

The manager continually emphasized that the employment rate would not be affected and that they would make every effort to place the employee on the most feasible unit for him or her.

This obviously asked a lot of consultation with the managers of UZ Leuven, which were convinced to carefully pay attention for the huge emotions that caused this change for some employees.

After consultation with all employees and following consultation with the managers of the main campus of UZ Leuven, a plan was drawn up, which was submitted to the trade unions. The plan showed that about 60% of employees could work immediately after moving on the place they had chosen. During a second personal meeting, new destinations were proposed. For the people who found themselves in a different place than desired, a guidance plan was drawn up. The manager followed the plan in person until two months after moving in. Afterward, the personalized follow-up was guaranteed by the HR manager. Since turnover in such a large size hospital is quite high, almost all employees came on the unit of their choice after six months.

- *Inclusive actions in team formation for the new rehabilitation departments*

In Saint Barbara, one rehabilitation unit was already operational at the time of the removal operation. This formed the basis for the new to be developed department. The three floors that had become available were reconditioned so that they were suitable for rehabilitation patients. At one ward, an existing unit of another campus moved in. On the other two floors, new programs were launched for psychosomatic rehabilitation, pain rehabilitation, and geriatric rehabilitation. This meant that new teams had to be formed. It was decided to recruit internally. And following aspects of the circle of inclusion, the manager aimed to recruit based on competences and variety. Nurses who were looking for a new challenge for a while, got the opportunity to apply for the new programs. People of the other campuses were also approached for their specific expertise in one of the new themes: psychosomatics, pain, and geriatrics. As much as possibly, the age distribution as well as male–female ratio were taken into account. The latter is particularly not evident, given the historical imbalance of men to women in nursing. So, completely newly constituted teams started on the new wards. The classic stages of team formation (Raes et al. 2015) had to be completed rapidly. An intensive introduction program was set up, with the aim to welcome the people and to familiarize them with the new campus. Training courses were organized to increase the knowledge about the new themes. The storming phase was quickly visible: The different clinical backgrounds of the people, unleashing their habits, to adapt to a new situation, for many people also to other schedules, frequently caused tension. This required much attention from the clinical leaders (Van Emmerik and Euwema 2008). Following initiatives have been developed to meet this demand:

- The manager supported clinical leaders under the 'coach the coach' principle: This meant that the clinical leaders had an appointment with the manager every two weeks in which they could discuss issues concerning their employees in order to acquire the necessary skills for adequate coaching of their team members.
- A two-day course on participative leadership was arranged.
- The manager tried to visit at least twice a week the wards to keep in touch with the situation in the workplace, the staff of the units, and their clinical leaders: In case of tension or resistance of staff members, the local clinical leader was supported in developing an appropriate approach.
- The manager asked the union delegates, just like in the removal of Pneumology, to keep well in touch with the experiences of the people.
- When entering new schedules, the individual needs of the employees were taken into account and implemented in close consultation with the trade union delegates.

• *Inclusion of patients in multidisciplinary work design of the rehabilitation center*

A multidisciplinary approach was deliberately chosen for the elaboration of the rehabilitation concept. A core team was formed consisting of representatives from the various rehabilitation disciplines. They determined principles for the content of care, but also operational objectives. Some programs, such as psychosomatic rehabilitation and pain rehabilitation, had to be defined from scratch. The joint drafting of the program created a special spirit in Saint Barbara: everything was new, everyone was fully involved, and wanted to be fully committed. After only a few months, a series of creative and innovative initiatives was taken. There was even opted for making the switch from discipline-driven reporting to problem-driven reporting, which significantly strengthened the cooperation since the distinction between disciplines became less explicit. The most extreme form of inclusion was perhaps that they started with patients discussions where the patient and his family themselves were present. On the so-called round tables, solutions for the patient's life after rehabilitation were harmoniously discussed, with great respect for the patient.

13.5 Lessons Learned

This case holds important lessons with regard to inclusive policies:

- The development of a real inclusive policy starts with the conviction of the manager that *involvement of all coworkers* in a change project is a key factor to the success and the sustainability of the change. In this case, the manager applied a *shared leadership principle* (Verschueren et al. 2013), whereby he consequently integrated advice and opinions of the concerned staff in his decisions. He defined inclusion as intentions and actions to make people partner of his management, irrespective of their age, gender, ethnicity, level of seniority, or professional role.
- Inclusion implies careful attention for *information* and *transparency*. People feel more involved when they meet face to face with the change agents. Active listening, observing on the floor what staff reactions are, reduces the normal feelings of insecurity that are linked with change processes. Also, being present and visible helps coworkers in maintaining trust in their leaders, which in turn helps to adapt a positive mindset.
- The trade union delegates can help successfully the management in the implementation of change from *a position as partner*. By giving them explicitly the role as partner, their attitude toward management changes. Instead of being continuously in the opponent position, they develop a more constructive style.
- To keep people involved in change, it is appropriate to spend much time on the *individual needs* of all stakeholders. Listening to people, taking their emotions and their opinions seriously, costs a lot of time but has a guaranteed return on investment. It is a universal human need to be seen and to be respected. Aside of group interventions, individual consideration is really necessary. Essentially, inclusion here means recognizing and appreciating the differences between employees. This is beyond the 'surface level' diversity and addresses the 'deep level' diversity (Harrison et al. 2002), in terms of needs, values, and competencies.
- The formation of new teams should be given adequate attention; particularly investing in the *forming stage in terms* of good introduction, goals, appointments, is a success factor for the further operation.
- This case shows that *involving people* in the development of a new department results to a creative and an innovative spirit. Many caregivers have splendid ideas of how to improve services, it is worthwhile to invest in interaction between the different professional groups and their synergetic potential.

- An inclusive approach of a change project is not a one-shot action. In order to become sustainable, a change project needs not only an extensive preparation but also mostly a sound *follow-up*. People have to experience that leaders really stay approachable, that they are ready to make adjustments if needed.

13.6 Conclusion

An inclusive HR policy is feasible and possible, even in times of complex and systemic change. It requires the belief of management that through social dialogue, by focusing on all stakeholders, a culture of inclusion can be established, which ensures that the change is positive and sustainable.

References

Harrison, D. A., Price, K. H., Gavin, J. H., & Florey, A. T. (2002). Time, teams, and task performance: Changing effects of surface-and deep-level diversity on group functioning. *Academy of Management Journal, 45*(5), 1029–1045.

Raes, E., Kyndt, E., Decuyper, S., Van den Bossche, P., & Dochy, F. (2015). An exploratory study of group development and team learning. *Human Resource Development Quarterly, 26*(1), 5–30.

Van Emmerik, I. J., & Euwema, M. C. (2008). The aftermath of organizational restructuring: Destruction of old and development of new social capital. *Journal of Managerial Psychology, 23*(7), 833–849.

Verschueren, M., Kips, J., & Euwema, M. (2013). A review on leadership of head nurses and patient safety and quality of care. In T. Simons, H. Leroy, & G. T. Savage (Eds.), *Leading in health care organizations: Improving safety, satisfaction and financial performance* (pp. 3–34). Emerald Group Publishing Limited.

Chapter 14
Social Dialogue as a Sustainable Career Development Practice to Combat (Meta) Stereotyping

Pascale Peters, Beatrice Van der Heijden, Daniel Spurk, Ans de Vos and Renate Klaassen

14.1 Sustainable Career Development for Shaping Inclusive Workplaces

The notion of sustainable career development (SCD) (De Prins et al. 2015; De Vos et al. 2016) builds on the ROC model by De Lange and Koppens (2007) which stresses the need for respect for internal and external organizational stakeholders (R); openness or environmental awareness including an outside-in and inside-out perspective on Human Resource Management (HRM) (O); and continuity, that is a long-term approach to economic and societal sustainability, in particular individual employability (C). Consistent with the ROC model, this chapter addresses how an ongoing social dialogue between internal stakeholders at the shop-floor level can help to shape an inclusive workplace for all workers (respect dimension), including

P. Peters (✉) · B. Van der Heijden
Institute for Management Research (IMR)/GAINS, Radboud University, Nijmegen, The Netherlands
e-mail: p.peters@fm.ru.nl

B. Van der Heijden
Open University of the Netherlands, Heerlen, The Netherlands

B. Van der Heijden
Kingston University, London, UK

D. Spurk
Bern University, Bern, Switzerland

A. de Vos
Antwerp Management School, Antwerp, Belgium

A. de Vos
University of Antwerp, Antwerp, Belgium

R. Klaassen
Radboud University, Nijmegen, The Netherlands

A. Arenas et al. (eds.), *Shaping Inclusive Workplaces Through Social Dialogue*, Industrial Relations & Conflict Management,
DOI 10.1007/978-3-319-66393-7_14

vulnerable categories, by focusing on sustainable career development, in particular on employability (continuity dimension), and how this may be affected by negative (meta)stereotyping (openness dimension).

Employability is a key element of SCD and is believed to foster individual workers' career success over the life cycle (De Prins et al. 2015). We define employability as individuals' capacity of continuously fulfilling, acquiring, or creating work through the optimal use of competences, which enhances their labor market opportunities (Van der Heijde and Van der Heijden 2006) and, hence, career development. Several stakeholders are involved in safeguarding and enhancing employees' employability throughout the life course. Although the individual is the key actor, organizations directly and indirectly affect workers' employability both via their career and development policies and via the way these are enacted via daily interactions with employees (De Vos et al. 2011). The latter brings in the stakeholder perspective and emphasizes the importance of social dialogue in SCD (De Prins et al. 2015) and in particular the direct participation of employees and their supervisors herein (Nauta 2015).

In practice, social dialogue takes place in social contexts, which in some cases may be characterized by a climate of discrimination and negative stereotyping. Such a climate may impact stakeholders' attitudes, motivations, experiences, feelings, and behaviors (cf. Kunze et al. 2011), possibly resulting into organizations and HR managers refraining from the development of inclusive employability measures, or preventing supervisors and workers at the shop-floor level to actually use these in the intended way, affecting the effectiveness of the social dialogue. The process approach to HRM (Wright and Nishii 2007) underlines that employability and its effect on career development should be viewed as part of the HR-process which demands all organizational stakeholders to understand and make sense of the content and usefulness of inclusive employability policies and practices. To further the debate on SCD and inclusive workplaces, we argue that social dialogue at the shop-floor level (Bryson et al. 2012; Euwema et al. 2015; Nauta 2015) can be viewed as an important practice in the HR-process, as this provides room to monitor vulnerable workers' perceptions and ambitions, and to stimulate (new) career opportunities, possibly reversing negative (meta)stereotyping processes.

Stereotyping refers to unconsciously or consciously making generalizations about individuals based on the group (e.g., categorized by gender, race, or age) to which they belong (cf. Henkens 2005). However, individuals belonging to a particular group (e.g., older workers) may also hold beliefs regarding such stereotyped views they think that outgroup members may hold about them. This we refer to as metastereotypes (Finkelstein et al. 2013; Vorauer et al. 1998). Both stereotyping and metastereotyping may affect inclusion (Vauclair et al. 2016).

In this chapter, we outline how the concepts of social dialogue, employability, and (meta)stereotyping may be conceptualized and interrelated and how they play a role in the HR-process and, ultimately, affect workers' career development. This process is illustrated by a short summary of preliminary results from a study of supermarket workers in the Netherlands, particularly focusing on workers engaging in negative age-based (meta)stereotyping. In view of several interrelated trends, older workers (among other labor market categories) have become an increasingly vulnerable labor market category. On the one hand, aging and dejuvenization of the labor market have led to a rise of the legal retirement age across the globe and, hence, the need for workers to work longer over the life cycle. On the other, fiercer competition in globalizing markets and technological changes may cause older workers to be viewed as 'too expensive' to employ, while their skills may become obsolete, which stresses the importance of ongoing employability development. Although older and often more tenured workers may have gained more work experience and skills over the life span than their younger peers (cf. Froehlich et al. 2015), in contemporary labor markets, this may not suffice to remain employable throughout their careers. In addition, especially in the light of ever-increasing labor market flexibility and technological developments, (lower-skilled) work becomes more uncertain which demands a more proactive labor market orientation to other career paths than older workers use to display. The chapter concludes by suggesting organizations to implement HR practices to combat negative (meta)stereotyping in general, and older workers in particular, enabling them to shape more inclusive workplaces, for example, through social dialogue.

14.2 Social Dialogue, Employability, and (Meta) Stereotyping

14.2.1 Social Dialogue

Social dialogue refers to "discussions, consultations, negotiations, and joint actions involving organizations representing the two sides of the industry (employers and workers). Social dialogue is a process by which relevant parties seek to resolve employment-related differences via an information exchange" (Bryson et al. 2012, p. 5). It can take place at the European, national, and sector levels, but also within working organizations. Demographic changes and rapid technological innovations bring along many challenges for both employers and employees pertaining to sustainable careers and, hence, employability throughout the life course. This urges social partners to work out measures that respond to societal needs for an employable working population, to employers' needs for a high performing, flexible, and employable workforce, and to employees' needs for satisfying work and possibilities for career development and personal growth (De Vos et al. 2016).

Within the organizational context, the dialogue between the employer (CEO and/or HR-director) and the works council, in which they can consult each other about organization policies, especially HRM (Nauta 2015), is an important vehicle for installing collective measures for SCD. Recently, and in line with the growing emphasis on tailor-made HR solutions and a life course approach to careers, also the interpersonal dialogue between employees and their superiors and among employees, shaping their mutual relationship, has received greater attention. At this level, the social dialogue centers around formal and informal conversations on topics, such as performance appraisal or career development needs, thereby directly involving the employee.

This chapter primarily relates to these formal and informal types of direct employer and supervisor participation in the social dialogue which is an increasingly important HR-instrument that allows to discuss workers' career options, ambitions, and development needs, herewith stimulating engagement in employability activities, including education and training, but also proactive and flexible employee behaviors. It is important to recognize the perspectives both parties bring to the table, and which might shape their personal values and their views, beliefs, and attitudes about employability and the usefulness of investing in workers' employability-enhancing activities. Of course, the room for the social dialogue at the shop-floor level is also shaped by HR-policies, works councils, organizational strategies, Collective Labor Agreements (CLAs), national agreements, and even European directives (Nauta 2015).

14.2.2 Negative (Meta)Stereotyping Threatening Worker's Employability

In order to remain employable, within or outside the current organization, and to ensure lifelong employment and personal career success (Van der Heijde and Van der Heijden 2006), workers need to possess the right competences to do their work effectively. As workers need to adjust their focus on 'what are the right competences?' on an ongoing basis, this implies that workers not only need to invest in particular domain-specific expertise, but also need to develop competencies that enable them to be proactive and flexible, to handle ambiguity, and to manage multiple tasks simultaneously. Therefore, Van der Heijde and Van der Heijden (2006) distinguish five competence-based employability dimensions. The first focuses on domain-specific occupational expertise (knowledge, skills, including metacognitive ones, and social recognition by important key figures). The other four are more general competence dimensions which focus on job-related matters and broader career development aspects: anticipation and optimization; personal flexibility; corporate sense; and balance.

This conceptualization implies that all workers have to stay up-to-date and keep track with changes in one's occupation and the needed occupational expertise and competences following from these, which can be achieved through formal and informal learning (Froehlich et al. 2015). Simultaneously, however, it implies that workers need to proactively and reactively adapt to internal and external labor market changes, create career opportunities by investing in their social networks, and display commitment to organizational goals. Moreover, they need to protect a sound balance between striving to fulfill their personal, and often conflicting goals, and between one's own needs and those of their (potential) employer(s) (cf. Van der Heijde and Van der Heijden 2006).

The absence of an inclusive HR policy and associated practices which ideally signals an organization-wide diversity climate and stresses the importance of employability of all worker categories (cf. De Prins et al. 2015) may lead to a low level of worker motivation to invest in employability-enhancing activities. Moreover, previous research has shown that vulnerable worker categories, such as part-time workers, older workers, ethnic minorities, and temporary workers, may suffer from organizational climates characterized by stereotypical views and discrimination which may hinder their optimal participation (Henkens 2005; Owuamalam and Zagefka 2014; Peters and Lam 2015), and hence, their internal and external career opportunities and progress.

Stereotyping can be viewed as an often unconscious, although sometimes conscious, categorization process (cf. Henkens 2005). Organizational members may categorize workers based on certain assumptions about personal characteristics (e.g., gender, race, or age), regarding the category a person may be viewed to belong to. For example, older workers may be viewed to be less capable or willing to adopt new technologies or to be less committed to organizational change than their younger counterparts (see Drydakis et al., Chap. 6 in this volume). Of course, positive stereotyping regarding older workers is also possible. For example, older workers may be believed to be more experienced, loyal to the organization, and trustworthy (Henkens 2005).

Worker categories may be aware of, or may perceive them being negatively stereotyped (e.g., by their supervisor, HR managers, coworkers, or clients) and may form their own opinion about how they are being perceived by others. Their beliefs regarding the stereotypes that outgroup members may hold about their own group can be referred to as metastereotypes (Finkelstein et al. 2013; Vorauer et al. 1998). Workers may identify with their own perceptions of the beliefs that others may hold toward them, which may increase the potential for miscommunication and tension and affect their feelings of inclusion (Vauclair et al. 2016). Being largely negative in content, metastereotyping can undermine the stereotyped group's self-worth (Vorauer et al. 1998) and their employability beliefs (Owuamalam and Zagefka 2014), discouraging them to engage in employability-enhancing activities (cf. Dordoni et al. in progress). This, in turn, may affect their career opportunities in detrimental ways (De Lange et al. 2015). Although metastereotyping does not necessarily have to be in line with the actual beliefs that the other groups have about them (cf. Finkelstein et al. 2013), metastereotypes do form the lens through which workers themselves view the world. Therefore, these are likely to influence work attitudes and behaviors, which may lead to a self-fulfilling prophecy (cf. Van der Heijden 2005).

14.2.3 Preliminary Insights into How Metastereotyping of Older Workers Can Affect Their Self-reported Employability

While acknowledging that SCD promotes an inclusive employability climate for all worker categories, intending to prevent all types of negative (meta)stereotyping and discrimination, to illustrate the process through which metastereotyping of older workers can affect employability, this subsection briefly discusses some preliminary results of one of our studies in progress on age-related (meta)stereotyping on employability in a low-skilled work context, focusing on supervisors and service employees in seven different supermarket locations of a large Dutch supermarket chain. In this study conducted among 98 supermarket workers with permanent contracts for at least 12 h comprising team leaders and service workers, an old age group (50 or older) is contrasted against a young (under 30 years old) and a middle-aged group (30–49 years old). The focus is on the effects of metastereotyping on the self-reported perceived employability of older supermarket workers. Based on Henkens (2005), metastereotypes relate to the respondents' perceptions of the extent to which the organizational climate signals that older workers are less productive, less adaptable, and less reliable, respectively, than younger age groups. Employability was measured with five dimensions by Van der Heijde and Van der Heijden (2006): occupational expertise, anticipation and optimization, personal flexibility, corporate sense, and balance. Our preliminary results showed that:

- Older supermarket workers themselves reported lower levels of negative metastereotyping than the level of stereotyping about older workers as reported by the other two age groups;
- Older supermarket workers reported lower scores on (some dimensions of) self-perceived employability;
- Older supermarket workers are impacted more by negative (meta)stereotyping regarding older workers in terms of lowered self-perceived employability (compared to young or middle-aged workers).

In more detail, the results revealed that self-reported employability was lower for older supermarket workers than for both the youngest and middle age groups when it comes to corporate sense and anticipation and optimization, and lower only in comparison with the youngest age group when it comes to balance. Older supermarket workers did not perceive to have lower levels of occupational expertise than their younger counterparts, possibly because their jobs may not be that complex and may be less subject to change over time. The low level of job complexity may also facilitate all supermarket workers' personal flexibility, regardless of their age, and hence, their opportunities for internal or external mobility.

Although the older supermarket workers themselves, on average, reported lower levels of stereotyping regarding older workers than the level of stereotyping regarding older workers as perceived by the two younger age groups, those older supermarket workers who did engage in a process of metastereotyping reported lower levels on all the employability dimensions, with the exception of personal flexibility. That is, metastereotyping by older workers impacted their occupational expertise, anticipation and optimization, corporate sense, and balance. These older workers' lower motivation to invest in employability was clearly aggravated by their perceptions regarding the lack of an age-inclusive employability climate, possibly due to them having negative moods or experiencing anxiety or anger (King et al. 2008). In that case, older workers perceiving stereotyping from others regarding older workers may have a hard time to hold positive views about themselves, for example, regarding self-perceived employability (Van der Heijden 2005), and they may become less likely to invest in their employability.

Note that we found some differences in the comparisons across the older group of supermarket workers and the other two age groups, depending on the focus of metastereotyping: older workers' perceived productivity, adaptability, or reliability. Overall, the younger and middle-aged workers reported more employability. Another finding was that also middle-aged workers were negatively affected by the metastereotypes. Specifically, the relationship between the metastereotype of reliability and balance was negative for the middle age group, but not for the other groups. This finding implies that not only older age groups need to be focused on in the social dialogue, but that also other age groups need to be taken into account as negative perceptions regarding older workers may also impact other groups in the organization. The impact of negative perceptions regarding older workers' reliability on the middle-aged workers' balance may aggravate exclusion of older workers, strengthening the meta(stereotyping) process.

Our preliminary results suggest that inclusive career development practices need to pay particular attention to how not only age in itself, as a 'surface-level' aspect of diversity, but also the interaction with metastereotypes (a 'deep-level' aspect) affects employability and, hence, the career development of employees and might possibly lead to exclusion. A sound social dialogue between workers and their supervisors might be particularly relevant here since it may open up to discuss (meta)stereotyping, and ambitions and opportunities within or outside the current organization (De Prins et al. 2015).

14.3 Discussion and Conclusion

14.3.1 Shaping Inclusive Climates and Preventing Stereotyping in View of SCD

Securing employment throughout workers' careers by motivating them to invest in employability-enhancing activities is an important element of sustainable career development (De Prins et al. 2015). For employers, an employable workforce is important to remain competitive. Despite that employers are becoming increasingly aware of the importance of investing in all workers' employability through offering

SCD policies and practices (De Vos et al. 2016), there is a tendency to focus these efforts more on core workers or so-called ‘key talent’ within the organization, rather than taking an inclusive approach (Peters and Lam 2015). Consequently, more vulnerable workforce categories, such as older workers, run the risk of being out of the scope of corporate employability-enhancing initiatives. Moreover, when workers themselves do not feel confident in developing their own employability, they might refrain from participating in employability-enhancing activities, such as training opportunities, thereby creating a self-fulfilling prophecy. Stereotyping regarding and metastereotyping by vulnerable worker categories, such as older workers, might further impact this process.

With regard to older workers, the literature reveals a strong correlation between workers’ chronological age and future time perspective (cf. Lang and Carstensen 2002) which may affect older workers’ motivation to maintain and enhance their employability, since they are closer to their pension age. Just because older workers may attach less value themselves to opportunities for advancement and continuous learning, it is important for organizations and supervisors to actively motivate them to invest their (own) time, money, and energy in employability-enhancing activities by having regular dialogues on this topic. In order to combat (meta)stereotyping, HR practices, and in particular social dialogue and trainings, can contribute to a climate of inclusion by paying attention to employability, activating older workers’ ambition, and creating career opportunities for all, including older and other vulnerable worker categories. Our preliminary results on supermarket workers provided a valuable basis for discussing possible actions HR practitioners can take to implement HR practices aimed at shaping inclusive climates, where workers from all categories (e.g., age, gender, ethnicity, flexible workers, and intersections thereof) perceive that they are esteemed members, and receive equal opportunities for employability, thereby satisfying all workers’ needs for belongingness (i.e., to form and maintain strong, stable interpersonal relationships) and uniqueness (i.e., to maintain a distinctive and differentiated sense of self) (Shore et al. 2011).

The key imperative might be recognition and awareness of processes of (meta) stereotyping and biased perceptions regarding particular worker categories (such as older workers) and make all stakeholders in the organization aware of when and where (meta)stereotyping occurs and which stakeholders are involved, for example through trainings and workshops focused on how to combat stereotyping. One single training or workshop, however, might not suffice, and therefore, more structural HR practices should be implemented, which demands the support of line managers who should give the example, but also make others aware of possible (meta)stereotyping and discriminating behaviors. In addition, also organizational structures and systems should be checked for and mainstreamed regarding stereotyping or discriminating biases against (meta)stereotyped groups (Nahavandhi et al. 2015).

The mutual understanding and openness gained from these practices allows to shape an ongoing dialogue between managers and workers, and among worker categories, in order to respond to the differences in expectations with regard to work (and non-work) and personal development, in line with the differences in individual aspirations and capabilities. Both the more diverse working population and the increasing acknowledgment of the importance of non-work areas of life, such as 'quality time' with family and friends and leisure, but also informal care obligations, urge us to avoid thinking in categories regarding traditional ways of career development and career success alone. Organizing for social dialogue among multiple intra-organizational stakeholders increases the contact and interactions between groups that may not be inclined to regularly interact, but this would allow to learn about others' views, values, motives, and skills. This can help to suppress (meta)stereotyping and its negative impact on employability and career development.

Importantly, in order to enable all employees to 'take ownership' for their career development, a 'one-size-fits-all' approach will not work (De Prins et al. 2015). An inclusive approach to career development implies that during the interactions between managers and workers and among worker categories, the needs of individual workers, including older workers, are respected and being taken into consideration. As mentioned earlier, when parties engage in career dialogues on a more regular basis, supervisors and workers might be able to recognize, monitor, and overcome (meta)stereotyping processes. Current performance evaluation criteria, for example, may be biased toward stereotypical younger workers' characteristics and skills, which may undermine the career and work opportunities of other worker categories with other characteristics and skills.

In conclusion, social dialogues ought to be particularly centered around the five employability dimensions we examined in our study. In this way, supervisors and employees can engage in constructive conversations about sustainable careers through safeguarding workers' expertise and corporate sense, exploring how employees can be flexible and can anticipate and optimize their career strategies in light of future labor market requirements, meanwhile sustaining employees' work–life balance (Van der Heijde and Van der Heijden 2006). The insights obtained from social dialogues on these topics between employees and supervisors, in turn, can form important input for social dialogue between stakeholders at a collective level, e.g., when discussing employability-enhancing activities between HR and union representatives.

14.3.2 Avenues for Future Research

In this chapter, we have argued that social dialogue at the shop-floor level can be expected to contribute to an inclusive employability climate leading to higher career success of all workers. However, in view of the often incompatible multiple goals (rational efficiency, legitimacy, fairness, and ethical arguments) intra-organizational stakeholders (organizations, HRM, supervisors, and employees) might have, it should be realized that social dialogue at the shop-floor level will be surrounded by multiple (paradoxical) tensions that need to be acknowledged and that conflicts need to be addressed in constructive ways (Peters and Lam 2015). Since the sources of these tensions may originate from the wider economic, political, and sociocultural contexts, also external labor market stakeholders need to be aware of what their policies and practices entail for social dialogue at the shop-floor level where HRM, supervisors, and employees have to search for creative and more sustainable management solutions. This calls for more research into the relationships between macro-, meso-, and micro-level policies and how (paradoxical) tensions at these levels can spill over to affect HR processes and hence, social dialogue at the shop-floor level (cf. Nauta 2015; Peters and Lam 2015).

More concretely, future research could address how stereotyping by parties involved in SCD (e.g., workers, supervisors, HR managers, and clients) about vulnerable worker groups may not only affect workers' perceived employability, but also the career-related decisions intra-organizational parties take regarding these groups. In this chapter, we paid attention to an understudied population of workers when it comes to career development, i.e., older workers at the shop-floor level in a low-skilled work environment. Future research could include other types of vulnerable groups and further investigate the interactions between structural (e.g., job type) and individual (e.g., age and ethnic background) factors in explaining the role of (meta)stereotyping in SCD.

For long, it was assumed that having a 'career' only applied to professional or managerial workers (Lawrence et al. 2015). The current organizational reality makes it clear that organizations should not overlook other labor market categories when it comes to career development: Sustained employability of workers in all types of jobs, of all categories, and with all sorts of backgrounds and labor market contracts will be important not only for sustainable careers at the individual level, but also for organizational adaptability and sustainable growth, benefiting national and global economies. It will therefore be important to overcome obstacles that, overtly or implicitly, affect the ways in which workers look at themselves (e.g., metastereotyping).

14.3.3 Conclusion

To conclude, we would like to stress the importance of implementing policies, practices, and social norms that direct behaviors in organizations and promote tolerance and mutual respect in order to improve older people's aging experience (cf. Vauclair et al. 2016). In line with the insights gained from the Circle of Inclusion (Arenas et al., Chap. 1 in this volume), we advocate that organizations follow an integral approach that incorporates curative (focusing on groups that score lower on factors predicting career development), preventive (focusing on groups that run the risk of scoring lower on factors predicting career development), and amplition-related measures (focusing on vitalizing all worker categories through training, coaching, giving feedback, and allowing intra- and extra-organizational mobility) managing the employability of employees across the life span to promote worker well-being (cf. Van Vuuren 2012). We advise that HR managers and line managers alike pay serious attention to combatting the possible negative effects of metastereotyping, by striving for a positive social climate that enables social dialogue as an approach to strengthen inclusive workplaces. The latter should be characterized by a strong focus on motivating all stakeholders to be unprejudiced as a social norm and preferably should be reinforced in institutions both implicitly and explicitly, for instance in terms of how to refer to older workers and their legal rights (cf. Vauclair et al. 2016).

References

Bryson, A., Forth, J., & George, A. (2012). *Workplace social dialogue in Europe: An analysis of the European Company Survey 2009*. Dublin: Eurofound.

De Lange, W., & Koppens, J. (2007). *De duurzame arbeidsorganisatie: Een geloofwaardig vervolg op maatschappelijk verantwoord ondernemen*. Amsterdam: WEKA Uitgeverij.

De Lange, A. H., Kooij, D. T. A. M., & Van der Heijden, B. I. J. M. (2015). Human resource management and sustainability at work across the lifespan: An integrative perspective. In L. M. Finkelstein, D. M. Truxillo, F. Fraccaroli, & R. Kanfer (Eds.), *Facing the challenges of a multi-age workforce: A use-inspired approach* (pp. 50–79). SIOP Society for Industrial and Organizational Psychology. New York: Routledge.

De Prins, P., De Vos, A., Van Beirendonck, L., & Segers, J. (2015). Sustainable HRM for sustainable careers: Introducing the 'Respect Openness Continuity (ROC) model'. In A. De Vos & B. I. J. M. Van der Heijden (Eds.), *Handbook of research on sustainable careers* (pp. 319–334). Cheltenham, UK/Northampton, MA, USA: Edgar Elgar.

De Vos, A., De Hauw, S., & Van der Heijden, B. I. J. M. (2011). Competency development and career success: The mediating role of employability. *Journal of Vocational Behavior, 79*(2), 438–447.

De Vos, A., Dujardin, J. M., Gielens, T., & Meyers, C. (2016). *Developing sustainable careers across the lifespan: European Social Fund network on "Career and AGE (Age, Generations, Experience)*. Dordrecht: Springer.

Dordoni, P., Van der Heijden, B. I. J. M., Peters, P., Kraus-Hoogeveen, S., & Argentero, P. (in progress). Keep up the good work! Towards an age-moderated mediation model predicting intention to retire.

Euwema, M., Munduate, L., Elgoibar, P., Pender, E., & Garcia, A. (2015). *Promoting social dialogue in European organizations. Human Resources management and constructive conflict management*. Heidelberg/New York/Dordrecht/London: Springer.

Finkelstein, L. M., Ryan, K. M., & King, E. B. (2013). What do the young (old) people think of me? Content and accuracy of age-based metastereotypes. *European Journal of Work and Organizational Psychology, 22,* 633–657.

Froehlich, D. E., Beausaert, S. A. J., & Segers, M. S. R. (2015). Great expectations: The relationship between future time perspective, learning from others, and employability. *Vocations and Learning, 8,* 213–227.

Henkens, C. J. I. M. (2005). Stereotyping older workers and retirement: The managers' point of view. *Canadian Journal of Aging, 24,* 353–366.

King, E. B., Kaplan, S., & Zaccaro, S. (2008). Metaperceptions in diverse workgroups: Intrapersonal perspectives and intragroup processes. In B. Mannix, M. Neale, & C. Anderson (Eds.), *Research on managing groups and teams* (pp. 109–142). Oxford: Elsevier.

Kunze, F., Boehm, S., & Bruch, H. (2011). Age diversity, age discrimination, and performance consequences. A cross organizational study. *Journal of Organizational Behavior, 32*(2), 264–290.

Lang, F. R., & Carstensen, L. L. (2002). Time counts: Future time perspective, goals, and social relationships. *Psychology and Aging, 17*(1), 125–139.

Lawrence, B. S., Hall, D. T., & Arthur, M. B. (2015). Sustainable careers then and now. In A. De Vos & B. I. J. M. Van der Heijden (Eds.), *Handbook of research on sustainable careers* (pp. 432–449). Cheltenham, UK/Northampton, MA, USA: Edgar Elgar.

Nahavandhi, A., Denhardt, R.B., Denhardt, J.V., & Aristigueta, M.P. (2015). *Organizational Behavior*, First Edition. Thousand Oaks, CA: Sage Publications.

Nauta, A. (2015). Industrial relations and works councils in the Netherlands—Results from interviews and a survey among HR managers. In M. Euwema, L. Munduate, P. Elgoibar, E. Pender, & A. Garcia (Eds.), *Promoting social dialogue in European organizations. Human Resources management and constructive conflict management* (pp. 105–121). Heidelberg/New York/Dordrecht/London: Springer.

Owuamalam, C. K., & Zagefka, H. (2014). On the psychological barriers to the workplace: When and why metastereotyping undermines employability beliefs of women and ethnic minorities. *Cultural Diversity and Ethnic Minority Psychology, 20*(4), 521–528.

Peters, P., & Lam, W. (2015). Can employability do the trick? Revealing paradoxical tensions and responses in the process of adopting innovative employability enhancing policies and practices in organizations. *Zeitschrift für Personalforschung, 29*(3–4), 235–258.

Shore, L. M., Randel, A. E., Chung, B. G., Dean, M. A., Ehrhart, K. H., & Singh, G. (2011). Inclusion and diversity in work groups: A review and model for future research. *Journal of Management, 37,* 1262–1289.

Van der Heijde, C. M., & Van der Heijden, B. I. J. M. (2006). A competence-based and multi-dimensional operationalization and measurement of employability. *Human Resource Management, 45*(3), 449–476.

Van der Heijden, B. I. J. M. (2002). Prerequisites to guarantee life-long employability. *Personal Review, 31*(1), 44–61.

Van der Heijden, B. I. J. M. (2005). No one has ever promised you a rose garden" On shared responsibility and employability enhancing strategies throughout careers. Heerlen, the Netherlands, Open University of the Netherlands. Assen, the Netherlands: Van Gorcum.

Van Vuuren, T. (2012). Vitaliteitsmanagement: je hoeft niet ziek te zijn om beter te worden! Vergroot de duurzame inzetbaarheid van werknemers door hun vitaliteit, werkvermogen en employability te versterken [Vitality management: You don't have to be ill to get better! Enlarge the sustainable labour participation of workers by strengthening their vitality, work ability and employability]. *Gedrag & Organisatie, 25*(4), 400–418.

Vauclair, C. M., Lima, M. L., Abrams, D., Swift, H. J., & Bratt, C. (2016). What do older people think that others think of them, and does it matter? The role of meta-perceptions and social norms in the prediction of perceived age discrimination. *Psychology and Aging, 31*(7), 699–710.

Vorauer, J. D., Main, K. J., & O'Connell, G. B. (1998). How do individuals expect to be viewed by members of lower status groups? Content and implications of metastereotypes. *Journal of Personality and Social Psychology, 75*(4), 917–937.

Wright, P. M., & Nishii, L. H. (2007). *Strategic HRM and organizational behavior: Integrating multiple levels of analysis*. CAHRS Working Paper Series. Paper 468. Retrieved from http://digitalcommons.ilr.cornell.edu/cgi/viewcontent.cgi?article=1469&context=cahrswp.

Chapter 15
Developing Multiple Careers: Dealing with Work–Life Interaction

Ines Martinez-Corts and Evangelia Demerouti

15.1 Introduction

Considering heterogeneity of society, and drawing on the "Circle of Inclusion" (see Arenas et al. Chap. 1 in this volume), inclusive organizations should promote diverse career development and avoid excluding or adversely incorporate people and groups—i.e., women, older people. In this chapter, we highlight social dialogue[1] as a social innovation strategy to design diverse careers in which not only vulnerable groups, but also a wide range of heterogeneity may be present.

Inclusive organizations should be aware that in managing their careers, individuals may be motivated to fulfill values related to their different roles—i.e., work, self, family (Hall et al. 2013). For instance, younger employees show an increased desire to balance work and personal goals (Smola and Sutton 2002). Therefore, analyzing work–non-work interaction may highlight our understanding of contemporary and

This work was funded by the Spanish Ministry of Economy and Competitiveness (MINECO/FEDER),grant reference n. PSI2015-64894-P.

[1]Social dialogue is defined as "discussions, consultations, negotiations, and joint actions involving organizations representing the two sides of the industry (employers and workers). Social dialogue is a process by which relevant parties seek to resolve employment-related differences via an information exchange" (Bryson et al. 2012, p. 5).

I. Martinez-Corts (✉)
University of Seville, Seville, Spain
e-mail: corts@us.es

E. Demerouti
Eindhoven University of Technology, Eindhoven, The Netherlands

A. Arenas et al. (eds.), *Shaping Inclusive Workplaces Through Social Dialogue*, Industrial Relations & Conflict Management,
DOI 10.1007/978-3-319-66393-7_15

diverse career dynamics (Greenhaus and Kossek 2014). In this chapter, we focus on work–life interaction—work–life conflict[2] (WLC) and enrichment[3] (WLE)—as a relevant driver to promote diverse career development in organizations. Drawing on the job demands–resources model (Demerouti et al. 2001), we posit that WLC is a demand (a situation that costs effort), whereas WLE is a resource (a situation that motivates individuals to invest effort). In other words, reducing WLC is necessary to avoid the negative outcomes that impede individuals' career management. Complementary, promoting WLE enhances individuals' resources that promote their career development. For instance, work–family enrichment has been consistently related to career outcomes such as job satisfaction and affective commitment (McNall et al. 2010). Opposite, WLC have a direct negative relationship with career satisfaction (Martins et al. 2002), self-rated as well as manager-rated work performance and hierarchical level and salary (Hoobler et al. 2010).

Since WLC and WLE are two independent mechanisms and that employees can experience them simultaneously (Boz et al. 2016; Demerouti and Geurts 2004), social dialogue in organizations may contribute to reduce WLC and enhance WLE simultaneously. In doing so, we propose to focus specifically on structural or formal human resources policies and practices—work–life policies (WLPs), and on organizational cultural/relational support—organizational work–life culture (WLCU) (Kossek et al. 2010). Both WLPs and WLCU have been widely related to WLC and WLE experiences (i.e., Allen et al. 2013; Dikkers et al. 2004). Next, in this chapter, we analyze the potential of these two conditions for individuals to negotiate their work–non-work relationship and their career development.

WLPs and WLCU operate and are negotiated at workplace level by employers, representatives, and employees. Although social dialogue at national level has been widely analyzed, social dialogue at workplace level is underexplored. Specifically, we focus in social dialogue at the ground floor, where negotiations take place between individual employees and their superior on a daily basis (Nauta 2015). Although WLPs are usually negotiated in the first floor—between management, human resource managers, and work councils—in practice, social dialogue in a ground floor is a main issue for the implementation of WLPs. Moreover, daily negotiations in the ground floor also contribute to build a supportive WLCU. Therefore, we aim to shed light on the ground floor social dialogue by explaining why and how to provide employees' voice, opinions, and concerns about how to

[2]Work-family conflict has been defined by Greenhaus and Beutell as "a form of interrole conflict in which the role pressures from the work and family domains are mutually incompatible in some respect" (1985, p. 77). Work-family conflict occurs when demands of one role drain the resources —time, strain, and emotions—needed to meet the demands of the other role (Greenhaus and Beutell 1985).

[3]Work–family enrichment is the perception that the work/family role provides individuals with instrumental and affective resources that help them to improve affect and performance in their family/work domain (Greenhaus and Powell 2006). These resources refer to the two main components of work–family enrichment, one more instrumental, related to skills, abilities, and values, and another more affective, related to climate, mood, and emotions (Carlson et al. 2006).

manage work and non-work conditions in order to promote diverse career development.

First, we highlight gender and life stage as two main sources of diverse career development. We explain how work and life conditions determine men and women's and different life stage employees' career development. Second, drawing in a research review and our own empirical data, we provide evidence on working conditions—WLPs and WLCU—that may reduce WFC and increase WFE. In doing so, we aim to establish some key issues on working conditions to be negotiated between supervisors and employees through social dialogue. In the third section, we highlight some supervisors' characteristics to facilitate social dialogue in the ground floor. Finally, we provide some guidelines on how to improve social dialogue to negotiate diverse career development. We focus on how empowering employees, and specifically protected groups, to proactively manage their career.

15.1.1 Diverse Career Development. Considering Gender and Life Stage Diversity

In this section, we explain how work and family conditions may shape career developments across different life stages and between men and women. Powell and Greenhaus (2010) suggest that individuals in one life domain are influenced by the characteristics of the other domain. Specifically, they discriminated between three types of decisions. First, role entry decisions—decisions about whether to seek full-time or part-time employment, or to enhance one's credentials for an occupation, which are typically made during the exploration and/or establishment stage. Second, role participation decisions—decisions regarding the amount of investment of time and emotion at work, participation in role-related activities, etc., typically prevalent in middle adulthood. Third, role exit decisions—decisions to abandon an occupation or career path, to quit a job or leave an organization, to retire early, etc., typically made during late adulthood. All types of decisions are influenced by or based on family and work considerations and conditions, which may differ for women—i.e., postponing motherhood, taking care of older members of the family, partner work. Women are still the primary caregivers and have more non-work responsibilities than men, and have to address unexpected personal and family demands. Such responsibilities or demands force women to craft their career in response to their personal values and particular life situations (Valcour et al. 2007). Therefore, with special attention to women organizational inclusion, it is essential to focus on work and life conditions.

Another reason why we should focus on work and family conditions is that such conditions may explain how work–life management may change throughout one's career. Based on the assumption that work and family conditions change in the course of one's career, Demerouti et al. (2012) suggested in their review that young employees are expected to be exposed to high demands, and insufficient resources, in both the work and non-work domains. Not surprisingly, this group was found to experience high WLC and low WLE (Demerouti et al. 2012). During middle adulthood, employees were expected to possess high job demands, average home demands, and high resources in both the work and non-work domains. Literature suggests that this group experiences high work–family–conflict but also high family–work–conflict and high family–work enrichment (e.g., Matthews et al. 2010). During late adulthood, employees were expected to have average demands and high resources in both the work and non-work domains. Consequently, they were found to experience lower levels of inter-role conflict and higher levels of enrichment/facilitation compared to their younger and middle-aged counterparts (Demerouti et al. 2012). Linking career and life stages with daily WLC and WLE experiences enables to better guide worker's career development, finding ways to support them (see Peters et al. Chap. 14 in this volume). It is especially relevant when integrating diversity because employers are able to target interventions to specific work–family needs for each group.

A third reason is that research seems to suggest that the conditions not only at home but also at work differ between men and women. Dubbelt et al. (2016) studied whether gender discrimination had a relationship with the job characteristics of women working in two different work environments, namely a male-dominated work environment (more than 70% males) and a gender-balanced work environment (about 50% females). The results provide preliminary evidence that gender discrimination is related to experiences of a suboptimal work environment for women working in a male-dominated work environment and a more gender-balanced work environment. The more gender discrimination women perceived the higher their level of job demands was and the lower their level of job resources was. These results highlight that gender discrimination was related to suboptimal working conditions.

The above information highlights gender and life stage as two main determinants in diverse career management. Both types of diversity shape WLC and WLE experiences through perceived differences in work demands and work resources. Therefore, social dialogue in inclusive organizations should be a tool to provide enough resources to assure diverse career development, specifically between women, young, and middle adulthood employees.

15.2 Promoting Diverse Work–Life Experiences. Organizational Conditions for Social Dialogue at the Ground Floor

As the case "Utility" in the box shows, to better manage work and life interaction and allow for a diverse career development, organizations have two main challenges: provide with formal WLPs and provide with the cultural support toward work–life issues (Kossek et al. 2010). In this section, we provide evidence on how these organizational challenges may alter work–life experiences. We posit that meanwhile WLPs are focused on reducing WLC experiences; cultural support toward work–life issues may enhance WLE experiences. Drawing on the Accommodation Model and the Redesign Model (Perlow and Kelly 2014), we will explain the paradoxical outcomes when using WLPs and how culture may enhance WLE experiences.

Box: Case study "Utility"

"The 'Utility' is a for-profit public company with approximately 850 employees located in Southern Spain and is highly unionized. It is highly hierarchical structured. Although 'Utility' is a public company, it is considered to be very competitive as it is the leading firm in its sector in the country. This organization has been offering a wide range of WLPs via collective agreement since 2005. 'Utility' has been acknowledged as a family-friendly organization for it has been recently nominated for a national prize directed toward flexible workplaces. Surprisingly though, 'Utility' is male-dominated (80% of men). A gliding segregation phenomenon can be observed in 'Utility': Women with the same educational level as men often end up in more administrative and support positions instead of technical and strategic ones. In 'Utility,' there is a significant group of employees in a high commitment contract consisted of an agreement that formally requires total availability for more demanding job positions in exchange of a significant additional compensation. The implementation of this contract was part of the organizational strategy to increase employees' commitment toward to the company. High commitment contract is a management practice to assess performance since the 'greater commitment hours' have to be clocked in and out in the sites of 'Utility.' In 'Utility,' performance assessment is mainly based on time control even for those under the greater commitment contract, and business related targets exist for some positions only. Finally, the greater commitment contract is also perceived as an organizational barrier to an effective boundary management since it does not allow employees to organize their non-work time with total autonomy. Though this practice creates a specific context deeply embedded in assumptions and expectations related to availability, power relationships and fairness perceptions ultimately shape employees' experiences with WLPs utilization in the studied organization" (Boz et al. 2011).[4]

A quantitative study was conducted with 287 voluntary and anonym employees in "Utility" to analyze the mediation effect of organizational work–life culture in the relationship between the use of WLPs and WLC and

[4]The description of the case study has been extracted from a qualitative paper presented in 2011 at the IV International Conference of Work and Family (ICWF), IESE, Barcelona, Spain.

WLE experiences. As expected, based on the ideal worker model, WLPs utilization is positive related to WLCU hindrance, which increases levels of WLC. However, contrary to the organizational support theory, WLPs utilization is negatively related to WLCU support, which in turn relates to increased levels of conflict and reduced levels of WLE (Boz et al. 2014).

15.2.1 Dealing with Work–Life Policies to Reduce Work–Life Conflict: The Accommodation Model

WLPs are valuable resources that provide individuals with more time, skills, and material assets to allow them to enhance their participation in the private domain. By offering formal WLPs—i.e., flexible scheduling, telecommuting, daycare, and eldercare assistance— organizations expect to reduce employees work–life conflict and improve a number of work outcomes such as increased career and job satisfaction, work-related performance, and a reduced burnout, absenteeism, and turnover intention (Butts et al. 2013). From the *Accommodation Model*, WLPs "help individuals accommodate the work demand" (Perlow and Kelly 2014, p. 112) to reduce the incompatibilities between work, family, and life demands. Therefore, WLPs would be focused on reducing WLC.

These formal policies theoretically offered by the organization to all employees are in practice individually negotiated with supervisors and are individually implemented (Perlow and Kelly 2014). For instance, as can be seen in the Utility case, in many organizations, WLPs are only available to blue-collars (e.g., Lambert and Waxman 2005) and workers rewarded for their high performance (Kelly and Moen 2007). Moreover, although many organizations held a wide range of WLPs, in practice, flexible work policies are only used when managers are work–life supportive (Perlow and Kelly 2014). Therefore, we highlight the role of supervisor in social dialogue to negotiate WLPs implementation.

As in the Utility case, many organizations offer a wide range of WLPs as a strategy to attract, motivate, and retain talent. However, as it is observed in "Utility," their capacity to reduce WLC and promote positive outcomes can be limited. As highlighted by Allen et al. (2013), there are a number of factors that may affect the effectiveness of WLPs:

1. *The work–life conflict direction*. Drawing on Frone et al. (1994) domain specificity model, WLPs have been demonstrated to be more effective to reduce the conflict caused by work demands and less effective to reduce conflict initiated by family demands (Allen et al. 2013). This is not so strange though, as WLPs are targeted to work characteristics rather than family aspects.

2. *WLPs use and availability*. Differentiating between the use and availability of WLPs is important to understand why employees improve their attitudes and reduce WLC even though not using these policies. Drawing on Butts et al. (2013) model and based on Grover and Crooker (1995), WLPs availability operates through symbolic mechanisms creating a supportive and caring view of the organization. Drawing on the social exchange theory, when employees perceive that their organizations care about them, employees reciprocate their debt felt with positive attitudes. However, WLPs use operates by an instrumental mechanism in reducing WLC as they aim to help employees deal with job requirements. According with the self-interest theory (Sears and Funk 1991), employees would need to feel the benefits of WLPs to reduce WLC and improve work attitudes. Butts et al. (2013) provided empirical evidence of the mediation effect of family-supportive organization perceptions and work–family conflict as two mediating mechanisms in the symbolic and instrumental paths, respectively. In line with these results, Allen et al. (2013) found that flexplace use is more negatively related to work–life conflict than flexplace availability. Therefore, negotiating a wide range of policies may be positive to create a family-friendly organizational perception between employees, which in turn would reduce their work–family conflict, to finally improve work attitudes. However, to directly reduce work–life conflict would be necessary to facilitate the use of these policies. In doing so, supervisors have been identified as a main source of support to create an organizational culture positively oriented to work–life balance (Allen 2001). Specifically, they are a main source of instrumental and emotional support toward reducing employees' WLC (Kossek et al. 2011).
3. *Considering diversity*. WLPs use and its effectiveness to reduce WLC may vary as a function of individuals' differences. Results from Allen and colleagues' meta-analysis (Allen et al. 2013) show a stronger negative impact of WLPs on work–family conflict in workers married and with children. Butts et al. (2013) found consistent results with Allen et al. (2013) and also found gender differences. Thus, in samples with more women, the positive relationship between availability and use of WLPs was stronger, and the negative relationship between use of WLPs and work–family conflict was weaker. Therefore, according with empirical finding, WLPs may be more effective to reduce work–life conflict in married, parents, and women employees, i.e., those groups of employees who need them more. When representatives negotiate, formal WLPs should be prevented to highlight the needs of these specific groups of employees. Drawing on diversity, WLPs should also provide options to other different groups of employees—e.g., different generations, lifestyle, and family configuration—to allow them choosing how to manage their specific work–life interaction experiences. For instance, according to diverse motivational needs, Shockley and Allen (2010) found in a sample of university staff that employees' motivation to segmentation—motivation to keep physical and temporal boundaries between work and personal life—is negatively related to flextime and flexplace work–life policy use. Moreover, Shockley and Allen (2010) found that family responsibility moderated the relationship between employees'

occupational achievement needs and flextime use. Specifically, the relationship between employees' occupational achievement needs and the use of flextime policies was positive when family responsibilities were high, and negative when family responsibilities were low. Therefore, considering not only the individuals' differences but the interaction between these differences makes it more difficult for representatives to negotiate formal WLPs to satisfy all employees in an organization. Organizations must be aware of employees' diversity when providing different WLPs so that employees can choose what they need for their work–life interaction.

The previous Utility case exemplifies how the use of WLPs may result in a counterproductive outcome. As the Accommodation Model posits, employees using WLPs are seen as deviating from the ideal worker—full-time, on-site, without interruption career development. Thus, employees using WLPs are often perceived as less motivated because they are perceived to prioritize personal life beyond work (Leslie et al. 2012), and WLPs can have severe social and career development consequences. First, these employees may be stigmatized by co-workers, managers, and community (Williams et al. 2013). Second, organizations penalize employees' career development in terms of fewer career development opportunities for advancement and promotions (Hoobler et al. 2010) and slower wage growth (Coltrane et al. 2013).

As can be seen in the Utility case, WLPs leave the broader organizational culture unchallenged—characterized by the masculinized ideal worker norm—and may marginalize the employees who are more likely to use them—i.e., women, parents—(Ryan and Kossek 2008), reinforcing inequalities in the workplace—i.e., gender inequalities. As highlighted by many researchers (i.e., Allen 2001; Butts et al. 2013; Wayne and Casper 2016), although WLPs may help employees to increase their "sense of control" or even "control" their work–life interaction, there are fundamental aspects of the organization such as organizational WLCU, which can impede employees to successfully balance their career and private life.

15.2.2 Promoting Organizational Work–Life Culture to Increase Work–Life Enrichment: The Work Redesign Model

Organizational WLCU is defined as "the shared assumptions, beliefs, and values regarding the extent to which an organization supports and values the integration of employees' work and family lives" (Thompson et al. 1999: 394). WLCU encompasses aspects concerning support by managers (organization), supervisor, and co-workers toward employees' family responsibilities and also hindrance, such as perceptions of negative career development in relation to WLPs utilization and expectations that employees should spend much time visible at work (Dikkers et al. 2004). Both support and hindrance components are independent aspects of culture and may coexist (Boz et al. 2014; Peper et al. 2011). For example, Dikkers et al. (2004) suggest there could be a contradictory culture characterized by high support and high hindrance. Existing evidence has confirmed that perceived work–life hindrance has been directly related to increased levels of conflict (e.g., Peper et al. 2011). Opposite, perceived WLCU support is directly related to lower levels of conflict and higher levels of enrichment (e.g., Dikkers et al. 2004).

The *Work Redesign Model* (Perlow and Kelly 2014) posits that, beyond offering WLPs, organizations must provide with conditions—improving work process, collective cultural change—to promote a supportive work–life culture. When promoting work–life culture, organizations recognize and support persons with the different roles that they are involved in—work, self, family, community—and value what people bring to their business role from other roles. In other words, organizations recognize the positive effects of WLE experiences. Therefore, organizations should provide with enough resources—i.e., work redesign processes supporting WLCU—to promote WLE experiences. Moreover, WLCU moves from the ideal worker to diversity by providing with flexibility and support for all different employees' work–life interactions. Cultural change through work redesign processes is produced when employees find new ways of doing their work and in doing so they change norms about work schedules and employees interactions. Next, we describe two work redesign interventions and provide empirical evidence of their effectiveness. Both are interventions of social dialogue between co-workers and the supervisor–employee and provide the basis for the desired change—changing individual behavior and organizational norms.

Results-Only Work Environment (*ROWE*). Ressler and Thompson (2008) designed ROWE to promote an organizational culture change that increase employees' sense of schedule control using trust as a basic tool in the process. The slogan for ROWE is "free to do whatever they want, whenever they want, as long as the work gets done." Promoting a culture where the norm is flexibility implies a collective effort to change institutionalized expectations about performance norms. Specifically, ROWE intervention replaces face time workplace norms by rewarding productivity and job requirements (Ressler and Thompson 2008). It is a wide intervention as far as it incorporates changes in human resources policies, changes in informal organizational culture, and changes in the structure of work (Kossek and Distelberg 2009). Therefore, senior managers, executives, and managers must agree with the intervention. Group exercises, guided dialogue, and open discussion forums between employees promote critical thinking about the traditional model. Through these forms of direct participation in social dialogue, employees identify creative effective new ways of working and analyze how to implement changes. Kelly et al. (2011) found evidence of the effectiveness of ROWE intervention in reducing work–life conflict, improving work–family fit providing more time adequacy to develop different roles—work, family, self–increasing control over where and when they work, promoting healthy practices such as exercise, more sleeping hours, and also positive organizational outcomes—i.e., lower turnover intentions, higher perception of work–family-friendly culture, and greater organizational commitment and job satisfaction.

Predictable Time Off (PTO). It is a related strategy also aimed to change organizational culture toward a more equity and flexible organization culture. Perlow and her colleagues conducted an experiment in a consulting organization to improve the work process and consultant's personal lives (see Perlow 2012 for a depth description). Surprisingly, they identified the lack of predictability and not the long working hours as a problem in all levels, genders and marital status consultants. Perrow proposed to each member of the team to take a predictable night off. This should be a collective goal and felt owned by each team. In PTO teams, although support from managers is necessary, the focus is on negotiation at team level. Participation in different meetings is mandatory for participants to review how each member deals with the collective goal, helps others to get his/her night off, and identifies opportunities for change in case of fail. Trust, transparency, and openness about work and personal life are valued outcomes in the process to make change happens. In their studies, Perrow and colleagues demonstrated compelling work–life benefits (Perlow 2012). This strategy, that might be considered as a form of teams' direct participation, promoted different ways of organizing work avoiding unnecessary work and helped members to improve interpersonal communication.

15.3 The Role of Supervisors in Diverse Career Development

As already indicated, supervisors play a role in social dialogue at the ground floor, for instance, to provide resources or to promote a WLCU. In this section, we explain some specific mechanisms in doing so. Several studies have shown that a supportive relationship with one's supervisor is associated with diminished work–family conflict and positive work–life outcomes (Major et al. 2008). Employees are found to be less likely to experience work–family conflict (Thomas and Ganster 1995) and psychological strain (O'Driscoll et al. 2003) if their supervisors supported their efforts to balance work and family needs. Having an understanding and supportive supervisor is related to higher scores on positive indicators of life quality (coping/mastery) and lower scores on negative indicators of life quality (work/life conflict, overload, and stress) for both men and women (Moen and Yu 2000). Interestingly, Major et al. (2008) showed that a supportive work–family culture influences work–family interference through the experience of supportive supervisory and co-workers.

Kossek et al. (2011) found meta-analytic evidence that work–family-specific supervisor support is more strongly related to work–family conflict than general supervisor support and that general and work–family-specific supervisor indirectly relate to work–family conflict via organizational work–family support. However, supervisor work–family support was also directly related to work–family conflict indicating that other mediating variables could explain why supervisor support alleviates work-to-family conflict, e.g., decreasing job demands, workloads, and tight deadlines or increasing employee control over the timing and location of work through structural job design (Kossek et al. 2011).

Leadership is thus associated with employee (and organizational) outcomes, but the mechanisms through which leaders exert their influence on their followers' outcomes have not been adequately addressed in the literature (Avolio et al. 2004). Notable exceptions are the studies of Breevaart and colleagues (Breevaart et al. 2015, 2014a), who showed that followers in high-quality Leader Member exchange (LMX) relationships received more latitude to make decisions about how and when to perform their work (i.e., autonomy), received more opportunities to grow and develop (i.e., developmental opportunities), and more social support from their colleagues. In turn, these resources contribute to how engaged followers fell in their work and how well they performed their core tasks. Similarly, a transformational leader (i.e., inspiring, intellectual challenging and attentive of individual needs) makes employees more engaged in their work and better performing because their basic needs are fulfilled (Breevaart et al. 2014a), and employees' work environment is more resourceful (more autonomy and support) (Breevaart et al. 2014b).

These empirical findings suggest that leaders have great potential to contribute to the amount of job demands and resources of their employees. Leaders who develop high-quality relationships with their subordinates and who are transformational are likely to promote autonomy or valuable coaching in the work environment, to provide support and relevant feedback, and to adjust job demands such that they are more affordable. The availability of such job resources and the prevalence of affordable job demands are found to enhance followers' motivation and health and consequently is suggested to help them to effectively manage their work and nonwork roles. Moreover, when job demands are not overly high, employees need to invest less effort to fulfill them, which will leave them available resources (energy) to manage work and non-work roles.

On the basis of this empirical evidence, supervisors' leadership and specific support for work–life balance are key tools to facilitate social dialogue at the ground floor. As it has been explained, it is not a matter of negotiating a wide range of WLPs, but to individually negotiate resources with employees to better manage their career development. By providing with resources such as trust, autonomy, or feedback, supervisors stablish the optimal conditions for employees to negotiate specific work conditions on a daily basis.

Nevertheless, since supervisors may not always be present or willing to facilitate resource allocation, it is important to examine how employees may take responsibility to create a resourceful work environment for themselves.

15.4 Empowering Employees to Proactively Manage Their Career

In this section, we provide with some specific strategies on how employees may get greater control in their career management. We highlight the relevance of such strategies to integrate diversity in organizations, focusing specifically on vulnerable groups.

Social dialogue in the ground floor may constitute an innovative tool for individuals—specifically for individuals who belong to a vulnerable group—to proactively create a resourceful work environment to manage their career development. Through formal and informal dialogue between supervisors and employees and between co-workers, individuals, and specifically minorities are allowed to proactively manage their career development. In this way, employees can complement top-down approaches of job design or provided work–life policies to make them fit to their own situation and preferences. Dubbelt and colleagues (Dubbelt et al. 2016) studied proactive strategies that focused on managing the self-domain (time spend on personal interests) with work (i.e., self-regulation), and strategies that focused on altering the constellation of job characteristics (i.e., job crafting strategies). They chose to focus on these strategies, because women, particularly when they are in a minority position at work, have to compensate for a lack of resources in the work environment (e.g., Benschop and Doorewaard 2012) and may benefit from a proactive approach toward resources.

Specifically, Dubbelt et al. (2016) found that women can purposefully maximize self-work facilitation by using four self-regulation strategies, i.e., prevention focus (aiming to avoid making mistakes and to fulfill all responsibilities; Higgins 1998), mastery approach (persistently spend effort and regulate their behavior to achieve their goals; Elliot 1999), self-goal setting (the formation of personal goals to attain personal satisfaction or organizational goals; Marques-Quinteiro and Curral 2012), self-rewarding (e.g., rewarding themselves when individuals achieve their goal, Houghton and Neck 2002). The value of the personal domain for the work domain lies in the fact that it may provide employees with energy, motivation, and intention which can be used at work (i.e., self-work facilitation). These self-regulation strategies were beneficial for women to experience more daily self-work facilitation, but were not helpful for men. These strategies helped women to focus on the resources that are available and to ignore the things that are irrelevant for goal achievement (e.g., Locke and Latham 2002).

Next to self-regulation, job crafting has been studied as a way to increase optimal functioning of employees in general and women in particular. Job crafting is defined as making small changes within the boundaries, conditions, and relationships of one's job (Wrzesniewski and Dutton 2001) by seeking demands (e.g., acquiring new responsibilities), decreasing demands (e.g., combining tasks), or seeking resources (e.g., asking for feedback) (Petrou et al. 2012). Job crafting is a proactive behavior, and employees apply it when they feel that changes in their job is necessary (Petrou et al. 2012). As women have less access to job resources and more pressure to manage different roles, they may particularly profit from job crafting because it will help them to align existing job demands and resources with their needs such that can function effectively. Dubbelt et al. (2016) found that seeking challenges was positively related to career satisfaction, whereas seeking resources was positively related to task performance. Women benefitted more from seeking resources in terms of higher task performance compared to men, whereas men's task performance benefitted more from decreasing demands compared to women. These findings highlight the importance of proactive strategies that women can employ to create favorable work conditions for success and to survive (Eagly and Carli 2007). Through social dialogue at ground floor, employees and specifically those who belong to vulnerable groups would have equal career development opportunities. Diverse organizations' human resource policies (see the Circle of Inclusion) should be oriented to promote individuals proactive initiatives that have to be negotiated with supervisors and colleagues to assure diverse career development (Arenas et al., Chap. 1 in this volume).

15.5 Conclusion

As it has been explained in this chapter, promoting WLE and reducing WLC experience should be an organizational strategy to assure diverse career development. In doing so, organizations need to negotiate WLPs but also promote a work–life culture to assure employees' use of WLPs. The decision to include work–life interaction issue in social dialogue can be the result of a cost-benefit balance. As we have seen in this chapter, costs of engaging employees and workers' representatives in the process of work–life interaction decision-making are outweighed by benefits, such as increased diversity.

Some of the available WLPs in organizations can be the result of the implementation of existing legislation. Law is important to assure basic human rights but not enough to go deeply into individual employees needs to manage diverse careers. In this sense, social dialogue with representatives can play an important role to promote formal work–life support in individual workplaces and in public policy areas (Firestein 2009). Given social dialogue availability to solve differences via an information exchange process, employers may ask employees what WLPs would help them to better integrate work and life roles and negotiate them with employees' representatives. First, through collective bargaining agreements, it is secured that work–family programs are developed and implemented for diverse workers (i.e., all levels of workers, not only highly valued workers, women, parents). Second, these agreements can promote changes in public policies in going beyond state legislation.

Since formal benefits and programs are negotiated by workers' representatives and employers, it could be assumed that negotiated benefits and programs best suit to a majority of the employees. However, as it was said before, diverse workforce implies a wide range of individual differences that have to be considered. Moreover, some organizations penalize employees' career development when WLPs are used. Therefore, the availability of WLPs does not assure their use. As it was explained, it depends on supervisor leadership and support, co-workers support, and workplace work–life norms. In this chapter, we highlight the role of social dialogue to enable employees to manage diverse career development according to their specific work–life situation. It goes beyond negotiating WLPs, but to individually proactively negotiate work conditions with supervisors and co-workers to generate resources.

Acknowledgement This work was funded by the Spanish Ministry of Economy and Competitiveness (MINECO/FEDER), grant reference n. PSI2015-64894-P

References

Allen, T. D. (2001). Family-supportive work environments: The role of organizational perceptions. *Journal of Vocational Behavior, 58*(3), 414–435. doi:10.1006/jvbe.2000.1774.

Allen, T. D., Johnson, R. C., Kiburz, K., & Shockley, K. M. (2013). Work–family conflict and flexible work arrangements: Deconstructing flexibility. *Personnel Psychology, 66*(2), 345–376. doi:10.1111/peps.12012.

Avolio, B. J., Zhu, W., Koh, W., & Bhatia, P. (2004). Transformational leadership and organizational commitment: Mediating role of psychological empowerment and moderating role of structural distance. *Journal of Organizational Behavior, 25*(8), 951–968. doi:10.1002/job.283.

Benschop, Y., & Doorewaard, H. (2012). Gender subtext revisited. *Equality, Diversity and Inclusion: An International Journal, 31*(3), 225–235. doi:10.1108/02610151211209081.

Boz, M., Martínez-Corts, I., & Munduate, L. (2014). *The dark side of work-life policies: Perceived negative consequences of the use of dependent care benefits*. 74th Academy of Management Annual Meeting, Philadelphia, USA.

Boz, M., Martínez-Corts, I., & Munduate, L. (2016). Types of combined family-to-work conflict and enrichment and subjective health in Spain: A gender perspective. *Sex Roles, 74*(3), 136–153. doi:10.1007/s11199-015-0461-5.

Boz, M., Martínez-Corts, I., Munduate, L., & Lewis, S. (2011). *High performance work systems and work-life policies utilization: Implications for employees' work-life balance*. IV International Conference of Work & Family (ICWF), IESE, Barcelona, Spain.

Breevaart, K., Bakker, A. B., & Demerouti, E. (2014a). Daily self-management and employee work engagement. *Journal of Vocational Behavior, 84*(1), 31–38. doi:10.1016/j.jvb.2013.11.002.

Breevaart, K., Bakker, A. B., Demerouti, E., & Van den Heuvel, M. (2015). Leader-member exchange, work engagement, and job performance. *Journal of Managerial Psychology, 30*(7), 754–770. doi:10.1108/JMP-03-2013-0088.

Breevaart, K., Bakker, A. B., Hetland, J., Demerouti, E., Olsen, O. K., & Espevik, R. (2014b). Daily transactional and transformational leadership and daily employee engagement. *Journal of Occupational and Organizational Psychology, 87*(1), 138–157. doi:10.1111/joop.12041.

Bryson, A., Forth, J., & George, A. (2012). *Workplace social dialogue in Europe: An analysis of the European company survey 2009*. Dublin: Eurofound.

Butts, M. M., Casper, W. J., & Yang, T. S. (2013). How important are work-family support policies? A meta-analytic investigation of their effects on employee outcomes. *Journal of Applied Psychology, 98*(1), 1–25. doi:10.1037/a0030389.

Carlson, D. S., Kacmar, K. M., Wayne, J. H., & Grzywacz, J. G. (2006). Measuring the positive side of the work-family interface: Development and validation of a work-family enrichment scale. *Journal of Vocational Behavior, 68*, 131–164. doi:10.1016/j.jvb.2005.02.002.

Coltrane, S., Miller, E. C., DeHaan, T., & Stewart, L. (2013). Fathers and the flexibility stigma. *Journal of Social Issues, 69*(2), 279–302. doi:10.1111/josi.12015.

Demerouti, E., Bakker, A. B., Nachreiner, F., & Schaufeli, W. B. (2001). The job demands-resources model of burnout. *Journal of Applied Psychology, 86*(3), 499–512. doi:10.1037/0021-9010.86.3.499.

Demerouti, E., & Geurts, S. (2004). Towards a typology of work-home interaction. *Community, Work & Family, 7*(3), 285–309. doi:10.1080/1366880042000295727.

Demerouti, E., Martínez-Corts, I., & Boz, M. (2013). Issues in the development of research on interrole enrichment. In S. Poelmans, J. Greenhaus & M. Las Heras (Eds.), *New frontiers in work-family research: A vision for the future in global world*. Chicago: Palgrave.

Demerouti, E., Peeters, M. C. W., & van der Heijden, B. I. J. M. (2012). Work-family interface from a life and career stage perspective: The role of demands and resources. *International Journal of Psychology, 47*(4), 241–258. doi:10.1080/00207594.2012.699055.

Dikkers, J. S. E., Geurts, S. A. E., Dulk, L. D., Peper, B., & Kompier, M. A. J. (2004). Relations among work-home culture, the utilization of work-home arrangements, and work-home interference. *International Journal of Stress Management, 11*(4), 323–345. doi:10.1037/1072-5245.11.4.323.

Dubbelt, L., Rispens, S., & Demerouti, E. (2016). Work engagement and research output among female and male scientists: A diary study. *Journal of Personnel Psychology, 15*(2), 55–65. doi:10.1027/1866-5888/a000150.

Eagly, A. H., & Carli, L. L. (2007). *Through the labyrinth: The Truth about how women become leaders*. Boston: Harvard Business School Press.

Elliot, A. (1999). Approach and avoidance motivation and achievement goals. *Educational Psychologist, 34*(3), 169–189. doi:10.1207/s15326985ep3403_3.

Firestein, N. (2009). Union strategies for work-family policies. In A. C. Crouter & A. Booth (Eds.), *Work-Life Policies* (pp. 61–69). Washington: The Urgan Institute Press.

Frone, M. R., Russell, M., & Cooper, M. L. (1994). Relationship between job and family satisfaction: Causal or noncausal covariation? *Journal of Management, 20*(3), 565–579. doi:10.1177/014920639402000303.

Greenhaus, J. H., & Beutell, N. J. (1985). Sources of conflict between work and family roles. *Academy of Management Review, 10*(1), 76–88. doi:10.5465/AMR.1985.4277352.

Greenhaus, J. H., & Kossek, E. E. (2014). The contemporary career: A work-home perspective. *Annual Review of Organizational Psychology and Organizational Behavior, 1*(1), 361–388. doi:10.1146/annurev-orgpsych-031413-091324.

Greenhaus, J. H., & Powell, G. N. (2006). When work and family are allies: A theory of work–family enrichment. *Academy of Management Review, 31*(1), 72–92. doi:10.5465/AMR.2006.19379625.

Grover, S. L., & Crooker, K. J. (1995). Who appreciates family-responsive human resource policies: The impact of family-friendly policies on the organizational attachment of parents and non-parents. *Personnel Psychology, 48*(2), 271–288. doi:10.1111/j.1744-6570.1995.tb01757.x.

Hall, D. T., Kossek, E. E., Briscoe, J. P., Pichler, S., & Lee, M. D. (2013). Nonwork orientations relative to career: A multidimensional measure. *Journal of Vocational Behavior, 83*(3), 539–550. doi:10.1016/j.jvb.2013.07.005.

Higgins, E. T. (1998). Promotion and prevention: Regulatory focus as a motivational principle. *Advances in Experimental Social Psychology, 30*, 1–46. doi:10.1016/S0065-2601(08)60381-0.

Hoobler, J. M., Hu, J., & Wilson, M. (2010). Do workers who experience conflict between the work and family domains hit a "glass ceiling?" A meta-analytic examination. *Journal of Vocational Behavior, 77*(3), 481–494. doi:10.1016/j.jvb.2010.07.001.

Houghton, J. D., & Neck, C. P. (2002). The revised self-leadership questionnaire: Testing a hierarchical factor structure for self-leadership. *Journal of Managerial Psychology, 17*(8), 672–691. doi:10.1108/02683940210450484.

Kelly, E. L., & Moen, P. (2007). Rethinking the clockwork of work: Why schedule control may pay off at work and at home. *Advances in Developing Human Resources, 9*(4), 487–506. doi:10.1177/1523422307305489.

Kelly, E. L., Moen, P., & Tranby, E. (2011). Changing workplaces to reduce work-family conflict: Schedule control in a white—collar organization. *American Sociological Review, 76*(2), 265–290. doi:10.1177/0003122411400056.

Kossek, E. E., & Distelberg, B. (2009). Work and family employment policy for a transformed work force: Trends and themes. In N. Crouter & A. Booth (Eds.), *Work-life policies* (pp. 1–51). Washington, DC: Urban Institute Press.

Kossek, E. E., Lewis, S., & Hammer, L. B. (2010). Work-life initiatives and organizational change: Overcoming mixed messages to move from the margin to the mainstream. *Human Relations, 63*(1), 3–19. doi:10.1177/0018726709352385.

Kossek, E. E., Pichler, S., Bodner, T., & Hammer, L. B. (2011). Workplace social support and work–family conflict: A meta-analysis clarifying the influence of general and work–family-specific supervisor and organizational support. *Personnel Psychology, 64*(2), 289–313. doi:10.1111/j.1744-6570.2011.01211.x.

Lambert, S. J., & Waxman, E. (2005). Organizational stratification: Distributing opportunities for balancing work and personal life. In E. E. Kossek & S. J. Lambert (Eds.), *Work and life integration: Organizational, cultural, and individual perspectives* (pp. 103–126). Mahwah, NJ: Erlbaum.

Leslie, L. M., Manchester, C. F., Park, T., & Mehng, S. A. (2012). Flexible work practices: A source of career premiums or penalties? *Academy of Management Journal, 55*(6), 1407–1428. doi:10.5465/amj.2010.0651.

Locke, E. A., & Latham, G. P. (2002). Building a practically useful theory of goal setting and task motivation: A 35-year odyssey. *American Psychologist, 57*(9), 705–717. doi:10.1037/0003-066X.57.9.705.

Major, D. A., Fletcher, T. D., Davis, D. D., & Germano, L. M. (2008). The influence of work-family culture and workplace relationships on work interference with family: A multilevel model. *Journal of Organizational Behavior, 29*(7), 881–897. doi:10.1002/job.502.

Marques-Quinteiro, P., & Curral, L. A. (2012). Goal orientation and work role performance: Predicting adaptive and proactive work role performance through self-leadership strategies. *Journal of Psychology, 146*(6), 559–577. doi:10.1080/00223980.2012.656157.

Martins, L., Eddleston, K., & Veiga, J. (2002). Moderators of the relationship between work-family conflict and career satisfaction. *The Academy of Management Journal, 45*(2), 399–409. Retrieved from http://www.jstor.org/stable/3069354.

Matthews, R. A., Barnes-Farrell, J. L., & Bulger, C. (2010). Advancing measurement of work and family domain boundary characteristics. *Journal of Vocational Behavior, 77*, 447–60. https://doi.org/10.1016/j.jvb.2010.05.008.

McNall, L. A., Nicklin, J. M., & Masuda, A. D. (2010). A meta-analytic review of the consequences associated with work-family enrichment. *Journal of Business and Psychology, 25*(3), 381–396. doi:10.1007/s10869-009-9141-1.

Moen, P., & Yu, Y. (2000). Effective work/life strategies: Working couples, work conditions, gender, and life quality. *Social Problems, 47*(3), 291–326. doi:10.1525/sp.2000.47.3.03x0294h.

Nauta, A. (2015). Industrial relations and work councils in the Netherlands: Results from interviews and a survey among HR managers. In M. C. Euwema, L. Munduate, P. Elgoibar, E. Pender, & A. Belén García (Eds.), *Promoting Social Dialogue in European Organizations: Human resources management and constructive conflict management,* 105–121. doi:10.1007/978-3-319-08605-7_8.

O'Driscoll, M. P., Poelmans, S., Spector, P. E., Kalliath, T., Allen, T. D., Cooper, C. L., et al. (2003). Family-responsive interventions, perceived organizational and supervisor support, work-family conflict, and psychological strain. *International Journal of Stress Management, 10*(4), 326–344. doi:10.1037/1072-5245.10.4.326.

Peper, A., Dikkers, J. S. E., Engen, M. L. van., & Vinkenburg, C. J. (2011). Causes and consequences of the utilization of work-life policies by professionals: Unconditional supervisor support required. In S. Kaiser, M. Ringlstetter, M. Pina e Cunha, & D. R. Eikhof (Eds.), *Creating balance? International perspectives on the work-life integration of professionals*, 225–250. Berlin: Springer. doi:10.1007/978-3-642-16199-5.

Perlow, L. A. (2012). *Sleeping with your smartphone: How to break the 24/7 habit and change the way you work*. Cambridge: Harvard Business Review Press.

Perlow, L. A., & Kelly, E. L. (2014). Toward a model of work redesign for better work and better life. *Work and Occupations, 41*(1), 111–134. doi:10.1177/0730888413516473.

Petrou, P., Demerouti, E., Peeters, M. C. W., Schaufeli, W. B., & Hetland, J. (2012). Crafting a job on a daily basis: Contextual correlates and the link to work engagement. *Journal of Organizational Behavior, 33*(8), 1120–1141. doi:10.1002/job.1783.

Powell, G. N., & Greenhaus, J. H. (2010). Sex, gender, and decisions at the family-work interface. *Journal of Management, 36*(4), 1011–1039. doi:10.1177/0149206309350774.

Ressler, C., & Thompson, J. (2008). *Why work sucks and how to fix it*. New York, NY: Penguin Group.

Ryan, A. M., & Kossek, E. E. (2008). Work-life policy implementation: Breaking down or creating barriers to inclusiveness? *Human Resource Management, 47*(2), 295–310. doi:10.1002/hrm.20213.

Sears, D. O., & Funk, C. L. (1991). The role of self-interest in social and political attitudes. In M. P. Zanna (Ed.), *Advances in experimental social psychology* (pp. 1–91). San Diego, CA: Academic Press.

Shockley, K. M., & Allen, T. D. (2010). Investigating the missing link in flexible work arrangement utilization: An individual difference perspective. *Journal of Vocational Behavior, 76*(1), 131–142. doi:10.1016/j.jvb.2009.07.002.

Smola, K. W., & Sutton, C. D. (2002). Generational differences: Revisiting generational work values for the new millennium. *Journal of Organizational Behavior, 23*(4), 363–382. doi:10.1002/job.147.

Thomas, L. T., & Ganster, D. C. (1995). Impact of family-supportive work variables on work-family conflict and strain: A control perspective. *Journal of Applied Psychology, 80*(1), 6–15. doi:10.1037/0021-9010.80.1.6.

Thompson, C. A., Beauvais, L. L., & Lyness, K. S. (1999). When work-family benefits are not enough: The influences of work-family culture on benefit utilization, organizational attachment, and work-family conflict. *Journal of Vocational Behavior, 54*(3), 392–415. doi:10.1006/jvbe.1998.1681.

Valcour, M., Bailyn, L., & Quijada, M. A. (2007). Customized careers. In H. Gunz & M. Peiperl (Eds.), *Handbook of career studies* (pp. 188–210). Thousand Oaks: Sage Publications.

Wayne, J. H., & Casper, W. J. (2016). Why having a family-supportive culture, not just policies, matters to male and female job seekers: An examination of work-family conflict, values, and self-interest. *Sex Roles, 75*(9), 459–475. doi:10.1007/s11199-016-0645-7.

Williams, J. C., Blair-Loy, M., & Berdahl, J. L. (2013). Cultural schemas, social class, and the flexibility stigma. *Journal of Social Issues, 69*(2), 209–234. doi:10.1111/josi.12012.

Wrzesniewski, A., & Dutton, J. E. (2001). Crafting a job: Revisioning employees as active crafters of their work. *Academy of Management Review, 26*(2), 179–201. doi:10.5465/AMR.2001.4378011.

Chapter 16
Inclusive HRM in West Africa? Women's Religious Congregations in Nigeria

Innocentina Obi and Katalien Bollen

16.1 Introduction

Women's exclusion in Nigerian leadership is still a reality. Like in many other countries, Nigerian organizations are hierarchical, top-down and male-dominated. Although it is known that women are key stakeholders in the development of any society, including Nigeria (Okafor and Akokuwebe 2015), women usually face many challenges when it comes to obtaining a leadership position or having a say in things (Weyer 2007). This long-standing undervalued and under-represented position of women in different societies and organizations has been globally acknowledged (Eagly and Karau 2002; Ecklund 2006; Grandy 2013). The same is true for Africa and Nigeria (Agadjanian 2015; Aina and Olayode 2012; Akubue 2016; Okafor et al. 2011). In this chapter, we focus on Nigeria, being the largest African society in terms of population and gross domestic product (GDP). In Nigeria, HRM faces various challenges. Instead of relying on specific HRM procedures or policies to make work-related decisions, often is relied upon the ethnicity, religion and gender of the person at hand (Fajana et al. 2011) with clear consequences for female leadership. Until now, gender issues are not yet a point of attention in many Nigerian organizations (Nwagbara et al. 2012; Olufemi and David 2011). This is largely due to a patriarchal culture, male chauvinism and anarchy which are present in Nigeria (NGP 2007; Okeke 2017). This is also reflected in women's under-representation and male dominance in leadership

I. Obi (✉)
Faculty of Psychology and Educational Sciences, Department of Occupational and Organizational Psychology and Professional Learning, Katholieke Universiteit Leuven, Dekenstraat 2, 3725 Leuven, Belgium
e-mail: innocentina.obi@kuleuven.be

K. Bollen
Department of Educational Research and Development, University of Maastricht, Tongersestraat, 53, 6211 LM Maastricht, The Netherlands

A. Arenas et al. (eds.), *Shaping Inclusive Workplaces Through Social Dialogue*, Industrial Relations & Conflict Management,
DOI 10.1007/978-3-319-66393-7_16

positions (Anigwe 2014; Olojede 2004; Olowe 2001). Given this situation, a key question is how to empower Nigerian women. How can women gain influence in overall society and specific organizations, and realize their full potential without feeling threatened? We explore these questions in this chapter. We start with a short overview of the Nigerian background.

16.2 Nigerian Context: An Overview

Nigeria is located in sub-Saharan West Africa. It is the most populated country in Africa, with a rapidly growing population of approximately 192 million inhabitants in 2017. Nigeria embeds many different tribes and subcultures, and women's rights and opportunities have been undermined economically, socioculturally and politically in both public and private spheres (Okafor et al. 2011). Nigeria is made up of more than 250 ethnic groups with Christian and Muslim religions in the south-eastern and northern parts of the country respectively. Compared to Western societies, religion is much more central to African people including Nigeria. In 2017, Nigeria remains Africa's largest economy. The Nigerian labour force is made up of approximately 55 million people, with 70% working in agriculture, 10% in industry and 20% in services.

Although there exists a strong economic track record, poverty remains significant in Nigeria. One of the things that may account for this is the poor investment in education. In Nigeria, an estimated 9 million children have never gone to school. And when they go to school, 40% of primary school teachers are unqualified, and 80% of the students do not have textbooks. Especially girls do not have the chance to attend classes. In Africa, around 30 million girls are denied the basic human right to education. This has also affected women's participation as full political citizens in Nigerian society and may explain why the male literacy rate (69.2%) is significantly higher than the female one (49.7%). Instead of going to school, women get married at a very young age.

Consequently, men dominate the political arena. For example, since the recent Nigerian elections, women hold only about 20 out of 360 seats in the House of Representatives, and seven out of 108 seats in the Senate, which can account for a total of 5.7% female representation (Agbalajobi 2010). Once operating in this political arena, these women often encounter many barriers including harassment; threats, violence. Also in the Nigerian Federal Civil Service, 76% of civil servants are men while only 24% are women (CIDA Nigeria GSAA 2006).

Since its independence in 1960, Nigerian women have continuously strived to gain equal rights and opportunities. This is reflected in laws, however, hardly in daily reality. For instance, the ministry of women affairs created in 1989 with the aim to review substantive and procedural laws that affect women (Usman 2005), is not functional in reality. This implies that till date, Nigerian women are discriminated and marginalized in politics, overall decision-making processes and leadership positions (Anigwe 2014; Chuku 2009; Nebolisa 2009). Nowadays, the position of Nigerian women is strongly debated especially in relation to their access to different types of leadership positions (e.g. Okafor and Akokuwebe 2015).

There are several factors that make it difficult for Nigerian women to progress and take up leadership: First, the Nigerian culture can be characterized as a high power distance culture (Hofstede 1980, 2017), meaning that people in position of formal hierarchy (especially men) are overly respected and listened to. As such, hierarchy, which has been bureaucratic, reinforcing authority of top management, has negatively influenced women's roles in Nigerian organizations (Okeke 2017) but may also have hindered social dialogue. Because in Nigeria, there is no tradition of social dialogue between employers and employees who could have defended, for instance, the rights of female employees. Second, many studies indicated the patriarchal nature of Nigerian society as one of the key factors militating against women's participation in management and leadership roles (Agbalajobi 2010; Mathur-Helm 2005; Okafor and Akokuwebe 2015; Omotola 2007). As such, Nigerian cultural values have barricaded women from participating in political and leadership positions (Awofeso and Odeyemi 2014; Okeke 2017). Instead, many wives are battered by their husbands and widows dehumanized through which they lose self-confidence and end up in silence in both private and public spheres (Aina and Olayode 2012).

On an economical level, it is for women much more difficult than men to get access to land and credit facilities. Consequently, women are at higher risk to end up in poverty (Mathur-Helm 2005; Omotola 2007). When at work, Nigerian women often encounter difficulties since the notion of inclusive human resources management (IHRM) is hardly on the agenda (Olufemi and David 2011). Studies have also found that the practice of HRM in Nigeria is day by day becoming more and more challenging (Ovadje and Ankomah 2001; Fajana 2009; Fajana et al. 2011). Female managers face strong negative stereotypes and are mostly perceived and described as lacking self-confidence, emotionally unstable, uncritical, inconsistent and perceived as displaying almost no leadership skills, compared to male managers (Okafor et al. 2011).

Olufemi and David (2011) advocate affirmative actions, which implement equal opportunities for minorities including women. Barriers include strong gender stereotypes (Okafor et al. 2011; see also Peeters et al., in this handbook) and lack of women's access to resources (Aina and Olayode 2012; Usman 2005). It is clear that gender roles constitute one of the major constraints of women's access to leadership positions in Nigeria (Olojede 2004; Olowe 2001). It can be said that women in Nigeria are marginalized in almost all aspects of public life (Alyssa 2002; Okafor and Akokuwebe 2015). And, what is even worse, women often do not know their rights under the international and local laws (Nebolisa 2009).

In such a context, the notion of inclusive human resources management which focuses on how to make sure that different types of groups are able to work in an integrated way in the workforce is far away. In such cases, the starting point might be how to create a safe working environment for relatively deprived and discriminated groups, so that they can claim their rights and equality can be built in. Examples of these are communal forms of working, often seen in agriculture, worker-owned organizations or cooperation in which communities are formed. We elaborate here one such a traditional form.

16.3 Female Religious Congregations as Inclusive Organizations

One way to realize equality, gain influence and create a safe workplace in a complex country as Nigeria, is to come together and to develop an organization based on values of inclusion. Nigeria has shown over the past 80 years a steady increase of mostly indigenous women's (and also foreign) religious organizations. For example, two indigenous women's religious congregations were founded in the 1930's and Missionary Sisters from Ireland came to Nigeria more than three decades before Nigerian independence in 1960. These sisters improved largely the livelihood of girls through a network of schools for teacher training, nursing and technical instructions. Although these organizations were thriving, there was still need for more.

Shortly after Nigeria got her independence in 1960, a female indigenous organization was founded in the southeastern part of the country. This religious order started with a small group of young women. Nowadays, the organization consists of more than 1000 professed women (Rev. Sisters) living and working across all the continents of the globe. Our study is based on this organization, whose members not only contemplate God in prayer but also engage in societal development through investing in female leadership, empowerment and inclusive practices. The organization defines a strong mission to contribute to society. This can be observed in their inclusive human resource management present in their community life and works—care of the poor and needy, education, different forms of health care and pastoral works, both in their own established institutions as well as in (non-) governmental institutions. In this chapter, we focus on the leadership of this organization and how the organization fosters inclusiveness through female leadership. Although our study only focuses on this specific organization, we believe that our results are very relevant since other indigenous Nigerian religious organizations show comparable patterns and in Nigeria we observe many similar religious 'start ups'.

Typically, sisters (as these religious women are usually addressed) live together in religious communities (Njoku 2014) and have their job in society, either directly employed by their organization, or by others such as education and health care. The local communities (where they live) are relatively small. The size varies between 2 and 30 sisters living together. In each community, one of the sisters is appointed as formal local community leader. Sisters can be active in leadership roles in the job they fulfil, for example in the management of schools, hospitals, pastorals, elderly and foster homes. Sisters, both leaders and members, are typically 'a sister among the other sisters' in the community. A leader in the community is perceived as 'first among equals'. This reflects the core value—equality.

One of the aims of this organization is to be a learning organization—where people consistently maximize their potential, new and extensive thinking are fostered, and people stimulated to learn together (Senge 2006). The organization can be characterized as a servant-led organization that endeavours to empower women by supporting the development of their leadership competences and other essential skills to face the challenges of the changing world. As an inclusive organization, this organization employs workers, both women and men from diverse backgrounds, who work both within their communities (domestic staff) and in their institutions (staff at different levels). They have approximately 400 teaching staff in nursery, primary, secondary and vocational schools and hospitals. They employ about 150 domestic staff working in different areas in their various communities and institutions (e.g. cleaners, drivers, gardeners, chefs). Here, inclusive policies are key.

New members or candidates that wish to join this organization apply both in writing and in person. The most important aspect of recruitment in this organization is that there is no segregation when it comes to ethnicity and religion. Even though it is a female organization, men are welcomed and can join the specific 'brother organization'. The majority of the candidates that join this organization have no higher educational qualification but they will be given the opportunity to develop their competences to the highest level. This implies that lack of education is no barrier to recruitment and selection in this organization. These lines of thought depict the ways through which this organization promotes inclusiveness.

16.4 Leadership and Dialogue Within this Women's Religious Organization

Typically, leadership for this organization is a synonym to service.

16.4.1 Election of Leaders and Social Dialogue

The organization has three levels of leadership—the central administration, the regional level and the local community level. Election of the general leader (GL) takes place during the six-yearly General Chapter. The General Chapter (GC) is a general assembly that is typically composed of delegates from all groups of sisters within the same congregation. Its aim is to review the state of affairs of the organization and to make a decision to embrace a specific direction for the congregation for the next 6 years. The election of the general leader and the general councillors that make up the central leadership team then follows. The main function of the central leadership team is to help navigate the decisions of the GC and other organizational affairs. All professed sisters participate in the election of the general leader through voting. The candidate to be elected must meet the required organizational criteria for leadership; especially, the need to have completed certain number of years as a member of the organization and must not be less than 35 years of age. Chapter Delegates (CDs) are elected from each group of the sisters from the first group (foundation members) through the youngest professed sisters. The CDs attend the GC during which they elect a GL from the already elected sisters. They also elect the general councillors that make up the central leadership team as we have already mentioned. The office of the central leadership team lasts for six years but any of them may be re-elected, however, not immediately for the third time. So, essentially the structure is democratic, where sisters regularly elect their representatives, their leaders and collectively decide on strategic issues. Though it needs to be mentioned that this form of representatives is quite different from western models of employee representation (Euwema et al. 2015). In some ways, the influence of the representatives is here even larger.

The election of the regional leaders and their councillors takes place in different regions and all professed sisters also participate in this election as above. However, there is neither a GC nor chapter representatives in this regard. The regional leaders and councillors make up the regional leadership team, and there are at the moment 6 regions in this organization. The office of the regional leadership team lasts for three years, although any of them may be re-elected but not immediately for the third time. The GL with the consent of the team appoints a local leader for the local communities. The local leader and the sisters in the community form the local leadership team. In some cases, the regional leader may also appoint the local leader. The office of the local superior lasts three years. She can also be re-appointed but not immediately for a third time. The election of different leadership teams in this organization is done by the sisters themselves (the immediate members of the congregation) and not by any external body or group. Remarkably, the central leadership team and even the GL will step down after 6 years and move to different assigned communities. The same is applicable to other leaders at different levels.

16.4.2 Purpose of Leadership and Leadership Structure

The main purpose of leadership for this organization is rooted in service, towards building and rebuilding solid community of members holding values such as mutual respect, affection and reciprocal confidence. Leadership in this organization is structured to embrace the values of authority (ability and influence), subsidiarity, shared responsibility, service and accountability (responsibility). One may argue that these leadership values are mostly rooted in relational, person oriented, ethical, follower oriented and servant leadership style.

Authority

Authority for this organization is the leader's ability to promote the common good of the members. Authority enables the leader to be an inspiration to the sisters and influences the sisters to embrace their vocation of service to humanity with renewed zeal, compassionate love and vigour. Most importantly, authority in this organization is typically exercised in dialogue and in shared responsibility. The process of dialogue will be discussed in detail later on. Dialogue for this organization encompasses adequate and effective information, active participation in deliberations and discussions and gearing towards better decision-making. Thus, the general leader is usually able to influence the deliberations and negotiations towards a common goal.

Subsidiarity

The principle of subsidiarity is pragmatic. The higher authority will always be clear about the responsibility of each level of leadership for the sake of order and common good. In other words, the value of subsidiarity is respectfully practiced so that the higher leadership may not take up a responsibility that could be carried out by a lower level leadership unless the common good requires it. The principle of subsidiarity, therefore, requires reliable, unvarying, truthful and coherent communications, dialogue, clear information and trust. Furthermore, with the principle of subsidiarity, the leader creates personal autonomy (responsibility), clear goals and empowerment. With these potentials, the principle of subsidiarity makes explicit the respective quality of each organizational member and each community. The principle of subsidiarity implies decentralization of authority, collaboration, and teamwork to prevent potential conflicts in the organization.

Service and accountability

Leaders are committed to serve their members with sense of responsibility in the community. Both the local leader and the members embrace each other in service through humility and cooperate with each other towards their common goal. Every service is rendered with due and responsible accountability, which involves transparency and clear goal definition.

Shared responsibility

Shared responsibility consists of delegating roles and responsibilities to the sisters. Sisters are expected to exercise their right and duty towards formation of policies that relate to their own living. These values are expected to serve as a springboard towards the development of leadership competences within and outside the organization. Thus, these female leaders also promote inclusivity in this organization.

16.4.3 Social Dialogue

Social dialogue in this organization consists of sisters' participation in leadership and involvement in decision-making towards a common good. In the local communities, each sister participates in social dialogue. The community members (the leader and the sisters) meet at least monthly to discuss pertinent issues that concern them. These issues include crucial community affairs, life and works, projects and other vital issues bothering the local community. The local leader represents the concerns and opinions of the community to the larger organization.

Sometimes important issues surface at the central level that need the contribution of each member; in this case, the message is circulated with high importance for immediate attention. For example, prior to the GC (usually a year), the central leadership team compiles various issues that are pertinent to the organization and forward them to each local community for deliberation and feedback. Sisters' deliberation and feedback form the key deliberations of the GC. Social dialogue embraces discussions on the following key areas: the founding spirit and charism of the organization, organizational policies and decisions, leadership and administration, work, lifelong learning and development, formation, etc. Usually, the community members discuss these issues and send their feedback to the organization through their local leader or any other sister that the leader may delegate. Through social dialogue, the members of this organization feel part of the organization and practice leadership which prepares them for potential leadership positions.

Notably, respect for each sister is more visible during social dialogue. Sisters respect each other's points of view and respectfully assert or express their points when needed. Leaders also let the sisters understand that their contributions count. Fair treatment towards each sister is the key to justice and trust. Social dialogue of this sort is rare in Nigeria. Furthermore, members of this organization have equal access to opportunities and resources and, as a result, can contribute devotedly towards the success of the organization.

16.4.4 Further Education and Development of Leadership Skills

Education is a very important aspect of this organization through which it promotes inclusion. The organization provides sisters the opportunity for optimal learning, developing and upgrading their academic know-how. It is believed that education provides sisters the opportunity to acquire skills to face the complex society. Sisters are therefore trained in sound quality education. The organization promotes lifelong learning as a key competence for leadership. A recent study (Obi and Euwema 2017) shows that there is a strong positive relation between length of membership in this organization and level of education, with many sisters achieving academic degrees, varying from bachelors and masters to Ph.D.'s. Although this venture is rather expensive, each leadership team of the organization finds it pertinent and worth investing in. This is in contrast to the overall Nigerian opinion.

16.4.5 Servant Leadership as a Concept to Realize Inclusion

Servant leadership aims primarily at service to the followers' needs and interests (Greenleaf 1977; Patterson 2003, 2010). These needs include building strong competences such as listening skills, empowerment, stewardship, community building, conceptual vision and building relationships (Coetzer et al. 2017; Liden et al. 2008, 2015; van Dierendonck and Patterson 2015). The concept of servant leadership shows many similarities with the concept of leadership as viewed by this organization and evident in their leadership structure above. For this organization, formation is an ongoing lifelong process that influences all aspects of human life and stimulates nation building. Developing leadership competences is an important element in this respect. Servant leadership, more than other related leadership styles (e.g. transformational, ethical, spiritual and authentic leadership), is follower oriented (van Dierendonck and Patterson 2015).

The choice for the servant leadership paradigm by this congregation is informed by its aim to promote inclusiveness through women's leadership and by the current demand of leadership that is relational and person oriented, pro-social, ethical, authentic and spiritual and above all, follower focused (van Dierendonck 2011; Liden et al. 2015; Parris and Peachey 2013). It is also mostly informed by the servant leadership functions knotted with its respective objectives, characteristics and competences (Coetzer et al. 2017; Malingumu et al. 2016; Sousa and van Dierendonck 2017; Spears 2010) that gear towards love, reconciliation, respect, equity and fairness of every individual. Servant leadership skills have been outstanding and more closely related to virtues and characteristics that are usually linked with women (Emmerik and Euwema 2009), which are catalyst for inclusion practices.

This organization develops leadership competences in their sisters through training in servant leadership characteristics: listening, emotional healing, creating value for the community, conceptual skills, compassionate love, empowerment, helping followers grow and succeed, putting followers first and behaving ethically (Liden et al. 2008, 2015; van Dierendonck 2011; van Dierendonck and Patterson 2015). These qualities are the core vehicles towards inclusion in practice.

Worthy of note is that this organization embraces community living as one of its core values and strives daily towards building and rebuilding it, with a view to building the wider community through these sisters. Building community is one of the major characteristics of servant leadership. According to Greenleaf (1977):

> All that is needed to rebuild a community as a viable life form for large numbers of people is for enough servant leaders to show the way, not by mass movements, but by each servant leader demonstrating his or her unlimited liability for a quite specific community related group (p. 53).

The female leaders in this organization promote inclusiveness through developing many female servant leaders in order to build the Nigerian nation.

16.5 Conclusion: Servant Leadership as a Way to Promote Inclusion

Leaders of this organization are aware of the fact that they have been elected by their sisters to serve them. Hence, they are all sisters with equal rights and corresponding responsibilities in the organization. The leaders, therefore, approach their members with a sense of equality, respect and fairness. This implies that, although some sisters among them are leaders, they are all sisters among themselves. In this organization, every sister has equal rights to the resources of the organization. For example, sisters take education in turns. Those that are competent and interested in vocational skills and other important competences are trained in that line. Equality, respect and fairness for this organization depend not only on counting every sister but also demonstrating that every sister counts.

References

Agadjanian, V. (2015). Women's religious authority in a Sub-Saharan setting: Dialectics of empowerment and dependency. *Gender & Society*, *29*(6), 982–1008. doi:10.1177/08912432106.

Agbalajobi, D. T. (2010). Womens participation and the political process in Nigeria: Problems and prospects. *African Journal of Political Science and International Relations, 4*(2), 75–82.

Aina, O. I. & Olayode, K. (2012). Gender equality, governance and women empowerment agenda in a democratizing society issues, prospects, and challenges. *Nigerian Sociological and Anthropological Journal*.

Akubue, M. T. E. (2016). *Exploring women's advancement in top management positions in higher education in southeast Nigeria* (Doctoral dissertation, Grand Canyon University).

Alyssa, Q. (2002). Women in Nigeria today. African postcolonial literature in English. *In the postcolonial web*. Retrieved June 21, 2017 from http://www.postcolonialweb.org/nigeria/contwomen.html.

Anigwe, A. (2014). *Perceptions of women in political leadership positions in Nigeria* (Unpublished dissertation).

Awofeso, O., & Odeyemi, T. I. (2014). Gender and political participation in Nigeria: A cultural perspective. *Journal Research in peace, Gender and Development, 4*(6), 104–110.

Chuku, G. (2009). Igbo women and political participation in Nigeria, 1800s-2005. *International Journal of African Historical Studies, 42*(1), 81–104. Retrieved from http://www.jstor.org/stable/40282431.

Coetzer, M. F., Bussin, M., & Geldenhuys, M. (2017). The functions of a servant leader. *Administrative Sciences, 7*(1), 5.

Eagly, A. H., & Karau, S. J. (2002). Role congruity theory of prejudice toward female leaders. *Psychological Review, 109*(3), 573.

Ecklund, E. H. (2006). Organizational culture and women's leadership: A study of six catholic parishes. *Sociology of Religion, 67*(1), 81–98. doi:10.1093/socrel/67.1.81.

Emmerik, I. J., & Euwema, M. C. (2009). The international assignments of peacekeepers: What drives them to seek future expatriation? *Human Resource Management, 48*(1), 135–151.

Euwema, M., Munduate, L., Elgoibar, P., García, A., & Pender, E. (Eds.). (2015). *Promoting social dialogue in European organizations. Human resources management and constructive conflict behavior*. Dordrecht: Springer.

Fajana, S. (2009). HR management in Africa: The social and economic framework. *Personalfuhrung, 7,* 80–86.

Fajana, S., Owoyemi, O., Elegbede, T., & Gbajumo-Sheriff, M. (2011). Human resource management practices in Nigeria. *Journal of Management and Strategy, 2*(2) (57 numbers). doi:10.5430/jms.v2n2p57.

Georgetown Institute for Women, Peace and Security. (2015). Election-related violence against women in Nigeria. Retrieved from http://blog.giwps.georgetown.edu/election-related-violence-against-women-in-nigeria/.

Grandy, G. (2013). An exploratory study of strategic leadership in churches. *Leadership & Organization Development Journal, 34*(7), 616–638. doi:10.1108/lodj-08-2011-0081.

Greenleaf, R. K. (1977). *Servant leadership: A journey into the nature of legitimate power and greatness*. New York: Paulist Press.

Hofstede, G. (1980). *Culture's consequences: International differences in work related values*. Beverly Hill, CA: Sage.

Hofstede (2017) What about Nigeria? https://geert-hofstede.com/nigeria.html. Retrieved June 27, 2017.

Liden, R. C., Wayne, S. J., Zhao, H., & Henderson, D. (2008). Servant leadership: Development of a multidimensional measure and multi-level assessment. *The Leadership Quarterly, 19*(2), 161–177. doi:10.1016/j.leaqua.2008.01.006.

Liden, R. C., Wayne, S. J., Meuser, J. D., Hu, J., Wu, J., & Liao, C. (2015). Servant leadership: Validation of a short form of the SL-28. *The Leadership Quarterly, 26*(2), 254–269.

Malingumu, W., Stouten, J., Euwema, M., & Babyegeya, E. (2016). Servant leadership, organisational citizenship behavior and creativity: The mediating role of team-member exchange. *Psychologica Belgica, 56*(4).

Mathur-Helm, B. (2005). Equal opportunity and affirmative action for South African women: A benefit or barrier? *Women in Management Review, 20*(1), 56–71.

Nebolisa, E. (2009). Women and Politics. *Peace & Conflict Monitor, 13*. Retrieved from http://search.ebscohost.com (AN 37584095).

Njoku, M. B. (2014). *Consecrated life: Towards deepening its understanding*. Enugu: Snaap Press.

Nwagbara, E. N., Etuk, G. R., & Baghebo, M. (2012). The social phenomenon of women empowerment in Nigeria: A theoretical approach. *Sociology Mind, 2*(04), 388.

NGP. (2007). *National gender policy' federal republic of Nigeria*. Abuja: Federal Ministry of Women Affairs and Social Development.

Obi, I., & Euwema, M. C. (2017). *Servant leadership and conflict management in women's religious congregation in Nigeria* (Unpublished).

Okafor, E., & Akokuwebe, M. E. (2015). Women and leadership in Nigeria: Challenges and prospects. *Women, 5*(4), 1–10.

Okafor, E. E., Fagbemi, A. O., & Hassan, A. R. (2011). Barriers to women leadership and managerial aspirations in Lagos, Nigeria: An empirical analysis. *African Journal of Business Management, 5*(16), 67–71.

Okeke, O. J. P. (2017). Nigerian culture: A barrier to the career progress of women in Nigeria. *Global Journal of Human Resource Management, 5*(5), 1–11.

Olojede, I. (2004). Public policy and gender politics in Nigeria. Paradox of gender equality. In *Nigerian politics*. Lagos: Concept Publications limited.

Olowe, S. K. (2001). *Correlates of career advancement among female professionals in Lagos state: Implications for management* (Unpublished doctoral dissertation). University of Lagos, Lagos, Nigeria.

Olufemi, J., & David, K. (2011). Gender issues in human resource management in Nigerian public service. *African Journal of Political Science and International Relations, 5*(3), 112–119.

Omotola, S. J. (2007). What is this gender talk all about after all? Gender, power and politics in cotemporary Nigeria. *African Study Monographs, 28*(1).

Ovadje, F., & Ankomah, A. (2001). Human resource management in Nigeria. In P. S. Budhwar & Y. A. Debrah (Eds.), *Human resource management in developing countries* (pp. 174–89). London: Routledge.

Parris, D. L., & Peachey, J. W. (2013). A systematic literature review of servant leadership theory in organizational contexts. *Journal of Business Ethics, 113*(3), 377–393.

Patterson, K. A. (2003). Servant leadership: A theoretical model. *Doctoral dissertation*, Regent University. ATT No. 3082719.

Patterson, K. (2010). Servant leadership and love. In *Servant Leadership* (pp. 67–76). UK: Palgrave Macmillan.

Religious life in general. Abbaye de Scourmont, Armand Veilleux's Homepage http://www.scourmont.be/Armand/writings/ref-eng.htm downloaded on May 4, 2017.

Senge, P. (2006). *The fifth discipline: The art and practice of learning organizations*. New York: Double Day.

Sousa, M., & van Dierendonck, D. (2017). Servant leadership and the effect of the interaction between humility, action, and hierarchical power on follower engagement. *Journal of Business Ethics, 141*(1), 13–25.

Spears, L. C. (2010). Character and servant leadership: Ten characteristics of effective, caring leaders. *The Journal of Virtues & Leadership, 1*(1), 25–30.

Usman, N. E. (2005). Integration of gender perspectives in microeconomics. United Nations. Retrieved on June 22, 2017 from https://www.un.org/womenwatch/daw/Review/documents/panelVI/nigerian%20minister.pdf.

U.S. Central Intelligence Agency "Nigeria." (2014). The World Fact book. September 4, 2014. Retrieved from https://www.cia.gov/library/publications/the-world-factbook/geos/ni.html.

van Dierendonck, D. (2011). Servant leadership: A review and synthesis. *Journal of Management, 37*(4), 1228–1261.

van Dierendonck, D., & Patterson, K. (2015). Compassionate love as a cornerstone of servant leadership: An integration of previous theorizing and research. *Journal of Business Ethics, 128* (1), 119–131.

Weyer, B. (2007). Twenty years later: Explaining the persistence of the glass ceiling for women leaders. *Women in Management Review, 22*(6), 482–496. doi:10.1108/09649420710778718.

Women, U. N. (2013). *A transformative stand-alone goal on achieving gender equality, women's rights and women's empowerment: Imperatives and key components*. New York: UN Women, June.

World Economic Forum. (2014). The global gender gap report. Retrieved from http://www3.weforum.org/docs/GGGR14/GGGR_CompleteReport_2014.pdf.

Chapter 17
Showcase—Creating Inclusive Organizations: The Case of CIEE, a Nonprofit Study Abroad and Intercultural Exchange Organization

Jaime Ramirez-Fernandez and Jimena Ramirez-Marin

17.1 Introduction

The Council on International Education Exchange (CIEE) is the oldest and largest US nonprofit study abroad and intercultural exchange organization. This organization operates in 45 countries around the globe, employing nearly 800 people worldwide. The international exchange programs are bidirectional, including US students studying at overseas campuses and study centers, and international students traveling to the USA for either academic programs or cultural exchange programs at American organizations. Information reveals that in 2016, the organization brought over 30,000 participants into the USA, and over 12,000 students and participants overseas on various CIEE programs. In the last 10 years, more than 350,000 students have benefited from these programs.

After Dr. James P. Pellow became President and CEO in June 2011, the organization experienced tremendous growth in all its areas and departments with the objective of expanding access to internationalization by providing opportunities for increasingly diverse people in a growing number of locations. In only four years (2012–2016), the number of US-based employees increased by more than 50%. Despite the lack of a formal system for workplace representation (a trade union), CIEE has decided to commit to diversity and inclusion strategies internally as well as support every single employee, no matter his or her position, location or cultural background, as it grows and continues to expand access and success for diverse students.

J. Ramirez-Fernandez (✉)
Council on International Education Exchange (CIEE), Portland, Maine, USA
e-mail: jramirez@ciee.org

J. Ramirez-Marin
IÉSEG School of Management, Lille, France

A. Arenas et al. (eds.), *Shaping Inclusive Workplaces Through Social Dialogue*,
Industrial Relations & Conflict Management,
DOI 10.1007/978-3-319-66393-7_17

Dr. James P. Pellow was interviewed for his commitment and thoughts on diversity and inclusiveness at CIEE. As the fourth president and CEO in the organization's history, Dr. Pellow previously spent 20 years at St. John's University in Queens, New York, where he served as executive vice president and chief operations officer. With a doctorate in education from the Graduate School of Education at the University of Pennsylvania, Dr. Pellow also received an honorary doctorate from Kokushikan University in Japan for his commitment to global programs and international cultural exchanges. Dr. Pellow is completely aware that success is only possible if everyone is on board, especially leaders who are in a position to transmit values by encouraging people to participate and commit themselves to their teams as he exposed:

If you want an open and inclusive work environment, you need to have leaders who believe that this is vital. If they don't really believe, you will not get the environment you seek. So, the key is to ensure you are picking leaders that share your values. It's that simple, and that complex, all at the same time.

Inclusion requires attention, intention, effort, and ongoing learning. The role of CIEE leaders is vital in that process. CIEE leaders need not only to believe that inclusion is essential to the organization, but also to engage to openly communicate the importance of inclusion, diversity, and their benefits. They need to believe that their role is the key to create a climate in which differences are explored and valued. They need to commit to support others in being themselves; therefore, they do not have to hide their valued identities. Becoming culturally competent will enhance leaders to learn and appreciate different cultures, races, religions, and backgrounds represented at CIEE.

CIEE is not only working to recognize the potential benefits of its multicultural workforce but also to create a more inclusive work environment, giving voice to employees in all levels of the organization. The CIEE initiatives to be presented in this showcase are based on inclusion through intercultural development and fostering recognition and respect for the voices of all employees.

17.2 Organizational Characteristics. The CIEE Difference in Employment Relations

"The CIEE Difference" is comprised of the qualities that differentiate CIEE from other international education organizations. We emphasize, in this section, the CIEE differences that are aimed at promoting diverse and inclusive employment relations. Budd (2004) proposes efficiency, equity, and voice, as basic mechanisms through which organizations can build appropriate employment relationships. Efficiency is defined as the effective, profit maximizing use of scarce resources, and it captures concerns with productivity, competitiveness, and economic prosperity. Equity entails fairness in both the distribution of economic rewards and the administration of employment policies. Voice is the ability of employees to have meaningful input into workplace decisions (Budd 2004; Gartzia et al. 2016). CIEE's strategies are aimed at promoting efficiency as a standard of business performance, equity as a standard of treatment and voice as a standard of employee participation (Budd and Colvin 2008).

A summary of the CIEE employment relations strategies will be presented in the following paragraphs. With the aim of improving efficiency, equity, and voice, CIEE prohibits discrimination on the basis of race, color, religion, sex, age, national origin, sexual orientation, gender identity or expression, disability, veteran status, or marital status.

Indeed, CIEE's mission has been to develop and deliver international programs and support services to help people gain understanding, acquire knowledge, and develop skills for living in a globally interdependent and culturally diverse world since 1947. As a result, applications by ethnically diverse and underrepresented groups are strongly encouraged for any job opening position. In this sense, CIEE has specifically exceeded in the areas of *recruitment and selection*, and *socialization and training*.

Recruitment and selection: CIEE is a very diverse organization with roughly 50% of the staff hired internationally across more than 45 countries—Male 34% and Female 66%. As a multicultural corporation, the recruitment, hiring, and on boarding policies in these many countries have been oriented to attract and retain local employees for the different CIEE Study Centers operating worldwide. While the majority of the overseas workforce has been locally hired in Europe (45%), Latin America (21%), Asia (15%), Africa (10%), Middle East & North Africa (8%), and Australia (2%), the US headquarters is only slightly more diverse than the majority of other organizations in its location, Portland, Maine, as it was exposed in an interview with the CEO and President James P. Pellow:

Our organization is dedicated to finding the very best employees, especially those with diverse backgrounds who can enrich our efforts to fulfill our mission. At times, we have difficulty recruiting diverse employees, especially in Portland, ME, where our HQ is located, and so we go the extra mile in several ways. One example is opening domestic administrative offices in Boston and Washington, D.C. to broaden the pool of candidates for domestic employees. In Boston, after just 6 months, we have 12 employees including four employees who are Iranian, Pakistani, Haitian-American and Slovakian, seven women and five men, each of whom has excellent technical skills and a highly diverse personal story that enriches our effort to fulfill our mission.

Maine, a state of the northeastern USA, has a predominantly white population (94.9%) and a smaller proportion of racial minority populations compared with the nation (The US Census Bureau, 2015). According to the information provided to the Equal Employment Opportunity Commission (EEOC), CIEE is mainly white (85%); however, the Hispanic/Latino (4%), Asian (3%), and Black identities (1%) are also represented.

As CIEE keeps its commitment to fostering a more diverse and inclusive culture based on excellence, integrity, respect, collaboration, and innovation, the use of all pre-employment inquiries that disproportionately screen out members of minority groups (*Are you a US citizen? What country are your parents from? What is your native language? What religion are you?*) or members of one sex (*How many children do you have?*) has been excluded from CIEE employee recruitment interviews, following the USA and Equal Employment Opportunity Commission (EEOC) guidelines on discrimination. Disability-related questions are also prohibited, following the Americans with Disabilities Act (ADA). Under the ADA, an employer cannot lawfully ask an applicant whether he has a particular disability or ask questions that are closely related to a disability. Questions that disclose age (*How old are you When did you graduate from high school*) are also not allowed, following the Age Discrimination in Employment Act (ADEA), since they tend to deter older applicants, and may result in age discrimination.

Socialization and training: In 2007, CIEE consolidated all headquarters activity in Portland, Maine. The organization settled on building a new facility in the heart of the Old Port, the city's historic center. The five-story facility includes wide open spaces for meeting, interacting, and socialization among colleagues. However, socialization is no longer limited to coffee with coworkers or eating lunch with your team. CIEE is aware that socialization takes on new forms outside the workplace, and consequently, has promoted several social initiatives outside of the workplace, such as the "*CIEE Cultural games*" or the "*CIEE Olympic games*," to promote knowledge sharing, team bonding, and a larger sense of community. Dr. Pellow stated:

We have a robust set of colorful socialization activities from monthly Stammtisches, to Halloween parties, to Culture Games, to company parties and picnics; we also have significant training programs. Another example of our inclusiveness is our program of corporate social responsibility which includes a series of partnerships that embrace people from different backgrounds and cultures. One prime example is our partnership with the University of Maine School of Law and the Justice for Women Lecture Series. Each year for the last six years, CIEE sponsors the travel expenses for an exemplary world female leader to visit Maine and share their story of success. Our speakers have hailed from Botswana, Liberia, Afghanistan, India, Zimbabwe, and Malaysia. This sends a very big message to the entire company on what we value.

CIEE works to create more formal collaborative opportunities for employees such as the "*Visioning Initiative*" and the "*Employee Intercultural Development Program* (*EIDP*)" to promote personal and professional growth and serve the organization to achieve greater levels of employee welfare and productivity. For instance, the intensive three-month Visioning Initiative engages a diverse cross section of 30 high-performing CIEE staff that supports and informs CIEE's strategic plan. Consistently, over 100 talented staff from across the organization, located domestically and overseas, volunteer to participate in this initiative. This robust response demonstrates a profound and broad-based commitment to CIEE and an investment in its future.

Over a three-month period, three "Visioning teams" meet concurrently to explore crosscutting themes that represent potential challenges and opportunities for CIEE in the coming years. During this time frame, each team meets, brainstorms ideas, reviews data, and recommends actions that correspond with each team's topic. These recommendations may identify an expansion of best practices or business activities, strategies for confronting emerging challenges, or the launch of new programs or services. Teams present dynamic and visually engaging final reports to a senior management panel at the close of the initiative. Later, Visioning teams also present to their coworkers. Several of the recommendations and ideas that were presented by the 2016 Visioning teams were discussed, analyzed, and debated by the CIEE executive management team. While some of these ideas were transformed into more complex projects to be developed by the group of CIEE Summer Alumni Interns, others have been already implemented. In 2016, for example, CIEE launched the CIEE Mentorship and Apprenticeship Program (CIEE MAP), an idea put forth by a Visioning team, that allows interested staff to find mentors or teachers, based on interests, skill levels, and experience. As a result of the work of the dedicated Visioning teams, many new ideas and projects were included in the CIEE 5-year Strategic Plan 2016–2020.

CIEE is also committed to intercultural skill-building as part of its training plan for all employees in order to bolster cross-cultural competency and inclusive leadership skills. For example, CIEE launched the Employee Intercultural Development Program (EIDP) to train every CIEE employee worldwide on core intercultural skills in order to advance CIEE's mission:

Our company-wide commitment to the Employee Intercultural Development Program (EIDP) is one of the main examples that CIEE is dedicated to its founding purpose and guided by its core value of respecting all people. This is a two-day workshop for every employee worldwide designed to develop a baseline level of knowledge and ability in intercultural communication skills and competencies. The concept is simple: Our core mission is to bring together people from different countries, cultures, customs, religious beliefs, and lifestyles through high quality exchange programs that will teach participants the beauty of our differences (and how to respect those differences) as well as the many ways in which we are all similar (and how we humans are all interconnected). To live that mission successfully, we believe that everyone needs a base level of competency and vocabulary in intercultural communications and understanding. After nearly three years, we have certified nearly 90% of our global workforce.

The EIDP is an experiential training and development program designed to increase intercultural competency and the ability to work effectively and appropriately across cultural differences. The EIDP is intended to provide employees with the skills to achieve organizational goals, whether communicating with staff across the world, within Study Centers, or with diverse students from sending institutions. In order to become an inclusive organization, CIEE aims to provide its employees with the skills needed to view and respect their colleagues and clients as whole persons with different or similar identities. The learning outcomes of EIDP are to increase cultural and personal self-awareness; increase awareness of others; learn to understand and manage emotions in the face of ambiguity, change, and challenging circumstances and people; and bridge cultural gaps by learning to shift frames and adapt behavior to different cultural contexts. It is required for all full-time CIEE employees (including USA and international staff). The groups are designed such that each cohort consists of maximum 24 employees, with diverse representation of departments, roles, tenure, and locations.

Each course is facilitated by two CIEE Intercultural Trainers who have completed a comprehensive Train-the-Trainer program. Trainers are employees who showed strong interest in the initiative, demonstrated qualities associated with intercultural competence (such as curiosity and the ability to perceive experiences from multiple perspectives), and communicated a desire to support the idea of diversity and social inclusion. A group of 25 staff members were nominated as training corps and completed a one-year train-the-trainers certification program. These staff members have committed to delivering the multi-year training series that integrates employees from all levels, all divisions, and all countries. The content of the course is based on a customized intercultural communication program and in collaboration with an intercultural consultant, the CIEE HR team, and employees with prior experience teaching intercultural communication and interest in the project. Employees complete all components of the program over the course of several weeks, although the participation in the three-day training program represents the core of the experience. The workshops take place all over the world. By March 2017, a total of 30 training programs had been organized and over 90% of staff with at least one year of tenure had participated in the program. While English is the primary language of instruction, a few workshops have been offered in local languages. For example, the workshop organized in Santiago, Chile, was offered in Spanish to open the EIDP to those employees lacking English competency. Creating these workshops in the native language of a number of employees had a significant impact on employees' sense of inclusion and value for their unique linguistic and cultural contributions.

CIEE is also implementing new features in several other areas such as **performance appraisal and compensation, and developing careers**. CIEE pays special attention to the relationship between itself as a large organization and its individual employees with the belief that this bond must be a mutually supportive association in which each party contributes in specific ways to the success and development of the other. The CIEE Employee Relations Plan begins prior to employment, as the interview process helps a prospective staff member and his/her future supervisor to establish a mutual understanding of the nature of the organization and the new staff member's role in securing its success. This process continues when the new employee first reports to work with a comprehensive orientation and training program, and is then reinforced on an ongoing basis through discussion of goals and expectations, regular feedback between each staff member and his/her supervisor, and formal performance evaluations at specified intervals.

At CIEE, feedback is continuous and mutual. Staff members and supervisors have both formal and informal opportunities to help each other in various ways through coaching, suggesting new approaches to ongoing tasks, and providing constructive feedback. Performance Assessment is a formal assessment of the entire year's work conducted at the end of the fiscal year, which involves both verbal and written communication. In terms of fair compensation, CIEE respects region, job function, and industry-specific salary benchmarking information on an annual base.

The use of salary tables or formulas helps the organization to neutralize negotiation skills when determining an employee's salary and, thus, avoid penalizing those who lack negotiation skills. Studies have shown that women are unfairly affected by salary negotiation practices when it comes to negotiating for themselves, yet excel at negotiation on behalf of others. The CIEE Performance Assessment process enables the organization to deactivate that penalization and deactivate the possibility of gender discrimination.

Maintaining a work environment free from unlawful discrimination or harassment based on sex, sexual orientation, race, color, religious creed, national origin, ancestry, age, disability, and any other category protected by law is imperative for CIEE. CIEE prohibits such harassment, whether at the office, in outside work assignments, at CIEE-sponsored social or nonsocial functions, events, or programs, or after work hours and off company premises. Should such harassment occur, CIEE takes appropriate corrective action to prevent its continuation or recurrence. Moreover, CIEE does not permit retaliation of any kind against anyone who complains about harassment or participates in good faith in an investigation of a harassment complaint. The CIEE anti-harassment policy is an essential part of the CIEE new hire orientation and stated in the CIEE employee handbook. In fact, all CIEE US-based employees are required to complete an online ergonomics and anti-sexual harassment video and quiz. In addition, each CIEE employee with individuals under his or her supervision has a duty to maintain a workplace free of harassment and to assure that each individual under his or her supervision is aware of CIEE's policy on harassment and the policy's Harassment Resolution Procedure.

CIEE is today a Safe Place for all—is perhaps what we offer most richly due to our embracing the tenants of EIDP and mutual respect for all people from all backgrounds.

CIEE is committed to helping every staff member excel through a staff development program, which includes formal training and assistance components, as well as informal coaching, brainstorming, and sharing of ideas. In terms of gender diversity, the organization has excelled in employing and promoting women into management positions. Today, there are 33% more women in senior management positions at CIEE than the 2016 DiversityInc Top 50 Companies for diversity worldwide. Compared to US companies overall, CIEE has 43% more women in these positions according to the information published by Diversity Inc in April 2016, as it was stated by Dr. Pellow:

As many as 30–35% of open positions are filled by internal candidates, providing a sound path of promotion and internal transfers to different departments. Recruiting internally was discouraged by 2011 and now is considered a part of what makes CIEE attractive to young professionals. The most important attribute is to promote based on skills and achievement, which at times will lead to an internal promotion (remember that 2/3 of CIEE employees are women), and at times will lead us to an external candidate with exemplary skills. Four of my five senior team members are women and each is excellent at what they do.

With a majority of female employees (66%), many of them part of the Executive Management Team as mentioned previously, the organization is aware of the importance of maintaining a work-life balance and has established a series of special holidays in order to contribute to such balance including but not limited to winter Fridays off; summer Fridays off; birthdays off; day of service; etc. Moreover, some employees have been granted flexibility to work remotely based on their family situation.

We have added a lot of flexible work arrangements to allow young parents the flexibility to balance life and work; we've added vacation days during major holiday periods and offer staff flexible Fridays to take off during the summer and winter months. Many CIEE staff leave to pursue family or different career options and return to CIEE with a positive welcome from staff and peers.

17.3 Conclusion

CIEE has experienced tremendous growth in all its areas and departments with the objective of expanding access to internationalization by providing opportunities for increasingly diverse people in a growing number of locations in only four years (2012–2016). As discussed, CIEE is committed to diversity and inclusion strategies. There are several initiatives that intend to create a more inclusive work environment, giving voice to employees at all levels of the organization, as well as several ongoing initiatives to improve the current scenario according to the CEO and President James P. Pellow:

The most important efforts underway to improve our employee skills and competencies are (1) recruiting more broadly than the Portland, ME, area to secure senior management, IT skills, marketing skills, and sales skills; (2) working hard to recruit diverse candidates that bring a new and rich perspective to our work which is more important than ever as our participants are becoming more and more diverse; and (3) developing a rich training program around skills that matter most to employees to do their jobs, which requires listening to employees share what is holding them back.

References

Budd, J. (2004). *Employment with a human face: Balancing efficiency, equity, and voice*. New York: Cornell University Press.

Budd, J., & Colvin, A. (2008). Improved metrics for workplace dispute resolution procedures: Efficiency, equity, and voice. *Industrial Relations, 47*(3), 460–479.

Gartzia, L., Amillano, A., & Baniandres, J. (2016). Women in industrial relations: overcoming gender biases. In P. Elgoibar, M. Euwema, & L. Munduate (Eds.), *Building trust and constructive conflict management in organizations* (pp. 195–212). The Netherlands: Springer International.

Part III
Turning the Wheel of Inclusion

Chapter 18
The Circle of Inclusion: From Illusion to Reality

Donatella Di Marco, Alicia Arenas, Martin C. Euwema and Lourdes Munduate

> "About 12,000 doctors trained in European countries could quit the UK because they feel less welcome following the Brexit vote, according to a survey of overseas medics. [...] The British Medical Association's findings are based on a survey it undertook of 1193 European Economic Area doctors working in the UK. When asked if they were thinking about leaving the UK following last year's referendum vote, 500 (42%) said yes, 309 (26%) said no, 278 (23%) were unsure, while the other 106 did not answer" (The Guardian 2017, February 23).
>
> "Immigrants are the backbone of this country and the heart and soul of the service industry. Without them, our small businesses would crumble. They are also part of our family here at Little Red Fox, and I, too, am worried about their future under this administration" (Matt Carr, owner of the Little Red Fox restaurant in Washington, D.C, CNN, 2017, February 17).

18.1 The Long Journey to Inclusion

Diversity in the workforce, societal changes and social dialogue have been the drivers of the long journey to inclusive organizations. We are seeing that societies, labor markets, and work relationships face fast changes, and several dynamics are

---

This work was funded by the Spanish Ministry of Economy and Competitiveness (MINECO/FEDER),grant reference n. PSI2015-64894-P.

D. Di Marco (✉) · A. Arenas · L. Munduate
University of Seville, Seville, Spain
e-mail: ddimarco@us.es

M.C. Euwema
KU Leuven, Louvain, Belgium

A. Arenas et al. (eds.), *Shaping Inclusive Workplaces Through Social Dialogue*,
Industrial Relations & Conflict Management,
DOI 10.1007/978-3-319-66393-7_18

shaping a new landscape which includes workers with diverse cultures and backgrounds. However, if changes are not managed well, they might be perceived as chaotic, and the results might be different from those expected (Karp and Helgø 2009). Furthermore, there are also worldwide pressures which are not in favor of inclusion. Global and local competition and a race to the bottom when it comes to pricing puts pressures on working conditions, leaving little room for an inclusive and safe environment, and neither to implement such HR policies (D'Cruz and Noronha 2010; D'Cruz 2014; Obi and Bollen, Chap. 16 in this volume). Also, societal developments might push organizational policies and practices in directions of exclusion, or limited inclusion. This is visible in the recent political landscape, as is shown in the introductory examples. Two of the main influential countries in the world, UK, after the vote for Brexit in 2016, and USA, after the presidential election in 2016, are promoting a discourse which closes the doors to dialogue, building ideological (and maybe physical) walls between countries and people. Moreover, the economic crisis of the last few years has reinforced the position of populist parties in Europe: less immigration, the rejection of the Eurozone, and the war against Islam are some of the common battles of this new political trend. The picture described does not seem exalting the respect for diversity, specially when discriminative values are invoked.

Beyond the political landscape we are living, and the legal framework of countries involved, many organizational leaders recognize inclusive policies are not only the right thing to do, but also the smart thing to do. It is a business case to invest in inclusive policies for more and more organizations.

The experiences and experiments we present in this handbook offer benchmarks for those organizations that want to foster inclusive workplaces. A comprehensive model of human resource management (HRM) for inclusion has been presented through the Circle of Inclusion (see Fig. 18.1).

The journey through the Circle of Inclusion starts at the recruitment stage (see Bozani et al., Chap. 6 in this volume). Although at legislative level, many countries recognize the importance to provide the same opportunities to everybody in terms of access to the labor market, organizations and recruitment agencies can exclude specific categories of employees from the recruitment process, as is often the case for older people, or people with disabilities, or for a minority group. Bias and prejudice, many times settled on an unconscious level, can prevent organizations from including them, even if they demonstrate to hold the same skills and abilities as other applicants. This is also true for people who speak a minority dialect (Cocchiara et al. 2016), or show symbols of specific groups (Hebl et al. 2002). These mechanisms are well explained by fundamental social psychological theories on ingroup and outgroup differentiation and social-identity theory (Hogg and Terry 2014).

Unconscious bias and prejudice might intervene at other early stages of people entering organizations. Once applicants have been selected for the recruitment process, organizations have to guarantee a discrimination-free personnel selection, providing a fair and objective selection system and take into account candidates' perceptions of the whole process (see Salgado et al., Chap. 7 in this volume).

Fig. 18.1 Circle of Inclusion

Justice and fairness are elements that have to characterize the job offer for people selected. In that sense, the changing nature of work relationships and work arrangements, which involved the increase of freelancers, contract workers, etc. (Katz and Krueger 2016), might be affecting some groups more than others, such as women, ethnic minorities, and young people. These new work arrangements open a debate about the future of the job, but also about the safety of these employees. A new question related to the changing nature of the work is to how social dialogue and actors involved will redefine their role and how they will guarantee decent working conditions to everybody.

Recruitment and selection are probably the most studied activities of the HRM System, from the perspective of inclusion and diversity. However, once having guaranteed to everybody the same chances to enter, organizations also need to offer a supportive work environment fitting employees' needs, so they also stay and can develop productive work relations (ILO 2016). A first and important step is adjusting and accommodating the workplace to the needs of the workers. This can vary from entrance and workspace, for example for people with disabilities

(Nelissen et al. 2016), or conditions for women entering specific environment (working in the army), or meeting the different food needs in the company canteen. As we have seen in the previous chapters (see Zijlstra et al., Chap. 8 in this volume), configuring the opportunity to stay entails embarking on a structural change, creating new jobs for people with different capabilities. Accommodating the work environment is not enough to be inclusive: Organizations need to redesign the work processes, taking into account specificities of different groups. Working space and place, working hours, tasks, technology, and communication, all can contribute to motivation and inclusion for employees who are working with atypical work arrangements, allowing them to balance their personal and work life.

During a long time, it has been considered that inclusion is reached if several vulnerable groups are represented within the workplace. And, in some countries, quota has been one of the main tools to reach this goal. The debate about affirmative actions to promote inclusion in the workplace is ongoing and lively (Harrison et al. 2006; Noon, 2010; Sargeant et al. 2016). Affirmative actions have promoted diversity at work; however, this certainly not ensures the inclusion of diverse groups at the workplace (see Hoel and McBride, Chap. 3 in this volume; and Torres and Hanashiro, Chap. 10 in this volume). So, affirmative actions can create a pre-condition for inclusion. It is essential to manage such diversity, avoiding negative or discriminatory behaviors and facilitating the encounter of different groups. Indeed, diversity without inclusion might be counterproductive if not well managed (Bendick and Egan 2010).

In order to avoid negative behaviors or discrimination toward vulnerable groups, the socialization process is an essential step to integrate and include diversity. Medina and Gamero (Chap. 9, in this volume) tell the successful case of the socialization process of people with disabilities. Managers, co-workers, and people with disabilities were involved in specific interventions aiming to eliminate distances between them, and adjusting expectations of each group. In doing so, the participation of several actors, such as families and NGOs, was key to success of the socialization.

Training is another step that helps to clarify organizational values and policies toward inclusion (see Torres and Hanashiro, Chap. 10 in this volume). Training offers instruments to prevent and manage prejudices and stereotypes among employees. However, the results of training programs appear contradictory (Kalinoski et al. 2013). One typical reason for poor results of training is the lack of alignment between the different HR policies toward inclusion. For example, if managers are evaluated only on production targets, and not in team climate, it is unlikely diversity training will have much effect.

Obviously, it is unrealistic to believe that socialization and training alone can modify people's attitudes toward vulnerable groups (Dobbin and Kalev 2016), specially if they are conceived as isolated interventions. The Circle of Inclusion tries to overcome this limitation, fostering a comprehensive model that motivates the HRM System to implement an integrated strategy on inclusion.

Following the Circle of Inclusion (Fig. 18.1), we find career development, an important process to keep employees engaged, and to promote employability, in terms of workers' use of competences to create and identify employement opportunities (Van der Heijde and Van der Heijden 2006). During many years, employees with specific characteristics have been facing extra barriers to career development, related for example with age, sexual orientation, gender, and ethnicity (e.g., Adams et al. 2005; Ossenkop et al. 2015; Villanueva-Flores et al. 2014). Inclusive organizations are characterized by promoting career and development policies reducing stereotypes and prejudices, and fostering a climate for diversity (Hicks-Clarke and Iles 2000). For instance, in order to promote career development of employees with a high care-load in their personal life (young children, older parents), measures can be taken to meet individual needs to balance work and personal life (see Martínez-Corts and Demerouti, Chap. 15 in this volume). Also in this respect, discussions on affirmative actions are continuing. To what extent should organizations take personal and private conditions into account? Based on the studies in this book, we promote individual tailoring of working conditions as an important tool for career development, both horizontal and vertical. A call for sustainable career development, fostering workers' employability (see Peters et al., Chap. 14 in this volume), is required.

While pro-diversity researchers' efforts have been focused on some stages of the organizational circle, some others require more attention from academia and practitioners. There exist several studies about performance appraisal and compensation (DeNisi and Murphy 2017; Rynes et al. 2005), but few analyze to what extent they promote diversity (Feild and Holley 1982; Miller et al. 1990). They should not have been ignored from organizations that want to make possible an integral model of inclusion.

The last step of the Circle of Inclusion, farewell, is a process which seems relatively under developed. With an aging labor force, and senior citizens who are healthy, active, and in need of making contributions, there is a great potential for new forms of cooperation, also after formal retirement. Retirement is still seen as a natural end of a career (Kiefer and Briener 1998). Many studies have focused on timing and consequences of retirement (Davies and Jenkis 2013; Lee et al. 2016), however only few explore the options people have for a healthy transition from the point of view of inclusion and social dialogue. Organizations need an open dialogue addressing the needs of different (groups of) employees, when it comes to career planning and retirement. Many organizations face tensions between older and senior employees at top positions, and younger colleagues who are waiting for them to retire, so they can move up the ladder. Negotiating creative and inclusive solutions are needed in many sectors, meeting the interests of all parties involved.

Several organizations have applied retention policies, in order to maintain mature employees' knowledge and experience (Lee et al. 2016). In line with the policy applied, different organizational typologies have been identified, according to the possibility of leaving, following a standard procedure, or staying, crafting the mature employee's work contribution in several ways (e.g., part-time, mentoring programs, etc.) (see Lee et al. 2016). In order to identify the best solution for people and organizations, a participation and open communication process is required. Several actors might enter in the negotiation about the exit/staying process (Lee et al. 2016).

Taking in mind the steps of the Circle of Inclusion, in the next sections we are going to analyze some of the challenges inclusive organizations have to face to apply it and the role played by social dialogue.

"Mothers who return to work end up earning a third less than men as the birth of a child cuts their chances of getting promotions and pay rises, a study has found.

This is mainly as a result of mothers tending to work fewer hours than colleagues who are not parents, according to the Institute for Fiscal Studies (IFS).

"Men's wages tend to continue growing rapidly at this point in the life cycle (particularly for the highly-educated), while women's wages plateau" said the IFS. Before having a child the average female worker earns 10–15% less per hour than a male employee. After childbirth that steadily increases to 33% after around 12 years. The wage gap is particularly serious for women with low levels of education and few qualifications, as they receive lower pay at the same time as looking after children" (The Telegraph, 2016, August 23).

18.2 Go Forward: The Need of Organizational Change Through Social Dialogue

The Circle of Inclusion is not a group of single interventions at several stages of the HRM process. It is a comprehensive model in which inclusion and diversity are considered strategic resources, a reality which needs attention. But it goes further. It integrates the need to manage diversity with the awareness that building consensus around this new model is necessary. For many organizations, this implies a deep-level organizational development, primarily aiming at cultural change (Cummings & Worley, 2014). Such change entails an effort to incorporate inclusion as a feature of the HRM System and the organizational culture (see Elgoibar et al., Chap. 5; Ramírez and Ramírez, Chap. 17; Verschueren and Euwema, Chap. 13 in this volume).

Although organizations might take a stance against and ban any forms of discrimination, workers might carry out discriminative behaviors due to prejudice and negative stereotypes. Nowadays, organizations are more aware about the presence of unconscious biases (Bourke et al. 2017). Fostering an inclusive culture through an organizational change is a tool for inhibiting those negative behaviors against co-workers who belong to minority groups, or divert in any kind of way from the mainstream and implicit group norms. In fact, a strong organizational culture against any forms of discrimination can act as a normative or external motivational factor to inhibit discriminatory behaviors (Butz and Plant 2009; Cortina 2008; Hernandez et al. 2016). Previous research has shown that the presence of both a Human Resource Department and diversity policies work successfully as external motivators against discrimination (see Bozani et al., Chap. 6 in this volume).

Across the experiences that this handbook offers, we have seen that unions, works councils, and labor movements (Euwema et al. 2015b) are key players of this process. An organized social dialogue, where employees' representatives give voice to the variety within the employees, can be a powerful instrument to promote inclusion. However, when employee representatives are in reality not representative for this variety, mostly being white, 50+, heterosexual men, employees' representatives can become in fact an obstacle for this organizational development toward inclusive organizations (Munduate et al. 2012). Therefore, selecting and recruiting and training new employee representatives, who indeed are representing a diversified workforce, is a priority, both for unions, as well as for employers (Munduate et al. 2012).

In organizations, social dialogue can take many different forms. In the European model, often works councils will be the platform for such a dialogue. In other societies, models of participative decision-making can produce an organizational development process (Cummings and Worley, 2014). At the agenda, can be:

- Developing fundamental and fair practices and standards to foster inclusion of vulnerable groups.
- Monitor attempts of flouting the norms established and contained at legal or organizational level.
- Recognize employees' voice, pointing out those structural and cultural norms that hinder workers from speaking up.
- Adjust the expectations of people involved, in terms of the degree the organization is able to accomplish individual and career needs of diverse people, on the one hand, and of what it is needed in order to offer a satisfactory work environment, on the other hand.
- Promote mediation in case of conflict, trying to preserve the interest of all the parties involved, specially of those who have seen their rights violated.

18.2.1 Managing for Change, Managing for Inclusion

So far, we have described that inclusive policies and isolated measures are not enough. People who do not discriminate against vulnerable groups because externally motivated by norms stated at organizational or group level might fail to manage their bias under pressure or stressful situations, when it is more difficult to control (un)consciuous bias. (Hernandez et al. 2016). Implementing the Circle of Inclusion by starting from selecting people who show internal motivation to behave without prejudice might be a beginning (Hernandez et al. 2016). The following step is to promote a deeper change that fosters daily behaviors and practices rooted in inclusive values. One of the most important agents of such internal revolution are managers and supervisors, also when unions do exist and act effectively.

In order to integrate inclusion in the organizational daily life, supervisors and managers play a central task, being the role model for workers and representing organization mission in front of their employees. They are essential for successful implementation of organizational change directed to promote inclusion (see Hoel and McBride, Chap. 3 in this volume).

Management commitment with diversity has to be kept in mind when organizations select leaders, because they are key actors to facilitate the integration and inclusion of diverse groups (Medina and Gamero, Chap. 9 in this volume; Ramirez et al., Chap. 17 in this volume). Organizations need to look for inclusive leaders who have to realize that they are accountable for their actions (Bourke et al. 2017).

Promoting people who belong to specific groups is by no means a guarantee to inclusion, and might in fact result in negative dynamics. Recent research has highlighted that workplaces are becoming more segregated (e.g., Black people lead Black subordinates, and White people lead White subordinates) (Hernandez et al. 2016). Moreover, stigma might be transferred from stigmatized leaders to followers end or vice versa ("stigma-by-association"), leading to a negative appraisal of the whole group (Hernandez et al. 2016). As stated before, the presence of external factors which motivate people to take under control their biases allows to moderate the negative effect of the "stigma-by-association." Moreover, creating groups with a superordinate identity and common goals might help to weak the boundaries between the "in-group" and "out-group" (Cortina, 2008; Hernandez et al. 2016).

Inclusive leaders need to promote inclusion at all the internal and external steps of its productive chain. This means that leaders have to strive for making sure that all their partners are committed with diversity and inclusion (e.g., recruitment agencies, suppliers, etc.). HRM, Unions, Work Councils, and Labor Movements play an essential role to achieve of this goal.

18.3 Beyond the Business Case: The Social Justice Issue

Diversity and inclusion are a competitive advantage for organizations. Those ones which held a diverse workforce are more creative, more productive, and more effective to retain talent, more capable to understand the needs of the market (e.g., Bourke et al. 2017). For instance, a research on Fortune 500 organizations (Catalyst 2011) showed that those with higher rates of women representation on the board reach more positive outcomes in terms of return on sales, investment capital, and equity.

However, some studies have pointed out the difficulty to achieve the benefits that diversity promises (Kalinoski et al. 2013). At this point of the journey, it might be clearer that diversity without inclusion does not produce any benefits (Bendick and Egan 2010) and that all agents involved play a key role to make possible the Circle of Inclusion. The experiences collected in this handbook showed that implementing the Circle of Inclusion goes beyond the economic implications it entails: fostering inclusive organizations is an issue of social justice. Nowadays, offering a safe workplace where people are protected from any form of harassment (see Deakin, Chap. 11 in this volume), where anyone feels free to manage its identity as she/he considers appropriate (see Di Marco, Chap. 12 in this volume), and where everybody can have access to a decent and paid work (see Zijlstra et al., Chap. 8 in this volume), is not an option but an essential requisite for organizations (see Hoel and McBride, Chap. 3 in this volume). However, nowadays, not all societies start from the same beginning point. It is the case of those parts of the world where values such as diversity and inclusion are not widespread and where discrimination is the norm instead (see Obi and Bollen, Chap. 16 in this volume). Then, organizations might be key in empowering employees with diverse characteristics and starting a virtuous change which might benefit the entire society. Self-organizations, for instance, might represent a safe starting point for vulnerable workers who act in a risky environment.

As seen before, positive actions have been implemented as a measure to reach diversity. They have provoked a strong resistance, invoking the deficiencies of such measures. Anti-quota people, for instance, blame this system to foster "favoritisms" to the detrainment of those groups which does not receive any benefits from their implementations; they also point out the limitation of quotas in recruiting talented workers (Wiersema and Mors 2016), and in some countries is illegal. In line with detractors of such measures, positive actions reduce the value of meritocracy. This statement might be rooted on the "belief of a just world" (Hafer and Bègue 2005; Lerner 1980; Lerner and Miller 1978). According to this belief, people get what they deserve. However, such assumption might be a double-edged sword because it might normalize the unequal status which affects some groups in society and within organizations.

Meritocracy is an important pillar of many countries and industries and there are no doubts that it is necessary to foster the effectiveness of systems based on it. Positive actions are not the only and the best solution. However, positive actions might be an instrument to improve resources able to facilitate people to compete in a meritocratic system, equalizing and balancing the starting point of people who belong to a vulnerable group and people who do not. HRM System, Unions, Work Councils, Labor Movements, leaders, and employees should work together in order to achieve such balance.

When the change advocated by the Circle of Inclusion is aimed, policies and measures for diversity and inclusion come to be part of the organizational culture. At that moment, the Circle of Inclusion becomes a "turning wheel" that requires stakeholders monitor that such change is working successfully.

18.4 Conclusions

During the journey through the Circle of Inclusion, we have seen several steps and good practices possible to apply in order to shape an inclusive workplace through social dialogue. We pointed out the role of all the stakeholders involved. As the International Labour Organization pointed out in an encounter about the future of work (2017a, April 7), social dialogue might be an instrument to shape future work environments where more people are included and participate based on their competences, instead of being excluded for specific characteristics. A sustainable future where innovation and development are present but that does not leave anybody behind (ILO 2017b).

We have also explored the experience of groups with different characteristics, such as people with disabilities, elder people, LGB people, etc. However, we realize that some other important groups are not included in this handbook. For instance, refugees who, after having lost their home, are facing the exclusion from part of those societies which should receive them; people with special needs, such as those employees living with or affected by HIV, who needs a "reasonable accommodation" (ILO 2016, p. 11) at work; young people, who are increasingly out of the labor market; workers who might be stigmatized for their religious beliefs; also, transgender and intersexual people are not represented, even if their work experience is often marked by exclusion and discrimination. Another important concern refers to the intersectionality issue. Sometimes, stigmatized identities intersect in the same person, at the same time, increasing the possibility to be the victim of discrimination (McBride et al. 2015). Although the handbook has not focused on implications produced by intersectionality, this is a reality that needs further consideration.

The Circle of Inclusion is a comprehensive model that organizations can use in order to start organizational change, and to do so in a systematic way. More important, to develop this as a structured and continuous process of dialogue, representatives of all parties have to be involved at different levels in the organization. This can be presented with the Tree of Trust (Lewicki et al. 2016). Trees typically have different layers of branches. The Tree of Trust represents different levels of actors within organizations where dialogue needs to take place, so as to overcome conflicts of interest and develop integrative solutions, which might be decisive to foster inclusion. Conflicts of interest might coincide with social-identity conflicts. Fault lines in organizations are perceived between different groups, activating easily social identities (see Dovidio et al., Chap. 2 in this volume; Rink and Jehn 2010). And this drives complex conflicts. In order to foster dialogue for inclusion, role models, who can represent multiple identities (Fiol et al. 2009), and boundary spanners within organizations, can act to connect different groups (Ramarajan et al. 2011). These roles are often stressful and should therefore be cherished.

Trust and cooperation are the two important ingredients of the change required (Euwema et al. 2015a). The results might affect not exclusively the success of the organization, but might also shape a change toward inclusive and sustainable societies.

References

Adams, E. M., Cahill, B. J., & Ackerlinda, S. J. (2005). A qualitative study of Latino lesbian and gay youths' experiences with discrimination and the career development process. *Journal of Vocational Behavior, 66,* 199–218.

Bendick, M., Jr., & Egan, M. (2010). The business case for diversity and the perverse practice of matching employees to customers. *Personnel Review, 39,* 468–486.

Bourke, J., Garr, S., van Berkel, A., & Wong, J. (2017). Diversity and inclusion. The reality gap. In Deloitte (Eds.), *Rewriting the rules for the digital age 2017. Deloitte Global Human Capital Trends* (pp. 105–116). Brussel: Deloitte University Press.

Butz, D. A., & Plant, E. A. (2009). Prejudice control and interracial relations: The role of motivation to respond without prejudice. *Journal of Personality, 77,* 1311–1342.

Catalyst. (2011, June). *The bottom line: Corporate performance and women's representation on boards (2004–2008).* Retrieved from www.catalyst.org.

Cocchiara, F. K., Bell, M. P., & Casper, W. J. (2016). Sounding "different": The role of sociolinguistic cues in evaluating job candidates. *Human Resource Management, 55,* 463–477.

Cortina, L. M. (2008). Unseen injustice: Incivility as modern discrimination in organizations. *Academy of Management Review, 33,* 55–75.

Cumming. T. G., & Worley, C. G. (2014). Organization development and change (10th ed.). Stamford: Cengage Learning.

Davies, E., & Jenkis, A. (2013). The work-to-retirement transition of academic staff: attitudes and experiences. *Employee Relations, 35,* 322–338.

D'Cruz, P. (2014). *Workplace bullying in India.* London: Routledge.

D'Cruz, P., & Noronha, E. (2010). The exit coping response to workplace bullying: The contribution of inclusivist and exclusivist HRM strategies. *Employee Relations, 32*(2), 102–120.

DeNisi, A. S., & Murphy, K. R. (2017). Performance appraisal and performance management: 100 Years of progress? *Journal of Applied Psychology, 102,* 421–433.

Dobbin, F., & Kalev, A. (2016). Why diversity programs fail. *Harvard Business Review,* 52–60 (*July–August issue*).

Euwema, M. C., García, A. B., Munduate, L., Elgoibar, P., & Pender, E. (2015a). Employee representatives in European organizations. In M. Euwema, L. Munduate, P. Elgoibar, E. Pender, & A. B. García (Eds.), *Promoting social dialogue in European organizations* (pp. 1–17). The Netherlands: Springer International.

Euwema, M. C., Munduate, L., Elgoibar, P., Pender, E., & García, A. B. (Eds.). (2015b). *Promoting social dialogue in European organizations.* The Netherlands: Springer International.

Feild, H. S., & Holley, W. H. (1982). The relationship of performance appraisal system characteristics to verdicts in selected employment discrimination cases. *Academy of Management Journal, 25,* 392–406.

Fiol, C. M., Pratt, M. G., & O'Connor, E. J. (2009). Managing intractable identity conflicts. *Academy of Management Review, 34,* 32–55.

Harrison, D. A., Kravitz, D. A., Mayer, D. M., Leslie, L. M., & Lev-Arey, D. (2006). Understanding attitudes toward affirmative action programs in employment: Summary and meta-analysis of 35 years of research. *Journal of Applied Psychology, 91,* 1013–1036.

Hebl, M. R., Bigazzi, J., Mannix, L. M., & Dovidio, J. F. (2002). Formal and interpersonal discrimination: A field study of bias toward homosexual applicants. *Personality and Social Psychology Bulletin, 28,* 815–825.

Hafer, C. L., & Bègue, L. (2005). Experimental research on just-world theory: Problems, developments, and future challenges. *Psychological Bulletin, 131,* 128–167.

Hernandez, M., Avery, D. R., Tonidandel, S., Hebl, M. R., Smith, A. N., & McKay, P. F. (2016). The role of proximal social context: Assessing stigma-by-association effects on leader appraisals. *Journal of Applied Psychology, 101,* 68–85.

Hicks-Clarke, D., & Iles, P. (2000). Climate for diversity and its effects on career and organizational attitudes and perceptions. *Personnel Review, 29,* 324–345.

Hogg, M. A., & Terry, D. J. (Eds.). (2014). *Social identity processes in organizational contexts.* Hove, UK: Psychology Press.

ILO. (2016). *Promoting diversity and inclusion through workplace adjustments a practical guide.* Geneva: International Labour Organization.

ILO. (2017a, April 7th). *ILO says social dialogue key to shaping the future of work we want.* Retrieved from http://www.ilo.org/global/about-the-ilo/newsroom/news/WCMS_550238/lang–en/index.htm.

ILO. (2017b). *World employment social outlook. Trends 2017.* Geneva: International Labour Organization.

Kalinoski, Z. T., Steele-Johnson, D., Peyton, E. J., Leas, K. A., Steinke, J., & Bowling, N. A. (2013). A meta-analytic evaluation of diversity training outcomes. *Journal of Organizational Behavior, 34,* 1076–1104.

Karp, T., & Helgø, T. I. T. (2009). Reality revisited: leading people in chaotic change. *Journal of Management Development, 28,* 81–93.

Katz, L. F., & Krueger, A. B. (2016). *The rise and nature of alternative work arrangements in the United States, 1995–2015.* Working Paper No. 22667, The National Bureau of Economic Research.

Kiefer, T., & Briener, R. B. (1998). Managing retirement—rethinking links between individual and organization. *European Journal of Work and Organizational Psychology, 7,* 373–390.

Lee, M. D., Zikic, J., Noh, S., & Sargent, L. (2016). Human Resources approaches to retirement: gatekeeping, improvising, orchestrating, and partnering. *Human Resource Management,* 1–23. doi:10.1002/hrm.21775.

Lerner, M. J. (1980). *The belief in a just world: A fundamental delusion.* New York: Plenum Press.

Lerner, M. J., & Miller, D. T. (1978). Just world research and the attribution process: Looking back and ahead. *Psychological Bulletin, 85,* 1030–1051.

Lewicki, R., Elgoibar, P., & Euwema, M. (2016). The tree of trust: Building and repairing trust in organizations. In P. Elgoibar, M. Euwema, & L. Munduate (Eds.), *Building trust and constructive conflict management inorganizations* (pp. 93-117). The Netherlands: Springer International.

McBride, A., Hebson, G., & Holgate, J. (2015). Intersectionality: are we taking enough notice in the field of work and employment relations? *Work, Employment & Society, 29,* 331–341.

Miller, C. S., Kaspin, J. A., & Schuster, M. H. (1990). The Impact of performance appraisal methods on age discrimination in employment act cases. *Personnel Psychology, 43,* 555–578.

Nelissen, P. T. J. H., Hülsheger, U. R., van Ruitenbeek, G. M. C., & Zijlstra, F. R. H. (2016). How and when stereotypes relate to inclusive behavior toward people with disabilities. *The International Journal of Human Resource Management, 27,* 1610–1625.

Noon, M. (2010). The shackled runner: Time to rethink positive discrimination? *Work, Employment & Society, 24,* 728–739.

Munduate, L., Euwema, M., & Elgoibar, P. (2012). *Ten steps for empowering employee representatives in the new European industrial relations.* Madrid: McGraw-Hill.

Ossenkop, C., Vinkenburg, C. J., Jansen, P. G. W., & Ghorashi, H. (2015). Ethnic diversity and social capital in upward mobility systems. Problematizing the permeability of intra-organizational career boundaries. *Career Development International, 20,* 539–558.

Ramarajan, L., Bezrukova, K., Jehn, K. A., & Euwema, M. (2011). From the outside in: The negative spillover effects of boundary spanners' relations with members of other organizations. *Journal of Organizational Behavior, 32*, 886–905.

Rink, F. A., & Jehn, K. A. (2010). Divided we fall, or united we stand? *The Psychology of Social and Cultural Diversity*, 281–296.

Rynes, S. L., Gerhart, B., & Parks, L. (2005). Personnel psychology: Performance evaluation and pay for performance. *Annual Review of Psychology, 56,* 571–600.

Sargeant, M., Radevich-Katsaroumpa, E., & Innesti, A. (2016). Disability quotas: Past or future policy? *Economic and Industrial Democracy,* 1–18. doi:10.1177/0143831X16639655.

Van Der Heijde, C. M., & Van Der Heijden, B. I. J. M. (2006). A competence-based and multidimensional operationalization and measurement of employability. *Human Resource Management 45* (3), 449–476.

Villanueva-Flores, M., Valle-Cabrera, R., & Bornay-Barrachina, M. (2014). Career development and individuals with physical disabilities. *Career Development International, 19,* 222–243.

Wiersema, M. & Mors, L. (2016, November 14). What board directors really think of gender quotas. *Harvard Business Review,* 1–6 (*November issue*).

MIX
Papier aus verantwortungsvollen Quellen
Paper from responsible sources
FSC® C105338

If you have any concerns about our products,
you can contact us on
ProductSafety@springernature.com

In case Publisher is established outside the EU,
the EU authorized representative is:
Springer Nature Customer Service Center GmbH
Europaplatz 3, 69115 Heidelberg, Germany

Printed by Libri Plureos GmbH
in Hamburg, Germany